AF607987

ROMANTIC PROPHECY AND THE RESISTANCE TO HISTORICISM

Romantic Prophecy and the Resistance to Historicism

CHRISTOPHER M. BUNDOCK

UNIVERSITY OF TORONTO PRESS
Toronto Buffalo London

Toronto Buffalo London
www.utppublishing.com

ISBN 978-1-4426-3070-3 (cloth)

Library and Archives Canada Cataloguing in Publication

Bundock, Christopher M., 1980–, author
Romantic prophecy and the resistance to historicism
/ Christopher M. Bundock.

Includes bibliographical references and index.
ISBN 978-1-4426-3070-3 (hardback)

1. Romanticism – Europe. 2. Prophecy in literature.
3. Literature and history. 4. Time in literature. 5. European
literature – 18th century – History and criticism. I. Title.

PN751.B86 2016 809'.914509033 C2016-901903-9

This book has been published with the help of a grant from the Federation for the Humanities and Social Sciences, through the Awards to Scholarly Publications Program, using funds provided by the Social Sciences and Humanities Research Council of Canada.

University of Toronto Press acknowledges the financial assistance to its publishing program of the Canada Council for the Arts and the Ontario Arts Council, an Ontario government agency.

Canada Council for the Arts | Conseil des Arts du Canada

Funded by the Government of Canada | Financé par le gouvernement du Canada | Canada

Contents

List of Illustrations vii

Acknowledgments ix

Introduction: Prophecy and the Temporality of Being Historical 3

Part One

1 Secularization and the New Ends of History 27
2 Prophecy within the Limits of Reason Alone 51
3 Ghostlier Demarcations: Mysticism, Trauma, Anachronism 75
4 Beyond the Sign of History: Prophetic Semiotics and the Future's Reflection 103

Part Two

5 The Future of an Allusion: Temporalization and Figure in Lyrical Drama 123
6 Auguries of Experience: Impossible History and Infernal Redemption 141
7 The Preface and Other False Starts: Prophesying the Book to Come 168
8 "a woman clothed with the Sun": Female Prophecy and Catastrophe 195

Afterword 223

Notes 227

Bibliography 253

Index 267

Illustrations

Figure 1 John Flaxman, Compositions from the Tragedies of Aeschylus, Plate 29 135

Figure 2 William Blake, *Milton,* Plate 33 158

Figure 3 William Blake, *Jerusalem*, Plate 20 160

Figure 4 William Blake, *Milton*, Plate 17 161

Figure 5 Thomas Rowlandson, "A Medical Inspection. Or Miracles Will Never Cease" 201

Table Probable/improbable, possible/impossible diagram 145

Acknowledgments

I first began to think seriously about this project around 2005. Since then, a multitude of conferences, courses, workshops, and conversations have served as opportunities for generating and refining the work finally produced. This makes a comprehensive acknowledgment of every instance of support difficult – and yet, with this difficulty comes the immense pleasure of the attempt to re-collect, as far as is possible, some history that might offer at least a glimpse of how such a text, in spite of the single name on the cover, emerges out of a collective. The number of individuals who have informed the work – intentionally or otherwise – is countless. Let me try to count them.

My thanks to faculty and students at The Centre for the Study of Theory and Criticism and the Department of English at the University of Western Ontario. Thanks especially to participants, from both these units, in various iterations of the Romantic Reading Group (2005–present) and the conferences and workshops that emerged from these meetings; for their brilliance and commitment and generosity I am deeply indebted to Naqaa Abbas, Gord Barentsen, Elizabeth Effinger, Jim Hall, Nigel Joseph, Jeff King, Josh Lambier, Mark Mazur, Jared McGeough, Adrian Mioc, Shalon Noble, Diane Piccitto, Logan Rohde, Kaila Rose, Derek Shank, and John Vanderheide. Thanks to Josh Lambier (again!) and the members of the Public Humanities at Western whose vision of community-engaged scholarship is exciting and crucial for the evolution of higher education. It was a pleasure to work alongside Samantha Angove, Joel Burton, Donnie Calabrese, Michael Courey, Phil Glennie, Maryam Golafahani, Laura Kelvin, Jaxson Khan, Stephanie Oliver, Jaime Brenes Reyes, Jamie Rooney, and Cierra Webster. Several faculty members at Western made lasting impressions. They include David Bentley, Steven Bruhm, Jonathan Boulter, Tony Calcagno, Michael Gardiner, Chris Keep, John Leonard, Steve Lofts, Mark McDayter, Calin Mihailescu, Elias Polizoes, Allan Pero, Matthew Rowlinson,

Peter Schwenger, and Pauline Wakeham. For their mentorship, advice, and kindness, thanks to Cory Davies and Catherine Ross.

Thanks as well to colleagues at Western, Huron University College, and Fanshawe College whose dedication to teaching has helped me to reflect on and – I hope – improve that practice: Neil Brooks, Mark Blagrave, Amanda Di Ponio, Mark Feltham, Teresa Hubel, Dimitri Karkoulis, Paul Meahan, and Scott Schofield. To the students at these institutions: my thanks for your enthusiasm and curiosity. I also look forward to getting to know better my new colleagues at the University of Regina: Jesse Archibald-Barber, Jes Battis, Noel Chevalier, Marcel DeCoste, Troni Grande, Susan Johnston, Cindy MacKenzie, Alexis McQuigge, Craig Melhoff, Medrie Purdham, Jan Purnis, Christian Riegel, Nicholas Ruddick, Gary Sherbert, Michael Trussler and those I have yet to meet.

I am fortunate to have circles of friends that extend beyond the academy. Thanks to my football (soccer) teammates, especially Michael Koval, Dave Mimnagh, Mark Migueis, and Chris Power. Thanks to Laura Hansen-Kohls and Jason Kohls, friends who are, in truth, family. Thanks also to Justin Potts and Sarah Mitchell, Angela Scott and Ross Armstrong, Jeff and Sheila Caughell, Tyler Beaton and Rodrigo Farias: "therefore, ye soft pipes, play on / Not to the sensual ear ..." But seriously, please do send me the recordings.

Romantic Prophecy and the Resistance to Historicism, specifically, has evolved in a close, almost symbiotic relationship with conferences and special sessions organized by the North American Society for the Study of Romanticism. Participating in the annual and supernumerary conferences from 2006 as well as panels organized for the MLA and ACCUTE/Congress exposed me to exciting work in the field and offered opportunities to interact with people whose work I deeply admire and respect, including Jamie Allard, Ian Balfour, Christoph Bode, David L. Clark, Tristanne Connolly, Libby Fay, Steven Goldsmith, Noah Heringman, Kevin Hutchings, Jacques Khalip, Nat Leach, Peter Otto, Arkady Plotnitsky, Dahlia Porter, and Viv Soni. Thanks especially to Thomas Pfau, my post-doctoral supervisor, and David Collings, my external thesis examiner – both read versions or parts of this manuscript and made important recommendations. David Baulch has also read the manuscript and provided detailed, sensitive commentary – an act of rare and remarkable kindness. Thanks also to the anonymous readers for the University of Toronto Press, whose first and second reports urged me to "forge ahead with the whetted axe," making this a more cohesive and focused book.

The most substantial influences on this work – and, frankly, on me as a scholar – stem from a handful of faculty members at Western whose contributions are difficult to calculate because they are so profound. My thanks to Joel Faflak, in whose writing and conversation "there lives the dearest freshness deep down things," an energy that can churn up a person and make even "plough down sillion / Shine." Thanks to Jan Plug, second reader for my dissertation, whose insights always pushed me in new directions: "You must dream up beauty and goodness and justice. Tell me, do you know how to dream?" Thanks to Angela Esterhammer, from whom I learned that "a LION roars HIMSELF compleat from head to tail." And thanks to Ross Woodman, who was gathered to his people in 2014: "wish by spirit and if by yes." The largest single debt I owe to Tilottama Rajan, whose mentorship has evolved into one of my most treasured friendships. As a supervisor, she helped me to isolate the finer tone of my own thought, before it was quite audible to me. As a colleague, she sets a luminous example of dedication not just to Romanticism and the profession more broadly, but to critical thought. As a friend, that light is matched by the full measure of her warmth, her compassion, her humanity. "Cherish in hand, lift down, and not let fall": I hope I can be as careful in kind.

Thanks also to my family: my mother Linda and stepfather Alan; my father Mike and stepmother Susan; my sisters, Robyn and Shannon; my in-laws, Debbie and Steve – and, of course, Nanny Turt. The love and support of my wife, Sarah Rider, makes most of what I do possible. Her ingenuity, courage, and tremendous energy make life better than anything I could have imagined. It is to her I dedicate this work.

~

For the images included in this study, my thanks to the British Museum's Prints and Drawings Department, the Yale Centre for British Art, the Library of Congress, and the Gale Group, part of Cengage Learning. Detailed references, in the notes, accompany each image.

The Social Sciences and Humanities Research Council of Canada has provided financial support for this project in several ways: my thanks for both the Canadian Graduate Scholarship (PhD-level) and the two-year post-doctoral fellowship. Thanks also to SSHRC's Awards to Scholarly Publishing Program for supporting this book's publication. Thanks to Richard Ratzlaff at the University of Toronto Press for his consummate professionalism and patient shepherding of this manuscript over many months. Thanks also to Barbara Porter at UTP and Gillian Scobie for her careful copyediting of the manuscript. Thanks, finally, to Kel Pero not only for producing a comprehensive and sensitive index but also for her eagle eye.

Parts of chapter 1 appeared in an altered and shorter form in *Literature Compass* as "'And Thence from Jerusalems Ruins': Romantic Prophecy and the

End(s) of History" 10.11 (2013): 836–45. One subsection of chapter 3 appeared in *European Romantic Review* as "'A feeling that I was not for that hour / Nor for that place': Wordsworth's Modernity" 21.3 (2010): 383–9. A version of chapter 5 is collected as "Historicism, Temporalization, and Romantic Prophecy in Percy Shelley's *Hellas*" in *Rethinking British Romantic History: 1770–1845*, ed. Porscha Fermanis and John Regan (Oxford: Oxford UP, 2014), 144–64.

ROMANTIC PROPHECY AND THE RESISTANCE TO HISTORICISM

Introduction: Prophecy and the Temporality of Being Historical

For nearly seventy years I have observed, that before any war, or public calamity, England abounds in prophets, who confidently foretell many terrible things. They generally believe themselves, but are carried away by a vain imagination; and they are seldom undeceived, even by the failure of their predictions, but still believe they will be fulfilled some time or other.

John Wesley[1]

At this momentous period, teeming with signs, wonders, and extraordinary events, and promising still greater, it would be sinful to withhold the least idea that might tend to enlighten the public mind; and as the world has seen an age of Reason and an age of Infidelity, so also shall the world see an age of Prophecy.

"A Convert"[2]

When William Blake, in the early 1790s, was writing his first so-called minor prophecies, biblical prophecy was enjoying a massive revival in England. Prophecy had been a popular phenomenon at different, turbulent moments throughout the sixteenth and seventeenth centuries – especially around, as Christopher Hill notes, the Reformation and the Restoration.[3] And with the intensification of revolutionary violence in France, across the channel not only did this engender a reactionary politics but also a conservative prophetic discourse. To call such a discourse "conservative" may sound somewhat counterintuitive. Max Weber's distinction between prophet and priest implies that the prophet is an anti- or at least a para-institutional agent.[4] This certainly squares with the Romantic rehabilitation of prophecy as a form of, in contemporary parlance, speaking truth to power. And yet, Weber admits that "the transition from the prophet to the legislator is fluid, if one understands the latter to mean a personage who in any given case has been assigned the responsibility of codifying a law systematically."[5] While a prophet may be socially and politically disruptive, he or she also advocates for a new system. Hence, when Blake's artist-prophet, Los, announces "I must Create a System. or be enslav'd by another Mans," much depends upon whether we place emphasis on the libratory *create* or the confining *system*.[6] The prophet's confidence in making new systems stems from a claim to special knowledge, very often knowledge of metaphysical truths and of the future. Indeed, it is *against* a sort of normalized chaos that the prophet erects an alternative scheme.[7] From a historiographical perspective, this casts the predictive clairvoyant as an agent of synthesis, organization, order, and discipline. Likewise, epistemologically, the claim to know the future means that historical and political change is forced into available aesthetic and intellectual patterns, the "dull round[s]" that Blake will detest for being merely possible and probable.[8] Taken together, this means that the prophet's future may not be qualitatively different from the past. The result is a defensive, reactionary form of prophecy; Los and Urizen shade into one another.

Many Romantic, popular prophets demonstrate such defensiveness in their tendency to form analogies between biblical passages and their prevailing social conditions.[9] What in the mid-eighteenth century had been – thanks to Robert Lowth's 1753 *Lectures on the Sacred Poetry of the Hebrews* and J.G. Herder's 1782 *Vom Geist der ebräischen Poesie* – a growing interest in the aesthetics of Hebrew poetry gains new, political urgency when Richard Brothers proclaims "God's awful warnings to a giddy, careless, sinful world."[10] Just as Brothers, in 1794–5, stresses biblical prophecy's applicability to "the *present* time, the *present* war,"[11] so too does the anonymous author of "Analogy of sacred history and prophecy."[12] With impressive exegetical dexterity, this pamphlet proposes to "apply this remarkable and most important passage of the prophet Isaiah [i.e., Isa. 8.6–9], which involves in it the efficient causes of the fate of a nation [...], to the present state of that church in Europe; and above all, [...] to our own country."[13] In *A concise view from history and prophecy*, Francis Dobbs, comparing the "*miraculous signs*" identified in several books of both the Old and New Testaments with his own historical moment, asks rhetorically, "Is not the papacy on the eve of its destruction? Is not infidelity prevailing with rapid strides? and are we not called on to watch and be prepared?"[14] Another, similar tract, composed between 1792 and 1795, is even more specific, reading Micah's "I will make Samaria as an heap of the field" (1.6) to mean that the "systems of Government shall be thrown into disorder and confusion, or in other words an intire [sic] revolution" – something that "has been evidently fulfilled in *France*."[15] Nor was this sort of speculation limited to fringe figures, as attested by Joseph Priestley's 1794 *The Present State of Europe Compared with Ancient Prophecies*. It is hardly surprising then that, amid the veritable deluge of these and similar publications, James Franks, in his 1795 *Memoirs of Pretended Prophets*, should diagnose the 1790s as infected with "prophecy-mania."[16] Nor is it surprising that Thomas Paine, using more economic than psychological language, gestures to a whole trade sustained by "prophecy-mongers."[17]

"The need to interpret the French Revolution," notes W.H. Oliver, "stimulated a boom in prophetical publishing."[18] As a discourse for understanding revolutionary turmoil, biblical prophecy also informs – in different and implicit ways – historiographical projects taking shape through the eighteenth century, including Enlightened projects by Gibbon and Hume as well as the Rational historiography of Kant, Herder, and Hegel often grouped under the heading of the "philosophy of history." The offspring of Enlightenment logos and the Romantic revalorization of mythos, the philosophy of history is both a reaction against and a continuation of the Enlightenment. Prophecy, as one form of representing historical experience that exists outside and parallel to the systematic, variously scientific elaborations of historiography by thinkers from Voltaire and Hume to F.H. Bradley, manages to persist in its synthesizing and totalizing work despite a growing suspicion toward supernatural explanations for mundane phenomena. It does this precisely by finding a new form of expression *as* historiography.[19] But why, if it is so popular, does prophecy need to adopt such a disguise? One reason is that for every Richard Brothers, Emanuel Swedenborg, or Joanna Southcott, there was a small army of critics working to debunk and parody such figures. Hence, prophecy evolved and adopted a more ostensibly legitimate cultural form. When Romanticism is denominated the new "age of Prophecy," this is to say that it is an age where the claims of prophecy are both advanced and opposed with new energy, producing a Frankenstein's creature composed of elements of both the sacred and the secular. The appeal to biblical precedent, for example, parallels but also enters into competition with the Renaissance and Enlightenment topos of *historia magistra vitae* – the concept that history is life's best teacher.[20] It is also complicated by a broader thinking of what constitutes a historical fact.[21] Historiography's Enlightened practitioners redefine concepts like evidence and method along apparently secular lines: no longer will testimony be taken on faith, or opinion pass simply as truth.[22] Yet, they continue to organize data teleologically through concepts such as progress – what in itself "[i]n the later nineteenth century [...] became almost an article of faith"[23] – effectively sustaining a latent theodicy.

One reason for the revival of tensions concerning historical being stems from the failure to render a new, modern experience of time coherent. As evidenced by various reflections on history penned in the final decade of the eighteenth century and the inaugural decades of the nineteenth, there is a pervasive sense of increasing speed, of a change in the pace of life itself. Such a change complicates and so brings before consciousness the experience of continuity through time typically managed by tradition. Consider, for instance, William Eden, the First Baron of Auckland's "Some remarks on the apparent circumstances of the war in the fourth week of October 1795."[24] Eden reflects on the conflict with France from a position that seems almost one of hindsight. In spite of a title that draws attention to the text's precisely located historical moment – one that, retrospectively, places Eden in the midst of rather than at the conclusion to the conflict with France – Eden, banking on England's "great naval superiority" and France's economic woes productive of "the high price of the necessities of life" and "general scarcity," believes that "the system of the French government (whatever may become its particular form) is no longer likely to be an obstacle to [peace] negotiation."[25] What is more interesting than Eden's particularly sanguine expectation, however, is the experience he describes that makes possible his treatment of the future as if it is already concluded – as if the conflict is substantially past. His discussion of the "principles, temper, effects, and probable consequences of the French insurrection" are in part, he says, "carried forwards by a spirit of investigation, and a desire to pursue an eventful period of history, *in which a few years have given the experience of whole centuries.*"[26] Historical life in the 1790s is, for Eden, peculiarly dense: it produces more experiences in a concentrated duration than one might have at other times. Or, put differently, experience is speeding up.[27]

This raises a series of questions about how to understand this change phenomenologically. How "fast" can experience become? How much experience, typically measured out across a certain regular duration, could be packed into a decade, a year, a week – like, say, the fourth week of October 1795? And at what point does this intensification of historical time overflow the edges of the present such that one can see, with Blake,

> a world in a Grain of Sand
> And a Heaven in a Wild Flower
> Hold Infinity in the palm of your hand
> And Eternity in an hour.[28]

Can one "live" the End in advance? This is a question to which we will turn later, especially with William Wordsworth and Mary Shelley. Wordsworth, for instance, experiments with prophecy as a means to forestall traumatic, apocalyptic events by anticipating and thus rendering experience – to play on Caruthian terms – unmissable. Shelley, too, imagines living the end of humanity, though her aim – like Blake's – is to compel a fundamental change in the subject and, by extension, reframe the meaning of the future. Indeed, as we turn, in the second half of this study, toward Percy and Mary Shelley, Blake, Schelling, and Kierkegaard, we encounter literary and philosophical prophecies that would aim neither to leapfrog experience nor to store it up. There is, rather, the powerful sense that experience may never synchronize with history – a sense that dominates not only consciousness in the 1790s but also our contemporary historical moment. It is easy, for instance, to feel that one might not be "keeping pace" in any number of ways. "It is this traumatic dissonance," argues Rebecca Comay in a parallel context, "that determines our fundamental sociability: because the present is never caught up to itself, we encounter history virtually, vicariously, voyeuristically – forever latecomers and precursors to our experiences, outsiders to our most intimate affairs."[29] But, crucially, it is this very discontinuity that prophecy insinuates into history that becomes, for the writers in the second part of this book, a resource through which Romantic thought can complicate the ideology of progress. Popular prophecy in Romanticism reacts in order, ostensibly, to quell temporal dissonance or historical untimeliness – to resolve historical turmoil into, as Wordsworth puts it, "A loud prophetic blast of harmony."[30] Yet, we will see how just as often and in spite of its apparent motives, prophecy works as an *amplifier* for temporal, phenomenological, and historical discord. Prophecy thus becomes a mechanism for radically anti-institutional thought but not because of its alignment with rousing Bardic performance – that is, not for the reason typically imagined. Rather, what this study proposes is that prophecy's greatest potentiality stems from its negativity, fragility, and failure. The prophetic subject is powerful because of her or his capacity, through self-immolation, to clear spaces for new thought, especially genuinely different, unprethinkable futures. Prophecy is most important for Romantic revolutionaries not when it maps the future but when it disencumbers the future from the weight of the past and from attempts to entail the future to the past through prediction. As we will see, especially in the second half of the text, only once we attend to this darker side of prophecy can we come closest to its most powerful political, aesthetic, and subjective reformative potential.

In *The State of Society in France before the Revolution of 1789, and the Causes which Led to that Event*, Alexis de Tocqueville reflects similarly on this discontinuous and mobile relation between experience and time. Describing what Hegel might call unhappy consciousness, Tocqueville identifies a gap between European culture's self-idealization and its reality. "In the ten or fifteen years preceding the French Revolution," he notes, "the human mind was abandoned, throughout Europe, to strange, incoherent, and irregular impulses, symptoms of a new and extraordinary disease, which would have singularly alarmed the world if the world had understood them."[31] In fact, he continues,

> [a] conception of the greatness of man in general, and of the omnipotence of his reason and the boundless range of his intelligence, had penetrated and pervaded the spirit of the age; yet this lofty conception of mankind in general was commingled with a boundless contempt for the age in which men were living and the society to which they belonged. Never was so much humility united to so much pride – the pride of humanity was inflated to madness; the estimate each man formed of his age and country was singularly low.[32]

The convulsion presaged by this cognitive dissonance, the French Revolution, not only failed to ameliorate the situation, it deepened the rift in historical experience. One effect of the Revolution was that history, as the narrative synthesis of events, lost its capacity for producing complete accounts since the world it ostensibly mirrored became, itself, irreparably fractured and incoherent. It is not simply that time speeds up or slows down but that subjects encounter several parallel yet discordant historical times, at the same time – an experience to which we will return via Friedrich Schelling in chapter 7.

We see the nature of this change best through contrast. In *Democracy in America*, Tocqueville describes pre-Revolution historical existence as a sort of timelessness:

> Among aristocratic peoples, families remain for centuries in the same condition, and often in the same place. That, so to speak, makes all generations contemporaries. A man almost always knows his ancestors and respects them; he believes he already sees his grandsons, and loves them. He willingly assumes his duty toward both, and he often happens to sacrifice his personal enjoyments for these beings who are no more or who do not yet exist.[33]

This is *not* to be confused with the dislocating "contemporaneity of the non-contemporaneous," however, precisely because "Among the aristocratic nations of the Middle Ages generations succeeded each other in vain; each family was like an immortal and perpetually immobile man; ideas varied scarcely more than conditions."[34] It is, as Claude Lefort notes, the "contrast with this model [that] brings out the singularity of democracy" and, I would add, of history.[35] In the wake of the Revolution, "the thread of time is broken at every moment" and the experience of contemporaneity inverts itself from one of historical unity to one of forgetting and loss.[36] For Tocqueville, the "immobile man" is suddenly surrounded by people from different historical periods, almost like a scene from Shelley's *Triumph of Life*:

> Although what is termed in France the Ancien Regime is still very near to us, since we live in daily intercourse with men born under its laws, *that period seems already lost in the night of time*. The radical revolution which separates us from it has *produced the effect of ages*: it has obliterated all that it has not destroyed. Few people therefore can now give an accurate answer to a simple question – How were the rural districts of France administered before 1789?[37]

J.G. Herder, to whom we will turn in greater detail in the next chapter, articulates a similar point in his philosophy of history when he notes that, in spite of a certain kind of linear development and unfolding through history, the past remains uncannily present, though alien; even if "The oldest times of *human childhood* are past" still "there are *remains* and *monuments* enough" to unsettle the unity of the contemporary.[38] Indeed, given Herder's tendency to categorize history's phases through bio-cultural maps (the ancient Orient is humanity's "childhood," classical Greece its "adolescence," etc.), different times, different "generations," remain awkwardly contemporaneous with each other. It is a central argument of the present study that historiography and prophecy alike, as narrative exigencies, emerge with special force precisely as responses to this kind of historical multiplicity. The break from pre-modern notions of time produces a kind of historiographical mirror stage, revealing a crisis – a cut – in what had until that moment of reflection seemed whole. Thus, part of what identifies Romanticism as an "age of prophecy" is the confluence of different ages: Romanticism is the age *of* ages. And yet, this folding back of the age on itself does not mean that history resolves itself dialectically. Rather, "age of ages" means that it may be impossible to find a single historical container, a single medium into which different histories and forms of historiography could be translated. The following chapters suggest that it is this crisis at the level of historical form that shifts the Romantic imagination away from empirical history and toward a conflicted experience of time that eludes representation and is systematically repressed by empirical histories that bypass the existential question of their very possibility.

Like Tocqueville, Thomas Paine draws attention to this temporalization by addressing prophecy at length in *The Age of Reason*, suggesting, in the midst of his rejection of supernatural powers, that two different ages are in a curious and uncanny way the same. While Paine insists that a "prophet is a character useless and unnecessary," his assertion implies a certain degree of general prevalence.[39] In fact, he argues that prophecy as it is construed in the late eighteenth century "is a creature of modern invention" when, in the form of prediction, it "took charge of the future and rounded the tenses of fate."[40] In its original application, argues Paine, "the word prophet, to which latter times have affixed a new idea, was the Bible word for poet, and the word prophesying meant the art of making poetry. It also meant the art of playing poetry to a tune upon any instrument of music."[41] In other words, only in his contemporary era was "The supposed prophet [...] the supposed historian of times to come."[42] If Paine rejects the efficacy of prophecy's history of the future, he nevertheless confirms, in this rejection, the temporal overdetermination, the multiple ages of the world contained within the deceptively monistic, singular age of "reason."

Reinhart Koselleck uses the term "*Zeitschichten*" to describe this kind of temporal layering as a new distribution of temporal and historical experience in the eighteenth century.[43] Koselleck's research suggests, in fact, that a particularly acute awareness of, and ambivalence concerning, history emerges alongside an understanding of historical time localizable in the late eighteenth century. "The decade from 1789 to 1799 was," he claims, "experienced by the participants as the start of a future that had never yet existed."[44] Or as E.P. Thompson puts it, "It is as if the English nation entered a crucible in the 1790s and emerged after the Wars in a different form."[45] This signals a break in what for Classical and Enlightenment historians alike was an "additive model" of historical thought; such a model, corresponding to "a uniform and static experience of time," made possible the dominance of the above-noted *historia magistra vitae* – the notion that knowledge of the past could educate subjects on how to face the future.[46] It follows from the structure of this "prehistorical" world that "Precisely because nothing fundamentally new would arise, it was [therefore] quite possible to draw conclusions from the past for the future."[47] Such a temporality recalls what Mikhail Bakhtin termed folkloric time which models a form of predictability that renders prophecy superfluous.[48] In Bakhtin's description of this shape of historical existence, the regularity of seasons provides a rhythm wherein time and activity are seamlessly integrated, where each day might vary in detail but repeats a larger pattern implicitly reflective of cosmological harmony. Koselleck, however, identifies a qualitative change in historical consciousness precisely with the interruption of this kind of regularity, positing temporality and history in their modern senses as symptoms of a change in the subject's experience of temporal (in)coherence. One signal of this change is that the concept of the future transforms. Rather than marking a state of affairs relatively continuous with present life, the future becomes radically unlike life as it is known, something completely unlike – to paraphrase Koselleck – the futures of the past.

In the midst of vast political and social revolutions across Europe in the 1780s and 90s, the future becomes "the bearer of growing expectations."[49] These expectations, however, are no longer neatly assimilable to the prevailing social reality. "Events were constantly occurring," notes E.P. Whipple in 1844, reflecting on the Romantic generation of poets and Wordsworth specifically, "to which no parallel could be found in European history."[50] Indeed, "There had been no period in modern history, when those mighty external causes, generally supposed to stimulate the powers of the poet into intensest action, were in such uncontrollable operation as in the interval between the years 1790 and 1820."[51] If novelty, experienced within a world running on folkloric time, is understood merely as local variation within a basic orderliness, Koselleck, like Whipple, sees – in the wake of the American Revolution, in the midst of the French Revolution, and in anticipation of rebellion in Greece and Ireland – the emergence of an experience of novelty that would compel Western society to rearticulate its very sense *of* orderliness. In this transition, historical events are no longer just the content of a narrative that transcends and subsumes them but, rather, are capable of influencing the form of their very conceptualization. So if, as James Chandler remarks, the early nineteenth century is "the age of the spirit of the age – that is, the period when the normative status of the period becomes a central and self-conscious aspect of historical reflection" – this interest in establishing determinate historical categories reflects a new anxiety surrounding the very notion of being historical.[52]

Romantic Prophecy

As Raymond Williams said, "Ideas that we call Romantic have to be understood in terms of the problems of experience with which they were advanced to deal."[53] In the case of a "Romantic prophecy," the problem of experience to which it responds is the growing anxiety about the stability of historical life and what it means to be historical. Prophecy is supposed to help deal with this new feeling of speed and dislocation in time by narratively organizing the sudden appearance of multiple and overlapping ages – a task it continues in the guise of historiography. Yet, as the following chapters demonstrate, historiography's smoothing, organizing, predictive gestures cannot help but call attention to the same disturbances it aims to quell. The central paradox of Romantic prophecy is that with each cultural and literary expression, it revitalizes, elaborates, and exacerbates the very problem of historical experience it is supposed to correct. For this reason, the era of the rise of historicism is also the era of a crisis in historicity, a phase where historicity threatens to disclose a deeper, existential angst and is, therefore, repressed all the more violently. It is in this sense that

Romantic prophecy is both the origin of and resistance to historicism. This resistance is most obvious in those literary treatments – remarkably frequent – when prophecy performs what Blake calls self-annihilation or, more simply, moments where prophecy spectacularly fails to reproduce the kind of regulation that historicism attempts to proliferate under the name of science.

The key to reading this economy is the recognition that the *repression* of historical anxiety takes place through the very *proliferation* of positive, empirical histories. The logic here is articulated nicely by Lefort in his reflection on nineteenth-century historical consciousness as an effect of the French Revolution's revision – really, secularization – of concepts like immortality and eternity. Lefort argues that Chateaubriand, Marx, Balzac, Tocqueville and others register how "the notion of time itself has changed": "once the fracture between *before* and *after* has become immediately tangible [...] humanity's whole past – the Orient as well as Greece, the Middle Ages and Renaissance – emerges, is summoned into the present, and simultaneously becomes a sign of a world that is vanishing."[54] In Joan Copjec's gloss, "The great social revolutions at the end of the eighteenth century may have severed all ties with the past, but they did so, paradoxically, in order to establish a permanence in time, a durability of human deeds that was not possible previously."[55] What marks this emphatically terrestrial sense of permanence is that it emerges "across a historical *break*; what was thus brought forth was 'the idea of a conjunction between something that no longer exists and something that does not yet exist.'"[56] This is the abyss whence historiography springs.

This book is organized into two parts in terms of how different Romantic thinkers respond to historiography's efforts to construe – and, in essence, repress – a newly emergent sense of history. Part 1 (chapters 2 to 4) focuses on appeals to prophecy that attempt to shore up the historical subject. As we will see, Wordsworth and Kant adopt prophetic subject positions in order to, in different ways, assure themselves that subjectivity can master time and historical contingency. Yet, in the course of making their cases, each resorts to a different kind of willful blindness. For both writers, prophecy's healing and unifying promise proves to be unsatisfactory. However, given their deep investments in this discourse, neither can admit explicitly to this disappointment. Part 2 (chapters 5 to 8) concerns, by contrast, works that engage prophecy in an effort to exploit precisely its detotalizing energies, works that find in prophecy's negativity – including its predictive failure – something like Blake's "corrosives, which in Hell are salutary and medicinal."[57] In these chapters, Romantic prophecy most clearly resists its ostensible continuity with historicism.

To give prophecy its due requires that we rethink the long tradition in which the Romantics are read as apocalyptic writers. In different ways, Northrop Frye and M.H. Abrams singled out Romanticism as the discourse of imagination's turn away from history and into itself, in the effort to compensate – through spiritual abstraction – for the failures of political and social revolution. The obsession with the Kantian sublime as a concept through which to read Romanticism reflects a tendency to read the movement psychologically and as the product of escapist transcendentalism. As Steven Goldsmith argues, one might see this reflected in criticism that treats Romanticism as an occasion for making arguments about language or figuration in general. There is, he says, "a dominant strain of literary and cultural interpretation [that] has tended to reproduce the imperatives of formal apocalypse by minimizing the role of history in its investigations," an approach that "enact[s] figuratively what the Book of Revelation imagines will occur literally," namely "the displacement of history."[58] So, despite its attention to historical context, one might accuse Ian Balfour's *The Rhetoric of Romantic Prophecy*, among the most important books on Romantic prophecy, of a similar kind of abstraction since it continues a fundamentally de Manian form of rhetorical analysis.[59] Balfour is in many ways interested in prophecy as *the* discourse of figuration. Prophecy, for him, would be language reflexively "speaking itself," a performance oscillating between language as a positing power – of naming – and as a system of meaningful substitutions. As the ground of figuration, prophecy would remain strangely formless. Hence, at root, every prophecy is a "prophecy that is not about anything" while, at the same time, "all writing that matters may be prophetic."[60] Through an impressive range of philosophical and literary works, Balfour describes how prophecy becomes the field for understanding how language makes meaning. Hence, he details how prophecy and poetry bleed into one another in the late eighteenth century, creating an opportunity for the well-recognized prophetic strain in the voices of lyric Romanticism.

Where Balfour's stress falls on the *rhetoric* of Romantic prophecy, the present work stresses the *experience* of this phenomenon. This means reading prophecy – in popular, philosophical, and literary expressions – as a lived condition shaped in large part by a new sensitivity to time. It also means giving feeling and affect a much expanded role. Against the "anti-affective strain running from Wimsatt and Beardsley to de Man," the phenomenological approach here attends states of being that struggle to find adequate representation in rational discourse.[61] In Fredric Jameson's words, phenomenology "is precisely the attempt to tell not what a thought is, so much as what it feels like."[62] It is this methodological orientation that organizes the diverse collection of thinkers with whom this study dwells: Kant, Schelling, and Kierkegaard, but also Heidegger, Gadamer, Koselleck, Žižek, Deleuze, and, perhaps most important, Maurice Blanchot. As we will see in chapter 1, Blanchot speaks specifically about prophecy as a discourse of failure, negation, and interruption – in other words, in precisely the counterintuitive terms that neatly elucidate prophecy's paradoxical (mal)functioning in Romanticism. But, more than this, his reading of literature always asks, "How can the unknown be experienced without being dissipated?"[63] "Experience," as detailed in chapter 5, is the broader plane on which phenomenology operates and includes states of mind, feelings, moods, and other sub-conceptual registers of human life. And yet, as Blanchot's organizing question indicates, the danger is always that experience will sublate – will absorb and domesticate – what is other. This would turn the chaos of embodied existence in the world into "experience": a subject's possession. The hypothesis of this project is that prophecy is the cultural and literary symptom of a historical anxiety that has yet to find clear, rational, conceptual expression. This feeling is not yet available to discursive reason. If prophecy is, on the one hand, warped by its rationalizing translation into historiography, on the other hand, it spurs the impulse to find new languages that better express this condition of existence. It is in this latter vein that Blanchot's delicate approach to what he calls "the outside" – something obscure and without relation to the subject – is anticipated, in specific instances, by Kant, Wordsworth, Percy and Mary Shelley, Blake, Kierkegaard, and Schelling. In these contexts, the future is that obscure, hazy unknown that thought threatens to dissipate or – to use a Shelleyan image – condense into precipitation: to turn into something probable, possible, understandable, tangible, and ultimately continuous with the past. From "forgetful memory" in *Hellas* to "self-annihilation" in *Milton* to "worklessness" in Kierkegaard's *Prefaces* and Schelling's *Ages of the World* to, finally, "dystopic utopia" in *The Last Man*, Blanchot's "negative phenomenology" provides a new theoretical and philosophical lens for reading Romantic prophecy.[64] This study proposes, then, to reflect on a broad range of embodied experiences, experiences that include but also exceed their rhetorical encoding. Just as Blake's prophetic art operates at the level of dense and complex "states" understood simultaneously as political, psychological, historical, poetic, subjective, and ontological conditions, *Romantic Prophecy and the Resistance to Historicism* reflects on prophecy not only as a paradoxical form of speaking or writing, but also as a kind of mood, memory, and existential condition that – like Tocqueville's aforementioned "symptoms of a new and extraordinary disease" – is "Felt in the blood, and felt along the heart."[65]

David Erdman's seminal *Blake: Prophet Against Empire* illustrates a different kind of limitation with existing Romantic scholarship on prophecy. Reading Blake's poetry consistently as "historical allegory," Erdman treats Blakean prophecy as a form of displaced but engaged history.[66] Although Blake is clearly responding to actual episodes in his social and political moment, he is doing so in a way that is, however, far more impressionistic than Erdman's argument supposes – something indicated, ironically, by how often Erdman has to correct Blake's history. Thus, for all its remarkably wide-ranging and finely detailed scholarship on Blake's historical context, Erdman's methodology leads him to determine art *as* history in a manner that limits the hermeneutic potential of Blake's multifaceted work. Indeed, as Goldsmith observes, "The best recent work – by Jon Mee, Saree Makdisi, and others – has explicated Blake's enthusiasm by pointing it *backwards* in time."[67] This project, however, concerns how various Romantic prophets "orient that enthusiasm toward the future."[68] Rather than either limiting analysis to the philosophy of language or cultural history alone, the following chapters explore prophecy as a social and intellectual phenomenon that encrypts feelings about history that are largely indigestible. The study thus simultaneously heeds historicists' warnings of the tendency toward a Romantic (ahistorical) ideology while remaining critical of the polarizing tendency of some contemporary work that seems to think this means that empirical history and the statistical quantification of data ought to replace analysis of ideas, literature, or feeling. Taking a more balanced perspective, this project treats historiography *as* a Romantic idea, one born from the radical, existential feeling of being historical that initially vents itself as prophecy. For instance, chapter 1, "Secularization and the New Ends of History," demonstrates how the task of historical organization once handled by prophecy finds a more palatable – but basically analogous – medium of expression as the (ostensibly secular) philosophy of history, a science that refigures biblical eschatology as absolute historical consciousness. And yet, the prophecy of sacred history lives on in this "reoccupied"[69] form as the very drive to encompass the totality of cause-and-effect and so to explain historical events: a knowledge that aims ultimately to turn precedent into a template for living the future. Nevertheless, there is a way in which the incoherence that this historiography – as prophecy's proxy – is called on to ameliorate is never perfectly righted. In fact, in a line of argument potentiated by the materialist methodology of the biblical *höhere kritik* simultaneously emerging in the eighteenth century, prophecy's relationship to the future might also be thought of in terms of serial redaction.

Understanding prophecy as perpetual revision is of special importance for better understanding how and why prophecy in Romanticism can grow in cultural relevance in spite of so many failures to predict the future. For how can prophecy flourish if popular and literary prophecies so conspicuously fail to deliver insight? Given the urgency of historical being's existential crisis, how can prophecy afford to be so unreliable? We might sketch a response to this impasse through a brief consideration of a more modern study. In his classic analysis of cognitive dissonance, *When Prophecy Fails* (1956), Leon Festinger and a team of researchers infiltrated the "Seekers," a small group formed around Dorothy Martin (also known as Marian Keech). Martin predicted that on 21 December 1954, a massive flood would exterminate the entire human race save for her followers: these would be rescued by extraterrestrials. Placing the study within a longer history of prophetic disconfirmation, Festinger notes that the strange fallout from such "events" is paralleled in his case study: in his analysis of the Seekers he reports that, like the Sabbataians of the seventeenth century or the Millerites of the nineteenth century, "we observe the *increase* in proselyting following disconfirmation."[70] Dr Richard Reece makes a similar observation in 1815, following the death of Joanna Southcott.[71] In 1814 Reece discovered, much to his consternation, that Southcott's physical symptoms were consistent with her fantastic claim to be pregnant, at the age of sixty-four, with the Messiah. Instead of delivering a child, however, Southcott died late in December of that year. Reece is surprised to find among Southcott's followers a similar reaction to what Festinger observed with Martin's: "After the events that have occurred, would it be believed that the blinded followers of this infatuated woman still cling to her opinions, and that their faith should not be in the least abated?"[72] As we will see throughout this study, failed prophecies almost always prove weirdly productive. Rather than simply collapsing, prediction's apparent cancellation sets off new waves of hermeneutic re-evaluation. Like Chronos feasting on his own progeny, we will observe that it is, in fact, not at all unusual for prophecy to live on into the future through the very displacement of the end(s) it promises.

Mediating History

The logic here resembles how the proliferation of artistic media in Romanticism complicates the fantasy of immediacy. For instance, Jay David Bolter and Richard Grusin describe how the drive for experiential and perceptual immediacy leads, ironically, to hypermediation: the production of multiple media, their layering and combination. What they call the "double logic of *remediation*" names this counterproductive relationship between the desire for immediacy and the actual proliferation of media that this same desire spurs.[73] With each new medium, past media are not simply dissolved; rather, "As Marshall McLuhan reminds us, old media do not disappear: they are subsumed archaeologically, coexist with, or compete against new and emerging media forms, becoming the very 'content' that new media represent."[74] In this context, the term "medium" names a form of communication, a conduit, or a middle layer. But we should keep in mind that it also names "[a] person believed to be in contact with the spirits of the dead and to communicate between the living and the dead. Hence: a clairvoyant."[75] Indeed, if "'Remediation' [...] seems to offer a valuable corrective to our tendency to think of media and technology as successive regimes," it also hints at how the proliferation of prophetic "mediums," in the historiographical domain, often obscures or fractures the linear narratives they are supposed to render clear and transparent.[76]

Celeste Langan and Maureen N. McLane argue that, in spite of the image of Romanticism as anti-modern, we might better think of it as an era of multiplying media. In her reading of Walter Scott's *Lay of the Last Minstrel*, for instance, Langan observes that in the "representation of song, and that song's representation of image, text, music, the translation of one medium by another does not yield an equivalency – as in the ekphrastic model of *ut pictura poesis*. [...] [Rather,] [b]y using his own book to conjure the several arts – music, poetry, and architecture among them – Scott redefines print as a 'general medium' by contrasting it to the archaic 'arts' redefined as its content."[77] Print thus becomes the new, dominant medium through which other media are projected. Even figures whom we might think of as "antagonistic to the dominant print culture," such as William Blake, "identified with [print's associated] values of democratic inclusiveness"; indeed, as Goldsmith argues, with Blake, print becomes a potent medium capable of registering significant, if minute, particularities such that the generalizing that print makes possible need not imply idiocy.[78] The growth in print publication spurs important changes in reading behaviour, namely, silent reading: a practice that, bypassing verbal articulation, seems to allow for immediate communication between text and mind.[79] Through remediation, communication verges on spiritual communion; modern, material print technologies become, in effect, extensions of the mystical medium's paraphernalia.

This is explicitly so in Walter Scott's lesser-known tale "My Aunt Margaret's Mirror."[80] The titular Aunt Margaret, "in a ghost-seeing humour" one evening, relates a tale to her nephew about her grandmother's consultation with a mystic.[81] The story goes that her grandmother, Lady Bothwell, one day accompanied her younger sister, Jemima, to the strange abode of Doctor Baptista Damiotti, "a dangerous [...] expounder of futurity."[82] Jemima, driven to anxious desperation about the fate of her careless, adventure-seeking husband, Sir Philip, who has abandoned her for military excitement on the Continent, finally resorts to the "charms and unlawful arts" of the so-called Paduan Doctor.[83] Chief among his apparatus is a magic mirror through which the seer "could tell the fate of those absent friends, and the action in which they were engaged at the moment."[84] Damiotti is in possession of a televisual medium capable, it seems, of satisfying Jemima's desire for immediate knowledge. Indeed, as a reflection on Romantic mediation, the text thematizes the same fantasy of *telepathos*, or feeling at a distance, to which print and silent reading is also a response. In her analysis of Scott's story, Langan defines *telepathos* as "the prosthetic capacity to hear and see beyond the here-and-now, and its 'discomposing' effect on the experience of that here-and-now."[85] In a sense, then, we might see Romantic prophecy – its palliative *and* disruptive power – not only in terms of historiography but also as something encrypted within the rise of Romantic literary and visual media. This analogy is most apt when we recall that the proliferation of prophecy draws attention to its *inefficacy*, to its *failure* to ameliorate historical anxiety, just as the proliferation of Romantic media – responding tangibly to the desire for prophetic clairvoyance – produces works that are all the more complexly mediated, as the multiplying narrative and historical frames in Scott's story suggests.

Once rethought, prophecy offers a productive focus for reconsidering the interrelation of several major topics in Romanticism including not only media and mediation but, more broadly, the imagination, utopia, subjectivity, performativity, and history. Although prophecy is not identical to imagination, it might be thought of as a specific articulation of the creative mind as it is brought to bear on history and the prevailing political state in an effort to think the most radical possibilities of each. "The imagination is [often] assigned the responsibility," Forest Pyle observes, "of making a linkage, an articulation" between discordant realms.[86] The means by which this negotiation is attempted has, of course, spurred critical debate for years. Does the imagination rescue the subject from contradiction by simply ignoring reality? If so, then imagination is, as Mary Shelley's prophetess, Beatrice, complains in *Valperga*, just ideology: it merely distracts from rather than combats the persistent violence of things as they are. Ironically, then, imagination's attempt to "heal the gap between wanting and being" would mean excusing evil.[87] But what if, following Kant, we take the imagination as the faculty of representation itself? And what if we push this, as Hegel does, following Fichte, and suppose that, rather than transcend reality, this imagination plays an integral role in its active production? This is a world we recognize today as virtual reality, by which we mean not pseudo-reality but a reality that is the product of simulation. Rather than standing apart from the mind, human reality would be, substantially, the process of the unfolding of the mind (or *Geist*, more properly "spirit"). This suspends any neat opposition between ideology and truth and undermines critical claims to elude ideology through the distancing lens of history. Indeed, as Deborah White notes, the sense of the provisionality of this constructed – Pyle would say "instituted" – reality, rather than something enthusiastically bought into, remains for many Romantic writers an unsettling problem. If Percy Shelley's concept of imagination "compels a fragmented being into a whole," the poetic legislation behind this "remains famously 'unacknowledged,' and the 'whole' that imagines what it can know, can never know what it imagines."[88] So, while it is often "Deployed as a principle of coherence [...] or a medium of translation for the discourse of Romanticism, the imagination is simultaneously a principal site of its division and disjunction."[89] This is precisely how *Romantic Prophecy and the Resistance to Historicism* treats the concept of prophecy. Just as the Romantic imagination complicates its own consolidating operations, so does prophecy complicate the future(s) it ostensibly dictates and resist the historicism into which it is shaped by secular thought.

Odd as it is, prophecy's vitality is at its most intense in prediction's afterlife. Prophecy's typical image is, indeed, the reverse of this, its authenticity tied to a sincere conviction in prediction's realizability. It seems obvious that no prophet could be remotely compelling if she claimed, explicitly, that her revelations were merely preliminary to a series of revisions (or re-visions). As even a cursory glance at biblical and classical sources indicates, prophetic declarations, demands, or warnings almost always make historical pre-vision the basis for their legitimacy. As Gerhard von Rad notes of the ancient Hebrew context, prophecy is characterized in part by an "intensive view into the future."[90] Whether this be the hopeful view of Deutero-Isaiah that, in spite of the prevailing Exile, soon "Every valley shall be exalted, and every mountain and hill shall be made low: and the crooked shall be made straight, and the rough places plain:/ And the glory of the LORD shall be revealed" (40:4–5), or Jeremiah's warning to King Zedekiah on the verge of that same Exile – "Thou shalt be delivered into the hand of the king of Babylon" (37:17) – prophecy makes significant, sometimes very precise claims on and about the future.[91] Expanding on George Gleig's original article in the third edition of the *Encyclopedia Britannica* (1797) wherein, we are told, prophecy "in its original import [...] signifies the prediction of future events," William Robertson Smith, in the ninth edition, says that the "Prophetical Books of the Old Testament" are not only "predictive" but they lay "hold of the ideal elements of the theocratic conception, and [depict] the way in which, by God's grace, they shall be actually realized in a Messianic age, and in a nation purified by judgment and mercy."[92] This is the synthetic view of prophecy that William Blake, in his notes on Richard Watson's *Apology for the Bible,* boiled down to the formula, "If you go on So, the result is So"[93] – a formula, as we will see in chapter 6, that Blake finds to be inadequate for understanding history and future potential.

Prophecy aligned in this way with prediction is implicated with a particular concept of history. M.H. Abrams articulates their symbiotic relationship in his reading of Romanticism's secularization of theistic concepts as the naturalization of the supernatural; in his analysis, Christian theodicy remains active though somewhat disguised in both the neopagan return to nature and the internalization of spiritual transcendence as creative imagination.[94] Because, in this reading, prophecy is understood as the genre of metaphysical revelation, as apocalypse, texts so categorized become part of a literary tradition characterized by providential concepts of history. For Wordsworth, Abrams argues, this idea takes shape as a "holy marriage" of nature with spirit.[95] History is understood as essentially rational, that is, plotted and non-random. Prophecy can see into the future as well as through apparent surfaces to spiritual truths because there is assumed to be a history-in-itself – an *idea* of history – serving as a metaphysical ground. Abrams goes so far as asserting that one tenet held in common by major English and German Romantics is a "vision of an imminent culmination of history."[96] Indeed, many of the works considered in the chapters that follow advertise their participation in a literary tradition, presenting their own prophetic forms – at least it seems this way – as the penultimate stages before this completion. Very often, prophets in Romantic literature position themselves as sensitive souls who manage to intuit "the gigantic shadows which futurity casts upon the present."[97] Prophecy as prediction and revelation thus functions in tandem with a notion of history that has, at least in principle, a total shape – a history that has, in the Hegelian sense, already come to an end.

"The Shape of Things to Come"

This rather more conventional thinking of prophecy is characteristic of an earlier generation of scholarship from which the present study aims carefully but resolutely to break. We can perhaps take a series of studies by Joseph Anthony Wittreich as exemplary of this body of extant scholarship.[98] In this criticism, Romantic prophecy involves a form of subjectivity – a vatic self aiming to produce art and critique through revelation – and names a specific tradition and literary history. For example, in his studies of the "visionary tradition," Wittreich conceptualizes prophecy as a kind of complete – or at least completable – circuit. This means he reads prophecy as a literary-historical tradition that includes Chaucer, Langland, Sidney, and Spenser, but "whose great exemplar is Milton and whose holding spool is the Bible – its prophecies and especially the Book of Revelation."[99] Prophecy here is imagined to be a style of poetry that forms perfect "intrapoetic relationships" productive of "a whole system of aesthetics" that reciprocally – circularly – model and spur an analogous historical coherence. With the apocalyptic "Book of Revelation [as] a model for their art," prophetic poetry is considered to be a secular effort to reveal spiritual Truth.[100] "In union," says Wittreich, "epic and prophecy constitute the ultimate transcendental form" and effectively "equip man to enter the heavenly Jerusalem."[101]

By contrast to this established analysis, the present study situates Romantic prophecy between two forms of historiography – philosophical and empirical – that stress, by turns, its positive, predictive and negative, non-predictive relation to history and the future. Influenced by both, prophecy always points in two conflicting directions, generating what I call in chapter 1 a negative dialectic of prophetic historiography. Chapter 1 discusses how various efforts to think historically in Romanticism overlap but also displace (rather than simply enhance) each other, thus exacerbating the sense of acceleration and historical discontinuity characteristic of Romantic historical experience. Prophecy works less to rebuild an edifice of legitimacy than to splay out history's fragmentation. In light of this negative dialectic of prophetic historiography (*negative* because the oscillation between prediction and redaction, while generating complex and interrelated forms of historical knowledge, is never resolved by a third term that sublates the two), chapters 2, 3, and 4 present Kant and Wordsworth as Romantic prophets longing for a predictive, totalizing concept of prophecy – something that would control the spectre of contingency – in the era of its impossibility. In chapter 3, "Ghostlier Demarcations: Mysticism, Trauma, Anachronism," I argue that Wordsworth would like, for instance, to claim prophetic status as a means of transforming trauma, to which he is hypersensitive, into a mark of special election. And yet his sense of being "gifted" never quite compensates for the damage done to his ego as a result of that very sensitivity. Looking closely at works like "Home at Grasmere," *The Prelude,* and "Tintern Abbey" reveals Wordsworth's *assertion* of special powers as, in fact, a defensive manoeuvre, an implicit *wish* that attempts to produce absolute self-appropriation by fiat – an attempt that occasions a broader reflection on the paradoxes of prophetic language as performance in biblical sources. Wordsworth's assertions begin to look desperate and the effect, ultimately, is to raise doubts about the simplistic, stereotypical presentation of his prophetic and poetic energy – and "high Romanticism" more generally – as supremely confident in its expression of the imagination's vitality. In returning to the origins of historical experience, Wordsworth's prophetic poet finds a feeling too deep for history.

Chapter 2, "Prophecy Within the Limits of Reason Alone," and chapter 4, "Beyond the Sign of History: Prophetic Semiotics and the Future's Reflection," read Kant's pre- and post-Critical work, respectively, as, like Wordsworth's poetry, both fascinated with and terrified by prophetic enthusiasm. Based on an analysis of the skewed figures for judgment – such as the bisexual Tiresias – in Kant's 1766 "Dreams of a Spirit-Seer Elucidated by Dreams of Metaphysics" (a reading of Emanuel Swedenborg's prophecies), chapter 2 argues that Kant keeps closer company with "mystagogues" than he lets on. While Kant ultimately rejects Swedenborg's claims to intuit intellectual entities, he nevertheless entertains the possibility of both mystical communication and prophetic prediction, although he tries to argue that *reason itself* demands that these irrational claims not be dismissed entirely. Chapter 4, "Beyond the Sign of History," focuses on his later work in *The Conflict of the Faculties* (1798) and *Anthropology from a Pragmatic Point of View* (1798). Specifically, the chapter considers how Kant attempts to extend the demands for rational totality in the Critical work to history. This application leads to his endorsement of a "prophecy without foresight," or an enthusiasm not completely negated but perversely curbed. Hence, both Wordsworth and Kant retreat from an ecstatic consciousness imagined as harmful to the subject – or rather they *attempt* to retreat, although this effort simultaneously indicates how they remain haunted by a spirit outside subjective, rational, or historical appropriation.

Chapters 5, 6, and 7, by contrast, present works by writers who more happily take prophecy's failure as its essence and attempt to imagine the future and write history in the breach of time. Such ecstatic historiography is, in works like Shelley's *Hellas*, Blake's *Milton*, and Schelling's *Ages of the World*, translated into a dynamic process of re-vision rather than apocalyptic pre-vision. I argue in chapter 5, "The Future of an Allusion: Temporalization and Figure in Lyrical Drama," that, for Shelley, writing historically becomes a process of figuration and disfiguration sensitive to historical context but also oddly mobile given what Koselleck describes as an increasing gap – reflected in the drama – between the "horizon of expectation" and the "space of experience" in the Romantic period.[102] Even as Shelley, in his lyrical drama *Hellas*, puts the methodology of *historia magistra vitae* on stage by making prediction the central task of the prophet Ahasuerus, and even as he sets the text clearly within a classical literary tradition, at the same time the text's content is determined by the contingencies of the Greek revolution. In a display of what in the preface he calls "newspaper erudition," Shelley writes the drama in tandem with history as it unfolds throughout the spring of 1821. This forces synthesizing and dislocating conceptions of prophecy into direct conflict, such that the story of history *Hellas* tells raises meta-historical questions about the possibilities for historiography and the status of the knowledge it aims to produce in the era of Romantic temporalization.

Shelley's experimentation with form sets the stage for Blake's *Milton,* a work that expands on the disruptive potential of prophecy by rewriting the very concept of (historical) organization. Chapter 6, "Auguries of Experience: Impossible History and Infernal Redemption," focuses on the action of "Harrowing" at the heart of the Bard's tale that opens *Milton*, a concept that constellates Blake's material practice of engraving, the literary act of citation, and spiritual redemption. The chapter illustrates how the persistent narrative of Blake's *oeuvre* that presents his early texts, including the Lambeth books, as incomplete efforts at a systematic mythology realized only in the later illuminated books, *Milton* and *Jerusalem*, overlooks Blake's formulation of the prophetic imagination as a state of constant revision or what I call the "state of restating." It is in fact through his redundant layering of systems of organization – where he writes autobiography as personal myth, then as literary history, then again as cosmic geography and political allegory – that prophecy becomes the name for a process not of totalized recollection but ongoing "regeneration." Hence, one could agree with Jerome McGann that *Milton* is an "explicit [attempt] to recover the Divine Vision for, in, and through the world," but only if this is understood as a *power* of vision rather than some kind of final scene.[103] Prophecy, at this point, is almost the total reverse of what Wittreich claims it is when he says that "poets are the agents through which new, more perfect and enduring [orthodoxies] are created."[104] *Milton* writes the *impossibility* of such a history: history radically reinvents itself but through acts that cannot be anticipated. It is this impossible history that Blake complains, in the *Descriptive Catalogue*, is too often converted into a narrative of the probable and possible that removes from history any real revolutionary potential.

Chapter 7 transitions to a reading of Kierkegaard and Schelling via Blake's treatment of *The [First] Book of Urizen* as an interpolated preface in *Milton*. "The Preface and Other False Starts: Prophesying the Book to Come," discusses how prefatory media, while supposedly the foundation for the start of the work proper, tend in Schelling, Kierkegaard, and Blake to dissolve and suspend linear development. This formulation of Romantic prophecy's ambivalence – where prediction is coextensive with the unpredictability to which it responds – as the literary preface invokes even as it revokes the work to come. Kierkegaard's *Prefaces* and Schelling's *Ages of the World* are both, in different ways, locked into the preface and so unable decisively to begin. Rather than their hypermediation enabling access to the work proper, it suspends the anticipated body of the work. One consequence of this is that the works also delay the work of mourning the moment of radical originality, the strangely damaging instant of birth. In this way they become exemplary of what Maurice Blanchot calls the "work of the absence of the work." Such prefaces help to shed light on Blake's regressive temporality, where prophecy does not predict the future as much as explode anything like a stable present. Capitalizing on Hegel's annoyance with prefaces, this chapter foregrounds the place of irony in Romantic prophecy and situates this kind of negativity – where anything is possible, but *only* possible – in relation to Blakean impossibility.

Finally, chapter 8, "'a woman clothed with the Sun': Female Prophecy and Catastrophe," turns to Mary Shelley and reads her second novel, *Valperga,* in relation to her third novel, *The Last Man. Valperga* codes prophecy as confinement and even torture. In the same instant as Beatrice, the prophetess of Ferrera, discovers the truth of her powers she falls into the hands of the sadistic Battista Tripalda. Like Cassandra, Beatrice's clairvoyance comes at the cost of historical agency or even the ability to avoid her own abduction. Indeed, the text conspires against her, reflecting the broader campaign against charismatic women, like Joanna Southcott, who attempt to enter into the large and fractured field of Romantic history. *The Last Man* seems to extend Beatrice's anathema on the Romantic imagination as a mere lure, a power used by men to obscure persistent wrongs against women, by making her curse on the prophetic imagination into a plague that attacks the idealism of utopian Republicanism. However, *The Last Man* marks a significant refinement of Beatrice's suspicion toward the prophetic imagination – a refinement that succumbs *neither* to imagination's identification with false consciousness *nor* to the apocalyptic empiricism that finds the real in the elimination of the ideal. While the text retains a large measure of Beatrice's anger, gone is the naive assumption that truth lies outside ideology in, as Beatrice claims, "bitter experience."[105] In spite of its deeply depressing itinerary, then, *The Last Man* – through its complex engagement with the notion of "lastness" and the important, constitutive role of the imagination as described in the fictional Introduction set within the cave of the Sibyl – aims to purge history of flawed ideas in order to make way for an entirely new kind of future.

PART ONE

Chapter One

Secularization and the New Ends of History

"Israel's history with God thrusts forward violently into the future."

Gerhard von Rad

"When speech becomes prophetic, it is not the future that is given, it is the present that is taken away."

Maurice Blanchot

By 1791, Jean-Louis Carra's *System de la raison; ou, le prophète philosophe,* first published in London in 1773, was into its third edition. As the title suggests, the text hovers between Enlightenment rationality and what, from that perspective, must look like backward superstition. Curiously, the text blends these two antithetical mentalities together: "Je prédirai les progrès de la raison," says the speaker early on, "et annoncerai à la postérité, dans les transports d'une philosophie tendre et pieuse, des jours plus sereins, des vertus plus constantes, plus énergiques; des hommes plus éclairés, plus sensibles, plus justes."[1] Such "pious philosophy" and "prediction of reason's progress," in their awkward combination of rational and mythological language, suggests an uneasy marriage between pietism, with its stress on affect, and an Enlightenment focus on abstract, mathematical systematization. Indeed, in spite of the appeal to "le code des loix naturelles" (vii) that would render prediction possible through natural science – that would see humans as microcosms of the universe – there remains, in the prediction of progress, a quiet kind of fanaticism. In G.E. Lessing's description, the philosophical prophet, as a generic type, "takes well-judged prospects of the future," yet "cannot wait for the future. He wants this future to come more quickly, and he himself wants to accelerate it ... for what has he to gain if what he recognizes as the better is actually not to be realized as the better within his lifetime?"[2] This philosophy of history invites the future to arrive sooner, in a move that is strangely similar to the beckoning gestures of John's Apocalypse. Reinhart Koselleck notices the similarity as well. For Koselleck, the experience of history in Romanticism involves a break between previous Judeo-Christian schemes of narrative history and a modern sense of historical acceleration shorn of its telos. Yet, a "break" is always also a transition, through abrupt. So, while Christian history eclipses Classical circularity – think, say, of Aristotle's notion of historical revolution as recycling – by elaborating history as a narrative with beginning, middle, and end, that narrative begins to experience stronger and stronger g-forces (if you will) the longer history's end is deferred. "In the eighteenth century," Koselleck observes, "the acceleration of time that had previously belonged to eschatology became obligatory for worldly invention, [but] before technology completely opened up a space of experience adequate to this acceleration."[3] No wonder Hegel felt compelled to apply the brakes, to find a new end of history in the rational idea of freedom that he felt to be concretely at hand in the shape of Napoleon.

The pages that follow thus situate prophecy in the context of those historiographies that emerge in the eighteenth century from an attempt to cope with temporal and historical acceleration. In so doing, the chapter pursues a series of different but overlapping questions. For instance, what is prophecy's relationship to major forms of historiography in the eighteenth century, specifically the biblical higher criticism and the philosophy of history? What does a closer look at this kinship reveal about the internal mechanisms of prophecy itself and its ambivalent, even ironic, relationship to prediction? And how might prophecy's formulation in the period reflexively inform thought about history and historiography? Investigating such questions involves a comparison between types of narrative and epistemic negativity – Hegel's determinate, dialectical negativity and Kierkegaard's ironic negativity in particular. The narrative and epistemic reversibility we find in both prophecy and historiography – the way one kind of negativity might slip into the other – complicates how we can think about different historiographies as secularized incarnations of prophecy. For one way to frame Romantic history is to see it as the secularization of prophecy. Yet, this narrative is immediately complicated as a result of the complexity of all of the terms involved: historiography is not monolithic but rather encompasses several forms of mediation and remediation; prophecy oscillates between prediction and revision; and secularization itself is hardly a simplistic elimination of the sacred. So, while this chapter aims to offer framing contexts for thinking about Romantic prophecy as a type of historiography, it also serves to illustrate the intricacies of these same contexts. The result is a richer concept of historical periodization than that offered by the typical narrative that reads Romanticism as a rejection of the Enlightenment.

Koselleck's comments are especially useful for illustrating how secularization, for instance, might be conceptualized, not as the elimination of all concern for transcendence but rather as the reinvestment of that desire in a range of new knowledges. As John Milbank reminds us, the "secular" traditionally refers to a period within the narrative of Christian history: "the *saeculum*, in the medieval era, was not a space, a domain, but a time – the interval between fall and *eschaton* where coercive justice, private property, and impaired natural reason must make a shift to cope with the unredeemed effects of a sinful humanity."[4] This transitional moment is the time of recorded history; history as we know it coincides with that period in Christian history that is a prelude to redemptive apocalypse. The secular is encased by the sacred. This conceptual geography intimates that the process of secularization may have a more complicated relationship to belief that it may seem. The *saeculum* remains, indeed, defined by, even bracketed within, the Judeo-Christian conception of history and so takes its shape only in relation to the sacred. This is perhaps most obvious in eighteenth- and nineteenth-century historiography's assumption that history has a narrative arc, that it contains stages between a clear origin and decisive end: an apocalyptic notion of the historical. Hence, in Jean-Claude Monod's words, "it's also possible to think of secularization as a transfer [...] of schemes and models elaborated in the field of religion [such that] religion thus continues to nourish modernity without its knowledge."[5] In contrast to Koselleck's insistence on modernity's absolute novelty, "modernity would live only as something consisting of a bequest and inheritance," a phase of history where we experience "a '*worlding*' *of Christianity*."[6] This amounts to an extension into other fields of Carl Schmitt's influential claim that "all significant concepts of the modern theory of the state are secularized theological concepts" and also parallels M.H. Abrams argument about the constitution of Romanticism as such.[7] Put plainly, "secular modernity" would be oxymoronic since the concept "secular" would bind all processes, events, or concepts to the sacred narrative within which it is situated.

The secular is a wound or depression in sacred history. This is implicit in the legal application of the term. As Hans Blumenberg notes,

> The juristic act of secularization as the expropriation of church property was so practiced and named from the Peace of Westphalia onward. The canon-law use of *saecularisatio* designates the release of a cleric from the community and the obligations of his order into the status of a secular priest. [...] [T]he "Final Resolution of the Reichstag's Special Commission" [*Reichsdeputationshauptshluss*] of

> 1803 established the term "as a concept of the usurpation of ecclesiastical rights, as a concept of the illegitimate emancipation of property from ecclesiastical care and custody." These defining elements make "the attribute of illegitimacy into a characteristic mark of the concept of secularization."[8]

In this view, the continuity of religious influence is imagined as somewhat monstrous and criminal. Sacred forms of cultural constitution live on but only, like Ahasuerus, the Wandering Jew, as melancholy figures exiled by God. Modernity marks a decline, its continuity with the past offering only the coldest of comforts since that continuity reveals the ongoing diminishment of spiritual life. So, if in "attempts to remake society carried out by secular authorities [...] there is always a religious component," though one perhaps "never exclusively defined in religious terms,"[9] then modernity, however it copes, will always pale in comparison to its own ancestors. Modernity remembers and in some senses rehearses the past, but always in a cruder tone. Yet, the purpose of this brief reflection on secularization is not to advance yet another reading of modernity's origins. Rather, the guiding question is: to what degree is historiography secular prophecy? This chapter argues that, yes, historiography in Romanticism is secularized prophecy. Yet, the terms "secular" and "prophecy" are both more complex than this simple equation would suggest. The secular, for one, is an invention of the sacred; so, while secularization might appear to be about a break from broad religious belief, this very conceptualization of a "break" is shot though by the concept from which it would ostensibly separate. Secularization as a concept for describing historical change cannot be claimed easily by either the historical continuity or the historical discontinuity camp. Likewise, prophecy, as we shall see, is a concept through which history can be rendered *either* more *or* less continuous with itself.

Focusing first on secularization, Blumenberg complicates this concept of transition by suggesting that "the continuity of history across the epochal threshold [consists] not in the permanence of ideal substances but rather in the inheritance of problems, which obliges the heir, in turn, to know again what was known once before."[10] Modern empirical science may, for instance, be able to furnish responses to questions pertaining to natural phenomena that are richer, more complex, and coherent than what was possible from a strictly deductive, a priori kind of reasoning. At the same time, it may be unable to offer satisfying responses to other kinds of questions that had enjoyed more satisfying answers in an earlier context. This is not to endorse as "true" whatever passed for ethical understanding within earlier societies; what it does mean, though, is that modernity sacrifices the ability to make, for instance, ethical judgments in a way that is broadly compelling since there no longer exists a context – a language and a world view – wherein ethical problems can be effectively posed. Blumenberg says something similar and ties this problem back to historiography as another contested field. In fact, he outs the philosophy of history as the modern attempt to respond to the question of historical totality and the meaning in history – questions that had been answered previously by apocalyptic thought and that force secular thought, should it attempt them, to invent some kind of teleological stance, some new End.

"The modern age," Blumenberg argues, "found it impossible to decline to answer the question about the totality of history. To that extent the philosophy of history is an attempt to answer a medieval question with the means available to a postmedieval age."[11] The philosophy of history could be said to "reoccupy" a cosmological ideal of another era; indeed, Abrams remarks that what the Germans call *Universalgeschichte* gained great popularity among Romantic thinkers like Herder, Hegel, and Friedrich Schlegel, and that this is "a philosophical scheme of the human past, present, and predictable future."[12] The concept of "reoccupation" registers an ongoing tension within secularization and neatly frames modernity's oxymoronic discontinuous continuity with theological precedents. While this sounds like confirmation of the continuity thesis of modernity, Blumenberg in fact stresses this same narrative's tenuousness – he heightens rather than dissipates the danger of putting new wine in old wineskins. For "The concept of 'reoccupation' designates [...] the *minimum* of identity that it must be possible to discover, or at least to presuppose and to search for, in even the most agitated movement of history."[13] While indicative of a certain kind of linkage, the language of reoccupation, with its connotation of invasion and displacement, suggests that this continuity is troubled by an insistent violation. The integration of secular modernity with its sacred heritage through this concept of reoccupation turns history into a series of uncanny doubles, of imperfect refigurations, wherein the more things remain the same the more they change: this is a history wherein the same questions are repeated in different moments but yield radically different kinds of responses.

Prophecy holds a significant place at the heart of the schematization of secularization. On the one hand, prophecy is reimagined through the philosophy of history: that is, the philosophy of history takes up questions of continuity, change, and historical representation traditionally addressed by prophecy. On the other hand, since the prophecy from which the philosophy of history inherits the mantle of historiography is – as noted in the introduction – *not* identical to prediction, we observe in this philosophy a struggle between the organization and disorganization of historical knowledge, a struggle between proffering and revoking ideas about the future. The outcome is a negative dialectic of prophetic historiography. This is a rhythm of positive determination and ironic negation that takes place in historical thought. We can see this play out more clearly and concretely by comparing the treatment of prophecy in the philosophy of history to its treatment in the higher criticism. As the following pages argue, prophecy, under its negating, deflating aspect, becomes exemplary as a form for the kind of historical thinking developed in the higher criticism in biblical studies. This will stand in a persistent, unresolved tension (hence, a "negative" dialectical tension) to the prophetic form of the philosophy of history: for in the latter case, prophecy's predictive quality manifests in the claims to positive knowledge of historical trends and the confidence in identifying causes, effects, and ultimate ends.

The story of Romantic history as the secularization of prophecy thus takes on a much stranger shape than we might expect. Initially, the philosophy of history looks simply enough like a secular version of prophecy given its rational teleology that mobilizes post-Enlightenment thought around a basically sacred idea of Revelation. But this philosophy's claim to be "secular" is problematic from the start – and not just because, as noted above, that term is derived from a sacred vocabulary. Voltaire explicitly repudiates visionary prophecy, oracles, and other supernatural phenomena throughout his 1764 *La philosophie de l'histoire*; yet, the philosophy of history he inaugurates remains a theodicy at root, in its *form,* as later exponents in the movement, like Hegel, make clear. What is more, the concept of prophecy implicit in its form is of the synthetic, predictive sort. The higher criticism also adopts a secular historical approach and, like the philosophy of history, retains a latent prophetic quality. And yet, for the higher criticism, prophecy's legacy for historical thought consists of negation, of prophecy's (fruitful) tendency to fail in its predictions. These two modes of historiography, both claiming to be secular in nature, turn out to be continuations of prophecy. Their difference is that they understand and redeploy prophecy in two different ways or along two different lines. This is not to say, however, that division into different discourses eliminates prophecy's internal conflicts – its drive toward prediction and the revelation of unpredictability this same drive exposes. It does, however, help us to see more clearly how prophecy, in spite of the sincerity with which prophets make their demands and declarations and predictions, is also fundamentally ironic. Blake's wary bard in *Milton*, Wordsworth's speaker in *The Prelude*, and Percy Shelley's Ahasuerus, to take just a small sample, are entirely earnest figures – figures who speak if not always plainly, certainly bluntly. Yet, they enact a larger kind of irony insofar as the texts that host their performances present in various ways the tenuousness, fragility, and ultimate failure of their efforts to dictate history.

Since Hayden White's *Metahistory* (1973) and *Tropics of Discourse* (1978), we have been better able to recognize the literary dimension of historical writing. "The historian *shapes* his materials," White argues, "if not in accordance with what Popper calls (and criticizes) a 'framework of preconceived ideas,' then in response to the imperatives of narrative discourse in general."[14] This happens not through any conscious decision to be literary but from the fact that it is narrative as such that "transforms [...] events from the meaninglessness of their serial arrangement in a chronicle into a hypotactically arranged structure of occurrences about which meaningful questions (what, where, when, how, and why) can be asked."[15] Not only do historians necessarily adopt a "generic story form" (say, epic, comedy, tragedy, romance, or what have you) within which facts become meaningful, they also employ various tropes that betray the cool calculation of a scientist who "wants to show only what actually happened."[16] Put in White's terms, prophecy is historiography that is simultaneously comedic – history is completed under its aegis – and ironic, for it can unbind, in an instant, the neatly knotted threads of that comedic narrative. Prophecy's historiographical irony should not, then, be confused with Hume's "typically ironic [...] historical distance," for prophetic irony is a more radical form of narrative self-cancellation.[17] For instance, the history of prophecy's failure, written in the higher criticism, does less to eliminate prophecy from secular historiography than to reveal its ironic productivity and its persistence in how history continues to be imagined and lived. Especially in Søren Kierkegaard's analysis we see that irony short-circuits Hegel's progressive, essentially comedic dialectic, exposing history's "story forms" for what they are. Crucially, irony does not itself provide a new form but rather is the mechanism through which negativity introduces opportunities for revision. It is through that formulation of thought thinking itself, or absolute consciousness, that Hegel effectively ends history. This giving of the subject to itself is the achievement of freedom, which is for Hegel the goal of history. Against this powerful closure of both history and thought on itself, Kierkegaard's irony introduces a form of negativity that opens to the unknowable. Between Hegel and Kierkegaard, then, we see prophecy's positive and predictive form juxtaposed to prophecy's equally potent revocation of determinate knowledge of the future, all in terms of story forms or literary frameworks.

Irony and Mediation

Reduced to prediction, prophecy is the defensive attempt to transform the most dangerously unpredictable activity – its own reflection on the future – into a figure of prediction as such. However, Maurice Blanchot stresses the abyssal negativity of prophetic speech and illustrates how, as a linguistic performance, prophecy remains deeply opaque: "to foresee and announce some future event does not amount to much, if this future takes place in the ordinary course of events and finds its expression in the regularity of language. But prophetic speech announces an impossible future, or makes the future it announces, because it announces it, something impossible, a future one would not know how to live and that must upset all the sure givens of existence."[18] Rather than providing foreknowledge, Blanchot argues that "when speech becomes prophetic, it is not the future that is given, it is the present that is taken away, and with it any possibility of a firm, stable, lasting presence."[19] Blanchot's counterintuitive reflection on prophecy offers the most concise articulation of the form prophecy takes, as we will see, for Percy Shelley, William Blake, Friedrich Schelling, and Mary Shelley. His thinking of the future here also articulates an alterity that registers for the subject as something both rhetorical and experiential, taking us beyond language and into realms of incipient thought and obscure impression: a region we will also traverse with Wordsworth and Kant. Consequently, Blanchot's reflections on prophecy, literature, and Romanticism recur throughout this study.[20]

In his short essay "On Prophetic Speech," Blanchot evacuates the presumed fullness of prophecy, placing emphasis on its often ignored disruptiveness. Typically, prophecy is imagined to follow an itinerary similar that of to the sublime, where a moment of psychic disaster is ultimately recuperated by a greater, transcendent order. Prophecy would in this instance be, in Morton D. Paley's terms, apocalypse followed by millennium.[21] For Blanchot, prophecy is not, however, this divine speech, is not the mystical merger of being and meaning as *Logos*. This is because, in the first instance, prophetic language

> only repeats the speech confided to it, [and is] an affirmation in which by a beginning word something that has actually already been said is expressed. That is its originality. It [i.e., prophetic speech] is first, and yet there is always before it already a speech to which it answers by repeating it. As if all speech that begins began by answering, an answer in which is heard, in order to be lead back to silence, the speech of the Outside that does not cease: "my incessant Word," says God.[22]

The prophet's "original" utterance is always already displaced by the interval of repetition. If, as Mary Jacobus argues, "Blanchot's definition of conversation" incorporates and is formed thought "interruption, pause, or intermittency," then we might here talk about prophetic conversation as a multiplication of voices.[23] The "medium" of prophecy tends toward a sort of hypermediation. Rather than achieving direct contact between prophet and God, prophetic speech actually generates additional layers of mediation that dilate the very distance they are supposed to collapse. Indeed, the rhetorical complications become existential complications when we note how the impression of prophetic univocity is disrupted by the mere existence of the prophet as intermediary. Blanchot describes this ironic duplication by noting that "prophetic speech is originally dialogue";[24] even if it is a simple echo – the prophet relaying the word of God – Blanchot sees this minimal distortion of the immediate as proof of a latent multiplicity. In a move that recalls Kierkegaard's tendency to treat rhetorical phenomena existentially – for example, Socrates not only speaks ironically but *is* irony – Blanchot extends his rhetorical discussion to an analysis of embodied life. The prophet himself becomes a split personality, a subject who has lost possession of himself in becoming possessed by God.[25] Finally, Blanchot's reading links this sense of subjective displacement back to the geographically unsettled condition of the Israelites' priest class as described in the Old Testament: "prophetic speech is a wandering speech that returns to the original demand of movement by opposing all stillness, all settling, any taking root that would be rest."[26] Prophetic language reflects the historical condition of the Levites – the one tribe denied a specific plot in the Promised Land.[27] Shelley's Wandering Jew, discussed later in chapter 5, reflects this older record of an essentially Judaic placelessness that becomes the Passion of an indefinitely exiled nationalism. Like Blake's thinking of the "state" called "Milton" as something simultaneously psychological, political, and rhetorical, Blanchot thinks prophecy as simultaneously a rhetorical, existential, geographical, and historical phenomenon. This multifaceted reflection means that prophecy's irony – that it is at its most vital in prediction's collapse – can invert and displace expectations in multiple domains.

Splitting prophecy between, on the one hand, clear, reliable foresight and, on the other, radical difference and hypermediation is only possible because prophecy perpetuates the cognitive dissonance of the newly emerging historical subject. How can we characterize this dissonance? The negative pole of prophecy is Kierkegaard's "infinite absolute negativity."[28] Romantic prophecy is not accidentally related to this negativity: prophecy and irony each elaborate a workless, non-dialectical negativity that suspends positive projects, including narratives composed by historians. This irony produces what David Collings calls reversibility, the notion that while "The past may be determining, [...] it is also determined, the object of a continuous interpretive activity by which we refigure the meaning of our historical position and the possibilities available to us."[29] Irony is the historical trope through which prophecy and temporality reveal themselves as counter-apocalyptic forces; it both creates the desire for predictive, teleological history (precisely by ensuring the impossibility of actual prediction or historical completeness) while thwarting that same desire.

Kierkegaard's analysis of irony extends and elaborates on infinite absolute negativity, a concept borrowed from Hegel's description of Romantic irony in the *Aesthetics*:

> Solger was not content, like others, with superficial philosophical culture; on the contrary[,] his genuinely speculative inmost need impelled him to plumb the depths of the philosophical Idea. In this process he came to the dialectical moment of the Idea, to the point which I call "infinite absolute negativity," to the activity of the Idea in so negating itself as infinite and universal as to become finitude and particularity, and in nevertheless cancelling this negation in turn and so reestablishing the universal and infinite in the finite and particular. To this negativity Solger firmly clung, and of course it is *one element* in the speculative Idea, yet interpreted as this purely dialectical unrest and dissolution of both infinite and finite, only *one element*, and not, as Solger will have it, the *whole* Idea. Unfortunately Solger's life was broken off too soon for him to have been able to reach the concrete development of the philosophical Idea. So he got no further than this aspect of negativity which has an affinity with the ironic dissolution of the determinate and the inherently substantial alike, and in which he also saw the principle of artistic activity.[30]

Hegel criticizes irony not for its negativity or its suspension of the actual. Indeed, it is only through a thoroughgoing negation that the universal and the particular achieve the productive synthesis that Hegel, in the *Phenomenology*, calls individuality. He is wary, rather, of stalling the dialectic in its negative moment, of failing to negate negation into a higher synthesis. Later in the *Aesthetics* he casts the problem as irony's inactivity, its refusal to put negation back to work or to make negation effective in a project that would involve concretization: a "purely universal consciousness" of the sort indulged by irony "cannot attain to any specific action."[31] The ironic shape of consciousness "ends in mere heartfelt longing instead of acting and doing," suffers a kind of hypochondria that, as with the beautiful soul, "will not let itself go into actual action and production, because it is frightened of being polluted by contact with finitude, although at the same time it senses the deficiency of this abstraction."[32] Irony is too "one-sided"[33] since its form of negation remains polar, remains infinite and absolutely negative rather than "reestablishing the universal and infinite in the finite and particular." Hegel's real problem with irony is that, in it, negativity stops short or attempts a shortcut to make truth instantly and immediately tangible to itself.[34] Such intellectual intuition – that is, sensing ideas – represents an advance over Kant's "optimistic form of skepticism"[35] insofar as it asserts a fundamental continuity in knowledge: Hegel thinks that thought can know itself and its conditions of possibility, that thought can be Absolute in a way Kant could hope for but never claim to achieve. Yet, Hegel is suspicious of any intellectual intuition that would replace the careful, patient work of dialectical unfolding with enthusiastic rapture. Already we might sense the basis for a Hegelian critique of prophecy: not that it makes a non-Critical leap into the metaphysical but that it fails to return to earth.

Kierkegaard, however, finds in irony's hyper-negativity a more ambivalent relationship to actuality, a relationship that is useful for describing the full range of the prophetic mode in dialectical philosophy. Ironic negativity is meaningful and historically effective for Kierkegaard even if its negativity is resolutely workless and, as Hegel complained, abstract and infinite. Irony suspends the drive to make all negativity productive in the name of an overarching project, therein opening the possibility of altogether new projects. Glossing Hegel, Kierkegaard remarks that "irony *sensu eminentiori* is directed not against this or that particular existing entity but against the entire given actuality at a certain time and under certain conditions."[36] Irony at this level is existential, a way of being in the world – or of *not* being in the world – rather than something merely verbal. In words that parallel Blanchot's description of prophecy, Kierkegaard continues that "the whole of existence [becomes] alien to the ironic subject and the ironic subject in turn [becomes] alien to existence."[37] What for Hume is an ironic distance from history that regulates sympathy is, for Kierkegaard, an abyss in which history becomes unrecognizable. Like Blanchot's prophets who are forced to become strangers to themselves, "actuality has lost its validity for the ironic subject" such that "he himself has to a certain degree become unactual."[38]

When Kierkegaard explicitly addresses the prophetic quality of this irony, his ironic subject merges with Blanchot's disruptive prophet:

> For the ironic subject, the given actuality has lost its validity entirely; it has become for him an imperfect form that is a hindrance everywhere. But on the other hand he does not possess the new. He knows only that the present does not match the idea. He is the one who must pass judgment. In one sense the ironist is certainly prophetic, because he is continually pointing to something impending, but what it is he does not know. He is prophetic, but his position and situation are the reverse of the prophet's.[39]

Blanchot's concept of prophecy argues that there is no need to call this a reversal of prophecy. Rather, Kierkegaardian irony perfectly articulates the prophetic negativity that undermines prediction. The ironic prophet, then, opens a new way to think about the performance of prophecy in Romanticism as a certain dis-actualization and detotalization in the hermeneutic relation to history as an object of figuration. This prophet is a historical consciousness that is sensitive to the limitations and inadequacies of his own situation. Just as "the ironic figure of speech cancels itself," so the Romantic prophet revokes the very futures he seems to project.[40] Infinite absolute negativity haunts historiography's aspirations to coherence just as irony, for Paul de Man, lives within but "is the undoing, the necessary undoing, of any theory of narrative."[41]

Sacred and Profane Histories

Before turning to philosophical, literary, and popular examples of prophecy to investigate how prophecy deranges rather than stabilizes history, it is necessary to establish more clearly prophecy's place in eighteenth-century historiography, something we can begin to accomplish by looking at the philosophy of history and the higher criticism in more detail. That the philosophy of history is not a single or simple doctrine is clear from the fact that the movement is closely associated with thinkers as different as Voltaire and J.G. Herder. One of Voltaire's central concerns in *La philosophie de l'histoire* is to confine himself to "prophane" history – and yet this is hardly a confinement in any real sense.[42] That is, he treats Jewish, sacred history in the same terms as the history of any nation.[43] Voltaire appears, unsurprisingly, to be diametrically opposed to St Augustine on this point, for whom sacred and secular history ought to remain distinct (though related). Indeed, Voltaire's absorption of sacred history into empirical history seems like a clear rejection of prophecy, given the central place it is afforded by Augustine in his historiography. This is more complicated, however, since for the mature Augustine, prophecy does not mean predicting the future but rather names the power of rational judgment. Prophecy is the lens through which history becomes a narrative because it is the power to determine which moments should stand out as meaningful within a broad, confusing field.[44] Such a pattern is something that goes undiscerned in the chronicles of Greek and Roman writers. Any history that does not involve a minimum of perspectival transcendence must fail to distinguish the essential events of a narrative from the chaos of human activities as a whole. By the same token, secular history finds its centre in a variety of places, from the political history of nations, to social history, economic history, literary and art history, and so forth. This became possible since, as Dugald Stewart believed, it was increasingly imagined that the human "mind, not property" should form "the connecting principle" in histories.[45] While some of these events may be part of sacred history, their place in a universal narrative can only be determined by the inspired historian, that is, the prophet. Hence, somewhat surprisingly, what makes sacred history sacred is not its content – the particular acts or events of history that happen to be recorded – but its form, that is, the narrative architecture. And Voltaire hardly wishes to do away with history's narrativity, since he wants to tell a story of universal progress.

Voltaire's withering commentary on divine oracles, prophets, and Judaism's claims to special historical status thus seem slightly to miss the mark insofar as the sacredness of history does not base its claims on fantastic, supernatural events but rather on faith in a rational form. In this respect, Voltaire's own history, in its aim to be above all useful for future generations, is remarkably similar to what it attacks. The first line of *La philosophie de l'histoire* makes this pretty clear: "You wish that antient history had been written by philosophers, because you are desirous of reading it as a philosopher. You seek for nothing but useful truths, and you say you have scarce found any thing but useless errors."[46] For all its apparent practicality, there remains in this call a move toward transcendence; if history "has reference beyond itself to the future," its utility and meaningfulness relies on some kind of "total pattern," some kind of whole, traditionally visible only to the prophet (this is "redemptive history") but now also ostensibly visible to the philosopher.[47] As Hans Adler and Ernest A. Menze note, Voltaire, intending to subordinate theological to philosophical discourse, nevertheless "wanted to draw principles and regularities from the contingencies of successive and simultaneous historical events, in order to render history more comprehensible on the basis of its immanent rationality."[48] While undertaken in a spirit sceptical of religious faith and putatively confined "to mere history," Voltaire's universalist aims are similar in essence to what Augustine understood as prophetic history.[49] Herman Cohen puts it bluntly: "The concept of [universal] history is a product of prophetism."[50] Whereas "To the Greeks history remains something we can know because it is a matter of 'fact' [*factum*], that is, of the past," in the philosophy of history "Time becomes primarily future, and future the primary content of our historical thought. [...] Instead of a golden age in the mythological past, the true historical existence on earth is constituted by an eschatological future."[51] This dovetails with Herder's argument that what sets history apart from earlier chronicles and what makes it a specifically philosophical category is the effort to establish cause and effect relations such that we can approach not simply a record of the past but also an *explanation* for the present condition.[52]

This is also the gist of the "conjectural history" of the Scottish Enlightenment, where history is "not a political narrative governed by classical rhetorical prescriptions, but a moral science held together by the desire to investigate fundamental principles of human nature," in other words the "ends of man."[53] Hence, as Stephen Bann argues, Romanticism's "remarkable enhancement of the consciousness of history" is intimately linked to how in this time – in a statement that echoes Celeste Langan's discussion, in the introduction, of print as the universal medium of Romanticism – "history became [...] the paradigmatic form of knowledge to which all others aspired."[54] And yet, this philosophical orientation immediately returns us to the traditional function of prophecy. If we are concerned with a "subject matter's *inner aspect*, [...] the causes of its origination" – if this is precisely what makes the philosophy of history philosophical – then at this same point "historical seeing stops and prophecy begins."[55] For Herder, historical coherence is real and yet also ideal, its truth the product of an "ordering together of occurrences into a vision" by what must be called an "historical artist."[56]

The question therefore is: despite Voltaire's hostility toward "pre-Enlightened" thought and the special claims of sacred history, does the philosophy of history he inaugurates differ in essence from the basic assumptions of *Heilsgeschichte*, that is, from the salvational history encoded in Judaism and, later and differently, Christianity? Might even the gap between cause and effect amount to secular historiography's *felix culpa*, the "fortunate fall" that is so agreeable since it makes interpretative, scientific "redemption" possible? Koselleck argues that historical writing and thought does indeed become a complex mixture of Enlightenment rationalism and Judeo-Christian teleology that renders the historiographical thought in the eighteenth century deeply self-conflicted. For if "There enters into the philosophy of progress a typical eighteenth-century mixture of rational prediction and salvational expectation," this Enlightened "Progress unfolded [ironically only] to the degree that the state and its prognostics were never able to satisfy soteriological demands which persisted within a state whose existence depended on the elimination of millenarian expectations."[57] Generating an ironic loop, the motivating impulse of Enlightenment progressivism is here imagined as an extension of an unsatisfied desire for apocalyptic salvation, the very sort of desire that an Enlightened, mechanistic, utilitarian modernity would deem retrograde.

But then, this is precisely not the kind of future to which several major Romantic thinkers looked forward. It comes as no surprise, for instance, that Friedrich Schlegel, in his 1828 *Philosophy of history, in a course of lectures, delivered at Vienna*, should identify the "object of [his] 'Philosophy of History'" as "the progressive restoration in humanity of the effaced image of God, according to the gradation of grace in the various periods of the world, from the revelation of the beginning, down to the middle revelation of redemption and love, and from the latter to the last consummation."[58] Likewise, in the "Introduction" to his *Lectures on the Philosophy of History*, Hegel describes history as "a series of increasingly adequate expressions or manifestations of Freedom."[59]

"[T]ranslating the language of Religion into that of Thought,"[60] Hegel reads history as theodicy: "Our mode of treating the subject is, in this aspect, a *Theodicaea* – a justification of the ways of God – which Leibnitz attempted metaphysically, in his method, *i.e.*, in indefinite abstract categories – so that the ill that is found in the World may be comprehended, and the thinking Spirit reconciled with the fact of the existence of evil. Indeed, nowhere is such a harmonizing view more pressingly demanded than in Universal History."[61] The apparent chaos of conflicting human passions – the unreliable surface of history that philosophy must "redeem" – is subsumed by "the *cunning of reason*" such that even counterproductive events that would threaten the realization of the ideal of freedom can be read, rather audaciously, as evidence confirming progress.[62] That Hegel's philosophy of history is modernity's negative theology is made clear when he reads the most discouraging and confused data as evidence of a hopeful and coherent universal narrative. Not unlike Kant, to whom we will turn in chapters 2 and 4, the "general aim" of history can appear "only in an *implicit* form" – it is "a hidden, most profoundly hidden, unconscious instinct."[63] Empirical data gains its historical legitimacy only within a prevailing narrative of rational totalizability that subordinates that data, a priori, to the interpretive system. Seen through Augustinian, prophetic eyes, it is clear that "It is not the general idea" – that is, that history is the concrete form of freedom's unfolding – "that is implicated in opposition and combat, and that is exposed to danger. [...] [I]t is [rather] *phenomenal* being that is so treated [...]. The Idea pays the penalty of determinate existence and of corruptibility, not from itself, but from the passions of individuals."[64] History has already been worked out ideally; it just does not know this until Hegel makes it public.

Is it fair, however, to represent Romanticism as simply counter-Enlightenment, as merely reactive or, worse, regressive? If there is a certain revival of concepts like theodicy and prophecy in the discussion of history in the late eighteenth century, it would be naive to think of this as a simple return to the past – especially when a thinker like Hegel is under consideration. Just as "Being must not be conceived as a substance unmoved by thought,"[65] history cannot return simply to its own past any more than one could unstir cream from coffee: with each ostensible reversion, history adds to itself a layer of complexity. It would then be more accurate, as Louis Dupré argues, to see Romanticism as both a reaction against the extremes of Enlightenment mechanicalism and as a complex continuation of a movement based, essentially, on critical self-reflection.[66] Especially in the aesthetic turn from imitation to expression, "Romanticism rather than being a mere reversal of the principles of the Enlightenment fully developed their implications."[67] In the case specifically of historical consciousness, Herder's sympathetic attitude toward "pre-enlightened" traditions and peoples did not simply dismiss Voltaire's insistence on a qualitative difference between past civilizations and his contemporary Europe. But rather than construing that difference as one between ignorance and understanding, barbarity and civilization, darkness and light, he imagines a process of historical *bildung* on the model of human growth. For Herder, the world develops like a human being – phylogeny recapitulating ontogeny – and this serves as the philosophical basis for an interpretation of different ages and different peoples. Egypt and Phoenicia are, for instance, described as "*twins* from one mother, the *Orient,* who afterwards together formed *Greece* and hence *the world beyond it.*"[68] Continuing in this vein, he remarks that "in the history of humanity *Greece* will forever remain the place where humanity spent her *most beautiful youth* and her *bridal bloom.*"[69] At this stage, the "*oracular pronouncements of childhood*" represented by the ancient Hebrews "and the *instructive images* of the *laborious school*" of Egypt "were now almost forgotten" but nevertheless remain valuable, indeed essential, as initial steps in a longer journey.[70] In contrast to Voltaire, for whom history takes a basically dichotomous shape (modernity is knowledge, tradition a comedy of errors), for Herder every new unfolding follows from the "developments of primally ancient seeds" up to and including the Romans with whom "There came the *manhood of human forces* and *strivings.*"[71] One cannot judge the past by the standards of the present any more than one would call infancy or adolescence "wrong" in light of adult maturity. Such phases in development may, by comparison, be limited and yet they can only really be judged by internal standards.

As is evident in his most direct reply to Voltaire's historiography, *This Too, a Philosophy of History,* Herder takes a complex position between Enlightenment and counter-Enlightenment sensibilities. On the one hand, he mocks the concept of progress as the "pet idea" of Enlightenment ideology, an idea that demonstrates a very self-serving attention to historical events and a tendency to confuse "*enlightenment* for *happiness,* more and subtler *ideas* for *virtue*" in ways that prove utterly unconvincing to "the true pupil of *history* and the *human heart.*"[72] On the other hand, Herder is not a sceptic and mocks just as vigorously the idea that history has no plan at all and is a mere "*Penelope-work.*"[73] Ultimately, Herder argues that there *is* progress and improvement in history. However, he thinks that this improvement cannot be empirically measured. For instance, "the *formation* and *progressive formation of a nation* is," he asserts, "never anything but a *work of fate* – the result of a thousand *cooperating causes* of the *whole element in which they live,* so to speak."[74] Progress remains, then, incalculable. The number of variables at play in shaping history exceeds human understanding, rendering causation in discrete historical moments unreadable, a sort of mathematical sublime. This is not, to be sure, scepticism, since cause remains effective: it is merely beyond human understanding. In fact, Herder holds out the possibility that humans can use the imagination as a proxy for a knowledge that is, strictly, denied: "The Egyptian was not able to exist without the Oriental, the Greek built upon them, the Roman raised himself onto the back of the whole world – truly *progress, progressive development*, even if no individual won in the process! Its goal is on the large scale!"[75] Like a river – to borrow one of Herder's most interesting images[76] – that might meander, like a current that may eddy or even flow backward at certain points, there is a deeper "*guiding intention on earth*!, even if we should not be able to see the final intention, the state of the deity, [...] if only through *openings* and *ruins of individual scenes*."[77] In short, there is a progressive development in history but the Enlightenment is not its apex because there is no apex, just a movement that, from the broadest perspective, continues to become richer and more mature.

If progress implies an end in relation to which particular stages are measured, Herder reimagines and repositions that teleology by naming it "humanity." Unlike the abstraction called "*European culture*," humanity "shoots forth everywhere *in accordance with place and time*."[78] This idea of humanity is both universal and yet not identical across cultures. Herder insists on the necessary plurality of humanity in its active expression. "It is fine by this spirit if the Frenchman and the Englishman depict their humanité and humanity for themselves in English and French," since the unity of the idea in no way demands uniformity in expression – just as the same song may not only be sung by many voices but be enhanced by these differences in sonorous quality.[79] For Herder, "the *prototype of humanity* hence lies not in a single nation of a single region of the earth" but is instead "the abstracted concept from all exemplars of human nature in both hemispheres."[80] If history is teleologically oriented toward the expression of a universal "humanity," in Herder's thinking this in no way proposes confining the real to an idea. Instead, the idea itself comes into view and then evolves organically through the actual lives of peoples embedded in specific cultures and traditions. Put otherwise: there is for Herder something called "human nature"; however, this essence is determined by culture, physiology, and geography – from the ground up, so to speak – and as such is a dynamic idea.[81]

Herder here offers a prime example of a broader movement in Romanticism. As Hans Eichner describes, the Romantics, "Who had done away with the notion of an unchanging universe, also abandoned the concept of unchanging human nature."[82] Herder does think of the subject as something unified; by "subject" and "unity," however, he does not mean static states but rather the drives, urges, and impulses toward "something evermore about to be."[83] The Enlightenment's "admiration for the timeless, the universal, and the general made way," continues Eichner, "for a decided preference for the temporal, the local, and the individual."[84] History continues to be understood as meaningful, teleological, and as an expression of "man"; and yet, what emerges as more or less meaningful can change since both human nature and humanity's ends remain ideas in process – a concept that Mary Shelley will, in *The Last Man*, take to an extreme as we will see in chapter 8.[85] Jennifer J. Baker neatly summarizes the interesting consequences of this response to the Enlightenment philosophy of history: "Organically understood, the universe does not run predictably like a machine but, as with all living things, grows and develops. Growth means irreversible change, and hence history does not unfold in accordance with immutable laws but instead registers contingency. The romantics saw history as susceptible to rupture: a new era might be unlike anything that had come before."[86]

This has both epistemological and aesthetic implications that spur new forms of expression in Romantic philosophy and art. For instance, as Michael N. Forster notes, in Herder's estimation "history *is* governed by efficient causation and we should try to discover as far as possible the specific ways in which it is so." And yet, quite reasonably, Herder "remains skeptical about the *extent* to which such an undertaking can be successful, and hence about how far it can take us toward real explanations of the past, or toward predicting or controlling the future."[87] The problem is that history is massively causally overdetermined; the difficulty of interpreting history stems not from an absence but from an excess of determination. This excess makes tracing the precise lines of influence nearly impossible:

> Behold the whole *universe from heaven to earth* – what is means?, what is purpose? Is not everything means for *millions of purposes*? Is not everything the purpose of *millions of means*? The chain of almighty, all-wise goodness is entwined one part *into* and *through* the other a thousandfold – but each member of the chain is in its place a *member* – hangs on the chain and does not see *where in the end the chain hangs*. Each in its delusion feels itself to be the *central point*, in its delusion feels everything *around itself only to the extent* that it pours rays or waves on this point – beautiful delusion![88]

Various and competing human interests combined with various contingent circumstances mean that history is never produced in a simple, linear way but by and as a network of aims and inhibitions that can be understood at a local or micro-level but that rapidly increase in complexity when one tries to shift to a general perspective. History follows a plan but one that is inventing itself through history. So if "in eighteenth-century Europe, history was newly conceived as an independent complex whole, which had its own dynamics," that is, if "Transcendence was put aside" and, ostensibly, "history explained itself," such explanation was always provisional.[89] No wonder, then, that Herder and others – Wordsworth, Shelley, Blake, Schelling – appeal to the prophetic visionary, the artist of history, as the only figure capable of producing a historiography potentially adequate to the reality of life's complexity and then of actually reading that same text.

Historiography can no longer in good conscience confine itself to narrating events since such narratives fail to take into account the contingency of their hindsight. The problem with Hume and Voltaire and Robertson, says Herder, is that they "*model all centuries* after the *one form of their time*."[90] The disturbing insight of this objection is that standards themselves, the very ideas that regulate judgments about specific periods in history and form the basis for applying knowledge of the past to the present and future, are themselves subject to development – that is, to history. Judging the movement of an object is easy enough if the observer is stationary; it becomes far more difficult, perhaps even impossible, if the observer, too, is in motion. As Romanticism is discovering, history is multidimensional, its inner structure a tissue of competing forces. Typically, though, human intelligence has "a merely one-sided viewpoint" rendering "a one-sided sketch" of a "many-sided subject matter."[91] Accounting for this mobile and multidimensional history becomes possible only when "historical seeing stops and prophecy begins."[92] This sort of seeing would be the inverse of the self-fulfilling prophecy of historicism where "I sought what I wanted to find, and [find] it the better the more I wanted to find it."[93] The interestedness typical of – and in a sense, necessary for – most historical writing tends to "bind us to these or those prospects and [to] make a certain state of the historical soul into the most comfortable one, then into the necessary one, and finally into the sole one for us."[94] Herder – like Schelling – here does not predict the future but solicits "the true historical artist, the great painter of the most excellent composition" and "the true creator of history"[95] – a genius for history who might be able to grasp the whole of efficient causality in one grand symbol.[96] And yet, strangely, this would be a prophet who could see all the better precisely by being blind to any one view, who would grasp history's motion only by welcoming his or her own loss of footing.

Redaction and Protraction

As the foregoing suggests, in spite of Enlightenment secularization, prophecy continues to play an important role in concepts of history throughout the eighteenth century. As much as prophetism comes in for ridicule, in Voltaire for instance, it seems nevertheless to set the deeper, hermeneutic agenda for secular historiography. Moreover, when it makes a more obvious reappearance in the work of Schlegel, Schelling, Hegel, and Herder – and even, indirectly, in the "conjectural history" of the Scottish Enlightenment – this prophetic mode is neither identical to prediction nor does it inhabit a sacred, medieval world. A piece of religious property that is pressed into service outside its original context, prophecy continues to figure prominently in how Romantic culture understands history – especially its own history and its own moment as history. The so-called higher criticism movement in biblical scholarship is another important context for understanding this transformation of prophecy's relationship with historiography in the eighteenth century and Romanticism. Indeed, this approach to the Bible, especially to the prophetic books of the Old Testament, proves so productive that Gerhard von Rad, in the second volume of *Old Testament Theology*, argues that "Prophecy, as an independent religious phenomenon, was not discovered until the nineteenth century, when a whole new area of the Bible was brought to light."[97] The higher criticism illustrates how prophecy – as it were – becomes secular and how secularization is a process not opposed to but weirdly continuous with biblical prophecy. For, rather than disappear in the wake of scientific rationalization, or in light of its own long history of disconfirmation, prophecy continues to play a prominent role in framing historical experience. Indeed, as the higher criticism reveals, prophecy's modern, secular form may be as old as the writing and canonization of the books that constitute the Bible.

E.S. Shaffer argues that the broad shift in consciousness von Rad alludes to begins more precisely in the late eighteenth century.[98] J.G. Eichhorn, in his five-volume *Introduction to the Study of the Old Testament* published between 1780 and 1783, coins the phrase "*die höhere Kritik*" to name the textual and archaeological methodology for analysing biblical works as cultural products composed by human beings in particular, localizable historical contexts.[99] The higher criticism rejects the Bible's traditionally held pretensions to purely divine authorship, understanding the text as, rather, the product of various and necessarily fallible human authors. "A complete history of the Hebrew text would," Eichhorn argues, "enumerate, with reference to causes and consequences, all the essential and accidental changes, whether for good or evil, which it has undergone in the process of thousands of years and in its passage through men's hands, from the time of its first composition down to the latest periods."[100] While not incompatible with "the exceeding wisdom of the Divine dispensation" as such, the higher criticism poses major challenges to traditional exegesis and demands that theology adapt itself to historical discoveries concerning, for instance, the corrected chronology of textual composition, the political affiliations of specific authors, and multiple instances of apparent redaction.[101] Viewed from this perspective, a major question emerges concerning prophecy. Why, specifically, do the prophetic books of the Bible bear the traces of so much revision? More specifically, why not simply eliminate failed prophecies from the record entirely? Extant records of prophetic episodes, in other words, are conspicuous vestiges of an apparently dead discourse. How and why does prophecy live on in such a prominent way in the Bible in spite of its apparent exhaustion?[102] One compelling response to this phenomenon is that once prophecy is canonized and formalized as a *book* in the textual life of the Bible it becomes an altogether different thing. As an emphatically textual production, biblical prophecy's significance can no longer be judged in terms of promissory efficacy. With perhaps the exception of end-time prophecies, the future toward which biblical prophecies typically gesture represents moments, even at the time of their writing, belonging to the past. So, if prophecy nevertheless lives on in culture, it is not because it predicts what will happen tomorrow but because it serves as a cultural archive out of which subjects might draw rich material for reinvention.

As biblical scholars working in the tradition of the higher criticism have been among the first to see clearly, "What makes the Hebrew Bible different from any other ancient Near Eastern source [concerning prophecy] is the length, the depth and the purpose of the editorial activity that turned prophecy into literature."[103] Martti Nissinen, echoing Ehud Ben Zvi and Michael Floyd, goes so far as to assert that the function of the prophetic books of the Bible "is to transcend the message of ancient prophets for new audiences, not to conserve the 'original' word of the prophet."[104] Von Rad develops this reading of prophecy as a discourse that abandons its predictive, synthetic exigency to become a linguistic and cultural archive. The anticipation characteristic of prophecy metamorphoses into an exigency through which "Israel's history with God thrusts forward violently into the future," in the form not of a priori determination but of iterability.[105] For instance, von Rad points out the curious fact that whether the promises announced are unfulfilled or fulfilled – in either case, ostensibly exhausted – prophetic texts for the Hebrews "could never in any circumstances become void" and therefore "were retained as prophecies which concerned Israel and could always have fresh meaning extracted from them."[106] Hence, what Marshall McLuhan observed of media – that old media never disappear but become rather the very content of new media – also well describes Hebrew prophecy's ongoing self-remediation. Objects of a "centuries-long incessant process of continual reinterpretation of tradition," prophetic oracles open a new futurity by gathering together a record of Judaism's most pressing concerns about its own national and historical prospects.[107] What this record preserves is not a story of fulfilled expectations but rather the history of the reshaping and reformulation of expectations in light of routine disappointment. If "the way in which [Judaic] tradition mounts and grows can be closely followed in the prophetic writings," this means only that these writings encode a negativity – what was above identified as an irony – within their production that sustains the possibility of perpetual rewriting.[108] That is, the close textual analysis of the higher criticism reveals textual revision (a complex history of cutting, pasting, citation, and redaction) to be the *defining* feature of biblical prophecy. Embracing rather than ignoring this history calls, therefore, for a form of "Exegesis [that] must be less ready than at present to look on this infusion of new blood into the prophetic tradition as 'spurious' or an unhappy distortion of the original. The process is in reality a sign of the living force with which the old message was handed on and adapted to new situations."[109] In von Rad's analysis, prophecy's cultural fecundity is intimately related to prediction's failure, as if it were made to be "reoccupied" in Blumenberg's sense. This would make prophecy the ideal medium for secularization, for a process of cultural auto-remediation. Prophecy would also be elevated to the status of literature insofar as it embraces the irony that dissolves any generic story form, whether comic or tragic, that this same prophecy is called on to compose.

This negativity is neither accidental nor a late supplement added to an original, full biblical text. Biblical prophecy, in the *first* instance, is formulated as a *response* to its own imminent failure. As Robert Carroll notes, "the very failure of prophecy was to become the necessary condition for the growth of subsequent movements of reinterpretation of the traditions."[110] Carroll's close textual analysis of the Bible reveals a series of loose ends in the prophetic books indicative of editing and re-editing, what he takes as "responses to regular frustration of hopes."[111] If prophecy is formed out of prediction's strangely vital afterlife, then, as Carroll continues,

> The important task of interpretation is not demonstrating that the predictions were wrong but showing how they were treated by the later communities as ongoing possibilities for their future. Had being right or wrong been the main consideration then perhaps the traditions would never have survived[.] [Yet, evidently] small groups went on reinterpreting those traditions because they kept alive the vision of the earlier prophets. That vision was to have a creative significance repeatedly in the following centuries.[112]

If ever a voice aspired to self-presence, it is the prophetic voice. And yet, we see here a textual expression of what Blanchot identified as the doubling and displacement inherent in prophetic speech. What biblical scholarship in the tradition of the higher criticism indicates is that the prophet's voice is, in the first instance, a trace: instead of vatic fullness, the prophetic utterance anticipates – first and foremost – its own remediation, in effect evacuating itself pre-emptively, turning itself into a shell of its own non-origin.[113] Redaction rather than preservation of an original utterance is the defining characteristic of written biblical prophecy. Hence, the "so-called *ipsissima verba*" or prophet's original utterance is "unreachable."[114] Textual scholarship thus provides a path to a thinking of prophecy as a peculiar kind of negativity, opening history to the possibility of active refiguration, though at the price of disfiguring all narrative formulations that claim, decisively and finally, to align cause with effect and establish, to borrow Karl Löwith's phrase, "the meaning in history."[115]

Prophecy's relation to the future is now inverted. Rather than projecting (into) the future as the continuation and realization of the prophet's word, that word becomes the track that future readers regard retrospectively while retreating into an unknown tomorrow. As Schlegel writes, "the historian is a prophet facing backwards" and as such the tracks he sees are his own, are the failed prophecies that, like the ruins in Benjamin's adaptation of this image, blow the angel of history into the future.[116] This ambiguity concerning the prophet's temporal orientation is only intensified by the curious nature of ancient Hebrew. As Carroll notes, "the vexed problem of determining the precise meaning of the phrase *lōʾ-nābîʾ ʾānōkî welōʾ ben-nābîʾ ʾānōkî* indicates something of the ambiguity of prophetic speech. It may be taken as 'I am not a prophet,' or 'I was not a prophet' (but now am one), or 'Am I not a prophet?', or even as an emphatic 'I am a prophet.'"[117] Capturing some of the irony of prophetic speech, this ostensibly clear statement of identity turns out to be reversible and to invite all kinds of possible meanings while accepting none as decisive. No wonder, then, if Hebrew prophecy remains an active element in the formulation of historical futurity and that it remains equally available to gradualist and catastrophist formulations of that futurity. Prophecy's ambivalence makes synthetic, progressive historiography possible even as it suspends those same narratives or renders their sense episodic and provisional.

The foregoing pages have sketched, in a broad way, Romantic prophecy's genetic relationship to eighteenth-century historiography. This relationship is complex, however, since concepts like secularization and prophecy deconstruct the very continuities they seem to reinforce. This means that ideas of history in Romanticism are often inhabited by the spirits of a bygone time, complicating both their basis in a secular thinking that repudiates all transcendence and the operation of secularization itself. As a mode of sacred and (as it were) prehistorical historiography, we might well expect prophecy to be purged from the work of Enlightenment historians and philosophers working in ostensibly secular registers. Yet, when Enlightenment and post-Enlightenment historiography attempts to distinguish itself from earlier approaches to the past – chronicles, myths, legends, etc. – it does so on the claim that it can offer insight about cause, effect, and, ultimately, meaning. As Jan Plug puts it, "history takes place as the fulfillment of the promise of meaning," which means that a form of prophecy is the condition for history's possible meaningfulness.[118] This move, which Herder saw as fundamentally philosophical and reflexive rather than neutrally documentary and empirical, encrypts Judeo-Christian teleology as rational, systematic completeness. History's potential meaningfulness depends upon its re-elaboration as narrative amenable to story types – whether progressive or degenerative. And this is a holdover from the very tradition the enlightened sciences would repudiate.

Yet, the reoccupation of prophecy by new, rational ends is only half of the story. Prophecy itself turns out *not* to be a story form that offers completeness and coherence, in spite of appearing to be decidedly, even fanatically, teleological. Rather, prophecy is deeply ironic. With one hand, prophecy sketches history's completion while, with the other hand, it revokes any stable, lasting present. We see this most vividly in the higher criticism. This school brings documentary and archaeological methods to bear on sacred texts, indeed, on biblical prophecies themselves. Given this mode of scrutiny, we may well expect prophecy to be dismissed as an illegitimate category of historical understanding, as pseudo-knowledge and superstition. Instead, the higher criticism illustrates how prophecy itself functions differently from expectation. We discover that prophecy's relationship to the future is not anticipatory but rather revisionist, that Hebrew prophecy's defining feature is its redactibility, its availability for revision. It is this second, ironic mode of prophecy that the Romantics discussed in the second half of this study evoke in their own attempts to think historically.

As noted, this chapter has taken a general perspective on the history of ideas of history, including and especially prophecy in the eighteenth century, roughly from the Enlightenment to Romanticism. The aim was to provide a larger context for subsequent readings that will focus more particularly on specific thinkers and works of literature and philosophy. Indeed, the following chapter continues to ask the question, "in what way is historiography secularized prophecy?" but does so in terms of a specific case: Immanuel Kant's reading of Emanuel Swedenborg. The following looks with greater precision at how Critical philosophy, as the pivot between Enlightenment and Romantic thought, confronts prophetic mysticism. In cordoning off metaphysics, Kant seems to be the last thinker to approve of prophecy. And yet, we will see how his philosophy does not eliminate but rather appropriates – absorbs and transforms – prophecy in the name of reason itself, performing philosophically an operation that Wordsworth, as we will see in chapter three, aims to accomplish poetically.

Chapter Two

Prophecy within the Limits of Reason Alone

The growth of higher feeling within us is like the growth of faculty, bringing with it a sense of added strength: we can no more wish to return to a narrower sympathy, than a painter or a musician can wish to return to his crude manner, or a philosopher to his less complete formula.

George Eliot, *Adam Bede*

In 1936, Paul Valéry posed a question interesting not only for its content but also for its form. "How," he asked, "is a Swedenborg possible?" That is,

> What must be assumed to consider the coexistence of the qualities of a learned engineer, an eminent government official, of a man who was wise in practical matters and learned in every field, with the characteristics of a visionary who has no hesitation in writing out and publishing visions, in allowing himself to be known as one visited by the inhabitants of another world, taught by them, and living a part of his life in their mysterious company?[1]

Valéry here asks what circumstances, what influences must conspire to produce the unlikely combination that was Emanuel Swedenborg. The question is difficult to answer in this case given Swedenborg's sudden turn, in 1744, from a life of science and administration in the Swedish Bureau of Mining to mysticism – the result of a series of prophetic dreams. What inspired such dreams and, perhaps more important, what informed Swedenborg's response to them remains beyond the purview of typical narrative history that, as William Blake complains, accounts only for the narrow story of the possible and the probable.[2] But the importance of Valéry's question has also to do with its strikingly Kantian shape. Echoing the first *Critique*, Valéry asks not what Swedenborg is or was in himself (as it were) but only about the conditions of his possibility, restricting inquiry – in a perfectly Kantian way – to the thinkable conditions of a phenomenon. Indeed, in channelling the sage of Königsberg to address the spirit of Stockholm, Valéry pays subtle tribute to an intellectual influence the depth of which is difficult to discern in the history of thought, thanks in no small part to Kant's explicit repudiation of all spiritualists, like Swedenborg, who adopt a "higher tone" in philosophy.[3] Yet, it is not an overstatement to say that Swedenborg remains one important condition of a possible Kantianism. Kant might awaken from Swedenborg's dogmatism but he will retain the outlines of the latter's dreams.

In what sense is dogmatism a form of sleep? In the *Prolegomena to Any Future Metaphysics*, Kant famously credits Hume with waking him up from his "dogmatic slumber."[4] Dogmatism is a sort of unconsciousness in part because it is so comfortable. Sleep does not visit the anxious, agitated mind. Unlike dogmatism, transcendental philosophy vigilantly polices the subject-object distinction, forestalling the simple reduction of the one to the other. Dogmatic sleep would be comfortable, in other words, because it would be dreamless: there are no serpents in this philosophical garden to guard against, no satanic toads sowing the seeds of transgression to slumbering innocence, because there *is* no injunction to defy, no netherworld to fear. Only if the subject is of the schizophrenic sort Kant posits – inhabited by "an alien will"[5] that urges us beyond material sense toward something transcendent, a realm of spirits that are different in kind and yet somehow in communication with matter – are dreams even possible. Extending Kant's invocation of the prophet Tiresias, we might say dreams are the hermaphrodites of metaphysics: they are the understanding's attempt to represent in intuitable terms the pure spirit, the active life-force that inhabits a universe of ghosts. Hence,

> when a person dreams, he is not completely asleep; to a certain degree he has clear sensations, and weaves the actions of his spirit into the impressions of external senses. Hence it is that he subsequently remembers them in part; and hence it is that he also finds in them nothing but wild and extravagant chimeras, as must happen, since the ideas of the imagination and those of external sensation have been jumbled together with each other. (325)

The more one attempts to retain the metaphor of sleeping and wakening to describe Kant's change in philosophical attitude, however, the more problematic it becomes. For to "awaken" from dogmatic slumber would mean, now, to sink into dream and consequently to become aware of the dream as a sign for a world about which knowledge must remain deeply uncertain. "Do I wake or do

I sleep?" is a question that occurs only to one who has awoken into a life that, populated not by things but phenomena, *is* a dream.[6]

According to Kant's romping 1766 essay, "Dreams of a Spirit-Seer Elucidated by Dreams of Metaphysics," dreaming nudges thought toward its own outside. Foreshadowing his later characterization of experience as the phenomenal expression of noumenal reality – where the thing-in-itself is both reflected by and yet occluded in its very recognition by consciousness – the dream is characterized as a symbol of sorts: "For these influences [i.e., spirits] can enter the personal consciousness of man, not, it is true, directly, but, nonetheless, in such a fashion that they, in accordance with the law of association of ideas, excite those images which are related to them, and awaken representations which bear an analogy with our senses. They are not, it is true, the spirit-concept itself, but they are symbols of it" (326). Hence, in one among several reversals or ironic inversions, to dream is to heighten consciousness and yet to remain within specific bounds.[7] To dream, to see life as a dream inviting analogy with a world of spirits beyond all direct intuition, does not mean gaining direct access to such a world. Rather, the dream demarcates a limit – and in this one glimpses an early articulation of Kant's Critical idealism that concerns itself with establishing the limits of possible knowledge. To transgress this limit is to become a mystic, a "seer" who claims to have an intellectual intuition, to have a sensorium heightened to such a pitch that he can feel, and so convert into actual experience, the purely ideal. Kant, even in this early essay decries what he will later call transcendental illusion. So, put in the preferred terms of the essay, Kant would save his reader all form of "expense" – intellectual, financial, and even perhaps sexual – by investigating on the reader's behalf the claims of renowned mystic Emanuel Swedenborg.

Swedenborg was the metaphysician the public hoped Kant would become. In the aftermath of his highly acclaimed "The Only Possible Basis of Proof for a Demonstration of God's Existence" (1763), Kant's readers "expected and hoped for [...] a new, deeper, and more tenable metaphysics – an abstract, analytic dissection of its presuppositions and a careful theoretical examination of its most general conclusions."[8] At this time, Christian Wolff's metaphysics, disseminated especially through Alexander Baumgarten, ventured into domains such as ontology, cosmology, psychology, and natural theology, blending empirical experience with ideal entities in a fashion that aimed to defeat scepticism by extending theoretical understanding all the way to the foundations of knowledge as such. As hinted in his Introduction to *Dreams*, Kant's goal is, however, to find a "third possibility" (305) that would borrow elements from empiricism and from idealism without succumbing to the limitations of either. In *Dreams*, these limitations are described in terms of the compelling data one would have to deny in order to remain strictly in one camp or the other. "To believe *none* of the many things which are recounted with some semblance of truth, and to do so without any reason, is as much a foolish prejudice as to believe *anything* which is spread by popular rumour, and to do so without examination" (306). Kant's apparently whimsical decision to invite conflicting forms of prejudice, and then to expose this very inconsistency formally in his essay's divisions, represents a serious effort to establish precisely what is necessary to retain of empiricism and idealism, respectively. With Kierkegaardian aplomb, Kant's "first part, which is dogmatic," speculates on the nature of "immaterial beings" (311), effectively ventriloquizing Swedenborg. In "the second part, which is historical," Kant adopts the opposite perspective, working from recorded narratives rather than a priori arguments from reason.

The outcome of this two-pronged approach is, ultimately, to discipline – but *not* to eliminate – prophecy. By attending to how Kant, in *Dreams,* negotiates between categories like the synthetic and the analytic, the a posteriori and the a priori – between material, tangible experience and spiritual, moral feeling – we can see how Kant sublimates prophecy and how the later Critical philosophy appropriates enthusiasm even as it tries to obscure its subtle, continuing contribution to his system. The form of Kant's argument, however, exposes what would like to remain hidden. Just as dreams hover between domains, Kant resembles Tiresias, whom he invokes as a figure suspended between worlds: the past and the future, man and woman. The Kant of *Dreams*, in other words, is a being with double organs. Yet, unlike the prophet, Kant insists on a kind of prophylactic reflection that forestalls production of the "mooncalves" of reckless self-insemination (353). Hence, if *Dreams*, as Susan Meld Shell argues, is "an exercise in metaphysical detumescence," this is but another way to describe Kant's flirtation with prophetic invention and his struggle with modes of counter-conception or, in short, contraception.[9] Yet, Kant's appeal to reason turns out to share in an orgiastic excess, or enthusiasm. Rather than advocate for a mode of judgment abstracted from lived experience, Kant's rationalism reveals its proximity to the Heideggerian and Gadamerian notion of pre-judgment – for, as we will see, Kant says his scales of the understanding are *by design* off kilter. Kant's analysis of reason has a deeply prophetic strain that functions as an implicit, Romantic critique of what Gadamer identifies as the Enlightenment's prejudicial rejection of prejudice, that is, fore-conception, as the necessary – and necessarily "skewed" or "unbalanced" – conditions for any judgment. Kant reformulates the Enlightenment rejection of prejudice, then, by making reason, the ostensible enemy of pre-judgment, *into* his own form of pre-judgment.

Seeing Double

What is spirit? In an important footnote in the first chapter of *Dreams*, Kant identifies "the principle *of life*" as one good example (315). This principle would inhabit matter, have "*external* relations" (i.e., a relation to matter), and yet would not conform to physical laws (309): "for the presence of such spirit-natures would involve *being active in* but not *filling* space" (311). One implication of this thoroughly uncanny relation is that it inoculates the "*spontaneously active*" power of reason against the determinism of nature (315). Spirit thus figures what will later become the central concern of Kant's practical philosophy, namely, freedom: "for all *life* is based upon the inner capacity to determine itself *voluntarily*" (315). Understood as this force of pure self articulation, spirit thus seems to relate to matter and yet remain both descriptively elusive and functionally mysterious. What Kant's opening chapter illustrates is that while spirit might be effective in nature, it cannot be represented in-itself. This is because spirit – to put it in his later, Critical language – is subject neither to the intuitions of space and time nor to the categories of understanding. It is on this point that Kant's confidence that "we may [...] accept the possibility of immaterial beings without any fear that we shall be refuted" butts up against the requirements of theoretical knowledge. Residing beyond the conditions of the understanding makes questions of spirit's shape, place, extension, or community impossible. Kant is thus "not willing [...] to become involved in one of those scholarly wrangles in which it is commonly the case that both sides have the most to say precisely when their ignorance of the subject is most complete" (314). And yet, while Kant is uninterested in Cartesian or Lucretian speculations on the place or physical constitution of the soul, there remains the "natural [...] incomprehensibility" – in effect, then, a comprehended incomprehensibility – of the body's liveliness and human freedom. There is an obvious relationship between matter and spirit that, nevertheless, cannot be understood.

In the second chapter of the first division, "A Fragment of Occult Philosophy, the Purpose of Which is to Reveal Our Community with the Spirit-World," Kant crosses over, so to speak, to the world of spirits to investigate, from the hither side, the "mysterious [...] community which exists between a spirit and a body." If spirit interacts with matter – an unlikely yet demonstrable fact – it would be less surprising if spirit formed a community unto itself. On this basis Kant posits an "*immaterial world*" wherein spirits would communicate with each other immediately, for this society "would not be based on the conditions which limit the relationship of bodies" (317, 319). For Kant, this would be community par excellence in that "distance in space and separation in time, which constitute the great chasm of the visible world which cancels all community, would vanish" (319). The text thus places humans on a precarious isthmus situated between matter and spirit: "The human soul, already in this present life, would therefore have to be regarded as simultaneously linked to two worlds" (319). The situation is precarious in that the human being, subject to different states of consciousness, can on occasion lose sight of one territory or the other. Losing touch with spirit's obscurity induces dogmatic slumber; losing touch with matter's opacity renders one fanatical or insane. An additional challenge, though, is to understand the nature of the bond between matter and spirit located in the subject in a way that does not simply defer the problem by carving that subject in two. Initially, Kant does appear to be sharpening his analytic saw when he says that the human soul "has an effect upon [immaterial natures], though the human soul *qua* human being is not conscious of them" (320). But the argument quickly turns away from such parcelling and enters onto a crucial digression ("it will, admittedly, take me some distance from my path" [321]) that aims to recast the matter/spirit opposition in terms that make possible a new, more satisfying form of relation.

Spiritual and material beings intuit their worlds in radically different ways. Spirit-being's concepts, "in so far as they are intuitive representations of immaterial things," are not subject to the conditions of knowledge that apply to all corporeal beings, and vice versa (320). So, in an effort to conceptualize how the immaterial world might gain traction on matter, Kant changes the ground of the relation, entering into a discussion of the social impulse. Drawing in several ways on Rousseau, Kant notes that "among the forces which move the human heart, some of the most powerful seem to lie outside the heart" (321). As Cassirer remarks, whereas "Newton helped [Kant] to clarify the phenomenon of the world[,] Rousseau shows him the way to a deeper meaning of the noumenon of freedom."[10] By introducing the "*rule of the general will,*" the text rewrites the relationship between spirit and matter topographically (inside/outside) and socially (self/other) (322). This general will, experienced as a *moral* feeling that is at odds with the demands of merely corporeal desire, is a way to formulate spirit as an "imaginary focus" that draws the subject out of his self-imposed minority and into the larger world – that is, into the public – in accordance with what Kant will later identify as the defining characteristic of the enlightened use of reason. It is spirit, recast as a sort of moral gravitation, which manages to exercise a palpable influence on the composite subject. Or put differently, the general will disorganizes knowledge: it opens up the body and replaces the organs of sensation with a different kind of sensorium all together. For even if spirit can be figured as the "secret power" (322) that directs humans toward a higher order of moral interest, the subject's spiritual intuitions and material intuitions remain fundamentally divided: while the moral law acts on us, it remains impossible to have an "intuitive empirical concept" of one's spiritual self or to cognize this impulse theoretically (325).

It is precisely the claim to be able to understand the universal will intuitively that leads Kant to his condemnation of visionaries. This condemnation takes shape as a problem of the body's organization, of a confusion of different ways of sensing and knowing in relation to corporeal intuitions. Kant's allusion to the prophet Tiresias in the final paragraph of his second chapter offers a rich figural nexus for conceptualizing the key tensions of this issue. For not only is Tiresias the archetypal prophet of antiquity, he (or is it she?) is poised precariously between the visible and invisible and, on account of her (or is it his?) mobile sexuality, is uniquely able to reorganize the body. Tiresias appears in several Classical texts including Aeschylus' *Seven Against Thebes,* Euripides' *Bacchae*, and Sophocles' *Oedipus Rex* and *Antigone.* He also makes a cameo in Book 11 of Homer's *Odyssey* and later, in Dante's *Inferno*, inhabits the eighth circle of Hell. There are, in addition, two basic versions of the origin and nature of Tiresias' prophetic powers, one best represented in Callimachus' Fifth Hymn, "The Bath of Pallas," and the other derived from Book Three of Ovid's *Metamorphosis,* a collection with which Kant, given other instances of allusion, appears to have been familiar.[11] According to Callimachus, Chariclo, Tiresias' mother, was a favourite of Athena. One day, Tiresias stumbled across Chariclo and Athena while they were bathing in a spring and he "unwittingly saw what god's law forbids" – that is, the god's nakedness.[12] As punishment, Athena, citing "Cronos' law," blinds Tiresias.[13] Chariclo pleads for mercy and, as the law cannot be reversed, Athena compensates Tiresias with "many gifts" including the power to "know the birds, the auspicious and those that fly to no purpose and which have ill-omened wings."[14]

Ovid's version is considerably stranger and contains some elements that complicate Kant's particular evocation of the prophet. In Book Three of *Metamorphosis*, Ovid recounts the curious tale of Tiresias' sexual transformation. One day Tiresias struck two mating serpents with his staff. Consequently, he was transformed into a woman and remained so for seven years until spying the serpents yet again: another strike changed him back. Sometime later, on account of his unique perspective, Jove and Juno call on Tiresias to answer the question of whether men or women experience greater sexual pleasure. Tiresias agrees with Jove that women have greater pleasure. This annoys Juno so she blinds him. Jove, considering this punishment harsh but unable to reverse the curse of another god, chooses to compensate the unfortunate arbiter by granting him "the power to know the future, lightening the penalty by this honour."[15] While Callimachus' version of the story codes visual transgression as erotic, Ovid's version goes much further. For Ovid, the prerequisite for prophetic insight is not only the loss of sensual vision but a kind of organic plasticity. Tiresias' loss and recovery of the phallus suggests a reversibility, a Möbius-like folding of the outside into the inside, that echoes the co-penetration of matter and spirit, of tumescence and detumescence, of self and other that is also important for Kant. For visionaries, according to Kant, suffer from an organic derangement akin to Tiresias' sexual ambivalence.

Kant's allusion to Tiresias in *Dreams* seems to mix together the two versions of the legend and only to hint, obliquely, at sexual transformation:

> If one draws up a balance on the advantages and disadvantages which could accrue to someone who was to a certain extent organized not only for the visible world but also for the invisible (assuming that there ever was such a person), such a balance would seem to be a gift like that with which Juno honoured Tiresias: she first made him blind, so that she could grant him the gift of prophecy. For to judge from the above propositions, intuitive knowledge of the *other* world can only ever be attained here by forfeiting something of that understanding which one needs for this *present* world. (328)

The reference to Juno suggests that Kant has Ovid in mind. Yet the notion of being "doubly organized" is restricted to the dichotomy of vision and insight. Kant seems to suppress or at least skirt around that aspect of the story that explains why Tiresias is in conversation with Juno in the first place: his sex change. Prophecy is presented as a compensation for a sacrifice, suggesting that to be doubly organized is ultimately untenable. Hence, Kant bypasses the experience of sexual duality that does *not* demand such either/or determinations – for Tiresias clearly retains his experience of one sex while living as another. It is perhaps because Kant is asserting the mutual exclusivity of the realm of matter and the spirit world that he, therefore, somewhat misrepresents Juno's actions. It is a stretch to say that Juno "honoured Tiresias" with prophecy – at best, and this requires mixing Ovid's with Callimachus' account, she grudgingly repents of her anger. And yet if Kant softens her behaviour it is because he is keen to disguise his own affiliation with her. Kant characterizes as crippled or sick one who claims to have "organs [...] endowed with an exceptionally high degree of sensitivity" (327). In a way, Kant reacts as if the visionary has seen nature's nakedness and must therefore be blinded. The move is defensive and yet reproduces the very inversion Kant tries to avoid falling victim to by paralleling Juno's either/or logic: one can *either* see her *or* retain his normal senses, but not both; one can *either* have intuitive knowledge of spirit *or* of material beings, but not both. Hence, in yet one more gender bend, in his very effort to reassert sexual mutual exclusivity Kant acts the part of the female god.

Kant's reasoning in *Dreams* follows Dante's treatment of prophecy in the *Inferno*. As Farinata degli Uberti explains in Canto 10, prophecy in hell is a form of punishment: a certain class of sinner is cursed with a vision of the future that excludes knowledge of the present.[16] The same holds for Kant: to gain *intuitive* knowledge of the *other* world would mean to lose intuitive knowledge of the present world. The subject loses her sense and sanity. In other words, excessive sensitivity can wound sense – something we will see again in chapter 3, in the context of Wordsworth's poetic sensitivity. In Greek myth, "Perception and sexuality are both ultra-sensitive in experiences of the divine (often interdependently so), and sacred madness, as after encounter with the divine, may cause radical changes in either or both."[17] In Kant, the relationship between oversensitivity and madness can be understood specifically as a confusion of inner for outer sense. Spirit-sensations can enter into consciousness but only when they are wrought up by the imagination into figures of external perception, which they never really are: "in this way, ideas which are communicated by means of spirit-influence," following not mechanical but what he earlier calls "pneumatic" laws, "would clothe themselves in the signs of that *language*, which that human being normally uses: the sensed presence of a spirit would be clothed in all the images of *human figure*; the order and beauty of the immaterial world would be clothed in the images of our imagination which normally delights our senses in life, and so forth" (327). In a twist, the transgression here articulated involves not a vision of nakedness but illicit dressing up, or maybe even cross-dressing.

The imagination imposes the figures and forms drawn from and useful for cognizing objects of outer sense onto entities that, while "based upon a true spirit influence," do not have an outer sense, therein creating "wild chimeras and wondrous caricatures" (328). This rogue imagination suffers from a "genuine malady," then, as it aims to produce a-socially, as it were (327). Inside and outside, imagination and reality, have been confused by the "sick mind" (335). The visionary experiences a metamorphosis where his inside becomes his outside. In this, he fits Kant's earlier image of life's mobile organicism: "Boerhaave says somewhere: *The animal is a plant which has its root in its stomach* (inside itself). Someone else might, with equal propriety, play with these concepts and say: *the plant is an animal which has its stomach in its root* (outside itself)" (318). Again, the problem Kant has is not so much with one form or the other but the notion of being both at once, of being both stomach and root, both woman and man – to have a sensible intuition of a spiritual entity. The visionary, consequently, claims the power of self-insemination. Kant returns almost obsessively to the image of such isolated reproduction: "reveries" are, he says, "hatched out by the dreamer himself," "hatched out by his ever fertile imagination" (330).

The problem is thus akin to dreaming. In daydreams, the subject's sense of his body provides a background against which to distinguish inner from outer sense. Appealing to the language of optics, Kant explains that,

> in the case of the clear sensations of waking life, the *focus imaginarius*, at which point the object is represented, is placed outside me, whereas, in the case of images of imagination, which I may entertain at the same time as the clear sensations of my waking life, the *focus imaginarius* is located within me. For this reason, I cannot, as long as I am awake, fail to distinguish my imaginings, as the figments of my own imagination, from the impression of the senses. (333)

While fully conscious, the subject is capable of a parallax view, "the only method for preventing optical deception" (336). Kant's appeals to a double vision that enables comparison – like his image of changing pans on a weigh scale (336) – threatens, however, to slip into the very double vision "of someone who is drunk who, in his drunken condition, sees double with both eyes" (334). In dreaming, one loses the point of distinction, the metaphysical fulcrum, as it were, that enables one to perceive stereoscopically without confusing sources; the mind loses its "natural balance" (333). Just as one at sea cannot easily calculate longitude – the problem that so occupied Swedenborg in his first trip to England – so in dreaming is it difficult to calculate the precise difference between states. In sleep, the body's outer sense is suppressed – in effect, the body disappears – and with it the distinction between the two imaginary foci. Dreaming has the same effect as visionary "derangement" (333). In the case of visions, the oversensitive subject attempts to feel ideas or subordinate spirit to matter: the body swallows spirit. Contrastingly, dreams permit spirits to masquerade as tangible, sensible beings by diminishing outer sense: once the body is distracted from monitoring the border between inner and outer sense, spirit infiltrates and occupies the vestiges of intuition.

Anticipating his later, Critical work, Kant aims ultimately to "*purge*" (336) philosophy of metaphysics, not by denying metaphysical reality but by restricting attention to objects of possible theoretical knowledge. Fulfilling his appeal to instrumentality in the preface – that one ought "not to meddle with such prying or *idle* questions, but to concern oneself only with what is *useful*" (306) – he proposes to close the book on any future metaphysics of a reckless, speculative sort: "Since I now find myself at the conclusion of the theory of spirits, I venture to add one more remark: this reflection, if properly used by the reader, will bring the whole of our philosophical understanding of such beings [i.e., spirits] to completion. From now on it will be possible, perhaps, *to have all sorts of opinions* about but no longer *knowledge* of such beings" (338).

Kant, then, is concerned to confine philosophy to the production of viable thoughts. The chimeras produced through Tiresian mixing are for Kant the mules of the imagination, that is, incapable of reproduction, suggesting that an investment in Swedenborg proves fruitless. Yet, Kant insists that, having "paid for" the experience of reading the visionary, "such an effort [is] not to be wasted" (306). Indeed, this concern with profit, even if all it yields is knowledge "in the *negative* sense" (339) – that of finding the limit to knowledge – weds Kant to the visionary in a manner that invites contamination. To establish the limits of knowledge, Kant implicitly transgresses those same limits.

Inclinations and Deviations

As noted above, in Ovid's version of the legend of Tiresias he was called on to help arbitrate a dispute about sexual difference. He was, in a manner of speaking, called on to weigh alternatives. As a being who had lived as both a man and a woman, he is deemed uniquely impartial. And in spite of Juno's reaction, there is no hint in the text that Tiresias has lied. Impartiality is, ostensibly, the explicit requirement of any kind of judgment just as the scales of commerce are expected to be balanced before being put to use. Kant employs this image of the scale in the closing passages of the first division of *Dreams* as a technological analogy of the parallax view he cites as a requirement for performing due circumspection in philosophical investigation. Yet, in piling up analogies, Kant introduces a distortion. Tiresias is a problematic substitute for the figure of the weigh scale since his story can turn in two different directions. On the one hand, his experience of organ inversion could mean Tiresias is impartial, that he is deciding from a basis of equal knowledge about both sexes. Clearly Juno and Jupiter appeal to him with this expectation. On the other hand, the mobility of sexuality could mean Tiresias is, in another sense, completely unbalanced or unstable since he resists perfect identification. Indeed, Kant's allusion to Tiresias suggests this latter figuration – that, as an example of visionary excess, he confuses or blends together worlds that ought to remain distinct rather than simply measuring this difference. The difficulty is, however, that the ability to translate between terms – to weigh alternatives – requires intimate contact with both elements in question. As the very point of rational unification, as the power to calculate a ratio that establishes a finite relationship between one thing and another regardless of their differences, the medium (in every sense of that word) is under enormous stress. How can "he" remain impartial and yet accurate? And how does "he" stabilize himself when tasked with mediating between two worlds that differ not just in quantity but in kind? And how can "he" accomplish this without being torn apart? The key to Tiresias' power of judgment may, ultimately, lie in his *partiality*.

Recall Maurice Blanchot's short but potent meditation on prophecy discussed in chapter 1 where he identifies the problem of the body in prophetic mediation. In the Judeo-Christian tradition of prophecy, like the Classical tradition invoked by Kant, the visionary's mediation is intimately connected with a crisis in sexuality and identity. The prophet suffers from a split personality as a subject who has lost possession of himself in becoming possessed by Divine powers:

> Suddenly a man becomes other. Jeremiah, gentle and sensitive, must become a pillar of fire, a rampart of bronze, for he will have to condemn and destroy all that he loves. Isaiah, decent and respectable, must strip off his clothes: for three years, he walks naked. Ezekiel, scrupulous priest who was never lacking in purity, feeds himself on food cooked in excrement and soils his body. To Hosea, the Eternal says, "Marry a woman of whoredom; let her give you a prostitute's children, for the country is prostituting itself," and this is not an image.[18]

The prophet is thus what Heidegger calls "sacred." In terms that echo the paradox of remediation touched on in the introduction, the sacred is "the immediate [...], the immediate that is never communicated but is the principle of all possibility of communicating."[19] The sacred stands "between" and yet outside of the play between phenomenal revelation and concealment; it is the name for that fantastic, utopian medium that actually could prove so efficient that it would disappear. The revolution within the prophet's subjectivity reflects his or her struggle and failure to function as this immediacy of mediation – failure since one must be the impossible, must be simultaneously both self and other to shuttle between the domains with which she or he communicates. Like Blake's or Schelling's or Kierkegaard's self-annihilating prefaces to works that can never be completed, to which we will turn in chapters 6 and 7, the sacred is the immediate that sacrifices itself to enable mediation: a gesture that is, says Blanchot, impossible and yet necessary. It is therefore difficult to describe such an existence as anything other than a radical self-displacement.

Kant's *Dreams* offers a rendition of the prophet's existential ambivalence in the larger organization of its presentation. That is, *Dreams* makes an explicitly unbalanced argument. In doing this Kant weaves the instability at the heart of prophetic mediation into his attempt to measure the difference between several incommensurable elements. The essay aims not only to weigh different arguments about, say, the reality of spirits, the truth of ghost stories, and the limits of knowledge. The text is also and primarily concerned with judgment as such, with the constitution of the scales of the understanding and its analogous instruments of mediation – is concerned with the *form* as well as the content of decision. To be somewhat schematic about it, we could say that the image of judgment as a balanced scale nicely represents determinate judgment whereas the scale skewed by reason represents reflective judgment, or judging without a determinate concept. In determinate judgment the concept subsumes the particular. As such, it is equal to the task of the particular. Reflective judgment, however, involves a particular that does not correspond to an extant general concept and thus must go in search of one. Aesthetic judgment, in fact, describes precisely this kind of judgment. In the case of the beautiful the imagination tarries with an indeterminate concept of the understanding whereas in the sublime the imagination struggles with an indeterminate concept of reason. Reason thus carries away the imagination and changes the conceptual shape of judgment from one of adequacy between terms to one where terms remain incommensurable. Determination is displaced by a relation of aspiration, of desire, where judgment suffers a kind of internal schism in being unequal to one of its terms. This opposition in the structure of judgment formulates prophetic ambivalence in terms of the two opposed yet inextricable characterizations of Tiresias' prophetic mobility: while, on the one hand, he can stand as the balanced mediator between two different realms, he can, on the other, embody the immediacy of contact that must eliminate his neutrality. Kant's text is thus concerned with the broader Romantic conception of prophecy insofar as it is a reflection on the power of judgment as such.

Kant begins to complicate the image of "the scales of understanding" as soon as he introduces them in chapter 4 of the first part of *Dreams*:

> Scales, intended by civil law to be a standard of measure in trade, may be shown to be inaccurate if the wares and the weights are made to change pans. The bias of the scales of understanding is revealed by exactly the same stratagem, and in philosophical judgments, too, it would not be possible, unless one adopted this stratagem, to arrive at a unanimous result by comparing the different weights. (336)

The figure of commercial scales evokes a larger populous and civil society. The test here recommended is necessary in order to persuade the general public of fair dealing. What is key, then, is unanimity: the values must be established within a community of participants and gain general assent. The operation of reversal, thus, aims to quell any suspicions among traders by displaying the soundness of the measuring tool itself. Hence, Kant publicly performs a self-diagnostic: "I have purified my soul," he says, "of prejudices; I have eradicated every blind attachment which may have insinuated itself into my soul in a surreptitious manner with a view to securing an entry for a great deal of bogus knowledge" (336). Kant here describes a kind of mental evacuation. The subject has become analogous to a pan: empty and passive, available for any content, a total evacuation of self akin to what biblical prophet's experience. Kant extends the notion of subjective displacement when he develops his metaphor, such that "switching pans" represents seeing from another's perspective: "I formerly used to regard the human understanding in general merely from the point of view of my own understanding. Now I put myself in the position of someone else's reason, which is independent of myself and external to me, and regard my judgments, along with their most secret causes, from the point of view of other people" (336).

There is a measure of both irony and sincerity in this curious analogy – though not an equal measure. For it appears to be patently foolish to evacuate oneself of bias to the point that "a great deal of bogus knowledge" is welcome. The notion that impartiality can appear only through utter passivity and that this passivity should guarantee sound judgment seems absurd, especially when we consider that it is Kant, the vocal defender of the enlightened use of reason, who ostensibly advocates for this. While Kant is genuinely interested in the question of judgment and the elimination of bias, the extreme to which he goes here better illustrates what Hans-Georg Gadamer, many years later, would identify as the Enlightenment's prejudice against prejudice. This agreement is somewhat surprising in that Gadamer thinks Kant's narrowing of taste to aesthetic judgment (his effective hollowing-out of the Renaissance conception of the *sensus communus* as a way of thinking about the social that might usefully oppose "the violent anatomization of nature through experiment and calculation") essentially "discredit[s] any kind of theoretical knowledge except that of natural science, [...] compell[ing] the human sciences to rely on the methodology of the natural sciences in conceptualizing themselves."[20] Yet, in *Dreams* Kant seems to be closer to Gadamer's own position wherein the inevitable prejudgment of phenomena by a consciousness embedded in a world (what Gadamer calls *wirkungsgeschichtliches Bewußtsein*) is not an obstacle to judgment but rather its very condition of possibility.

Gadamer will argue that interpretation and understanding is made possible only thanks to a human being's ontological situatedness in a world of relationships about which that subject takes an interest. In Heideggerian terms – terms Gadamer in part adopts – it is *Dasein*'s very nature, part of its structure, to be concerned about itself. This means that part of what makes a human being the specific being that it is, is that it takes itself up as a project. *Dasein* "understands" itself then not merely in a psychological sense but ontologically by actively appropriating its own thrown projection toward its ownmost possibility, or death. In actively taking up this being-toward-death, *Dasein* stands under (i.e., under-stands) itself. This taking up is only possible, though, thanks to the radical thrownness of *Dasein*: a human being is always dwelling *in* a world. While *Dasein* cannot be reduced to being a mere thing, it has no existence outside of a world of things where it is always already engaged in projects that involve the surrounding world. After all, if "*Sein*" is not "*da*" – if "being" is not "there" – it is pure "*Sein*," being as such and in general. Being in the world thus means being part of a network of interrelatedness that makes *Dasein*'s world coherent; everything in such a world is intended for something else, and ultimately it is for *Dasein* – that is, a means through which *Dasein* takes up projects and pro-jects itself in a directed way into life. Gadamer develops this fundamental "dialogue" with the world in his discussion of pre-judgment and his critique of the Enlightenment's promotion of reason over tradition in rendering judgments.

Revising its pejorative connotation, pre-judgment or prejudice names merely the necessary situatedness of all consciousness. Just as the precondition for anything like conscious understanding is *Dasein*'s ontological self-understanding – *Dasein*'s radical "knowledge" of itself as a finite end in itself – so does understanding for Gadamer stress the enabling character of the finitude of consciousness. Understanding is nothing other than the rhythm of the revision of "fore-conceptions" and "fore-meanings."[21] Prejudice, then, names the radical interest that must ground any effort at judgment. Rather than clear this ground, Gadamer argues that one must better understand one's own prejudices and fore-conceptions in order to revise these conceptions in the face of new evidence. Hence Gadamer's famous criticism of the Enlightenment's "prejudice against prejudices."[22] Citing Descartes' methodical doubt as exemplary, Gadamer argues that "the Enlightenment tends to accept no authority and to decide everything before the judgment seat of reason."[23] Put in terms of Kant's competing images of evaluation, the Enlightenment would dismiss Tiresias – an authority on sexual difference who has earned his status as such – and turn to the mechanical commercial scales precisely because they know nothing, are not prejudiced.

This decision may, to contemporary eyes, appear apt. In fact, however, this appearance results from a modern and problematic tendency to apply natural scientific methods to the human sciences and related hermeneutic problems in art and philosophy – that is, to fields of enquiry that do not have objects of study in the same way as natural science does. Human sciences *constitute* their objects in dialogical relation to them. Hence the Enlightenment model of non-prejudice, which is what Kant somewhat mockingly invokes in his image of an inane human balance, is, particularly from the perspective of practical philosophy, *a false universality*. Rationalization reduces universality to generalization – indeed it confuses, as Kant says in the third *Critique*, "the theory of that which belongs to the nature of things" with practical philosophy.[24] Recalling the image in *Dreams*, Kant notes that "the solution to the problem in mechanics of finding the respective lengths of the arms of a lever by means of which a given force will be in equilibrium with a given weight, is of course expressed as a practical formula."[25] However, such a formula "contains nothing other than the theoretical proposition that the length of the arms is in inverse proportion to the force of the weight if these are in equilibrium."[26] By identifying judgment as such with an abstract mechanism divorced from the moral subject – a subject that would actually demand the reformulation of the mechanism of evaluation – Enlightenment thought suggests that to make a universal claim demands either (imaginatively) occupying all determinate subjective positions such that any authority is cancelled out democratically, or (and this amounts to the same thing) existing outside of any determinate position whatever. In a sense, then, Enlightened reason seeks to eliminate a form of rational fore-sight, a sort of prophecy that, like tradition, remains open and mobile even as it retains an attachment to its past and present. Is it any wonder, then, that the prophet makes a return in Romantic thought, even in the eminently enlightened Kant?

That Tiresias is unbalanced may be, ironically, precisely what makes him a suitable supplement to Kant's scales. Kant announces that "the scales of the understanding are not, after all, wholly impartial. One of the arms, which bears the inscription: *Hope for the future*, has a mechanical advantage" (337). Indeed, Kant cannot – nor would he want to – eliminate this bias, as it is the bias *of* reason. As Shell puts it, "Reason itself bears this hope inscribed upon one of its arms" in that it, reflexively, puts "reason in the pan of its own scale."[27] Reason will accord greater weight to a rational conception of spirits insofar as spirit names reason's power to transcend understanding. Reason itself opens a future beyond the empirical determination of the present, investing the "fond hope that one will somehow survive death" (337) into history. Kant is inclined, then, toward a minimal optimism of reason, prophesying not what the future will hold but that there *will be* a future. Because of this inherent inclination, even something as light as a phantom is able to tip Kant's scale. In this respect he shares something important with the atomist Lucretius whom he evokes midway through the second division of *Dreams.* Kant's willingness to be "swayed" recalls the atomist's appeal to the *clinamen* or swerve. Lucretius' material universe is destined to an "unalterable succession" and utter determination unless, he says, there is some event that interrupts that uniformity.[28] This swerve asserts freedom's reality. To be clear, the swerve is not an explanation or proof of freedom. Rather, the swerve is posited as necessary in order to account for the reality of freedom; the swerve does not prove freedom overcomes necessity but rather declares that this overcoming is a fact that finds its material expression in this unpredictable atomic action. Lucretius' materialist "inclination" thus prefigures Kant's ghostlier inclinations, his skewed scale of reason. The rational demand for totality reveals itself as a kind of prejudice in Gadamer's sense: this is not the Enlightenment rationalistic prejudice against prejudice but rather Kant's prejudice – his pre-judgment, his radical swerve – toward reason. The ironic consequence is that this rationalism becomes the shape of Kantian fore-conception.

Conspiracy of Reason

Kant turns the Enlightenment prejudice against prejudice on its ear by making reason into his own form of pre-judgment. This is odd since reason was apparently the Enlightenment's champion in the elimination of pre-judgment. What Kant's text illuminates, however, is that enlightened reason's attempt to ground itself on itself does not eliminate "bias" so much as reformulate the concept of truth to make it reducible to methodological consistency. Adopting physics and mathematics as its models, reason would not only seek to judge from a position uninfluenced by embodied existence or previous experience; it would, additionally, find its "truth" only in method. As a consequence of the Enlightenment rejection of earlier forms of authority, says Gadamer,

> The only thing that gives a judgment dignity is its having a basis, a methodological justification (and not the fact that it may be correct). For the Enlightenment the absence of such a basis does not mean that there might be other kinds of certainty, but rather that the judgment has no foundation in the things themselves – i.e., that it is "unfounded." This conclusion follows only in the spirit of rationalism. It is the reason for discrediting prejudices and the reason scientific knowledge claims to exclude them completely.[29]

By "method," Gadamer means a form of legitimation for thought that attempts to work autonomously: that is, with reference only to itself. When the hermeneutic task expands from the relatively narrow horizon of textual meaning determined by comparing, say, the sentence to the paragraph and the paragraph to the total work, to a much broader, historical horizon in the philosophies of history of the eighteenth century, the basis for the legitimacy of interpretation widens in tandem. No longer is the work, the *oeuvre*, or even the life of the author a sufficiently complete whole within which to organize the parts. Thought, rather, must reach "back beyond the concerns of each [narrower circuit of understanding] to the more fundamental relation – the understanding of thoughts."[30] Lacking a tangible, finite object to limit the work of interpretation, hermeneutics not only becomes universal but must seek its ground now not in an object but in an operation or "the unity of a procedure."[31] This shift in the basis of understanding means that judgment and interpretation aim not for truth – a concept too freighted with lingering elements of unenlightened authority – but rather the elimination of misunderstanding, resulting in something like the method of Cartesian doubt. This approach to judgment gains universality and autonomy but does so at the cost of evacuating force from judgment. If the transformation of judgment into method gains a certain neutrality, it is this same neutrality that makes it unfit for problems, like moral problems, that only come to subjects who are embedded in the world and embody reason in particular, concrete, finite ways. Or, as Louis Dupré puts it, Enlightenment thinkers often "imposed the rules of the one science that the mind could indeed claim full authorship of and which depended on no external content, namely, mathematics. The mind thereby acquired an unprecedented control over nature, yet it ceased to be an integral part of it."[32]

Throughout *Dreams*, Kant wrestles with the implications of this reduction of judgment to method. The title of the work itself is, for instance, significant in this respect: "Dreams of a Spirit-Seer Elucidated by Dreams of Metaphysics." The ostensible strategy wherein one kind of dream is to "elucidate" another kind of dream turns quickly into a fearful symmetry: how should one form of delusion clarify another? Indeed, Kant's paper suggests, ultimately, that the only thing these two kinds of dreams share is that neither can be placed in the scales of the understanding – that while a realm beyond the understanding may exist, we can *know* nothing about it. What, then, is elucidating what? How is one form of non-understanding – Swedenborg's visions, say – supposed to tell us anything about a metaphysical community of spirits that exist outside the conditions of possible knowledge? The apparent balance of the title anticipates Kant's strategic bias reflected in the structure of the essay itself. That is, Kant skews not only scale of understanding in favour of reason – or rather, reveals "neutral" reason itself to be a form of interested judgment – but confesses that the organization of his work into two parts (the first, which is dogmatic, and the second, which is historical) is also a calculated *trompe l'oeil*. What makes this trick particularly strange, however, is that Kant exposes it as a trick.

The first sentence of the second chapter in the second division of *Dreams* draws attention toward a rhetorical strategy – a specific method of argument – Kant employs in an effort to sway his reader. His method of "proceeding in a cunning fashion" refers to the larger, organizational decision to place the dogmatic section before the historical section (344). Such ordering generates the impression that conclusions suggested through "abstract observations" find fortuitous confirmation with historical, empirical data (344). Having, however, composed his a priori reflections on the nature of spirits with the information gleaned inductively and a posteriori in the back of his mind all along, Kant admits to stacking the deck. The truth is that there remains a gap between the two sections insofar as the a priori and a posteriori sides of the discussion are unified only by a manufactured parallelism. On the one hand, in Dupré's words, "observation never results in apodictic truth" and only ever "asymptotically approaches mathematical certainty."[33] Kant says as much when he notes that no matter how many "empirical cognitions" the inductive scientist gathers together, this process still leads "to a *Why?* to which no answer can be given" (344). On the other hand, working deductively has its corresponding limitations: beginning "from the pinnacle of metaphysics" merely means "one starts, I know not whence, and arrives, I know not where" since "the advance of the argument refuses to correspond to experience" (345).

Making the Lucretian undertones of his earlier "inclination" toward reason explicit, Kant here describes the conspiratorial nature of philosophy – where a priori and a posteriori argument secretly "glance" at each other – as a kind of atomic swerve: while each camp of philosophers "would adopt his own starting point," subsequently, "rather than following the straight line of [deductive] reasoning, they would rather impart to their arguments an imperceptible clinamen by stealthily squinting at the target of certain experiences or testimonies" (345). Philosophy conducted in this fashion begins to look like gothic fiction, where parallel but ostensibly distinct plots are finally brought, by some mysterious force of convergence, into sudden contact. "Ginotti is Nompere" and "Eloise is the sister of Wolfstein," announces Percy Shelley's narrator in the final page on his gothic novella, *St. Irvyne*;[34] reason posits the existence of a spirit world and Swedenborg, thanks to a singular sensorium, has been able to experience just such a world! Kant, however, attempts to dismiss by exposing this conspiracy, suggesting that if the historical record of Swedenborg's predictions and visions should correlate with his own metaphysical reflections, that very correlation ought to cast doubt on the philosophy rather than breed confidence in supernatural tales. At best "frenzied poets" might, like a broken clock, be correct twice per day: if "their prophecies now and again correspond to what actually happens," this is "a matter of pure chance" (346).

Anticipating his later insistence in the Critical work on establishing the conditions of possible knowledge, Kant concludes *Dreams* by arguing that what his reader has gained is really a warning. Delving into Swedenborg's fantastical claims – the dreams of the spirit seer – do not really elucidate (the dreams of) metaphysics: one gains no insights into metaphysical reality except the insight that such insight is impossible. Hence, Kant claims to gain through this loss. "I have wasted my time," he says, "in order to save it. I have deceived my reader in order to benefit him" (354). Playing his part as Juno, he has blinded us so we can see all the better. The compensation described here pertains to thought's future projects: by establishing the impossibility of "metaphysical understanding," thought can take up a different, more modest, and yet ultimately more fruitful direction. Still, as David Tarbet notes in a reading of Kant's rather attractive metaphors for speculation deployed in the first *Critique* – Kant's rejection of images and examples in the preface to the first edition not withstanding – the philosopher "experienced a struggle in leaving metaphysics behind. [...] One may awaken from 'dogmatic slumbers' without wanting to forget the dream."[35] Hence the trace of transgression that seems to haunt even Kant's *limiting* of philosophy to useful tasks: "in order to choose rationally one must already have *knowledge of what is* superfluous, indeed, *impossible*" (355, my emphasis).

To say that metaphysics haunts Kant is perhaps putting it too mildly. For just as Thomas De Quincey sees in Kant's rigorous regimentation of his own desires a kind of addiction to limitation,[36] so Kant's attempt to bracket metaphysics, or more accurately, to temper his metaphysical desire, means that it remains active throughout his Critical work. This is perhaps clearest when considering how the first *Critique* rewrites the conspiracy between a priori and a posteriori that Kant exposes in *Dreams*. Such a conspiracy remains active in Kant through the mediation of the opposition between analytic and synthetic as forms of relating subjects and objects in propositions. As seen in *Dreams*, Kant overlaps different figures for judgment: Tiresias and commercial scales. While each is a metaphor for adjudication, these metaphors are not perfectly interchangeable. Indeed, the figure of Tiresias contaminates the figure of the scales by introducing more clearly the paradox of evaluation that the prophet typically embodies: as the point of relation between two terms, the mediator must be intimately related to each term; and yet, this intimacy seems to violate the (enlightened) ideal of disinterested judgment.

In the first *Critique,* Kant similarly complicates two systems that appear at first to be neatly parallel. The opposition between a priori and a posteriori forms of reflection appears to correlate simply to two forms of propositions: analytic and synthetic, respectively. Analytic propositions are defined by a kind of redundancy insofar as the truth of the proposition can be established internally with reference only to the terms involved, whereas the truth of synthetic propositions can be established only through empirical confirmation. Kant's best-recognized description of an analytic proposition states that in such forms of knowledge, "B belongs to the subject A as something that is (covertly) contained in the concept A."[37] Such propositions do not add information but rather clarify the concept by "breaking it up into its components."[38] Analytic propositions might therefore "also be called *elucidatory.*"[39] Indeed, this term should recall the full title of Kant's *Dreams*. The term "elucidate" (*erläutert*) marks the relationship between the dreams of the spirit-seer and of metaphysics as analytic in nature – though, again, the irony is that such analysis reveals both sorts of dreams merely to be similarly groundless and ultimately off limits for the understanding. What is elucidated is the impossibility of theoretical elucidation.

As Stephen Palmquist argues, a helpful though "less frequently cited description of [the] distinction [between synthesis and analysis] is Kant's claim that judgments are analytic only if their truth is 'based entirely on the principle of [non]contradiction,' while judgments are synthetic only 'under the condition that an intuition underlies the concept of their subject.'"[40] Whereas analytic propositions follow logical relations and can be evaluated on the basis of their internal consistency, synthetic propositions involve existential relationships and gain confirmation only empirically. For instance, "coffee is a beverage" is an analytic proposition since each term can be inferred from the other; in this relationship, one term effectively restates the other and the outcome is a more refined sense of both terms. In contrast, the proposition "coffee is Kant's favourite beverage" is synthetic, as one could not infer this relation from one of the terms alone. Whereas the object in an analytic proposition is contained in its subject (coffee is "within" the concept of beverage), in a synthetic proposition the terms exist in an indeterminate proximity to each other: there is "coffee," there are "Kant's favourite things," and, in the sample proposition, these two fields overlap at one point if it is a true statement. Hence, the truth of this proposition would depend not merely on logical relations but on factual or historical data concerning Kant's tastes.

From the example provided, it is clear that analytic and synthetic propositions have different relationships to a priori and a posteriori reflective knowledge. Since analytic propositions ground their truth only on logical relationships, thought can reflect a priori or without experiential data in such cases, producing, for instance, analytic a priori knowledge. In contrast, synthetic judgments appear necessarily grounded through a posteriori reflection, producing synthetic a posteriori knowledge. There are, however, two additional pairings of terms made possible by placing forms of reflection in relation to forms of proposition: synthetic a priori and analytic a posteriori. Kant dismisses the latter because experience would add nothing to analytic insights. (And yet this dismissal may prove trickier than it appears. We will return to it in a moment). Synthetic a priori judgments form, of course, the most philosophically important form of knowledge for Kant, as only through their investigation can metaphysics become a science. Expanding on Kant's attempt to eliminate useless speculation in *Dreams*, the first *Critique* proceeds through a transcendental deduction, asking, how is synthetic a priori knowledge possible, how must we be constituted a priori as subjects to be capable of synthesizing phenomena in the ways that we clearly can? The only way it is possible is if objects conform, at least in part, to a subject who brings with him into the world innate intuitions (space and time) and categories of understanding. Transcendental philosophy thus becomes the work of establishing these formal limits for thought, establishing what can and cannot be possibly known as an object through these synthesizing mechanisms that exist a priori. The first *Critique* thus effectively domesticates prophecy by granting limited reign to a priori knowledge, that is, knowledge that exists in advance of experience. Kant here "prophesies the future by uncovering the limits of the possible – not the limits of what can possibly exist, for here our ignorance of ultimate grounds obscures our vision, but the limits of what we can possibly know about existence."[41]

Yet, prophecy does not remain so neatly contained. As with other instantiations of prophetic thinking in Romanticism, the appeal to prophecy as a regulative discourse cannot eliminate its more radical negativity. The first *Critique* registers this resistance when Kant describes the trade-off between knowledge and faith: "I had to deny **knowledge**," he says in the Preface, "in order to make room for **faith**."[42] This faith or belief refers to the form of relation to ideas like God, freedom, and immortality that are necessary for morality and yet, because they lack objective status, cannot be known theoretically. For Kant, this belief is rationally necessary. And yet, does Kant reduce this faith to a secular morality? In *Dreams,* Kant identified the collusion between the a priori and a posteriori approaches to investigation; his Critical philosophy is not perhaps as candid as *Dreams* is about the relationships between these forms of knowledge in relation to analytic and synthetic propositions. Specifically, what Kant calls rational belief and describes as synthetic a priori in the second *Critique* masks the return of the analytic a posteriori construction of knowledge earlier repudiated.

In the introduction to the second edition of the first *Critique*, Kant states that "it would be absurd to ground an analytic judgment on experience, since I do not need to go beyond my concept at all in order to formulate the judgment, and therefore need no testimony from experience for that."[43] Such analytic a posteriori knowledge would be conceptually autonomous and yet somehow contingent on experience – the inverse of a synthetic a priori knowledge that has an intuitive ground but is nevertheless necessary and universal. And yet, this rejected branch of knowledge may be useful for understanding how terms in analytic propositions are assigned meaning. That is, from within an analytic proposition there is no way to account for the givenness of the meaning of each term. It is for this reason that an analytic proposition may *look* synthetic from the perspective of someone for whom one or both terms is unfamiliar. If, for instance, one does not know what coffee is, then to hear it identified as a beverage makes the proposition function, as it were, synthetically. Indeed, we learn the names of all things through experience, that is, a posteriori. Thus any subsequent analytic definitions based on these words always retain an element of that radical contingency. As Palmquist puts it, "To name requires that we adopt a *practical* perspective, according to which we act 'as if' (or stipulate that) a certain object is to be rigidly designated by a certain word. That is, we subsume an object of experience (a posteriori) under a given concept (analytically)."[44] In this way, analytic a posteriori "knowledge" may be slightly misnamed insofar as it creeps beyond the boundaries Kant sets to what can be known. While the analyticity of the proposition remains intact, the implicit "as if" nature of the terms in relation denies the proposition the universality and necessity required by science.

In this respect, the first *Critique* already reflects on the rational faith of the second, though fleetingly. That is, the demand exercised by moral ideas on actual subjects could be viewed as both analytic (in that particular freedoms, for instance, are included analytically – or do not logically contradict – pure practical freedom) and also as a posteriori since such ideas demand to be instantiated in lived experience and only gain existential weight as such. The a posteriority here is, however, peculiarly protracted. As ideas, concepts of practical reason exercise a real, palpable force via the categorical imperative; and yet, they are never, as such, objects of possible knowledge. Thus, if analytic a posteriori reflection is a legitimate category of knowledge, it represents the space occupied, from the transcendental perspective, by a kind of prophecy: there is a strange way that propositions are suddenly revealed, after a transformative experience on the part of the subject, to have been enveloped in each other all along. What is a flash of insight from the theoretical perspective gestures, however, to the possibility of a new perspective altogether, namely the perspective of practical reason. In the latter case, it is as if consciousness has come to terms with and thus absorbed what looks, from the perspective of the first *Critique*, like prophecy. From the practical perspective, the a posteriori experience of nature is viewed "as if" it conforms analytically to an idea that is *not yet* known. If analytic knowledge is "late" in recognizing itself in cases of the analytic a posteriori knowledge viewed from within the limits of the understanding, the practical perspective aims, in contrast, to anticipate this revelation and to assume an analytical relationship between ideas and empirical reality *before* knowledge of this relation is even possible.

From this point of view, empirical life is tied to an idea the expression of which is assured thanks to an analytical form of involvement between subject and predicate. And yet the exact moment of the idea's historical revelation remains entirely contingent. With this formulation we anticipate the itinerary of the sign of history to which we will turn in chapter 4. Indeed, if the concept of prophecy is given greater attention in texts such as *The Conflict of the Faculties* and "Dreams of a Spirit-Seer" that are peripheral to Kant's major philosophical contributions, the three *Critiques*, this is not to say the concept is minor. The same impulse that compels Kant, in *Dreams*, to tilt the scales of understanding through a fore-conception of reason and, in *The Conflict*, to claim to prophesy without foresight is also at work in the midst of his critical project in the transformation of the speculative into the hypothetical and then into the categorical forms of reflection. For in spite of his frequent location within a tradition of Enlightenment thought characterized, in part, by its sweeping rejection of earlier forms of judgment on grounds that they do not achieve methodological purity, Kant must in fact go beyond his own theoretical limitations in order to meet reason's demands for systematic completeness. In fact, Kant here and, as we shall see, in *The Conflict*, proves to be remarkably *sensitive* to history. Kant's figuration and manipulation of reason in *Dreams* finds alternative expression in a concept of historical progress that is less an idea than a feeling, an obscure, ghostly sense that the human race is indeed progressing. How does one register such a feeling? How does one become sensitive to history, to the future? It is to these sorts of questions that Wordsworth offers vital insight.

Chapter Three

Ghostlier Demarcations: Mysticism, Trauma, Anachronism

"The revolution which did *not* happen in England was fully as devastating, and in some features more divisive, than that which did happen in France"

E.P. Thompson, *The Making of the English Working Class*

In Immanuel Kant's reading of Emanuel Swedenborg, prophecy faces a direct challenge from a refined version of Enlightenment scepticism. So refined is this scepticism that, on reflection, it makes surprising allowances for the supersensible. Indeed, as the preceding chapter argued, even in his cautious efforts to limit philosophy to objects of possible knowledge – that is, to mark metaphysics off limits and portray prophetic seers as kooks – the transcendent impulse of prophetic vision is encrypted within Kant's concept of reason itself. Just as prophecy, as discussed in chapter 1, continues in various ways to shape secular historiographies, so do Swedenborg's dreams linger even after Kant's awakening from his dogmatic sleep. Indeed, a carefully famed enthusiasm may even be a *necessary* prerequisite for practical philosophy, an issue we will revisit in chapter 4. For in spite of his own warnings against intellectual intuition, Kant appears to be swayed by ideas, to be pulled toward reason as if by a force working on him bodily. As much as anything else, it is Kant's sympathy with ideas – his prejudice *for* reason that is also the prejudice *of* reason – that casts him as a kind of prophet. Whereas Kant's desire emerges against the grain of the Critical philosophy, William Wordsworth actively cultivates a supernatural affect in an effort to achieve a prophetic sensitivity so potent that it can reach beyond worldly phenomena to the existence of what, in "Tintern Abbey," he calls, mystically, "something far more deeply interfused." We also see Wordsworth's prophetic aspirations in his treatment of memory as a broadly unifying and synthesizing operation – something to which we will turn in more detail in a reading of his famous spots of time later in this chapter. Indeed, the spots bring memory and feeling together in episodes that are powerful largely for being disturbing and depressing, for shaking the subject to his emotional core such that he gains a special susceptibility to the most elusive of ideas. One such elusive idea is time. Another, the future. Feeling and therein knowing both these ideas is like remembering a ghost, the spectral past serving as a conduit to a possible future. Yet, how should memory be a form of relation to the future? Maybe we should ask not the spirit-seer but the spirits themselves.

In *Essays upon Epitaphs*, Wordsworth cites John Weever's *Discourse of Funeral Monuments*, agreeing that the impulse to commemorate the dead "proceed[s] from the presage of fore-feeling of Immortality, implanted in all men naturally."[1] Somewhat surprisingly, the epitaph is cast as an aspirational genre of writing, a product of human sensitivity to the soul's immortality. In fact, in an unusual interpretation of causality, Wordsworth thinks that the very existence of epitaphs stands as empirical proof of the soul's supermundane future:

> If, then, in a creature endowed with the faculties of foresight and reason, the social affections could not have unfolded themselves uncountenanced by the faith that Man is an immortal being; and if, consequently, neither could the individual dying have had a desire to survive in the remembrance of his fellows, nor on their side could they have felt a wish to preserve for future times vestiges of the departed; it follows, as a final inference, that without the belief in immortality, wherein these several desires originate, neither monuments nor epitaphs, in affectionate or laudatory commemoration of the deceased, could have existed in the world.[2]

The phrasing here, especially in the final line, suggests that immortality is the condition of possibility for memorial graves. Reciprocally, that such observable markers do exist is supposed to stand, then, as evidence for the tangibility of the rational idea of immortality. Were subjects not moved by this larger idea, this passage implies, any interest in a historical individual would remain narrowly punctual. Via the epitaph, we are able not merely to pay "tribute to a man as a human being" but – in a line that echoes the imagination's sense of "something evermore about to be"[3] – are able to touch on "something more."[4] Wordsworth's hesitation to name what this something is, like his use of double negatives and hypotheticals in the passage above, sounds like a weaker version of the Kantian injunction to keep concepts distinct from things. Rather than proffer a detailed description – like Swedenborg and Blake – of heaven and hell, Wordsworth here stops short of intuiting what is intellectual. But, he suggests that we might have experiences that give us distinct impressions that such things exist just beyond our reach. Wordsworth, in accord with what we saw in the last chapter and will see again in the next, would allow for a sort of rational prophecy. For he, like Kant, wishes to ensure that human life is not confined to natural life, that one's own history operates also on a higher horizon – one perhaps forgotten at birth, as the "Intimations Ode" has it, but nonetheless within the compass of recollection. It is crucial, in other words, that we be able to gain, if only vaguely, "a still sense/ Of permanent and universal sway," gain palpable confirmation of the "spirt, that impels/ All thinking things" and that "rolls through all things."[5] Yet, if prophecy is one conduit through which this metaphysical comfort is supposed to descend (another is nature, as has been discussed at length in extant scholarship), we find that, in several instances, Wordsworth's prophetic experiments veer dangerously close to a world not spiritually calming but deeply agitating. Wordsworth would like to treat prophecy as a sort of hyper-memory, would like, as it were, preemptively to live through the danger of the future by taking prophecy as a mechanism for integrating historical experience. The effect of this is that the prophetic subject *becomes* his own epitaph. We can see this Wordsworthian death drive, so to speak, peaking out at several points, not least those points where Wordsworth (or his speaker) seems most confident, when history seems most happily redeemed through and as the growth of the poet's mind.[6]

When enthusiasm is successfully curbed, memory is the form foreknowledge takes. "Tintern Abbey" offers a good illustration of this. The speaker's recollection of his youthful "dizzy raptures" (85) is, ultimately, converted into a promise of future restoration:

> While here I stand, not only with the sense
> Of present pleasure, but with pleasing thoughts
> That in this moment here is life and food
> For future years. (62–5)

In fact, with the introduction of Dorothy toward the end of the poem, Wordsworth seems to gather time together or, to use his recurring figure, to harmonize different temporalities. Wordsworth casts Dorothy as an image of his own youthful self, such that, as he says to her, "I behold in thee what I once was" (120). If this turns Dorothy's present consciousness in to Wordsworth's past – a form of "animal" (74) consciousness, so he says, that had not achieved the self-consciousness of his mature "purer mind" (29), one sensitive to the "still, sad music of humanity" (91) – then he attempts, within this analeptic gesture, also to turn his own present consciousness into the shape of Dorothy's future. With this subjective remediation – a process where the speaker meets himself, as it were, face to face, but through the mediation of another – Wordsworth aims to galvanize his biography. According to this itinerary, no experience ought to be "unprofitable" (53) and youthful error and "loss" must somehow yield "abundant recompense" (87, 88). In the context of *The Prelude*, we will see this as attempting to profit from prophecy. Yet, even in this most famous attempt to convert difference into harmony, the speaker is almost too successful, for he manages both to "recover" and to "anticipate" something that is altogether outside empirical experience. His memory, for instance, goes beyond recalling details of the Abbey and his previous self to include "feelings too/ Of unremembered pleasure" (30–1) and "little, nameless, unremembered, acts/ Of kindness and of love" (34–5). If we take him at his word, this seems to suggest that memory somehow remembers the unremembered. While this might be read optimistically – that nothing can be absolutely beyond all recollection, that history is never lost, just perhaps obscured – it may also give us pause. Does this mean that the speaker's mind performs a deeper and wider surveillance than he realizes? Does memory bypass consciousness and lodge somewhere in "the blood" or "the heart," some sensitive primitive tissue? If so, could this sensitivity that is supposed to help the subject master himself – to ascend into the rarefied company of the prophets – turn out to render him only *more* vulnerable to the contingencies of disappointment and the disappointment of contingencies?

In such moments prophecy not only compensates for the mystery of future prospects but *over*compensates. Something similar can be said of the most obviously prophetic episode in *The Prelude*: the dream of the Arab. In Book Fifth, Wordsworth relates an obscure, prophetic dream, one that comes on the heels of an acute sadness played in the same key as in "Tintern Abbey." The speaker's pain has a specific root: "it grieves me for thy state, O man," but, he says, "not for woes" so much as for the honest labour of "study and hard thought/ The honours of thy high endowments," since these noble and worthwhile efforts will ultimately be superfluous as "the immortal being/ No more shall need such garments" (5.3, 5, 8–9, 23). The contradiction between human frailty –

> Oh, why hath not the mind
> Some element to stamp her image on
> In nature somewhat nearer to her own[?] (5.42–6)

– and the "highest reason in a soul sublime" (5.40) recalls the tension between the mortal and the immortal in the *Essays upon Epitaphs*. But where Wordsworth's *Essays* turn to the funeral monument as one place where the immortal soul might leave its "stamp," here books are the monuments in question. If the appeal to something "in nature" closer to the intellect seems abandoned by the adoption of this most cultural of artefacts, the framework of the dream in fact permits freer movement between realms than is permitted to the conscious, critical mind. The "book of poetry," after all, is condensed, in the Freudian sense, into a shell, a fossil remnant of bygone organic life. And yet this is not to say the object is dead since it manages somehow to speak:

"at the word,
The stranger," said my friend continuing,
"Stretched forth the shell towards me, with command
That I should hold it to my ear. I did so
And heard that instant in an unknown tongue,
Which yet I understood, articulate sounds,
A loud prophetic blast of harmony,
An ode in passion uttered, which foretold
Destruction to the children of the earth
By deluge now at hand." (5.90–9)

The clarity of the apocalyptic content announced at the conclusion of the passage contrasts the radical obscurity of the voice. The language is unknown, yet known at least to *be* language. Hence, strictly speaking, no translation takes place here. Instead, unknown sounds manage to be not only recognizable as language but, bypassing the understanding, to be understood. The idea punches through the conditions that make knowledge possible, communicating a thought via a medium that remains alien. There is also the confusion of voice with music, of song with sense. The materiality of the voice, the sonority of physical articulation, and the resonance of mere sound are, as it were, silenced when they are called "articulate." For when sound is articulated as language, we typically – except perhaps in song or poetry – cease to hear it as sound. How these different elements combine into a coherent vision thus remains impossible to understand. So while it looks like Wordsworth here rehearses the strategy of "Tintern Abbey," where harmony is the form through which poetry gathers different existential temporalities, this mechanism has in fact become wildly overwrought.

Following in a tradition of such associations, this prophecy also suggests that history follows some kind of mathematical necessity.[7] This is where the other "book" in this vision, a stone that is also Classical geometry, comes into play:

The Arab told him [i.e., the dreamer] that the stone –
To give it in the language of the dream –
Was *Euclid's Elements.* (5.86–8)

Given its placement in Wordsworth's book of Books, this book of Elements – an early text on geometrical sciences – might raise questions about the elements *of* books: the elements of figurative language, say, that populate literary texts. And yet, there is something ironic in this invitation to scrutinize literary elements since the dreamworld encountered in the vision precisely does *not* adhere to the kinds of laws sketched in Euclid's treatise. In a violation of Aristotle's law of non-contradiction – a law implicit in Euclid's rigorously analytic system – it *is* possible here for one thing to be itself and something else at the same time:[8]

> Strange as it may seem
> I wondered not, although I plainly saw
> The one to be a stone, th' other a shell,
> Nor doubted once but that they both were books,
> Having perfect faith in all that passed. (5.110–14)

With this invitation to consider the elements (of books) and to think of literature in terms of a mathematical system, we seem instantly to move beyond the purview of mathematical relation: the epistemology represented by Euclid's *Elements* reaches the limit of its relevance when one poses the question of the elements of books because the latter violate Classical physical (and metaphysical) laws. Rather than inspiring art to function with the structural coherence of math, Wordsworth's fusion of language and number tends instead to make number vulnerable to absurd equations. So when these "elements/ Of geometric science" supposedly return later to inspire in the speaker "a still sense/ Of permanent and universal sway" named simply "God," we might wonder if this is a wish parading as a fact (6.136–7, 151–2, 157). For what the unifying "blast of harmony" does is precisely to undercut axiomatic truths, truths that are supposed by definition, says Aristotle, to "hold good for everything that is and not for some special genius apart from others."[9] The harmony hits a sour note – one that cannot, however, neatly resolve its tension. At this apocalyptic moment, Wordsworth's poetry works at cross-purposes with its ostensible aim: rather than establish a language for universal translation or a mathematical ratio between various systems of ordering, the dream of the Arab mixes up forms of understanding and leaves us no closer to a genuine intuition of an idea.

Later in Book Fifth, Wordsworth compares the Arab in this dream to a poet and, ultimately, to himself. Ignoring Critical philosophy's protests, Wordsworth opts for an apocalyptic strain through which he might overcome by fiat the Kantian barriers between sensibility and timeless truth. Taking other poets as his guides, Wordsworth plays the Arab-prophet – literally follows in his footsteps – in an effort to join the kind of select artistic company that is granted cultural permission to represent the ineffable:

> yea, will I say,
> In sober contemplation of the approach
> Of such great overthrow, made manifest
> By certain evidence, that I methinks
> Could share that maniac's anxiousness, could go
> Upon like errand. Oftentimes at least
> Me hath such deep entrancement half-possessed
> When I have held a volume in my hand –
> Poor earthly casket of immortal verse –
> Shakespeare, or Milton, labourers divine! (5.157–65)

According to this reasoning – familiar from Homer and Virgil and Dante and Milton – genuine poets have special permission to participate in the spirit realm, to shuttle between the material and the incorporeal in ways that would, presumably for a less competent traveller, induce psychosis. The question that lingers is, then: can Wordsworth successfully navigate this route unscathed? For, "immortal verse" behaves rather like a restless ghost.[10] Will the apprentice poet, the would-be spirit-seer, relish such visitations or swoon? Upon perusing various poets' "poor earthly casket[s]" – in other words, upon wandering in the graveyard of their compositions, decaying never to be decayed – the speaker feels himself charged up with enough anxious inspiration to take on the burden of the mystery. These shades of "labourers divine" do not, we are assured, frighten so much as seduce the speaker into joining their disembodied company. Soon, we take it, the speaker will begin enthusiastically to craft his own coffin.

We sense a similar ambivalence later, in Book Tenth, when Wordsworth again associates himself and his poetic vocation with prophecy:

> But as the ancient prophets were enflamed,
> Nor wanted consolations of their own
> And majesty of mind, when they denounced
> On towns and cities, wallowing in the abyss
> Of their offences, punishment to come;
> Or saw like other men with bodily eyes
> Before them in some desolated place
> The consummation of the wrath of Heaven;

So did some portion of that spirit fall
On me to uphold me through those evil times,
And in their rage and dog-day heat I found
Something to glory in, as just and fit,
And in the order of sublimest laws. (10.401–13)

As in the dream of the Arab, Wordsworth here imagines that prophetic vision discloses "sublimest laws" through the "consummation of the wrath of Heaven," effectively turning the violence of the French Revolution – the topic of Book Tenth – into a Kantian sign of history. That the French Revolution is the context for this claim to special power is no accident: the supplementary order prophecy is supposed to offer is all the more important when mundane law and order has given way to political upheaval. Wordsworth's verse would, then, counter the "Change and subversion" (10.233) that "might be named/ A revolution" (10.236–7) not only in history but also in Wordsworth's own mind by revealing a larger, encompassing narrative of self and history.

Yet, it remains unclear if Wordsworth's poet–prophet brings order to chaos or if, in this encounter, history deranges the would-be prophet. This touches on the much larger question of whether Wordsworth's poetry is or is not historically sensitive. For instance, in *Wordsworth: The Sense of History*, Alan Liu reads the displacement of Druidic sacrifice from *Salisbury Plain* (1793) to the 1805 *Prelude* as a species of historical repression that undermines the contemporary urgency of the Revolution by retreating to prehistory. Wordsworth's poetry, he argues, makes "a sustained effort to deny history," is "a refugee flight of forms, a rush to escape history."[11] Yet, one may read the same pattern and conclude, to the contrary, that Wordsworth engages in a different mode of historiography altogether, one that, far from repressing history, *cannot* repress history successfully and therefore succumbs to a more recursive, obsessive action. But for Liu, this would not count as history: his positivism necessitates that whatever constitutes history be an object of consciousness. That is, Liu, wisely, refuses to deal in metaphysical terms; hence, "*There is no nature [...]. There is no time. There is no affection. There is no self or mind. Therefore, there is no Imagination*" (38; Liu's emphasis) – at least, not in any transcendental sense. Or as he puts it later on, "there is no nature except as it is constituted by acts of political definition made possible by particular forms of government," a condition that we must presumably extend to his other categories as well: time, affection, self, etc. (104). There is here nothing aside from phenomena and the discursive apparatus that make phenomena possible. In the absence, then, of any grounding being, Liu can suggest, "if there 'is' no history, then the relevant problem becomes the knowledge or *sense* of history in the full sense" (40): history *is*, only insofar as it is sensed. This in effect says that we can positively know history in an intuition because there is nothing that can be called history in itself, there is no idea of history.

Liu's argument has the virtue of undermining transcendental schemes of history and, instead, understanding history as a discourse constructed by human agents. Known only in its "determinate arbitrariness" (43), history is both non-rational yet theoretically understandable: while its particular shape may not be steered by some higher idea (hence, its arbitrariness), it can be known since it is composed of finite instances (is determinate). The problem, however, is that in eliminating the idea of history we also lose any way to think about the senseless and the irrational in the *emergence of* historiography as such. "Senseless" and "irrational" here does not refer merely to strange or unpleasant events in history. More fundamentally, these terms indicate the *ground* of historical consciousness. Unless Liu thinks consciousness is qualitatively unchanging, the particular shape of consciousness concerned about history – the historical "sense" – must itself have a history. Yet, how should we write this history of historical consciousness, given that it emerges over time and through development, if history is only and always the object of the understanding? How would we look at the formation of the very interest in history, what Stephen Bann calls "the desire for history," without admitting the possibility of a kind of Kantian leap, like the one taken in Critical idealism from objects to the *conditions* of their existence?[12] To anticipate a line of thinking similar to Kant's and explored in the next chapter, as well as chapters 6 and 7, we might think of the emergence of historical consciousness as an event and, therefore, as partly virtual. The virtual names the potentiality to which an event remains irreducible qua cause. Just as "one can play indefinitely the historicist game of sources and influences" without fully penetrating an event, so the emergence of historical consciousness itself cannot be fully narrated or, in Liu's sense, historicized.[13]

The reading of the spots of time later in this chapter provides an example of what happens when we do try to locate the originary moment of historical sensitivity. The subject, as we will see, does not become better grounded by history but is, instead, threatened by a force that is alien and other. This awareness of vulnerability produces a defensive reaction, one where the self-proclaimed prophet insists on being set apart such that the utopian idea of a nation of prophets – of a world wherein everyone enjoys a sensuous knowledge of ideas like freedom and immortality – must be excluded. That is, in the midst of his thinking about the French Revolution's potential for social and political liberation, Wordsworth echoes Moses' democratizing wish that "all the LORD's people were prophets."[14]

Yea, I could almost
Have prayed that throughout the earth upon all souls
Worthy of liberty, upon every soul
Matured to live in plainness and in truth,
The gift of tongues might fall, and men arrive
From the four quarters of the winds to do
For France what without help she could not do. (10.117–23)[15]

The speaker's language denies his ostensible desire by erecting barriers to this universalization. That is, he reserves insight for only those souls "matured to live in plainness and in truth," that is, souls that are in essence already enlightened. Moreover, the rhetorical framework, "I could *almost* have prayed," suggests that the speaker might in fact withhold his efforts: the grammatical formulation of the passage as a wish contains a latent rhetorical negation of that same wish. The rhetoric here squares with the privatization implicit in Wordsworth's persistent claims to special election – a not uncommon trait among self-styled prophets.[16] Early in *The Prelude* Wordsworth makes clear that not just anyone can be a poet and that, like the prophet, a higher power chooses this vocation on the subject's behalf:

To the open fields I told
A prophesy; poetic numbers came
Spontaneously, and clothed in priestly robe
My spirit, thus singled out, as it might seem,
For holy services. (1.59–63)

Wordsworth believes himself "gifted." Later on, he describes his mind as "gifted with such powers to send abroad/ Her spirit" (5.44, 47–8). The usage here connotes generosity. Yet, we have again to pause given the implications of this concept's several connotations. If poets and prophets, echoing Shelley's *Defence of Poetry*,

Have each his own peculiar faculty,
Heaven's gift, a sense that fits him to perceive
Objects unseen before (1850: 13.303–5)

then what is the relationship between the sense of a gift as something offered freely and this sense of giftedness as a special insight belonging only to an elected subject? What are the consequences for thinking about prophecy if the concept of the gift involves the conflation of these two diametrically opposed gestures – one of democratization and one of exclusion? And finally, how does this privatization of prophecy – Wordsworth's effort to turn prophecy into a *property* of the elected subject – undermine its social and political force in the context of the Revolution in France? There is a fault-line in Wordsworth's ambition that becomes most apparent in moments of prophetic self-election. In these moments of identity formation, prophecy offers a model for poetic subjectivity and a path to literary canonization – though at the risk of the subject's pre-emptive interment. Prophecy's double edge manifests in the way the spots of time are both restorative and traumatizing for the subject. The method – election to the status of "prophet" – through which Wordsworth would shore up the subject against the threats of contingency and history and loss turns out to unspool that same subject. Like what we witness even more violently in Blake's *The [First] Book of Urizen*, prophetic self-composition looks remarkably like a sort of self-destruction. But before we can assess what it is the spots "give" the subject, we need to look more carefully at prophecy's peculiar generosity.

"As are unheard by all but gifted ear"

What exactly does it mean to call the Romantic prophet "gifted"? This word has to be read in Wordsworth's double sense, as signifying both generosity and a particular, exclusive ability – specifically the *ability to give*. The prophet gives to his or her people a narrative that warns, threatens, and promises … something. That is, the prophet's generosity is particularly complicated, restaging for historiography the paradox of gift giving. In Jacques Derrida's words, "if the gift appears or signifies itself, if it exists or if it is presently *as gift*, as what it is, then it is not, it annuls itself."[17] When a gift is recognized as a gift, it is immediately taken up in an economy of exchange. Any such exchange of gifts, however, levels down the event of the gift through a formula of equalization. Put otherwise, exchange – as an essential component of the notion of economy as such – when applied to gifts, annihilates the pure giving of the gift by placing it in terms that make returnability possible. Such returnability is, further, easily and almost seamlessly appropriated by ulterior motives, translating generosity into an implicit demand for restitution. Due to this nature of economy and exchange, the gift is thus figured, for the receiver, as a debt. In order to prevent the gift's appropriation as debt through economization and to try, instead, to think about the gift as such, Derrida turns to strategies involving dissimulation, secrecy, and forgetfulness. The gift, apparently, must be disguised – must appear, but not as what it is – in order to function as a gift. But Derrida goes further than this, arguing that the *essence* of the gift is entangled in a paradox that undermines presence metaphysically. It is not simply that the gift must look different from what it is; it must, in fact, not be what it is, in order to be what it is. Or in Derrida's words, "the truth of the gift is equivalent to the non-gift or to the non-truth of the gift."[18] Only through a deeply and consistently aporetic movement can the gift, for Derrida, be approached – which is to say that the gift, like the auratic original work of art Walter Benjamin describes, must remain "at a distance, however close it may be."[19]

The implication of this thinking is that the only truly generous act is to give nothing. It is possible to make some sense out of this by considering again the concept of false prophecy, the apparent failure successfully to offer knowledge of the future as a positive content. Take, for example, the Book of Jonah. Jonah's credibility takes a major knock when God cancels the prophecy of Nin'eveh's destruction after having him announce this event. The prophecy, the peoples' repentance, and God's reconsideration all take place within just a few lines:

> Jonah began to go into the city, going a day's journey. And he cried, "Yet forty days, and Nin'eveh shall be overthrown!" And the people of Nin'eveh believed God; they proclaimed a fast, and put on sackcloth, from the greatest of them to the least of them. Then tidings reached the king of Nin'eveh, and he arose from his throne, removed his robe, and covered himself with sackcloth, and sat in ashes. And he made proclamation and published through Nin'eveh, "By the decree of the king and his nobles: Let neither man nor beast, herd nor flock, taste anything; let them not feed, or drink water, but let man and beast be covered with sackcloth, and let them cry mightily to God; yea, let every one turn from his evil way and from the violence which is in his hands. Who knows, God may yet repent and turn from his fierce anger, so that we perish not?" When God saw what they did, how they turned from their evil way, God repented of the evil which he had said he would do to them; and he did not do it.[20]

Given the definition of false prophecy offered in Deuteronomy, God's intervention proves disastrous to Jonah's reputation: "And if you say in your heart, 'How may we know the word which the LORD has not spoken?' – when a prophet speaks in the name of the LORD, if the word does not come to pass or come true, that is a word which the LORD has not spoken; the prophet has spoken it presumptuously, you need not be afraid of him."[21] Jonah's *success* – the people of Nin'eveh do change and forestall the anticipated catastrophe – makes him appear to be a *false* prophet. Jonah's story suggests that a successful prophet is, strangely, indistinguishable from a false prophet, since nothing that is threatened materializes if the warning is, as warning, successful.[22] The social or effective force of the language (the effect of the prophecy-as-threat) runs counter to the content of the language (prophecy-as-promise), producing a kind of schizophrenic speech. Prophecy, here, involves not the anticipation of the future in the present but a conflict, where an utterance's content contradicts its immediate effect. But what proves most curious about this strange story is that, ultimately, the text's paradoxical status, the double voice whereby it revokes what it also says, is what makes Jonah's prophecy a genuine gift. Precisely because he is unable to take credit for this result – because it runs counter to his intention – Jonah's prophecy could be called a genuine gift.

We can approach prophecy's rich negativity not only in terms of how the content of a prophetic utterance, its poetic language, deconstructs itself but also in the form of many self-identified prophetic works. With Wordsworth's *Prelude* in mind, we can pose the problem of prophetic inauguration structurally by focusing on anticipatory texts such as preludes and prefaces. Indeed, if apocalypse is concerned with the *end* of history, prophecy is concerned with how history – as figure, narrative, genre, or experience – opens to novelty and how one gains a sense for time through history, even if that means sensing time indirectly in the rhythm of its arrest. Inaugurating para-texts, like prophetic texts, do not simply begin works but attempt to *anticipate* the disruptive, alienating gift of the future by writing the beginning in light of that future. The preface, for example, attempts properly to locate a beginning by placing itself in a time before the beginning, such that *beginning* can be understood as something yet to come. However, if with this gesture a preface tries to give the beginning, it can do so only through an intense self-negation that reproduces textually the prophet's physical mutilation: his or her disfiguration and defacement or in Jonah's case discredit.[23] In fact, this negation opens another (even an absolute) gap between origin and goal, beginning and end, given the infinite regress implied by such negativity. When or how, one could ask, does a prelude *itself* begin? Can there be – or must there be – a prelude to a prelude, a preface to a preface that would dig ever deeper into absence in an attempt to stage the beginning as something continuous with the future? While we will return to this problem in chapter 7 via Blake, Kierkegaard, and Schelling, it is worth considering, if briefly, in the context of Wordsworth and in light of what it tells us about prophetic generosity and the productivity of negation.

Maurice Blanchot argues that such an abyss does indeed haunt literary beginnings of the sort Wordsworth, in his attempted auto-election to the pantheon of gifted poets, tries to overleap. There is the lingering paradox, says Blanchot, that a writer "has no talent until he has written, but he needs talent in order to write."[24] Such existential writer's block cannot be mitigated except by fiat or prefatory extemporaneity, as the musical connotations of the word *prelude* suggest[25] – a usage consonant with Wordsworth's "grosser prelude" (2.433) designating an external stimulus in distinction from the "one life" that is "invisible, yet liveth to the heart" (2.430, 424). Hence, Blanchot: "let us suppose that the work has been written."[26] Such a beginning would have to be irreducibly abrupt; the beginning is unprecedented and inescapably unexpected. This sense of a prelude as pure positing conflicts with the other sense of a prelude as an anticipation of beginning: a "prelude" would be both what is without precedent and that which serves as precedent, such that defining the word one way or the other inevitably solicits its opposed counterpart. Like prophecy itself, the prelude is both the ecstatic fiat that welcomes time's corrosive negativity and the defensive attempt to discipline that same negativity by presenting it as its perfect opposite: a plan for all that will follow. This duplicity is responsible for the conflation of the gift of prophecy with its own other, namely, trauma. The gift of prophecy makes the beginning into something inevitably traumatic because prophecy announces a future unlike any futures past, a future for which one cannot prepare.

Like the spots of time, there is something both palliative and distressing about the prophetic utterance; indeed, for both a "sense of creative donation traverses trauma but not smoothly."[27] On the one hand, prophecy, as prediction or as a preface (something that prepares for the beginning), attempts to remove any discontinuity in history through a contractual pattern that economizes the new by rendering it, in effect, always already old. In Koselleck's terminology, the preface under this aspect establishes a horizon of expectation, a framework for encountering novelty such that novelty's alterity can be absorbed within the prevailing space of experience. On the other hand, prophecy as an impossible speech, as a radical positing for which no preface can prepare history (this is where the preface emerges under its second aspect, as a perpetual retreat into absence) creates a rupture in time or opens the rupture *of* time – a cut or crisis in which thought and life's relation to the future has become intensely problematic. Blanchot hints at prophecy's violent prodigality when he concludes that,

> We owe much, then, to the poet whose poetry, translated by the prophets, knew how to transmit the essential to us: the primal eagerness, this haste, this refusal to be delayed and attached. Rare and almost threatening gift, for he must above all make perceptible, in all *true* speech, by the devotion to rhythm and primitive accent, that speech always spoken and never heard that doubles it with pre-echo, rumour of wind and impatient murmur destined to repeat in advance, at the risk of destroying it by preceding it.[28]

If the "essential" here has something to do with radical difference rather than full being – just as prophecy's essence as a form of writing resides in its redactability – the poetry of prophecy gives voice to such "primal eagerness" or "haste" of an inauguration that must always be a depression in or loss of self-command. If this ability to articulate origination is a "rare and almost threatening gift," it is because the Nothing that the gift gives is really indistinguishable from retracting assurance about the future of life and suspending narrative continuity altogether.

Self-Fulfilling Trauma

Let us suppose that *The Prelude* has been written. In the first effort at his epic proper, Book One of *The Recluse*, "Home at Grasmere," Wordsworth invokes the tradition of prophetic inspiration. At this point, however, such an appeal seems strangely belated. Has he not already begun and has he not already called on his muse – that "voice/ That flowed along" (1.6–7 [1799]) his childhood dreams – the river Derwent? Why this redundancy of invocation? In fact, the entire passage hovers in limbo between assertion and wish, poetic self-confidence and an "anxiety of hope" (11.371) – that is, somewhere between the poetic subject's assertions of predetermined, almost Calvinist election and his restless appeals to uncertain redemption:

> Come, thou prophetic Spirit, that inspirest
> The human Soul of universal earth,
> Dreaming on things to come; and dost possess
> A metropolitan temple in the hearts
> Of mighty Poets; upon me bestow
> A gift of genuine insight; that my Song
> With star-like virtue in its place may shine,
> Shedding benignant influence, and secure
> Itself from all malevolent effect
> Of those mutations that extend their sway
> Throughout the nether sphere! And if with this
> I mix more lowly matter – with the thing
> Contemplated describe the Mind and Man
> Contemplating, and who and what he was,
> The transitory Being that beheld
> This Vision, when and where, and how he lived –
> Be not this labour useless. (836–52)[29]

When the speaker asserts his availability for inspiration, he solicits the prophetic Spirit. This raises a question concerning poetic invocation as such: if inspiration must be solicited, is the act of solicitation itself inspired? Such a call *to* prophecy would seem to be an act performed before inspiration and as such to be, itself, necessarily *un*inspired.[30] The ambiguity concerning the usefulness of this poetic labour in the final line is supposed to be clarified by the "gift of genuine insight." Yet, given that such assurances issue from a speech itself apparently spiritless, any confidence in this clarification to come is difficult to sustain. As this misplaced confidence suggests, however, the invocation *already* performs the mixing it, ostensibly, *preemptively* apologizes for. The disconnection between the "lowly matter" of "the Mind of Man" and the "Vision" that this "transitory Being" is privileged to behold is something already dissolved in the very moment that the difference is asserted. In a somewhat camouflaged rhetorical manoeuvre, the echo between the object "contemplated" and the mind actively "contemplating" – the inspiring Spirit and the lowly speaker, respectively – mixes up subject and object. The speaker's mind is cast, grammatically, as the active force while the inspiring Vision is comparatively static: the object of an activity but itself inactive. Like the boy of Winander, it is as if the echo of his own voice here returns to and touches the speaker as something strange. His *appeal* to the "prophetic Spirit" returns to *fulfil* that same request, carrying far into "the human Soul of universal earth" the gentle shock, the "gift of genuine insight."

This self-fulfilling prophecy of prophetic inspiration means that it is difficult in Wordsworth to separate assertion from solicitation, fact from desire. And this confusion is one of the most interesting aspects of Wordsworth's prophetic mode. For, as Blanchot suggests, "literature encounters its most dangerous meaning – that of interrogating itself in a declarative mode – at times triumphantly, and in so doing discovering that everything belongs to it, at other times, in distress, discovering it is lacking everything since it only affirms *itself* by default."[31] Like literature's unsettlingly declarative interrogatives that place works always on the pivot between everything and nothing, prophecy's assertive solicitation of inspiration oscillates between absolute self-confidence and crippling self-doubt, vatic fullness and infinite absolute negativity.[32] In fact, this grammatical and affective overlapping of opposites reflects the more familiar temporal manipulations of prophecy, where it becomes difficult to parse past and present and future. In Wordsworth's (in)harmonious condensation of temporal difference, in his echo logic that sees the other as the self (but also the self as alien), the arrival of the future is indistinguishable from a return of the past. This interlacing of time structures those most well-known moments of inspiration in *The Prelude*, the spots of time.[33] Given the frequent repetition of this phrase, as Alan Richardson notes, "We no longer hear the paradox of Wordsworth's conflation of time with space" that aims "to halt the reading process."[34]

Attending closely to their disruptive energy, the insistence on failure in these moments of supposed "future restoration" illustrates not only the double gesture of the ecstatic gift (that gives by revoking) but also a more depressing double gesture, where an affirmative orientation to the future cannot be separated from a retrograde, traumatic itinerary. If Romantic prophecy is a gift that gives nothing objective – if the prophet "embodies" this absence as his or her giftedness, the generosity of a temporality both offered and hidden by the antinomic nature of prophecy as promise and threat – then it is no surprise really that, in Wordsworth, in the same instance as the future is proffered it is also revoked by the very trauma that spurred projection in the first place. The arrival of the future is confused with the return of the repressed – that is, the future is produced by the prospect of its loss. To be clear: this is not to say that Wordsworth is a failed prophet, per se, but rather that Romantic prophecy is often a disfiguring mode for representing history, reflective of the unprecedented temporalization of history and the epistemic break coincident with this new kind of time. The opaque surface of the future resembles a painful, originary beginning by fiat, so that when Wordsworth looks forward he cannot help but also look back.

This is not as obvious a statement as it may seem. We know, for instance, that throughout *The Prelude*, Wordsworth's goal is the origin, where this origin figures variously as the home, nature, the mother and father, the original self, and the original impressions experienced by that self: "How shall I trace the history, where seek/ The origin of what I then have felt?" (1.365–6), the speaker muses in Book First. In the wake of increasing industrialization and the subject's subsequent instrumentalization, Wordsworth would telescope the past through the present and suture the increasingly compartmentalized self together across time and space. But if the spots of time serve as so many quilting points – original impressions that transcend and organize history – such points are deceptive since their restorative power cannot be distinguished from their capacity for damage; the same intensity that causes these moments to stand out of time also scars the psyche. The various origins to which Wordsworth would return thus spring from yet deeper and stranger origins. Thus the desire to return to the past overlaps with an anxiety that, with this return, that speaker might descend too far, all the way to the origin's ground, such that "the fear gone by/ Pressed on [him] almost like a fear to come" (10.62–3). The spots of time, these original impressions that transport the speaker back to various points in childhood and draw his life together, are at the same time indistinguishable from damaging events, instances that alienate the subject from himself. With an insight reiterated later in psychoanalysis, subjectivity is for Wordsworth traumatic; it is not that trauma affects some coherent, pre-social subject but that the subject comes into being only with a radical cut or alienation in being.

The notion of an original subjective unity is the fiction of nostalgic fantasy, a form of life that never actually existed. Wordsworth's original moments have then both a centripetal and centrifugal force: as points around which the self turns, the spots of time derange the tidy, dialectical development they also make possible.

The temporal conflation and the attendant affective disjunction in Wordsworth's effort to secure subjectivity against contingency is couched in particularly gothic terms when the ostensibly inspired speaker of "Home at Grasmere" describes his ultimate project, namely, an epic on the sublimity of the human mind:

For I must tread on shadowy ground, must sink
Deep, and, aloft ascending, breathe in worlds
To which the heaven of heavens is but a veil.
All strength, all terror, single or in bands,
That ever was put forth in personal form –
Jehovah, with his thunder, and the choir
Of shouting Angels and the empyreal thrones –
I pass them unalarmed. Not Chaos, not
The darkest pit of lowest Erebus,
Nor aught of blinder vacancy, scooped out
By help of dreams – can breed such fear and awe
As fall upon us often when we look
Into our Minds, into the Mind of Man,
My haunt and the main region of my song. (781–94)

At one level, this passage appears simply to take up the epical tradition of overgoing the predecessor; just as Milton aspired to transcend Classical epic with his treatment of the Fall and redemption of humankind, so Wordsworth would pass Milton's "Jehovah" and "choir/ Of shouting Angels" coolly "unalarmed." There is, however, something troubling about this description of the mind. The speaker is on "shadowy ground" and has to "sink/ Deep" to regard a sublime, a higher power. The mind is presented as darker than might be expected from a speaker who "did [...] drink the visionary power" (2.331). Indeed, Wordsworth falls, Hyperion-like, into the "deep/ Recesses in man's heart" (1.233) and finds himself amid "huge and mighty forms that do not live" (1.424). Such "Unnam'd forms,"[35] as Blake might call them, refuse, however, passively to submit to reason, and move "slowly through" the mature poet's mind just as they had the mind of the young boy following his theft of the "elfin pinnace" (1.425, 401). In other words, if the mind is the speaker's "haunt" in the sense of "home" or a well-known space, it is also a *haunted* region.

Nor is this the first time that anxiety will be confused with ease. In Book Four of *The Prelude*, the summer vacation strangely imposes itself upon the speaker:

> comfort seemed to touch
> A heart that had not been disconsolate,
> Strength came where weakness was not known to be,
> At least not felt; and restoration came
> Like an intruder knocking at the door
> Of unacknowledged weariness. (4.143–8)

While in "Home at Grasmere," insistent claims to homeliness contribute to an unhomely atmosphere,[36] in Book Fourth of *The Prelude*, anxiety masquerades as restoration. Given the internal–external topography implied by the image of an approaching intruder, this scene sees the home compromised. When "restoration," the (as it were) true master of the home, returns to his dwelling, he finds it occupied by his enemy. And if restoration is initially mistaken for a threat, then the logic of the simile produces a moment of uncanny revelation: in a sudden reversal, those barricaded inside the metaphorical house must recognize that their presiding host is *not* comfort, that he is, then, something else and other.

The human mind and the childhood home, two places referred to by the speaker as the "haunt, and the main region of [his] song" in "Home at Grasmere," are also haunted. This illustrates the problem mentioned above, where attempts to return to an original impression or place in order to stabilize the self may actually involve a paradoxical self-alienation or re-traumatization. Wordsworth's effort to recuperate missed experience through subjective *Bildung* may therefore undermine itself not for failing to revive the past in the present but for doing so *too* vividly. Thus, reliving the past may not necessarily refine especially recalcitrant materials into objects over which the ego might rule. This is not to say that negative experiences – fear, suffering, anxiety, etc. – cannot have a dialectical, positive resolution in Wordsworth; there is certainly a strength that follows from being "fostered alike by beauty and by fear" (1.302). Nevertheless, this optimism might overlook a different quality of negativity that cannot be so easily appropriated. David Collings notes, for instance, that Wordsworth is playing a dangerous game throughout *The Prelude* when he attempts to metamorphose error into exception, errancy into a confidence that,

> should the guide [he] chuse
> Be nothing better than a wandering cloud
> [He] cannot miss [his] way.[37] (1.17–19)

Collings argues that Wordsworth defensively and desperately attempts to read failure *as* success, damage *as* inspiration. Following his decision not to pursue a Cambridge fellowship, for instance, Wordsworth claims, punningly, to find recompense in "poetic fellowship" with a company of authors (6.72–5). This, among many other instances, suggests that the ego relies on a particularly perverse economy, summed up in Wordsworth's conviction "that he was elected as a poet, set apart not merely by the gods but by God himself, in a moment of masochistic wounding."[38] In other words, Wordsworth's claims to prophetic inspiration often tackle negativity directly, going so far as claiming the prophet's physical and psychological trauma as the path – a kind of *via negativa* – to transcendence. Yet, this makes it impossible to separate an orientation to the future from the regressive, traumatic origin *of* that very visionary perspective. Hence, Collings' description of Wordsworthian masochism serves as an apt description of prophetic inspiration more broadly, precisely because the latter follows from psychic or even ontological violence, a radical penetration of the individual that is both damaging and yet, strangely, welcomed.[39] If the poet returns to past traumas with the aim to narrate missed experiences, it appears that the power to generate that superior, recuperative narrative itself rests on the careful *maintenance* of a trauma that must *never* be exposed as such. To eliminate the trauma would be to risk abdicating the very inspiration necessary for writing. Prophetic power is predicated on traumatic damage and retains its inspired, motivating potential only insofar as it wounds.

"A sensitive, and a *creative* soul"

Book Eleventh of the 1805 *Prelude* opens with the promise to document the trials of the "Imagination, How Impaired and Restored," suggesting a predictable itinerary of mourning and restitution. To this end, the poem turns to those "Points […] within our souls/ Where all stand single" (3.186–7), the spots of time. Such moments, with their "renovating Virtue" (11.259), "Are scattered everywhere, taking their date/ From our first childhood" (11.274–5). The speaker, then, suggests that such instants originate from a moment of intense consciousness:

> This efficacious spirit chiefly lurks
> Among those passages of life in which
> We have had deepest feeling that the mind
> Is lord and master, and that outward sense
> Is but the obedient servant of her will. (11.268–72)

This valorization of the controlling mind is, however, somewhat doubtful or, recalling the prophetic call to prophecy in "Home at Grasmere," wishful.

Consider the episode of the gibbet-mast: while the scene of "visionary dreariness" (11.311) that stands out in the poet's memory might indeed be the product of intense consciousness, that consciousness is itself the consequence of an unconscious tension that primes or readies the mind. While the "feeling, and diversity of strength" (11.327) in this moment is enshrined for "future restoration," it only has this power thanks to residual anxiety.

Thomas De Quincey, in 1839, recorded how Wordsworth understood this psychological operation. De Quincey recalls an occasion when the expectation of important news concerning the Peninsular War prompted him, with Wordsworth, to walk out and linger near the road. De Quincey describes waiting patiently, Wordsworth occasionally applying his ear to the ground in hopes of detecting horses. This proves fruitless, however, as the mail never arrives. Wordsworth then reflects on the effect of this disappointment in terms that will prove useful for reading key passages in his poetry:

> I have remarked from my earliest days that if, under any circumstances, the attention is energetically braced up to an act of steady observation, or of steady expectation, then, if this intense condition of vigilance should then relax, at that moment any beautiful, any impressive visual object, or collection of objects, falling upon the eye, is carried to the heart with a power not known under any other circumstances.[40]

This is how Wordsworth explains his vivid memory of a single star hanging in the darkening sky, an object on which, rising from the ground and preparing to return home, his eye on this day happened to fall.

Compare this to the case of the gibbet-mast in *The Prelude*. The young Wordsworth's consciousness is similarly primed by an imminent apparition when he witnesses obsessive engraving, that is, writing designed to keep a ghost confined by literally en-graving its murderous spirit:

> Some unknown hand had carved the murderer's name.
> The monumental writing was engraven
> In times long past, and still from year to year
> By superstition of the neighbourhood
> The grass is cleared away; and to this hour
> The letters are fresh and visible. (11.293–8)

The townsfolk's persistent repression of unruly spirits is tantamount to the "attention" and "intense vigilance" mentioned by De Quincey.[41] Yet, insofar as this repression successfully forestalls the ghost's return, so does the intense expectation of that return "inspire" the speaker.

That is, for all of the effort, there is a sense that the letter cannot, finally, repress the spirit. According to the *Essays upon Epitaphs*, "to raise a Monument is a sober and reflective act," one wherein "The passions should be subdued, the emotions controlled."[42] And yet at the gibbet-mast, trepidation transcends localization. In the perpetual postponement of the ghost, restless anticipation haunts the subject. If the grave site is supposed to be "a tranquilizing object,"[43] this episode presents us with something quite the opposite. For the spirit of the gibbet-mast escapes engraving precisely when anxiety "possesses" the young Wordsworth, making him *impressionable*. In this, a certain notion of history – history as linear narrative – could be said, also, to escape from inscription or interment: for the past is perhaps not so decidedly past, nor the future something that can be confidently predicted via precedent, as the unlikely intensity of the subsequent experience attests. More specifically, there is here an existential awaking, as the protagonist is not exactly impressed by the experience of the gallows, but rather made capable, subsequently, of *bearing impressions*. As Peter Larkin says, the "gibbet mast is an ordinary sight but on a site where trauma has ripped off the surface, exposing a newly vulnerable but intensified retina of perception."[44] This describes the speaker's historical receptivity, his being-historical or historicity. Hence, the episode complicates its own empirical language and the sense of history and time at play. The child-Wordsworth is left *un*marked by his experience at the gibbet only because he has been made eminently *re*markable. Becoming remarkable does not, itself, leave a mark – only perhaps an "obscure sense/ Of possible sublimity" (2.335–6). So, while the scene of the gibbet-mast itself is not taken as the restorative spot to which the mature speaker "repairs" in times of hardship, it is what makes possible the deep impression left by the otherwise "ordinary sight" (11.309) of a "A girl who bore a pitcher on her head" (11.305) walking against the wind in the hills – a scene that *will* be one of these reparative spots. The renovating impression in Wordsworth's memory thus contains a double reference. On the one hand, it points toward a singular, (extra)ordinary scene. On the other, it necessarily, if secretly, gestures to the gibbet-mast: to the preface of the impression, the unhallowed ground of engraving, or the disembodied intensity of vigilance. In fact, this episode of exceptional impression deconstructs the empirical logic of impression at work elsewhere in *The Prelude*.

The language of sensible impression is especially prominent in the 1799 *Prelude*. There, for example, the speaker apostrophizes the "powers of the earth" (1799, 1.186) as agents who

> Impressed upon all forms the characters
> Of danger and desire, and thus did make
> The surface of the universal earth

With meanings of delight, of hope and fear,
Work like a sea. (1799, 1.194–8)

Moreover, this monumental writing *on* the earth becomes the writing *of* the earth when the speaker becomes the ultimate archive and even the grave of history:

Distresses and disasters, tragic facts
Of rural history, that impressed my mind
With images to which in following years
Far other feelings were attached – with forms
That yet exist with independent life,
And, like their archetypes, know no decay. (1799, 1.282–7)

The speaker is eminently engravable. The impressions, moreover, are not superficial but take on an "independent life" that emulates changeless ideas or "archetypes," importing a dubious kind of stability. For it is clear, as noted above, that the spots of time are the products of scarring and borrow their traumatic itinerary from the imagery of Druidic sacrifice that punctuates so much of Wordsworth's poetry – moments that do not so much evade history as take narrative to its trembling limit in uncanny repetition. This shift from engraving nature to engraving the subject parallels the gibbet-mast scene as there, also, the speaker becomes the ultimate surface of impression. As such, we might recall John Locke's subject – particularly in his characterization of the mind as "white paper, void of all characters."[45] As Hugh Sykes Davies suggests, "So far as the notion of 'impulse' [and perhaps "impression"] goes, he [Wordsworth] was in general agreement with them [the empirical philosophers], and his use of the word is not very different from the way it is used in [...] Locke."[46] However, Wordsworth also departs significantly, if subtly, from strictly Lockean epistemology given, for instance, "his insistence upon the potential significance of '*one* impulse,' of one experience rather than a host of others."[47] Wordsworth, in contrast to Locke, suggests that there can be *exceptional impressions*. These impressions are not made exceptional through perception, attention, or higher-order operations of reflection. They are exceptional, rather, because of the preexisting conditions of the receptive subject, one specially "gifted" in the art of feeling. Whereas the Lockean subject is "essentially passive and inactive," at least in terms of the formation of "simple ideas," Wordsworth's subject, on the contrary, is radically agitated.[48]

The exceptional impression in the gibbet-mast episode is lighter and yet more profound than any other, as it stages what Wordsworth, in the

"Mutability" sonnet, calls "the unimaginable touch of Time." In the caesura at the centre of empirical impression, Wordsworth's subject (paradoxically) senses the radical openness and uncertainty of temporalized history. This is to suggest that time itself is a kind of missed experience and that the prophet's suffering – taken either traumatically or ecstatically – is a function of his or her immediate relationship to time's own extemporaneity. Anticipating the upcoming discussion of forgetful memory in chapter 5 – a phenomenon that leaves Blanchot with a strange epistemological residue, the sense that he *will have* known something – Wordsworth has the impression not that he knows time but that he will have known it, that he had known it once before but now only senses that loss. For if all we ever have of time is a memory, this is a strange, self-displacing kind of memory that recalls us not to something objective but to the absence of presence or, better, the presence of absence. Wordsworth will always come back to time's absent impression, will always experience the *missing of* experience, in his spots of time precisely because he does not directly return to the gibbet-mast episode but rather to the gap it makes possible, the impression that *covers over* even as it gently discloses its senseless condition.

There is a sense even in Locke that the lightness of time's impression troubles empiricism. This is especially evident in Locke's own version of the gibbet-mast episode. For beyond his three best-known images of the mind – an "empty cabinet," the aforementioned blank paper, and a "dark room" – there is an often-overlooked fourth image: the mind as a tomb, its surface engraved by memory.[49] In Book Two of *An Essay Concerning Human Understanding*, in the chapter "Of Retention," Locke suggests, in a strangely gothic passage, that memories fade just as actual memorials erode over time: "Thus the ideas, as well as children, of our youth, often die before us: and our minds represent to us those tombs to which we are approaching; where, though the brass and marble remain, yet the inscriptions are effaced by time, and the imagery moulders away."[50] Locke's metaphor here requires that we think of ideas as buried corpses. Memorial plaques and epitaphs – memories – constitute a temporary and fragile index: signs on dissolving surfaces that attempt, against time's exhausting violence, to "plot" ideas. As in Wordsworth, there is a pressing danger here that engraving, in every sense, will fail. Even when engraving (in the sense of writing) in Locke's metaphor *succeeds*, engraving (in the sense of "keeping in the grave") *fails*, as it would call-up – literally re-member – the "corpse" of meaning. Similarly, successful engraving (in the sense of writing) in Wordsworth's gibbet-mast episode does not prevent but actually sustains a residual, haunting anxiety. This failure is, in each case, linked directly to the properties of the respective impressionable surfaces.

That is, *sensitivity* is the necessary condition of impression, even as sensitivity itself withdraws from positive impression with "steps/ Almost as silent as the turf they trod" (1799, 1.331–2). Indeed, this sensing of senseless sensitivity has the oxymoronic structure Kenneth Burke calls "The incongruity of the grotesque-mystical," a condition in which "one hears silence, peoples [*sic*] loneliness, feels distance, and sees in the dark."[51] In Wordsworth's semi-mystical state of agitation, sensitivity is what at once grounds and eludes impression, disclosing time's unruliness through subtle fluctuations on the very edges of empiricism.

It is this return of the violent, though strangely impalpable – so, empirically missed – experience of time itself that structures, also, the Christmas vacation spot of time. The Christmas scene involves what Wordsworth, elsewhere, calls "the usury of time," an error or injustice committed by predictive "sages, who in their prescience would controul/ All accidents" (5.379). This predictive exigency recalls the young Wordsworth's position as he waits above two roads, expecting, along one or the other route, the arrival of a carriage to convey him home for the holiday. The schoolmasters addressed in Book Fifth force the speaker down one of these paths, teaching the student a lesson about mastering time that he will wish, later, not to have learned so well:

> These mighty workmen of our later age
> Who with a broad highway have overbridged
> The froward chaos of futurity (5.370–2)

manage, laments the speaker, to "Confine us down/ Like engines" (5.382–3). In an echo of Sin and Death who, in *Paradise Lost*,

> Pav'd after him [i.e., Satan] a broad and beat'n way
> Over the dark Abyss, whose boiling Gulph
> Tamely endur'd a Bridge of wondrous length,[52]

these stern instructors would impose a deadly predictability on the "unreasoning progress of the world," failing to see that "a wiser spirit is at work for us" in such ostensible errancy, or "even in what seem out most unfruitful hours" (5.384, 385, 388).

In the second major spot of time in Book Eleventh, such "usury of time" backfires. The passage is well-known. An "impatient" Wordsworth recalls climbing "Up to the highest summit" to view "the meeting-point/ Of two highways," along one of which "the expected steeds might come" that would convey him and his brothers home for Christmas (11.347, 355, 350–1, 353).

As in the passage above recalled by De Quincey, Wordsworth concentrates his attention –

> I watched,
> Straining my eyes intensely as the mist
> Gave intermitting prospect of the wood
> And plain beneath (11.360–3)

– but is finally disappointed and returns to school. What happens to this surcharged anticipation? Where does it go? It is not simply reinvested in another experience, as with the "ordinary sight" glimpsed following the encounter with the gibbet-mast. Instead, it turns out that the form it takes, the "anxiety of hope" (11.371), is really a sort of orientation to the future. Geoffrey Hartman notes that the speaker's protracted anticipation – the affect that is fuelled by the non-event of arrival – is complicated by his father's abrupt death: "the father's death, which supervenes as an 'event' (1.309), converts that moment of hope into an ominous, even murderous anticipation."[53] In light of his father's death, history takes on a suddenly new shape, suggesting that the speaker's anxious hope had not been experienced, as it were, felicitously. This feeling, this deep impression, was somehow misfelt; the moment's presence is strangely missensed or incompletely sensed. Similar to the consolation that comes like an intruder in Book Fourth, the desire to return to home's comfort somehow harbours another, secret, hostile affect. In the terms of Book Fifth, we could say that Wordsworth's initially excessive hope to see his holiday carriage constitutes temporal usury: he demands an experience from the future that "over taxes" the future's uncertainty. "In retrospect, then, a perfectly ordinary mood is seen to involve a sin against time" as the speaker's desire to return home quickly "seems to find retributive fulfillment when the father's life is cut short ten days later."[54]

The temporality and phenomenology of this moment is more complex than that of the gibbet-mast in part because it collapses several stages of experience. That is, the *entire* psychic complex of concentration, disappointment, and contingent reinvestment happens retroactively. Wordsworth's sparse, unremarkable surroundings during his wait – a "naked wall," a "single sheep," a "whistling hawthorne" – gain their aura not from the non-arrival of the horses but, later, from the conversion of impatient hope into guilt, from the recognition that the silent wish to hasten the holiday also, through some kind of mystical correspondence, hastened his father's death. This means that the "remarkable" moment of temporal sensitivity really comes *after* the visionary dreariness of the scene. The scene is impressive *ex post facto* for *introducing impressionability itself after the moment of impression*. It is not simply that Wordsworth feels the acuteness of his wish to return home as a sin; rather, he only feels acutely – acutely hopeful, acutely guilty, acutely anything – ten days later. The quality of sensitivity necessary to render this second ordinary sight into a spot of time comes back from the future such that the speaker is rendered more present, more alive to the moment, once it is history. These different experiences relative to anticipation (hope, guilt) seem to be chronologically distinct: hope appears to precede and turn into guilt. But in fact, the instant of recollection in tranquility *produces* powerful feeling. In spite of a logical difference between the two affects, the sense of hope is always already infused by guilt since both gain their special potency at the same time, namely, after Wordsworth is rendered extra-sensitive by his father's death. What this passage suggests, then, is that temporal usury, the effort to calculate the future, is a desperate strategy. It is not the case that the future builds on the past and present and could, with enough study, be narrowed down to the probable. This is because the empirical sense of history relies on a nebulous and elusive sensitivity, the temporality of which remains indeterminate. In a very literal way, the past may only make sense in the future.

As noted in the introduction, Max Weber makes a distinction between the prophet and the priest. The prophet undermines legal codes and institutional power, resists the "One Law" that Blake calls "Oppression," whereas the priest institutes such laws.[55] For Weber, what really "distinguishes the prophet [...] from the [priestly] types [...] is an economic factor, i.e., that his prophecy is unremunerated."[56] The prophet threatens, by operating outside of, prevailing social forms of valuation and exchange. Prophetic generosity – the gift of prophecy – is socially and politically disruptive because it threatens to puncture the deification of the economy, rendering its systematic violence obvious and impotent. Yet, with Wordsworth, we witness a retreat from prophet to priest. Like the infant in the "Intimations Ode" born into a world "Apparell'd in celestial light" only, through his growth, to see that light "fade into the common light of day," upon which he adopts his role not as nature's prophet but rather "Nature's *priest*," so does Wordsworth's poetry seem bent on profiting from his debts. This "profit" is not literally financial as it is for Weber but rather aesthetic and emotional "recompense," the "food for future years" that the speaker in *The Prelude* banks. In this shift toward a "priestly" mentality, Wordsworth resembles Kant: for Kant, too, insists, in rather perverse and even slightly absurd ways, on converting loss into gain. Recall, for instance, Kant's remarks discussed in chapter 2 about his motivation for reading Swedenborg: since he had "paid for" the texts, both literally and figuratively, "such an effort" ought "not to be wasted."[57] As we saw, Kant proceeded to extract from Swedenborg whatever philosophical value he could, treating the mystic as a limit case for what can and cannot possibly be known.

In the following chapter we return to Kant as he, now in his post-Critical phase, attempts to recuperate losses of another sort. Addressing social, political, and historical organizations of knowledge in *The Conflict of the Faculties* (1798), Kant explicitly adopts the position of a prophet in an effort to locate the historical coordinates for the completion of his system. The foregoing discussion of Wordsworth prepares us for this analysis because Kant's argument relies on his claim to a very peculiar sort of sympathy with the witnesses to world-shattering events. That is, Kant proceeds to read historical moments that would seem to be signs of degeneration – like, for instance, the regressive violence of the French Revolution – as, in fact, signs of human progress, in his own way, as spots of time. Revisiting questions of evidence, historical sensitivity, and irony that we have touched on in the preceding chapters, *The Conflict* offers the most paradoxical elaboration of Romantic prophecy we have yet encountered.

Chapter Four

Beyond the Sign of History: Prophetic Semiotics and the Future's Reflection

"And don't forget that Kant himself wrote a treatise on 'the end of all things.'"

Maurice Blanchot

Several of Kant's later, post-Critical texts are concerned with the political and historical ramifications of his epistemology. At this apparent turn to history we should not be surprised. For when Thomas De Quincey follows Kant, Godwin-like, into his closet in his selective translation of E.A.C. Wasianski's *Immanuel Kant in seinen letzten Lebensjahren,* we find at the centre of Kant's day a dinner table carefully managed to sustain lively conversation on topics "drawn chiefly from natural philosophy, chemistry, meteorology, natural history, and above all, from politics."[1] Kant's interest in the political is significant; yet, it finds access to his philosophical work only somewhat obliquely. One specific marker of the uneasy merger of political and philosophical thought is Kant's response to the question posed by the Royal Academy in Berlin in 1793: "What real progress has metaphysics made in Germany since the time of Liebniz and Wolff?" Kant attempted but never completed the essay; in 1804, shortly after Kant's death, Friedrich Theodor Rink produced the extant version of the essay from Kant's notes.[2] While contingent factors may have played a supplementary role, Kant's decision to shelve the piece reflects a genuine philosophical impasse in his thinking about history more broadly: his abandonment of the essay marks a realization that he must reorient his thinking about history if he is positively to address rather than merely avoid the question of the relationship between history and reason. What emerges from this reorientation is a surprising kinship with Wordsworth. As we saw in chapter 3, Wordsworth tries to adopt a mystical response to the pressure of history's contingency, tries to translate subjective wounding into a form of sensitivity indicative of special election. Given Kant's sceptical reaction to Swedenborg, we might expect him to reject such measures. And yet, his discussion of historical violence in his post-Critical work takes on a mystical cast, projecting reason into the future on the winds stirred by regressive trauma.

In his fragmentary notes toward a response to the prize question, Kant frames the concept of progress in two ways: empirically and philosophically. Empirically, he sketches a historical movement from dogmatic, to sceptical, and then to his own Critical philosophy. However, "philosophizing is a gradual development of human reason," says Kant, "and this," unlike descriptive history, "cannot have set forth, or even begun, upon the empirical path."[3] What is called for, then, is an account of the drive or desire that compelled reason "to ascend from its judgments about things to the grounds thereof," and that account would constitute what Kant calls "a philosophical history of philosophy."[4] "A philosophical history of philosophy is itself possible," he continues, "not historically or empirically, but rationally, i.e., *a priori*."[5] In a reversal of most Enlightenment historiography, Kant's philosophical history of philosophy "does not borrow [facts of reason] from historical narrative, but draws them from the nature of human reason [itself], as philosophical archaeology."[6] Such history without history is thus dubbed "archaeology." And if the archaeology of reason represents the place to which the history of philosophy has progressed, the fold in the story is that this system, in seeking the limits of possible knowledge rather than making claims to supersensible intuition or metaphysical knowledge in any dogmatic sense, identifies its progressiveness with theoretical philosophy's circumscription. Progress in philosophy is coincident with the determination of its own finitude, with the recognition of its unsurpassable horizon.

To Kant's credit, he appears to be aware that limiting the concept of progress in metaphysics to, on the one hand, theoretical cautiousness and, on the other, practical Duty, avoids the gist of the Academy's question. His attempt to respond more directly, then, can be measured in the reformulation of this problem in the second section of his 1798 book, *The Conflict of the Faculties*.[7] There, Kant asks not "is metaphysics progressing?" – by his own analysis, really an unhistorical question – but rather, "is the human race progressing?" Both questions, at root, face the same challenge as the third *Critique*. And, indeed, both find ostensible resolution in a concept akin to the third *Critique's* concept of purposiveness, namely, the "natural sign." Kant turns to what he calls the sign of history to illustrate how the sympathy it evokes – and then, with a positively Wordsworthian modulation, carefully regulates – constitutes a prophetic promise that reason and nature will agree actually, even as it projects the day of that realization into an unspecified future. Reading several of Kant's later political texts through the concept of the sign described in his final publication, *Anthropology from a Pragmatic Point of View*, reveals a Kant more ironic, conflicted, risky, and even perverse than one would expect from the form and content of the Critical work alone. Kant adopts what Ian Balfour calls the "prophetic mode," a style of thinking that is at odds with his attack, in "A Recently Prominent Tone of Superiority in Philosophy," on the "mystagogue[s]" and other self-styled "philosopher[s] of *vision*" of his age.[8] Kant's system, in order to reconcile itself with reason, must keep closer truck with irrationality than ever expected – something David Clark has unfolded in his careful reading of Kant's uncanny proximity to De Quincey, where the latter exposes the former's addictions to regimentation as forms of perverse pleasure.[9]

Enthusiasm, to be sure, is another version of intoxication. And, as we saw in his reading of Swedenborg, intoxication is not by Kant wholly condemned. In the third *Critique*, Kant describes a bout of enthusiasm as a "**delusion of sense** [...] which occasionally affects the most healthy understanding."[10] Like "getting drunk," a method which is "meant to serve the purpose of making man forget the burden which seems to be an integral part of life itself," these carefully managed departures from immediate experience are analogous with the drive, noted above, of consciousness to ascend from objects to a thinking of their conditions of possibility.[11] In fact, this not only echoes the double vision discussed in "Dreams of a Spirit-Seer" but also recalls what Kant identifies, in the preface to the first *Critique*, as Reason's "peculiar fate": the rational subject is compelled, driven, urged to address "questions which it cannot dismiss, since they are given to [human reason] as problems by the nature of reason itself, but which it also cannot answer, since they transcend every capacity of human reason."[12] Kant is not an ascetic.[13] Epistemologically, this means that Kant does not simply ignore empirical information. Rather, he tries to master its contingency through various assimilative strategies, metabolic and metaphorical, that keep its excess both close and at a safe distance. In a gesture oddly reminiscent of Wordsworth's Stoic intensification of affect, Clark notes how Kant

> "attends" to the never-ending contingency of daily life, but "negatively," that is, "as if it had nothing to do with me" (OP 189). As in so many places in Kant's work, that "as if" opens a space of play that involves a turning from that is also always a turning to, and that works to separate worlds without making them inaccessible to each other. In Kant "negative attentiveness" [negative *Aufmerksamkeit*] ensures that disinterestedness and renunciation are not the opposite of interest but rather its most subtilized expression. It means never having finally to say no to no.[14]

Negative attentiveness – or what both Rebecca Comay and Jacques Khalip, in separate reflections, call "disinterest"[15] – aptly describes Kant's relationship to history in his late philosophy. The sign of history manifested in and as the French Revolution orients attention specifically toward history but in the form of non-participation. The Revolution *qua* sign is the phenomenon on which Kant can pivot between the present and the future of the human race, temporalizing a promise that is spatialized at the end of the *Anthropology* by contemplating alien worlds.[16] Reflecting his complex investment in (by withdrawal from) the actions of French revolutionaries, Kant's figure for reading history as a sign oscillates between a medical doctor and a prophet, the former producing history as a body as if to balance the latter's rapturous dismemberment. Ultimately, however, Kant's "doctor," the agent representing Kant's strongest claims to offer prognoses (predictions) of the future that stitch history together, produces history as a Frankenstein's Creature: an entity desired in prospect but instantly monstrous in life and thus condemned to death.

Wonders Taken for Signs

The second section of *The Conflict of the Faculties* concerns the relationship between the Philosophy faculty and the "higher" faculty of Law. Hence, we ought not to be surprised that Kant is here concerned with how different forms of judgment, of legislation, relate tangible experience to higher ideas in terms recalling the *Critique of the Power of Judgment*. The title of this second book in *The Conflict*, "An Old Question Raised Again: Is the Human Race Constantly Progressing?," stages the kind of inquiry that had over the course of the eighteenth century – upon the reconsideration of biblical narratives compelled by the two prongs of the philosophy of history and the higher criticism – become urgent. Indeed, traditionally, this question was the territory of neither lawyers nor philosophers but prophets. Yet, the ground had shifted by Kant's day. "It was all very well for the Jewish prophets," says Kant, "to prophesy that sooner or later not simply decadence but complete dissolution awaited their state, for they themselves were the authors of this fate."[17] As Peter Fenves elaborates, this kind of prophecy involves not vatic fullness but rather forgetting: prophecy coincides with the prophet's ignorance concerning his efficient, active role in what he "predicts."[18] The irony – or hypocrisy – of the Hebrew prophets involves, then, a contrived discontinuity between prediction and determination. Read as conservative agents promoting nationalism though the reassertion of religious laws, these prophets exaggerate social degeneration and yet, perversely, enjoy the conditions they loudly protest. That is, without such deviant behaviour, regulation could not take the sadistic forms of discipline and punishment that act out a fantasy of justice in the space of God's retreat from direct intervention.

While it retains a trace of this self-fulfilling sort of prophecy, something quite different, however, takes place in the conclusion to Kant's chapter, with an irony based not on the secret determination of actuality by the prophet but on the apparent unreliability of empirical data as such: "A doctor who consoled his patients from one day to the next with hopes of a speedy convalescence, pledging to one that his pulse beat better, to another an improvement in his stool, to a third the same regarding his perspiration, etc., received a visit from one of his friends. 'How is your illness, my friend,' was [the doctor's] first question. 'How should it be? I'm dying of improvement, pure and simple!'"[19] This passage is an allegory for Kant's counterintuitive analysis of the sign of history, that is, the French Revolution. In an effort to ground what he might call "rational belief" (rather than theoretical knowledge) that the human race, as he asserts, *is* progressing morally, Kant first characterizes empirical evidence of either progression or regression as fundamentally misleading. He aims, rather, for "the standpoint of Providence [...] which extends to the free actions of man";[20] only from this place of safety – like the safe distance afforded the subject of the natural sublime – does the event become properly sensible. As Comay says, for the historical spectator "The *Ereignis* is an *Eräugnen*: an event viewed from the vantage point of those eyewitnesses able to convert mesmerizing visual impression into clairvoyant legible inscription, spectacle into sign, seeing into reading, and inspection into introspection."[21] Echoing his unfinished notes for the aforementioned progress in his metaphysics essay, Kant here proposes something resembling an archaeological analysis that turns away from history and toward reason, but now with the express – and deeply problematic – intention of reading rather than bracketing that same empirical history. The future, in its freedom, necessarily retains some empirical indeterminacy. Hence, Kant's predictive claim is grounded in the groundlessness of that very freedom – that is, in freedom as an idea known, rationally, in-itself and thus outside existential, intuitive conditioning. Freedom is the "cause distinct from Nature" that he describes, in the *Anthropology*, as the law of prophecy.[22] Freedom is also the idea that, as long as it expands its domain, constitutes progress. It is not enough, however, to "predict" the future's unpredictability, for this only defers rather than addresses the epistemological and theoretical problem of a rational totality that includes empirical history. As he says in *The Conflict*, "The prophetic history of the human race must be connected to some *experience*."[23] Or to appropriate Deleuze's comments apropos Kant's metaphysical deduction in the first *Critique,* "We would quickly lose the opportunity to exercise our principles if experience did not itself come to confirm and, as it were, give substance to our going beyond" tangible phenomena of the present.[24] A purely philosophical history of history would be only half the story and could not satisfy the desire for a complete account.

The shape or symbol of the translation from one domain to another, the object of consciousness' negative attentiveness, is the "historical sign (*signum rememorativum, demonstrativum, prognostikon*)."[25] This is the tangible phenomenon "demonstrating the tendency of the human race viewed in its entirety."[26] Why does Kant call the historical event a "sign"? In Section 39 of the *Anthropology*, Kant identifies three categories of signs: voluntary, natural, and miraculous. Within the category of natural signs he identifies three types, distinguished according to the temporality of the signifier's relationship to its referent. These three types elaborate on the parenthetical list that supplements somewhat cryptically in *The Conflict* the introduction, there, of the concept of the historical sign. Remonstrative signs, "like burial mounds and tombs[,] are signs of remembrance"; demonstrative signs represent something present but implicit, "just as smoke signifies fire"; and prognostic signs, like "allegorical signs in the heavens," predict "impending human destines."[27] Kant dilates on this allegorical approach with an example that recalls the anecdote of the physician from *The Conflict*, implying that the sign of history should be located within this particular semiological subset:

> Natural, prognostic signs of an impending illness or convalescence, or (like the *facies Hippocratica*) of impending death, are phenomena which, based upon long and frequent experience, serve the physician as a guide in administering his cure even after the discovery of the relation between cause and effect. The same holds true for the so-called critical days. Yet the auguries and haruspices, set up by the Romans for political purposes, were a superstition sanctioned by the government in order to direct the people in perilous times.[28]

Kant's sign of history, then, is a natural, prognostic sign. Just as an illness, beyond the empirical causes and symptoms of a particular case, can give the experienced doctor a clue how to proceed in his treatment, so can the French Revolution, as the specific event or *Begebenheit* Kant identifies as a sign of history, provide tangible information, in spite of actual regression, that "the human race has always been in progress toward the better and will continue to be henceforth."[29] *As a sign*, the event confirms a counterintuitive prognosis by producing a favourable *affect* that transcends the dire "symptoms" – namely, sympathy. Sympathy is a prognostic sign that overrules empirical conditions when it comes to how the future is anticipated. At the same time, this sympathy, as a feeling, provides the missing existential weight to the otherwise formal assertion of ethical progress.

Straddling the sensible and the intellectual, sympathy functions in historical and political contexts just as purposiveness functions in the third *Critique*.

Where purposiveness links rational and intuitive domains through the necessary fiction that we interpret contingent nature "as if" it were reasonable, sympathy draws the present to the future, though only insofar as that affect diminishes its own intensity. Clarifying how purposiveness functions by encouraging and yet curtailing the enthusiasm that excessive sympathy produces helps clarify how the sign of history couples empirical with rational history. It will also elucidate Kant's attempt to, as he says, "predict [...] even without prophetic insight."[30]

In the third *Critique*, Kant identifies purposiveness as judgment's autonomous concept, a concept responsible for offering palpable confirmation of the ability to realize ideas. This concept helps ground aesthetic judgments of taste as well as teleological concepts of nature. Such a concept is necessary since the challenge facing Kant following the *Critique of Pure Reason* and the *Critique of Practical Reason* remained how to connect practical ideas to sensible intuition, a task apparently impossible and yet demanded by reason itself. As Kant puts it,

> the concept of nature [or the domain of the understanding's categories] certainly makes its objects representable in intuition, but not as things in themselves, rather as mere appearances, while the concept of freedom in its object makes a thing representable in itself but not in intuition, and thus neither of the two can provide a theoretical cognition of its object (and even of the thinking subject) as a thing in itself, which would be the supersensible, the idea of which must underlie the possibility of all those objects of experience, but which itself can never be elevated and expanded into a cognition.[31]

Reason must overcome this divide if ethics is to be considered more than a mere fantasy. So, for Kant,

> Even though the moral law has its origin in our pure reason (rather than in our experience of nature) and even thought the freedom of our will has its place in the "supersensible" (or as [Kant] also calls it, the "noumenal") domain of things as they are in themselves rather than in the domain of appearances, the "final end" or purpose that morality sets for us [...] must nevertheless be realizable *in nature* and in accordance with its laws [that is, the final end must be able to appear within the forms of space and time and the categories of the understanding that make up the intuitable realm]. And *this* fact, [Kant] tells us, can be "cognized" or brought home to us by the power of judgment, through its concept of purposiveness.[32]

The highest Good needs to be coordinated to phenomenal experience, at least in principle, such that the possibility of the realization of what Kant, in the

Grounding for the Metaphysics of Morals, calls the "kingdom of ends" becomes palpable.[33] However, the very *tangibility of* objects in intuition *constitutes* the insuperable barrier to things-in-themselves, precisely because the unconditional cannot be rendered conditionally or understood in terms of the understanding's a priori forms of knowledge without being fundamentally distorted. But if the power of judgment – the reflective judgment of the third *Critique*, rather than the merely legislative, determinant judgment of the first *Critique* – through its concept of purposiveness is supposed to span the gap here by serving as the felt presentation of the possibility of the realization of ideas in nature, it has to perform this function without in fact reducing the idea to an appearance, or by limiting its appearance to something merely symbolic.

As Jan Plug argues, via the symbol, "critical philosophy continues to judge even in the absence of an empirical case by acting as if that empirical case existed."[34] The symbol enables a sort of fictional presentation of the idea through substitution. Yet, this strategy for grounding philosophy also introduces a play of serial mediation, or remediation, of the sort we touched on last chapter concerning preludes and will see dramatized again later in Percy Shelley's *Hellas,* Blake's *Milton*, and Schelling's *Ages of the World.* For, as Plug continues, "The analogy or symbol does not facilitate this transformation, making philosophy properly philosophical for the first time, however, by overcoming the lack of an empirical referent. Rather, it substitutes one absence for another ('another, "equally empirical" intuition'), or an 'as if' referent for an absent referent, one referent that is 'as if' a referent for another that is not a referent at all."[35] What is "felt" is not the idea but the imminence of its intuition. This is a kind of Wordsworthian sensitivity without sensation, a moment where the subject gains a clear impression that he *could* gain a clear impression of an idea. Likewise, when we read the sign of history, we should feel that freedom is on its way. Purposiveness, then, produces its own prognostic signs as a means of relating realms through the gap of semiotic referentiality. The difference is thus akin to that between the prognostic, natural signs that "serve the physician *as a guide*" (my emphasis) and the bolder Roman "auguries and haruspices" that make more bullying claims: just as the former works cautiously and reflexively, so does purposiveness' hypothetical nature stop short of determining actual purposes.

This is one reason why even Kant's prophecies are almost always presented in such cryptic terms. Recall Book Fifth of Wordsworth's *Prelude*, discussed in the preceding chapter. Michael Ragussis calls the dream of the Arab "one of the most puzzling moments of all of Wordsworth's poetry," an episode designed "by its very nature to elude our grasp."[36] While it inspires efforts at explanation (such as that undertaken in the preceding chapter), it is worth considering the function of its obscurity as such. Creating the impression of readability while also displacing any definitive explanation, the scene might also reflect the Kantian point that ideas cannot be rendered directly intuitable. The obscurity in prophetic episodes of this sort reflects Kant's insistence on the negative presentation of ideas or the fragmentary "unity" of his system. We are supposed, strangely, to feel reason itself in a deflected and indirect presentation of ideas – that is, in ideas' "actual possible" realization, where what is *actual* is the *possibility of* realization and not realization itself. Kant here hovers in the state described earlier, through Kierkegaard and Blanchot, as ironic. Intuiting without feeling – or feeling without feeling – generates the ironic economy in Kant's system that, when highlighted, clarifies the relationship between what Kant says in his Critical works and what he says in his later, prophetic comments on history. It also reframes the tension between reason and irrationality, suggesting that these two domains, while certainly different, are not in Kant diametrically opposed or mutually exclusive. Their relationship seems, rather, more uncanny and perverse in that reason relies on the careful regulation of an impulse that emerges from and yet attempts to transcend reason. Like the spots of time, feeling is dislocated from its conditions of possibility, and Kant asks us to take the proffered feelings as both confirmation of and sign for what remains elusive.

The promissory quality of purposiveness's mediation stretches analogy, as in Wordsworth's analogies that massively overdetermine rocks and shells, to its limits. Purposiveness is a guarantee of an agreement between reason and appearances, where it is the guarantee and not the actual agreement that is cognizable. The apparent contingency of aesthetic experience and nature itself is treated as if it were part of an organized whole. This whole is represented, analogically, as something akin to but infinitely more powerful than human understanding. So, while purposiveness does not claim to represent something in nature as such, it does offer the subject an orientation toward nature. With purposiveness, the demand of rational totality offers reflective judgment a guide – an "as if" (contingency were rational) that judgment's reflections can follow in order to allow theoretical reason to coincide with practical reason, that is, with the higher horizon of moral ideas. As Kant notes, "This transcendental concept of a purposiveness of nature is neither a concept of nature nor a concept of freedom [...] but rather only represents the unique way in which we must proceed in reflection on the objects of nature with the aim of [facilitating] a thoroughly interconnected experience."[37]

The power of aesthetic judgment in the third *Critique* marks one way Kant explores how ideas approach intuitability. He notes, for instance, that "without being transformed into a moral experience, the aesthetic experience of beauty nevertheless offers some palpable confirmation of our more abstract presupposition of the conditions of the possibility of morality."[38] Beauty, as another kind of sign or what Kant calls "hypotyposis," confirms a universal purposiveness while at the same time withholding a determinate purpose: aesthetics does not impose determinate judgments and beauty, in particular, is a mode of judging without a concept. Beauty can claim subjective universality since it is based *not* on an agreement concerning contingent data (i.e., whether subjects agree about the relative agreeableness of an object) but on an universalisable cognitive process, expressing the a priori harmony of the understanding's categories with nature – a capacity or power common to all subjects. The sublime, likewise, offers a sensible sign of universal coherence, although this coherence comes about in a counterintuitive mode of presentation by the imagination: "The experience of the sublime is the feeling (rather than mere idea) of our own power of reason, which is precisely what makes it an aesthetic experience, and palpable evidence for the existence of that faculty of mind that is presupposed but not actually experienced in morality itself."[39] Hence, Kant notes that "the beautiful seems to be taken as the presentation of an indeterminate concept of the understanding, but the sublime as that of a similar concept of reason," such that each brings theoretical and practical ideas, through their respective faculties, into a relationship with something intuitable – with something grounded in sense – without completely determining or objectifying their respective ideas.[40]

Aesthetic judgment aims to address the problem that Kant faced concerning the motivation guiding an ethical scheme as purely formal as the categorical imperative – a scheme that tells one not *what* to do but only in what *manner* to proceed. As Dale Snow notes,

> In order to be truly free, man's essence must be outside all causal connections and thus independent of time: nothing determines it but itself. It is a classic conundrum of Kantian moral theory that the good will is described as resisting all influence from inclinations, whether benign or malign, and determining itself by means of the moral law alone. Students of Kant have long been confessing themselves stymied by the notion of determination to action by reason alone; in fact we may speculate that enough of the original students of Kant found this a stumbling block that Kant attempted to clarify his meaning by invoking the feeling of respect for the moral law. This is not an inclination, Kant reminds us, but a pure feeling. A pure feeling – this expression, verging as it does on the oxymoronic, reflects Kant's struggles to capture the sense of self which we undeniably do have especially strongly at moments of moral choice.[41]

The "pure feeling" of respect reflects the precarious if also crucial place of feeling as a vanishing mediator of sorts between pure theoretical understanding and pure practical reason, for it is just as important that that Law be *felt* (as opposed to merely thought) as that this feeling gesture, sign-like, toward an ethical ideal that is always beyond intuition's grasp. Hence, the gesturality of the sign coincides with the disappearance of the feeling it makes possible, indicating the idea, in a melancholy sort of way, only in feeling's afterglow.

Kant's Fourth *Critique*

Kant's concept of the historical sign represents a prophecy of historical progress that attempts to form a similar kind of bridge – there, but in the process of crumbling – between ideas and appearances as that provided by purposiveness in aesthetic judgment. Just as "Kant will subsequently concede that 'principles of application' must be developed to mediate between the metaphysical and anthropological endeavours," so will prophecy and the prophetic sign constitute the historical means of joining and dividing times.[42] Kant argues that the higher aims of the human race are observable in the experience of sympathy that a third party feels for both factions of a conflict. Just as the power of aesthetic judgment is (subjectively) universal and disinterested (because it has no determined concept), the historical sign expresses a "universal yet disinterested sympathy."[43] As Gary Aylesworth explains,

> [since] the public display of enthusiasm for the Revolution is contrary to the self-interest of the spectators [...] it is a sign of progress in the development of the moral faculty [even though] as a motivating passion, it is ethically condemned, since if it were to affect our disposition to act, our will would not be purely motivated by law. Thus, for Kant, enthusiasm for the French Revolution may be uplifting as a sign (*Begebenheit*) of human progress (i.e., moral development), but is condemnable if it becomes a motive for joining the revolutionaries.[44]

If material, historical events – like the sick patient's vital signs – form an unreliable horizon for answering the question, "Is the human race progressing?," there remains an emotional residue bound up with but also aloof from history that is able to disclose with special force the possibility of realizing progress. The *Begebenheit* is not itself the realization of actual, historical progress. Yet, its complementary affect signifies the universality of a moral idea that must, according to rationality itself, play out historically. So even though it is not progress actually, the *Begebenheit* is also more than merely the formal idea of a progress to come: it is also something like the preface or prelude to historical progress in material terms, an actual opening toward progress.

The same event can figure, to use Jean-François Lyotard's terms, in two different phrase regimes simultaneously, such that history can always appear to be "dying of improvement." In one register – in public, specifically – the French Revolution is condemnable. It is clearly destructive. Indeed, it threatens to circumscribe the same freedom it inspires in the popular slogans of the late 1780s by producing a conservative, counter-revolutionary movement that imposes even narrower limits on the enlightened use of reason. In the other register – in the private feelings of the observer – it generates a sanguine sign, a hint that freedom and actual history must, at some point, coincide. This feeling may remain unconscious or "incognizant" but, nevertheless, it grounds, for the reader keen to find evidence, the rational idea of sustained peace on earth.[45] Hence, reading history demands an extraordinary kind of exegete, one recalling Kant's doubly organized Tiresias in "Dreams of a Spirit-Seer" and Wordsworth's hypersensitive poet–prophet. To one living between worlds, there emerges a prophecy of progress that is akin to purposiveness' (implicit) prophecy in the third *Critique* to unite theoretical and practical realms, the *as if* formula modelling the kind of totality reason can seek only *indirectly* through contingent historical circumstances. So, while the material, historical situation becomes a rather unreliable context for answering the question, "Is the human race progressing?," there remains a feeling – bound up with but separable from historical events – that is responsible for disclosing the possibility of the idea of progress. This affect inspired by the event, then, is *not* itself the idea of progress rendered immediately palpable but, like purposiveness, is a concept that aims to show history really *could* realize this idea, or that history is really *capable* of actual progress … eventually.

The temporality of Kant's prophecy is further complicated since this sign emerges, like Wordsworth's Christmas vacation spot of time, only retroactively. "We desire a fragment of human history," says Kant, "and one, indeed drawn not from the past but future time, therefore a predictive history."[46] As Ian Baucom argues, this demand turns the observer backward and forward in the same instant. Kant seeks this sign, this event that generates the optimistic affect in history, in a *history* of the *future*: "In troping his turn to the 'history of the past' as an 'extension' rather than a reversal of this forward-looking gaze, [Kant] seems, indeed, to wish to counter the suggestion that he has reversed field at all, to cover, or disavow, the dramatic shift in perspective that is about to ensue."[47] As noted a moment ago, we have noticed how the sign is supposed to be both the anticipation of progress and the inauguration of that progress. But it is also something recollected – a "*signum rememorativum.*" On this point Baucom turns to Alain Badiou and Slavoj Žižek's discussion of the time of the "event." As a happening that brings its own conditions of possibility to light only in or after its happening, the event involves, like the sign of history, a belated illumination of its circumstances. Again, such folding together of temporalities is something with which we are familiar from Wordsworth's spots of time. One of the most interesting aspects of the Christmas vacation spot discussed previously is that the speaker's future-orientations (hope, anxiety, and eventually guilt) *all* emerge retroactively. The present of the past proves to have hosted multiple futures that only become available for feeling and therefore realization in recollection. The belatedness of the speaker's sense of his own experience of anticipation turns the event into a spectre, an apparition: something that "happens" only after it has happened or (it amounts to the same) an experience that occurs for the first time only when revisited in memory.

The prophetic sign of history has, in other words, an ironic voice ("I'm dying by improvements!") and a convoluted temporality. For Lyotard, this is not so much a problem as it is a resource offering an opportunity to reflect on the usefulness of Kantian discontinuities for thinking about the political. As Georges van den Abbeele notes, "Lyotard is able to theorize dissonant forms of ethical and political activism *beyond the politics of consensus and representation*" – that is, beyond a dialectical program that puts all negativity to work – thanks precisely to "the reputedly static antithetic and dialectic" of Kant's system.[48] The absolute ambivalence the sign of history represents, as both regressive and progressive – its progressive promise realized only in the midst of actual regression (violence) and retroactivity (memory) – provides exactly the kind of tension that allows for "the theorization of nontraditional models of dissent (or 'dissensus,' as Lyotard liked to say) and unpresentable cases of injustice (eventually, his notion of the 'differend')."[49] Lyotard aims, in other words, not to sublate Kant's internal conflicts, but rather – in Lyotard's metaphor – to navigate between various islands in an "archipelago" of phrases "like an outfitter or an admiral who launches expeditions."[50] In other words, contact between these self-contained and perhaps conflicting realms does not mean smashing islands together by some manipulation of geological tectonics – or the philosophical architectonics Kant describes in his abandoned attempt to measure the progress of metaphysics – but rather welcomes persistent heterogeneity.

In the case of the historical sign more precisely, the conflicted promise (of synthesis) manifests itself as a peculiar, conflicted feeling, a species of sympathy analogous to the sublime: namely, as *enthusiasm* – a pejorative term, routinely ascribed to prophetic revolutionaries in the eighteenth century and indicative of immature thought.[51] In fact, the danger is, as Shaftesbury notes, contagious: "One may with good reason call every passion 'panick' which is raised in a multitude and convey'd by aspect or, as it were, by contact or sympathy."[52] Yet, as Kant notes, in combination with a republican constitution, "the passionate participation in the good, i.e., enthusiasm, (although not to be wholly esteemed, since passion as such deserves censure), provide[s] through this history the occasion for the following remark [...]: genuine enthusiasm always moves only toward what is ideal and, indeed, to what is purely moral, such as the concept of right, and it cannot be grafted onto self-interest."[53] Enthusiasm is the prophetic feeling *par excellence*. And for Kant, it is a laudable impulse provided it, like aesthetic feelings, stops short of becoming an interested feeling and, as with purposiveness, stops short of determining an actual purpose in aesthetic judgment. Indeed, a closer look at the third *Critique* reveals how Kant's attempt to negotiate between sublime enthusiasm and a more dangerous *Schwärmerei* can be read as an effort to regulate and discipline the prophecy he will only acknowledge explicitly in *The Conflict of the Faculties*.

As Kant says in Section 29 of the third *Critique*, enthusiasm is an "affect" rather than a "passion": "[affects] are related merely to feeling; [passions] belong to the faculty of desire [...]. [Affects] are tumultuous and unpremeditated, [passions] sustained and considered."[54] Proper enthusiasm, while excited at the prospect of ideas, lacks the hubris, as it were, of a passion that would seek to determine the idea sensuously – and therein fall victim to a transcendental illusion by ascribing thought's categories to reality itself. Kant even acknowledges that "enthusiasm is aesthetically sublime because it is a stretching of the powers through ideas, which give the mind a momentum that acts far more powerfully and persistently than the impetus given by sensory representations."[55] In other words, there is a reasonable amount of feeling – quantified as "affect" – that can attend thought's movement beyond the sensible, or that might spur the "the mind to soar above **certain** obstacles by means of moral principles."[56]

The experience of this feeling in a historical event guarantees human progress – the movement toward perpetual peace, or "the combination of the greatest possible virtue with the greatest possible happiness of all humanity" – because it proves that humans *have the capacity for* a peaceful society.[57] This mere having-the-capacity-for, expressed as the feeling of an ability or – to introduce a term important in chapters 6 and 7 for Blake and Schelling – potentiality, is the substance of the assurance. As Lyotard describes Kant's position, "If the history of humanity were but sound and fury, it would have to be admitted that this same nature that placed the 'seeds' of reason in man also prohibits man, through its own disorder, from developing the effects of those seeds in reality. Which is [for Kant] contradictory."[58] As such, the *Begebenheit* marks a deeply confusing prophecy: immediate improvement cannot be expected to manifest itself in empirical situations nor is it to be solicited through participation in actual, violent revolution. Kant asserts that history is indeed progressing, yet the empirical realization of this progress remains frustratingly indeterminate with respect to time:

> Now I claim to be able to predict to the human race – even without prophetic insight – according to the aspects and omens of our day, the attainment of this goal [i.e., a republican constitution]. That is, I predict its progress toward the better which, from now on, turns out to be no longer completely retrogressive. For such a phenomenon in human history *is not to be forgotten* [Kant's emphasis], because it has revealed a tendency and a faculty in human nature for improvement such that no politician, affecting wisdom, might have conjured out of the course of things hitherto existing, and one which nature and freedom alone, united in the human race in conformity with inner principles of right, could have promised. *But so far as time is concerned, it can promise this only indefinitely and as a contingent event* [my emphasis].[59]

Put otherwise, for Kant "revolutionary politics is based on a transcendental illusion in the political domain, confusing what can be presented as an object for a speculative and/or ethical phrase – in other words, it confuses schemata or examples with *analoga*. The progress of a common being for the better is not to be judged on the basis of empirical intuition, but on the basis of signs."[60] A sign, then, contrary to expectation, is tangible and yet not entirely empirical. While it is sensible and in this respect acts like an example, a sign also inspires feelings that exceed and reframe its manifest content. Hence, read as a sign, the French Revolution inspires an assurance of progress, and yet that progress to-come is *always* to-come. There is a sense that, just as the strength of the *promise* is untouched by regressive, empirical violence it is, at the same time, as an *actuality* perpetually suspended in this act of promising. And yet, this does not make the prophecy less "true" or cancel the promise of eventual and perpetual peace, as temporal suspension in no way undermines the promise as such. As Kant notes, in terms that strongly parallel the description of ironic, Romantic prophecy as the insinuation of discontinuity and the revocation of certainty, "philosophical prophecy still would lose nothing of its force" even if what it promises cannot have its fulfilment historically or temporally specified.[61]

Enthusiasm describes the feeling of transcending feeling, something akin to the oxymoronic "pure feeling" of respect for the moral law noted earlier. Hence, the danger enthusiasm generates lies in the possibility of feeling's persistence into the supersensible. While enthusiasm "is a modality," in fact, "an extreme form of the sublime feeling," its real virtue for Kant lies in its spectacular impotence.[62] As Lyotard says, in the sublime "the attempt to provide a presentation not only fails [...] but also, so to speak, is reversed or inverted so as to provide a supremely paradoxical presentation, which Kant calls a 'simply negative presentation,' and which he characterizes with some audacity as a 'presentation of the infinite.'"[63] The imagination's failure to present ideas is itself expressed as a painful pleasure, "pleasure," though, in a non-sensuous and disinterested register since this concerns the play *between* reason and understanding rather than anything *in* sensible intuition. This would be something like the idea of pleasure, the counterpart to the vacant feeling of the *possibility of* feeling ideas. In Kant's words from the third *Critique*, in the sublime "the imagination, although it certainly finds nothing beyond the sensible to which it can attach itself, nevertheless feels itself to be unbounded precisely because of this elimination of the limits *of* sensibility; and that separation is thus a presentation of the infinite, which for that reason can never be anything other than a merely negative presentation, which nevertheless expands the soul."[64] As an "extreme form" of this same paradoxical affect, enthusiasm is considered "genuine" only if it collapses and curtails its attempt to realize ideas, only if it finally keeps its distance from the unconditional. Enthusiasm, like aesthetic feeling more broadly, in its attempt to offer palpable evidence of the realisability of rational ideas, has to be maintained but equally disciplined or rigorously curbed. Kant, then, does not eliminate prophetic enthusiasm; in fact, he depends upon it. And yet, in order to abide by the rules of his system, this prophecy has to have its wings clipped, has to be (the force of) prophecy without prophecy.

Behind enthusiasm's ambivalent attitude toward ideals lies prophecy's ambivalent relationship to prediction. Just as prophecy's narrative supplementation intensifies the very temporal and historical discontinuity it is supposed to ameliorate, so is enthusiasm divided between promising and yet empirically repudiating historical progress. In this sense, Kant sounds almost like Walter Benjamin. Benjamin famously unmasks Shaftesburian historiographic sympathy as the perpetuation of triumphal violence; for, "with whom [do] the adherents of historicism actually empathize" but "the victor," and "empathy with the victor invariably benefits the rulers."[65] Kant retains but inverts the historian's sympathetic impulse such that the progress it confirms remains spectral. Kantian enthusiasm is thus the ironic reformulation of Wordsworth's sympathy, guaranteeing historical continuity by interrupting rather than intensifying identification between past, present, and future selves. Prophecy's schizophrenic structure is rewritten in Kant in terms of enthusiasm's barely restrained fanaticism, its oddly necessarily self-conflicting stance as a guarantee that relies on the *absence of* empirical evidence of the future it imagines in order to sustain this guarantee. In Lyotard's words, "*Schwärmerei* gives rise to an illusion, to 'seeing something beyond all limits of sensibility,' i.e., to thinking that there is a presentation when there is not. It makes a non-critical transition which is comparable to the transcendental illusion (the illusion of knowing something beyond all the limits of knowledge). Enthusiasm, on the other hand, sees nothing, or rather sees *the* nothing and refers it to the unrepresentable."[66] It is this nothing – the impressionless priming of receptivity – that Wordsworth also saw at the heart of empirical impression. It is, additionally, what the Kant of "Dreams of a Spirit-Seer" was keen to show us in refusing to pass judgment on the existence of a spirit world. "Genuine enthusiasm," then, as opposed to the fanaticism of *Schwärmerei*, seems to intuit ideas but then, like Oedipus, to pluck out its own eyes. The *Schwärmer* enjoys his or her obscenity, claims to feel ideas, or to be, in the case of history, engaged in making progress actually happen. Kant's very reasonable prophet castrates himself lest he – to recall the imagery of "Dreams" – give birth to monsters.

Kant does draw from empirical history to support his claim that history is progressing, but relies on this data, as it were, apophatically: it is only in registering an affect – namely, enthusiasm – that flashes up but disappears just as quickly that Kant is able to add intuitive content to his otherwise merely formal idea of progress. Or, as Lyotard puts it, while the reflective and cognitive phrases are heterogeneous they are also, in their very difference, compatible: "The same referent, a given phenomenon taken from the field of human history, may serve by way of example to present the object of the discourse of despair, but as a bit of guiding thread, it may also serve to present analogically the object of the discourse of emancipation."[67] With ironic flexibility, the historical phenomenon can, for Kant, say two diametrically opposed things at the same time, without generating, for him at least, either a dialectical (i.e., productive) contradiction or an utterly hopeless antinomy. Indeed, it is, so to speak, a hopeful contradiction. Phrases do not enter into a dialectical process – they do not speak to so much as speak past each other. And yet there remains an assurance – curiously, an assurance that is all the more self-assured for lack of its realization – that reason's ideas will be actualized, against all odds, in experience, that what we hear about progress in one regime will find a sympathetic ear in the other, that we will hear the alien language of Wordsworth's shell and yet, without translation, somehow know its truth. Kant, in the name of sobriety, effectively turns "every second of time [into] the strait gate through with the Messiah might enter."[68] In so doing, he engages the same historical affect as Wordsworth. For Wordsworth it was a subjective, psychological event that produced the conditions for feeling time in and as a distinct "spot." Universalizing this private experience, Kant charges the historical present with an "anxiety of hope" that recasts his present in terms of an impending, enlightened future.

The feeling at issue is also one close to what Steven Goldsmith calls "agitation." In the course of his "sustained phenomenology of critical excitement,"

Goldsmith turns to Kant's distinction between the private and public use of reason as well as Kant's sign of history in an effort to answer the question, "What did Blake mean by continuing to think of himself as a public figure despite his nonparticipation in *any* public sphere, middle or low, bourgeois or plebeian?"[69] Kant's sign, where the "event" shifts from actual historical violence to "a special kind of *reading* of the Revolution by nonparticipant spectators" marks an important moment where revolutionary feeling seems to be both private and public, both active and passive, at the same time.[70] Like Wordsworth's agitated subject discussed in chapter 3, the true enthusiasts of the French Revolution will be not those who act most dramatically and violently in the name of the idea of freedom. Rather, they will be those for whom fanaticism is curtailed into a feeling that "agitate[s] thought so fully, that the result is an experience that feels *like* participation in the stimulating object from which it is by definition detached."[71] Assailed by feelings and "Thoughts that do often lie too deep for tears," or for any available language, Wordsworth and Blake share an "affect [that] points toward a future whose idioms remain to be discovered."[72] Drawing together Wordsworth and Kant, and looking forward to Blake, we begin to see how a reading of Romantic prophecy complicates the picture of each writer in terms of his relationship to historical action and political agency. If Romantic revolutionary energy refuses on some occasions to enter the public, political sphere, this might not represent a failure of courage so much as an acute sense that available forms of participation remain fundamentally inhibiting, limited, and ill-fitting. This novel feeling of being historical remains in need of a form, of a language, that is still to come. Perhaps Percy Shelley, observing from the periphery another Revolution and another sign of history, can find a turn of phrase that will speak this agitation.

PART TWO

Chapter Five

The Future of an Allusion: Temporalization and Figure in Lyrical Drama

"It is not, however, to the revolutionary orators that the Romantics will turn for lessons in style, but to the Revolution in person, to this language become History that signifies itself through declarative events."

Maurice Blanchot

As the foregoing pages have illustrated, prophecy cannot simply be identified with or reduced to prediction. Imposing such equivalence would ignore the exceedingly delicate shape of the future that thrills, agitates, entices, and frightens the modern, "tensed" subject who occupies both Wordsworth's poetry and Kant's philosophy. We should recall Blanchot's alternative, disruptive theory of prophecy. For prophecy to be meaningful, he argued, it must "predict" something radically unexpected, something that is, strictly, *impossible* given the prevailing frame of social, intellectual, and political life. This way, any realization of the prophecy would mean a radical change in these established patterns. In terms we will explore shortly, prophecy has to eclipse and in a sense collapse the "space of experience"[1] in order to earn the name "prophecy." In a gesture that Blake, as we will see in the next chapter, takes quite seriously, this kind of prophecy places an actual state of being into conflict with an impossible and yet imminent historical Other. Reality, in a prophetic scene, has to contend with imminent acts like Milton's in *Milton* that are totally "unexampled" and evoke "State[s] about to be Created" unlike anything on record.[2] Rather than rescue the present from uncertainty through some kind of transcendent redetermination (as discussed in chapter 1, this is historicism's secret desire), prophecy, in its more turbulent aspect, only exacerbates the crisis. In this, we see why prophecy for Wordsworth and Kant backfired. Wordsworth's efforts to translate trauma into signs of prophetic election and to read his own personal history as a coherent tapestry of impressions was always doomed to fail: the very subtlety of detail Wordsworth achieves in his history of the growth of the poet's mind exposes the transcendental "conditions of possible history," so to speak, that remain, by necessity, below the threshold of any actual historical record, below the "sense of history" as a formed object for consciousness. By conceiving himself as a prophet, Wordsworth's defence against the slings and arrows of the future – of his futures past (his childhood's futures) as well as his futures present – in fact only exposes how prophecy itself *is* traumatic. Likewise, when Kant adopts a Swedenborgian enthusiasm in his transcendental leap from phenomena to their conditions of possibility, he opens a fissure in rationality that can only be sutured by taking that enthusiasm even further in the direction, according to his own analysis, of fanaticism. The prophetic sign of history that would proffer intuitive content for the idea of progress (i.e., expanding freedom) is one that, like Wordsworth's impressionability, cannot quite be fully felt. This leaves Kant's prophetic history in limbo since, with the sign of history, what is felt is not the idea (freedom, progress) but *the imminence of its intuition*; the feeling here is of a sort of becoming-tangible of the idea, but never the feeling of the idea as such. It is precisely this Critical limitation that leads Kant's prophet, on the verge of vision, to wound himself. Likewise, impressionability's intangibility means that Wordsworth-as-prophet will never, in fact, "feel it all" as he claims to do in the "Intimations Ode." Wordsworth's autobiography cannot achieve the resolved harmony and apocalyptic transparency of Hegel's absolute thought precisely because the mechanism of affect remains fundamentally opaque.

In contrast to Wordsworth and Kant, Percy Shelley evokes prophecy not to pursue narrative synthesis (problematic as that is) but to invite a sort of medicinal corrosion. We observe this vividly in his lyrical drama, *Hellas.* On the one hand, the text is deeply allusive, borrowing its literary form from Classical sources and its characters from recorded history. It even puts the *historia magistra vitae* on stage by making prediction the central task of the prophet, Ahasuerus. But, crucially, on the other hand, the text's content is determined by the twists, turns, and blind contingencies of the Greek revolution; in a display of what he calls in the Preface "newspaper erudition," "a mere improvise" that is "written at the suggestion of events of the moment," Shelley writes the drama in tandem with history as it unfolds through the spring of 1821.[3] The text performs the double movement of Romantic prophecy through its attempt to keep up with the acceleration of the present. That is, the text invokes prophecy in hopes of overcoming the violence and uncertainty of revolution. And yet, all of its organizing, harmonizing, and predictive efforts are inverted by its commitment to reportage. Synthesizing and detotalizing conceptions of prophecy enter into direct conflict; the story of history *Hellas* tells thus raises metahistorical questions about how writing history might itself transform under the pressure of a new experience of time.

But what is "Romantic temporalization"? Since the final decades of the eighteenth century, argues German historian Reinhart Koselleck, time has not been quite the same. Perhaps most well-known for his pathbreaking work in the multi-volume *Geschichtliche Grundbegriffe* (1972–97) exemplifying his practice of *Begriffsgeschichte* – that is, an analysis of the evolution of historical concepts – Koselleck presents some of the most richly suggestive and supple philosophical reflections on historical experience in contemporary research.[4] These reflections often place special weight on events of the Romantic period. As noted in the introduction, in Koselleck's view the concept of the future in the 1780s and 90s becomes "the bearer of growing expectations" that cannot be translated into available forms of thought and life.[5] In an effort to gauge the shift in the concept of historical orderliness itself, the effort to construct new forms for historical experience in light of indigestible content, Koselleck focuses attention on the relationship between what he calls the space of experience and the horizon of expectation. These are the two fields whose interaction is formative of nothing less than the "inner relationship between past and future, [...] without which history is neither possible nor conceivable."[6]

Koselleck's thesis is that "in modern time, the difference between experience and expectation has steadily increased," that "Modern time has only been conceived as such since expectations have moved away from all previous experiences."[7] In other words, this rupture cannot be confined to the philosophical struggles of the intelligentsia or writings of the cultural elite. The more ambitious claim is, rather, that there is a change in experience that cuts across social, economic, and even national differences within Western culture. What Koselleck gestures toward is nothing less than the interruption of the feeling of historical existence – an idea that finds support in the frequent attention to periodization in Romanticism. As long as experience and its horizon comprised an organic whole through which history could form and reform itself, novelty was never a problem. Even Gadamer's expanded notion of experience, one that seeks to go beyond its "scientific idealization" in empiricism, remains locked in a mutually regulative relationship to expectation.[8] On the one hand, experience is "acquired, suddenly, through this or that feature, unpredictably, and yet not without preparation, and is valid from then on until there is a new experience."[9] This openness of experience to what will interrupt it means it must stand in "an ineluctable opposition to knowledge and to the kind of instruction that follows from general theoretical or technical knowledge."[10] "Experience" suggests a kind of sensitivity that is "radically undogmatic" and even self-destructive in that "every experience worthy of the name thwarts an expectation."[11] Like a spot of time, an "experience" sets itself apart because it throws into crisis the patterns and paths through which we typically apprehend our world, exposing more fully the nerve of sensitivity that is typically somewhat numbed by our everyday life. On the other hand, however, this is clearly a dialectical kind of negativity. In Gadamer's thinking, the unexpected happening produces a new positivity, precisely *experience* as an attribute. In Wordsworth's thinking, this is what the spots of time turn into: memorial objects that he possesses completely and from which he can distill an analgesic to numb moments of painful feeling – ironically limiting the likelihood of his experiencing new spots of time. In this way, the unexpected remains basically harmonious with experience, providing only enough resistance so that the subject can (as in the Kantian sublime) enjoy his own momentary discomfiture or (as in Heidegger's system) gain a deeper, "authentic" sense of being through existential angst. This means that the unexpected, for all the friction it causes, is still essentially *possible* and can be accommodated within the space of experience without in fact causing any deep, structural alteration in experience as such.

What Koselleck sees, however, is a change in the relationship between experience and expectation where the future shifts from designating the realm of the merely unexpected to another order of novelty altogether, one where the new cannot be counted on to conform to the mediation of the prevailing horizon. In describing historical consciousness *before* this alteration in the structure of experience, Koselleck could easily be paraphrasing Gadamer: "Only the unexpected has the power to surprise, and this surprise involves a new experience. The penetration of the horizon of expectation, therefore, is creative of new experience. The gain in experience exceeds the limitation of the possible future presupposed by previous experience. The manner in which expectations are temporally exceeded thus reorders our two dimensions with respect to one another."[12] Insofar as the future, while perhaps improbable, is still relatable to the space of experience in such a way that experience is expanded rather than annihilated by the encounter, history retains, in its form and structure, a predictive quality. If the relationship between the space of experience and the horizon of expectation is dynamic and constitutive of "a temporal difference," this difference "has itself a prognostic structure."[13]

Viewed, however, from within the abyss that Koselleck sees opened between the space of experience and the horizon of expectation, the future becomes not merely improbable or unexpected but impossible. Experience now is strangely outside itself insofar as this "impossibility is nothing other than the mark of what we so readily call experience, for there is experience in the strict sense only where something radically *other* is in play."[14] This pits the actual state of affairs or existing space of experience against something it cannot prepare for. Without any possibility of provisionally construing history, we thus lose the basic operation of all hermeneutic practice, what Gadamer calls "prejudice" and by which he means – as we saw in chapter 2 – the subject's place in a world of intentions and projects. This loss can also be understood as the subtraction of mediation, a key characteristic of the new time of modernity. This new time, for instance, is "experienced, not *ex post facto* but directly," resulting in a concept of historiography that is "less a retrospective notion because it has arisen from the present, which is opening out toward the future."[15] What kind of historiography could contend with this temporalized history, this experience abandoned by precedents and therefore unable to prepare for the future? How could this be represented? How (in both senses) remediated? Shelley's closet-drama, *Hellas*, offers a fruitful case study of a response to these kinds of problems. Indeed, this text is especially important since it not only performs an innovative kind of historiography but makes the transition between traditional and "new time" into one of its major thematic concerns.

Hellas and the Dismemberment of History

Shelley's *Hellas* is at the mercy of history. Shelley relinquishes a large measure of authorial control to the unpredictable events immediately contemporary to the act of writing, namely, the Greek revolt that erupted in March 1821 against Turkish occupation. The text thus grounds its narrative historically, but in such a turbulent history that "history" (as a category) loses any claim to stand as the stable, if occluded, truth of narrative. Set into the chaos of nascent revolution, the text is forced to remain faithful less to particular established facts than to the reality of indeterminacy, and must therefore entertain mutually exclusive though co-present possibilities reflective of the overdetermined space of experience:

Semichorus I
If Heaven should resume thee [i.e., Greece],
  To Heaven shall her spirit ascend;

Semichorus II
If Hell should entomb thee,
  To Hell shall her high hearts bend. (102–5)

Shelley's drama consists of three scenes, book-ended and separated by visionary interludes, wherein Mahmud, the Turkish ruler residing in Constantinople, hosts various messengers who bring him news concerning the Turkish response to the Greek uprising. In an effort to gain insight concerning the fate of his Empire, Mahmud sends his agent, Hassan, to retrieve Ahasuerus, the Wandering Jew of medieval folklore, through whom he then solicits the ghost of Mohammed the Second – the famous sultan who captured Constantinople in 1453, thus ending the Byzantine Empire. Just as this pattern of summoning figures who, in turn, summon other figures, anticipates the rhythms of *The Triumph of Life* – where urgent questions are answered only by new scenes of obscure import – so Ahasuerus, when he does arrive, fails to offer useful predictions. Instead, and ironically, he confirms history's unpredictability. In spite of the assertion that Ahasuerus' is "a life of unconsumed thought which pierces/ The present, and the past, and the to-come" (147–8), he fails successfully to predict the revolt's outcome or to translate various signs into useful, strategic capital. By dramatizing his impotence, the text turns him into an anti-prophet, his incessant wandering foreshadowing the tread of the "shape all light" in *The Triumph*, whose

> feet, no less than the sweet tune
> To which they moved, seemed as they moved, to blot
> The thoughts of him who gazed on them, and soon
> All that was seemed as if it had been not. (352, 382–5)

Thanks to Ahasuerus' strange untimeliness, the future Mahmud and Shelley face could be unlike anything that has come before.

Ahasuerus performs the displacement of prediction in several ways. For instance, a key analogy in *Hellas*, one that ostensibly ties time together by repeating the past in the present, actually undermines historical continuity and dialectical progressivism. Just as the spectre of Mohammed the Second is about to appear to Mahmud, Ahasuerus remarks,

> the Past
> Now stands before thee like an Incarnation
> Of the To-come. (852–4)

William Ulmer reads this analogy as "plotting" history, where the repetition of events stabilizes the present and anticipates the future by incarnating precedents, in this case elective ancestors, such that the past is, as it were, *metaphorized*, that is, carried over into the present and future.[16] However, this reading overlooks the strangeness of this particular figure. If we consider again the structure of the analogy, we see that the past is *like* an incarnation. More specifically, this incarnation is qualified as the kind of incarnation demonstrated or modelled by the "to-come." But what kind of *incarnation* can this possibly be? The to-come is, precisely, not-yet – is possibility as opposed to actuality. In fact, if the to-come is understood rigorously, it is that which is *always* to-come and thus never really an imminent arrival or presence. Or rather, it is *only* an *imminent* arrival, arriving without arrival. The "figure" offered to the past in this comparison is a figure of that which, itself, has no clear figure. To rephrase the simile, then, what it says is: The past is incarnated in the same way as the to-come is incarnated, and is about to stand objectively before Mahmud in this form. The irony becomes evident when so phrased, as it seems that the quilting point between elements consists in their shared absence of body, or in a common dis-figuration or dis-incarnation. At this point, the figure's language of re-incarnation is completely inverted. So, while Ulmer is right that the "like" in this passage ought to be emphasized, it is not because this analogy simply accomplishes the identification of the past with the future. Rather, we have to pause, in the midst of this intensely telescopic moment, and ask: What does it mean to identify two things that, in Friedrich Schelling's terms, do not properly "have being" – namely, the past and future? How does the operation of synthesis function when the separate terms are themselves already in a kind of ontological limbo? Is there not something deeply ironic in this identity predicated on vacancy? And ultimately, what does this mean for the internal consistency of past, present, and future and, thus, of history?

This self-cancelling prophecy operates not only rhetorically but also phenomenologically in *Hellas* by unravelling synthesizing forms of consciousness. For instance, the specific job that Ahasuerus is tasked with goes beyond both prediction and dream interpretation. That is, Mahmud not only needs his troubled dreams – from which he "wake[s] to weep"[17] in the opening scene – interpreted; he also needs these dreams, in the first place, to be *remembered* for him. Hence Mahmud's special interest in Ahasuerus, whom he describes as "A Jew, whose spirit is a chronicle/ Of strange and secret and *forgotten things*" (133–4, my emphasis). Describing his situation, Mahmud reflects,

> Thrice has a gloomy vision hunted me
> As thus from sleep into the troubled day;
> It shakes me as the tempest shakes the sea,
> Leaving no figure upon memory's glass. (128–31)

Mahmud articulates a complex moment in consciousness, as he seems to have a memory of something forgotten – his soul, like Wordsworth's, "Remembering how she felt, but what she felt/ Remembering not."[18] This is exceptionally odd. For *what* does Mahmud remember when he remembers that he has forgotten? How can he know that there is anything to be remembered at all? How can an image leave its trace on the surface of a glass? Indeed, a mirror would seem only to function so long as it remembers to forget (so to speak) whatever crosses its surface, that it not retain anything that it happens to reflect. With this problem we might again see *Hellas* anticipating the cadence of Shelley's later poem, *The Triumph of Life*, where, as Paul de Man notes, "the movement of effacing and of forgetting becomes prominent in the text and dissolves any illusion of dialectical progress or regress."[19] The action of memory here, like the action of the simile noted above, eludes its own regulating action and suspends the history it might otherwise help to shape as an object – like, say, a spot of time – for consciousness.

What Mahmud recalls when he remembers his forgotten dream cannot be separated from the very action of forgetting, of bringing back forgetfulness itself. The result of this is what Blanchot calls "forgetful memory." For Blanchot, one key characteristic of Romantic writing is that it experiments with "an entirely new mode of accomplishment," one that affirms "totality, but in a form that, being all forms – that is, at the limit, being none at all – does not realize the whole, but signifies it by suspending it, even breaking it."[20] So, if "the task of Romanticism" is to imagine "an entirely new form of accomplishment" *through* fragmentation, Blanchot's reflection on prophetic speech, while undertaken without specific reference to Romanticism, suggests one way that literature answers that call.[21] Prophecy in his reading is, as noted earlier, not a full speech, is not the mystical merger of being and meaning in a divine *Logos*. It is, rather, much more like the language of Kantian signs – of analogies that exceed the economy of meaning, that burst their own seams – and of the experience of forgetful memory.

Blanchot's analysis of memory places the popular Romantic strand – typified by Wordsworth's spots of time and similar forays into spiritual recuperation through tranquil recollection – against another elaboration of memory, a version particularly illuminating for reading Shelley's figuration of history. In *The Infinite Conversation*, Blanchot reverses the expected trajectories of memory and forgetting in a way that helps to describe their relationship in *Hellas* and other of Shelley's texts, especially *The Triumph of Life*. Blanchot writes that "forgetting is the primordial divinity, the venerable ancestor and first presence of what, in a later generation, will give rise to Mnemosyne, mother of the Muses. The essence of memory is therefore forgetting; the forgetfulness of which one must drink in order to die."[22] This powerful, primordial forgetfulness is imagined, somewhat unexpectedly, as an excessive brightness: like the "shape all light" in *The Triumph*, the force resistant to figuration is here cast not as deficient but rather as overwhelming – invisible for being *too* visible. This is the transparency of pure visibility. As Blanchot puts it, "forgetting is the sun: memory gleams through reflection, reflecting forgetting and drawing from this reflection the light – amazement and clarity – of forgetting."[23] Memory would be the temporary *interruption* of brightness, the crease in light caused by reflection, shading, or other variations of the annihilating intensity of forgetfulness.

Such a reversal suggests a method for rereading Shelley's treatment of historical memory. Just as Prometheus' forgotten curse in *Prometheus Unbound* cannot – as Carol Jacobs points out – be recalled in the sense of *revoked* without, at the same time, being recalled in the sense of *repeated*, so Mahmud's memory of forgetfulness turns memory inside out.[24] Memory, we could say, is *dismembered* in every sense of that word: the synthesizing, recuperative action so important for Wordsworth's "future restoration" is poisoned by and transformed into what Shelley, in the *Hymn to Intellectual Beauty*, describes as "the memory of music fled" (10). That said, the result is not utterly cynical and the subject is not flatly abandoned by history. She is left, rather, with a very peculiar experiential residue suggesting that the oscillation between memory and forgetting, while objectively ungraspable, nevertheless produces something. What it produces is unclear since it is not an object so much as the sense that consciousness can open to – or change into – novel, yet-unconscious shapes through the generosity of temporality. "*I don't know*," writes Blanchot in *The Step Not Beyond*, "*but I have the feeling that I'm going to have known*."[25] Blanchot here indicates that if we ever come to historical knowledge it is only as a kind of future perfect knowledge as opposed to something graspable in the present – and yet that we *can* feel this *difference*. For the statement can be protracted and rewritten: I anticipate a time in the future when I will be able to remember having known something, even as precisely what that something is has faded from memory. Or: I can remember "the before" and "the after" of a memory that has, itself, dissolved, such that the ostensible continuity of experience figures as a strange kind of abridgement, as if something is always already missing. Like Kant's "feeling" of the possibility of intuition or Wordsworth's "feeling" of his own senseless impressionability, Blanchot imagines that we might, against all odds, gain the most delicate impression of the conditions of possible memory – namely, forgetting. This is not a spot of time but where one might have been.

Blanchot's sense, not that he knows but that he *will have known*, captures remarkably well the reader's reaction to *The Triumph of Life*. It also reproduces the experience of the characters depicted in the poem, "Shelley" and "Rousseau." From this perspective, the text is not exactly meaningless in the way it is for de Man, who sees the performance of the text as the annihilation of its meaning. While Blanchot draws attention to the radical negativity within figuration, memory's displacement does not result in a lament for apocalypse. The conversation with Shelley does not fall silent but is rather infinite, infinitely open to the future. In other words, Blanchot helps to extend Shelley's subversion of memory, revealing Shelley's attempt to represent what eludes representation as the same problem Koselleck identifies as the challenge modernized, temporalized life has with living not in the shadow of the future but, more problematically, precisely in the *absence* of any shadow and its implied object.

Even prophetic consciousness is infected by this inverted memory, a memory that lives on through its very deconstruction. On the surface, prophecy appears to be the most resolute form of historical ordering and discipline, one that masters contingency and time by relating to the future as if the future were already a memory. In this sense, prophecy is a kind of hyper-memory called on in precisely those moments of social and political revolution wherein consciousness loses its orientation or when the space of experience has lost its reciprocal relationship with expectation, as must happen when reduced, like Mahmud, to expecting the unthinkable. Yet, Ahasuerus' image of prophecy proves remarkably *dis*orienting when he attempts to recuperate order through yet another "figure" of absence. "Mistake me not!" he says toward the end of the text,

> All is contained in each.
> Dodona's forest to an acorn's cup
> Is that which has been, or will be, to that
> Which is – the absent to the present. Thought
> Alone, and its quick elements, Will, Passion,
> Reason, Imagination, cannot die. (792–7)[26]

Presented more schematically, the passage suggests that the past and the future are to the present what Dodona's forest is to the acorn. What complicates the analogy, however, is the implicit relationship between, on the one hand, time's horizons and, on the other, the seed to the full-grown forest. In accordance with its vegetable development, the *abundance* that the seed will grow into (viz., Dodona's forests) is analogous to – is identified with – the *absence* of past and future. While the seed implies immanent growth, its coordination with presence and absence (the forest identified with absence) means that growth is indistinguishable from vanishing, from an intensifying disappearance. In fact, while the metaphor recalls *The Defence of Poetry* where Dante's poetic language is compared to "the first acorn, which contained all oaks potentially" (528), it is also the case that, as Jerrold E. Hogle points out, we have here not an acorn but only its empty shell, indicating that the very representative of presence is already curiously inane, like the sky at the end of Act Three of *Prometheus Unbound*.[27] Once again, prophecy proves that it gives with one hand while it takes with the other. For the reference to Dodona's forests – the location of Zeus' oracle – makes the analogy itself, its aporetic structure, a figure of prophecy: this is an image that dissolves itself through its formation as an image, just as memory has become indistinguishable from the rhythm of forgetting.[28]

This inversion of prophecy helps to explain why Ahasuerus is in effect dismissed in the same moment that he arrives at Mahmud's court. Strangely, before Ahasuerus has a real opportunity to help Mahmud, the latter asserts

> but the unborn hour,
> Cradled in fear and hope, conflicting storms,
> Who shall unveil? Nor thou, nor I, nor any
> Mighty or wise. I apprehend not
> What thou has taught me, but now perceive
> That thou art no interpreter of dreams;
> Thou dost not own that art, device, or God,
> Can make the future present. (752–9)

Fulfilling Mahmud's prophecy of the impossibility of prophecy, when Ahasuerus does finally provide commentary on the revolution and Mahmud's dream his words "cast on all things surest, brightest, best,/ Doubt, insecurity, astonishment" (790–1). Recalling Asia's frustration with Demogorgon in *Prometheus Unbound* who responds to her passionate questions concerning the benevolence of God with the cryptic refrain, "He reigns" (2.4.28), Mahmud soon turns to other agents for information he hopes will prove more satisfying.

The larger point here is that Shelley's *Hellas* says more about historicization as an activity than about history as something objectively present. The play does not simply represent its historical moment – a task the text presents as rather pointless for the inevitable belatedness of its product. Rather, the text translates the re-formative energy of political revolt into a literary form, or better, a style of composition. In this sense, then, *Hellas* is "pre-historic," though in an affirmative as opposed to pejorative sense of the word. Since Shelley aims to represent not history (as something objective) but the unruly temporality that forms a pre-sense of the historical – the very *sensitivity to* history registered ever so delicately and variously in Kant, Wordsworth, and Blanchot – he translates poetry and consciousness's synthetic resources into dismembering forces. Active becoming can, subsequently, figure only *pre-figuratively*, where that term designates not so much an anticipatory sign as something not-yet-figured and perhaps resolutely unfigurable. History here is unfigurable, in other words, because it has become a technique; history is not a corpuscular substance but rather a power of representation, a type of imagination, of poetry. The inversions dramatized within analogy, memory, and prophecy throughout *Hellas* do not render history unreadable by equating history's claims to insight with blindness – basically de Man's conclusion in his reading of Shelley's *Triumph of Life*. Rather, Shelley elaborates on history's novel temporalization by turning Keatsian negative capability – the power to sustain "being in uncertainties, Mysteries, doubts, without any irritable reaching after fact & reason" – into a form of historical thought where consciousness resists the lure of prediction.[29] This is not an anti-historical stance but rather attempts to remain faithful to the difference in experience consistent with the emergence of new time. With this, Shelley renders forward thinking or pro-metheus truly *unbound* – that is, released from futures past. By explicitly obscuring the future's eventual shape while affirming futurity as such, the text opens history to a novel sense of time. *Hellas* thus embodies what Koselleck calls the Romantic "temporalization [*Verzeitlichung*] of history, at the end of which there is the peculiar form of acceleration which characterizes modernity."[30] *Hellas*' displacement of prediction expresses something not about the content of the future but about the reality of a qualitative difference, one traced in the negating power of temporality rather than spotted or claimed as property by an "apocalyptic prophecy [that] destroys time through its fixation on the End."[31]

Illusions of Allusion

Hellas' continual inversion of forms of historical synthesis, as a way of remaining responsive and sensitive to an unthinkable future that would only be misrepresented by any logic of entailment, is all the more striking since the text is also very clearly embedded in literary history. Shelley takes Aeschylus' *The Persians* as his formal template for *Hellas*. In so doing, he generates a higher level of reflexive gesturing through both allusion and more direct referencing. Just as Mahmud, in calling on Mohammed the Second, would "cite one out of the grave to tell/ How what was born in blood must die" (810–11), so does Shelley's text appeal to specific antecedents, though on at least two different plains. On the one hand, Mahmud performs the same action as Atossa in *The Persians* when she calls on the ghost of her late husband, Darius. On the other hand, Shelley's decision to echo Aeschylus' formal technique means that *Hellas*, as a whole, performs another kind of solicitation of the dead. Indeed, Shelley mines *The Persians* for the image of prophecy that will recur not only in *Hellas* but also, earlier, in *Prometheus Unbound,* producing a complex texture of historical reference across his *oeuvre.* That is, while Mahmud in *Hellas* has an obscure vision that involves a chorus of Greek women and disembodied voices – the vision he remembers forgetting – the "trouble in [her] heart"[32] that

Figure 1. Persia and Ionia upset the chariot of Xerxes. Aeschylus, and John Flaxman. *Compositions from the Tragedies of Aeschylus designed by Iohn Flaxman engraved by Thomas Piroli.* London: published for I. Flaxman by J. Matthews, 1795. Eighteenth Century Collections Online. Web. 16 July 2015. OCLC number 4352477. GDN: GALE | CW0106470345.

disturbs Atossa's dreams in *The Persians* seems to find clearer visual expression in *Prometheus Unbound*:

> Two beautifully dressed women seemed to appear to me, one decked out in Persian robes, the other in Doric clothing. In stature they were conspicuously larger than people are today, and they were faultlessly lovely; they were sisters of one race. One of them lived in her fatherland, Greece, which she had obtained by lot, the other in the land of the barbarians. A conflict between these two arose, as it seemed to me. When my son found out about it he tried to restrain and mollify them; he harnessed them both beneath his chariot and put a yolk-strap beneath their necks. One of them towered proudly in this gear, taking the reins submissively in her mouth, but the other struggled, tore the harness from the chariot with her hands, dragged it violently along without the bridle, and smashed the yoke by the middle. My son fell out. His father Dareios stood close by, pitying him.[33]

In his *Compositions from the Tragedies of Aeschylus* (1795), John Flaxman includes an engraving of this dream, labelling the refractory woman Ionia and the submissive woman Persia. Shelley seems to translate this allegorical vision of nations into Panthea and Asia. He adopts, for instance, the filial relationship between these spirits, Asia calling Panthea her "sweet sister" (2.1.14). More substantially, Asia, as the geographical quality of the name suggests, is a version of the woman "in Persian robes." Panthea represents "the other in the Doric clothing," or Shelley's revision of Aeschylus' figure of Greece: the Greek pantheon. The national struggle that "upsets" Xerxes in *The Persians* is rewritten as the fall of Jupiter, borrowing but inverting the dream's central image: rather than a single chariot toppled by "Greece's" refusal to cooperate (a political reading more directly represented in *Hellas*), *Prometheus Unbound* divides these conflicting impulses into two separate Cars of the Hours. Characteristic of Shelley's attempt to sustain a utopian vision of revolution by compartmentalizing violence, one Car, reflecting Ionia's resistance to Xerxes, is transformed into the "dark chariot" Demogorgon will ride up to Jove's throne on Olympus and upon which he will carry the tyrant "Dizzily down" (2.4.143, 3.2.81). Asia and Panthea are then free to ride on a second vehicle, an attractive "ivory shell inlaid with crimson fire" (2.4.157).

Asia and Panthea are avatars of allegorical figures encountered in *The Persians* and that later, in *Hellas*, haunt the dreams of Mahmud. Amid the new clash between nations, Atossa's dream is re-dreamed but only after its translation in *Prometheus Unbound*, where the lingering effect of that mediation has been to dehistoricize the characters. Hence, the earlier *Prometheus Unbound*, as an artistic work, looks like a prophetic spirit, one invoked by *Hellas* after the fashion of Mahmud's invocation of Ahasuerus. And, just as prophetic agents in Shelley's art – as noted above – often do not offer clear signs so much as make supplementary referrals, *Prometheus Unbound* does not so much clarify the text of *Hellas* in advance as present the possibility of reformulating historical elements in response to immediate pressures. Each work is thus another "waking dream" that is "hastening onward," another scene in a triumph of history that does not come to a decisive conclusion.[34] This means that, once read in terms of the series generated by Shelley's allusive composition, *Prometheus Unbound* forfeits its apparently apocalyptic totalization of history. *Prometheus Unbound*, in other words, "leaves [its] stamp visibly upon the shore" but only "Until the second bursts," until *Hellas*, again, reformulates Aeschylus' political imagery: "so on [the reader's] sight/ Burst a new Vision never seen before."[35] This meta-textual relationship unbinds what might otherwise seem like the fairly strong teleology in *Prometheus Unbound*, one that, as Steven Goldsmith describes, seeks spiritual perfection by ignoring actual historical life.[36]

Being set into the history of their composition and mediated by their Classical ancestors has, however, a counterintuitive effect on Shelley's texts. Rather than affirm a calculable influence of the past on the future, *Prometheus Unbound* and *Hellas* become distinct and juxtaposed horizons of expectation. "Merging" these horizons into a stable meta-history does not seem to be possible or even desirable; rather, read serially, the works represent the provisional nature of historical reflection. As much as Shelley borrows from *Prometheus Bound* and *The Persians*, he also – as his titles indicate – reverses certain polarities: bound becomes unbound, east moves west. Rather than a simple repetition, Shelley stresses, in an extremely visible way, that his homage will also make a marked deviation from originals; remaining essentially philhellenic, Shelley nevertheless effectively repudiates the common "fantasy of bypassing the violence of the French revolutionary experiment by returning to the bliss of an imaginary republican freedom à la grecque."[37] Instead, his "return" takes the form of revolution, difference in repetition, and hypermediation. The allusiveness produces a rhythm of the binding and unbinding of pro-metheus, of "forward dreaming": the messenger technique and the serial invocation of explanation *Hellas* clearly *borrows*, dramatizes the *impotence of precedents*. This is the formal version of Blanchot's forgetful memory. The form of literary–historical synthesis – allusion – is suspended when the material alluded to insists on the frailty of *historia magistra vitae*. Rather than locking history's action into some kind of narrative arc, allusion here has the reverse effect: the same Aeschylean motifs in Shelley's text that suggest the lyrical drama's place in a literary tradition simultaneously dramatize, in their particular functioning, the impossibility of deriving lessons from history for the future.

Again testifying to the text's remarkable ability to reflect on its own mechanisms, one can read *Hellas*' creative relationship to its own literary–historical debts in its conflicted treatment of branding, stamping, and other similar actions of marking. While *Hellas* seems clearly to display its literary and political stance, the drama suggests that determining the allegiances of various characters is substantially more complex. Hassan, for instance, gets so carried away describing the valour of the Greeks that when Mahmud chides him – "Your heart is Greek, Hassan" (454) – Hassan admits to a kind of temporary schizophrenia:

> It may be so:
> A spirit not my own wrenched me within
> And I have spoken words I fear and hate. (455–7)

Yet, it is not merely a matter of accidental apostasy; rather, theological alliances refuse to square perfectly with the political divisions. If, for instance, the Greeks are aligned with Christianity and the Turks with Islam, Ahasuerus' peculiar fate deranges the binary connotations of the holy crosses – they appear as encouraging beacons to the Greeks but as "ominous signs" (601) to the Turks. One cannot help but recall Ahasuerus' scarred face – the mark of God's anger – when one of the messengers relates how signs

> Are blazoned broadly on the noonday sky.
> One saw a red cross stamped upon the sun;
> It has rained blood, and monstrous births declare
> The secret wrath of Nature and her Lord. (602–5)

It is, similarly, ironic that Ahasuerus' advice to Mahmud to "look on that which cannot change – the One,/ Unborn and undying" (768–9), should recall the description of eternity a few lines earlier, within one of the interludes, that figures the continuity of history and of thought's eternity in terms of a stamp:

> But Greece and her foundations are
> Built below the tide of war,
> Based on the crystalline sea
> Of thought and its eternity;
> Her citizens, imperial spirits,
> Rule the present from the past,
> On all this world of men inherits
> Their seal is set. (696–703)

In the same moment as the text attempts to ensure Greece's victory through metaphysical appeals to the timeless realm of ideas, the language of stamping, the notion of the past indelibly marking the present, is explicitly correlated with a history of violence, repression, and servitude – as if a history that entails the future to the past perpetuates an ethically regressive mentality.

Given Ahasuerus' experience, the cross that is supposed to signal Greek liberation cannot avoid also signalling ongoing slavery. In fact, the Chorus of Greek women condemning "Slavery! thou frost of the world's prime" imposed by the Turks, describes bondage in terms strikingly close to Ahasuerus' circumstances:

> Thy [i.e., Slavery's] touch has stamped these limbs with crime,
> These brows thy branding garland bear,
> But the free heart, the impassive soul
> Scorn thy controul! (676, 678–81)

The cross cannot promise Christian liberation from Islamic oppression without also recalling, in the same breath, Ahasuerus' ongoing persecution. This skews the dualisms in the text, just as Blake does when he marries heaven and hell. Perhaps the most profound expression of this asymmetry's proliferation comes when the lyrical drama, ultimately, collapses victory into loss. While a call of "Victory!" ostensibly signals the defeat of the Greeks by the Turks, this is for Mahmud, the prospective victor, also a kind of curse since it promises the sad fate illustrated by the vision of Mohammed the Second – "for thy subjects thou,/ Like us, shalt rule the ghosts of murdered life" (882–3) – and a depressing repetition of violence:

> Spirit woe to all! –
> Woe to the wronged and the avenger! woe
> To the destroyer, woe to the destroyed!
> Woe to the dupe; and woe to the deceiver!
> Woe to the oppressed and woe to the oppressor!
> Woe both to those that suffer and inflict,
> To those who are born and those who die! (893–9)

As presaged by Ahasuerus' ambivalent semiotics, signs of victory and signs of loss – these signs of history – begin to lose their clear outlines and, with this, history loses any single directionality.

Edward Gibbon's *History of the Decline and Fall of the Roman Empire* describes Mohammed the Second's siege of Constantinople as the spur to Constantine Palaeologus' "funeral oration of the Roman empire."[38] Shelley's decision to "revive" Mohammed produces a sense of history that is, however, more uncertain and spectral than Gibbon's. As the title alone suggests, the *Decline* clearly reads history as unidirectional: it adopts, in Hayden White's terms, a tragic "generic story form."[39] Reaching the point of utter decomposition, Gibbon reads "the final extinction of the last two dynasties which [...] reigned in Constantinople" as the final "terminat[ion] the decline and fall of the Roman empire in the East."[40] It is here, with the death of Constantine and the transformation of St Sophia from Church into Mosque that decline finally realizes the inevitable conclusion in vast ruination. Indeed, history itself seems dealt a mortal blow when Gibbon singles out in the same chapter, amidst the victims, the complete works of Aristotle and Homer. Shelley, however, displaces this terminus, reopening the history of Greece through his invocation of the same instant on which Gibbon's history so emphatically ends. In the absence of a single clear arc of historical experience, *Hellas* adapts its form as a means of writing history in a mode that reflects the world's temporalization in the latter part of the eighteenth century. Rather than plug the Greek Revolution into a generic template of expectation, *Hellas* invokes historical precedents with the express goal of revealing their *inapplicability* to the contemporary moment's experience of the future. If the aim of remediation is typically, though paradoxically, to eliminate intervening frames, Shelley's treatment of historical precedents puts centre stage remediation's constant deferral of immediacy. *Hellas* resists the existential comfort provided by histories that remain prognostic in essence and aim – in their production of a knowledge that might be drawn on as a guide for historical subjects – in spite of their apparent rejection of predictive prophecy as unscientific. Indeed, *Hellas* dissolves *Prometheus Unbound*'s apocalypse into history. While readers have – with good reason – argued that Shelley, with *Prometheus*, indulges in an anti-humanistic vision of life "liberated from the constraints of history," *Hellas* places this earlier text into a series and relativizes its absolute vision, rewriting it as, rather, another failed prophecy.[41]

Shelley is not alone in his effort to unbind Prometheus from the narratives of futures past. William Blake, too, writes prophecies, the primary effects of which are to collapse the very apocalyptic vision he seems always on the verge of realizing. In fact, when Blake represents and embodies the prophetic mode, we encounter an artist working to sunder Wordsworth's unification of existential temporalities – indeed, we encounter someone intent on his own "self-annihilation," not the egotistical sublime. Blake's attitude toward prophecy as a form of historical consciousness fully engages its irony. This may be somewhat surprising given the utter sincerity of his voice, his declamatory and zealous form of address. But the irony at issue is not at all rhetorical. Nor does it diminish or undermine his trenchant social critique. Rather, Blake's prophecies stress their own impossibility. This does not mean that his prophecies or prophetic figures fail to take themselves seriously or that they do not mean what they say. Rather, impossibility is a form of emancipating negativity and it is Blake's way of talking about the potentiality of a revolution that would do more than simply repeat the same dull round of history. By mobilizing prophecy's anarchic power, Blake reveals how prevailing literary, social, and universal histories (for what is Milton's *Paradise Lost* if not a universal history!) are fictions composed by shackled imaginations. Hence, like Shelley, Blake's prophecies conspicuously fail to predict the future, even as they engage the imagination in an effort to represent history in the midst of an accelerating, modern experience of temporality.

Chapter Six

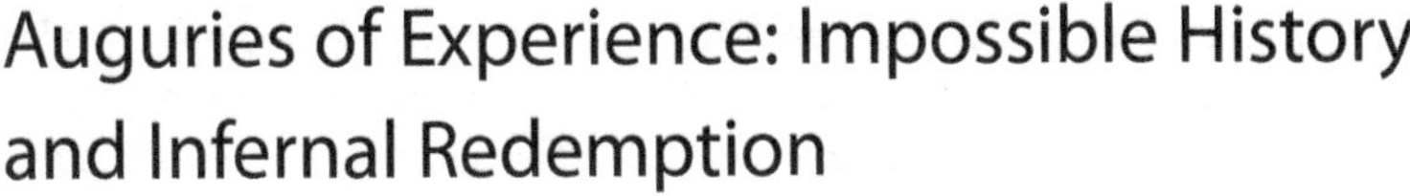

Auguries of Experience: Impossible History and Infernal Redemption

"Possibility is not the sole dimension of our existence"

Maurice Blanchot

As Saree Makdisi notes, "Blake's work, his art, his poetry, his political, philosophical, religious, and aesthetic beliefs, even he himself, were in his time understood – and indeed they usually still are – as both improbable and impossible."[1] One specific place where Blake writes history's impossibility is in his epic poem *Milton*. In this major prophecy he deviates from the typically dialectical brand of negativity we see in Enlightenment historiography and various philosophies of history; such forms of history stress history's rationality and treat history as a narrative, usually one of progress though, as noted last chapter, sometimes of decline. In either case, history is given a coherent and single form that makes certain futures more or less possible or probable. As mentioned earlier, J.G. Herder argues that when historians start identifying determinate causes for events "historical seeing stops and prophecy begins."[2] This is because making such determinations amounts to what Kant would see as a non-Critical operation of applying ideas concerning history's essence to contingent, natural phenomena. Yet, do Blake's prophecies elucidate historical action? Does Blake's representation of history offer a clear narrative of cause and effect? Do we glimpse in his art some outline of future forms? To the contrary. Alexander Gilchrist, speaking for generations of readers to come, complained that "In the 'Prophetic' and too often incoherent rhapsodies of later years this influence [of James Macpherson] increases unhappily, leading the prophet to indulge in vague impalpable personifications, as dim and monotonous as a moor in a mist."[3] Rather than transforming "these amorphous *Prophecies*" consisting of "profusely scattered the unhewn materials" into knowledge, Blake's historiography contends with how the narratives produced by historians fail if they limit history to the understandable.[4] The Hegelian operation that promises actual knowledge of what metaphysically exists just shackles history with "mind-forg'd manacles" to a logic of development that is, for Blake, deceptively smooth. The "daughters of memory" must give way, he insists, to "the daughters of inspiration" in a moment that will introduce more of enthusiasm to history than Enlightenment or Rational forms of historiography would accept as scientific.[5] Because *Milton* situates itself (like Shelley's *Hellas* and *Prometheus Unbound*) within a specific literary and political history, it serves as a particularly useful text for gauging how Blake alters concepts like influence and inspiration, operations that we expect work in only one historical direction. As David Collings reminds us, "The past may be determining, but it is also determined, the object of a continuous interpretive activity by which we refigure the meaning of our historical position and the possibilities available to us."[6]

Blake rewrites historiography (i.e., revises how history itself is written) with the "Harrow of the Almighty," the much-contested object at the centre of the Bard's Song. A harrow is an agricultural tool for plowing. The work it performs resembles Blake's practices of etching and engraving. Developing Nelson Hilton's discussion of Blake's use of the word "grave," Jared Richman notes, for example, that "Blake could use his burin (an engraver's tool) to incise or, quite literally, to plow into the copper plate; however, in *Milton a Poem*, Blake used an etching needle to plow the acid resistant substance (called the 'ground') to expose the copper plate thus allowing the acid to carve narrow grooves into the metal and thereby preparing the plate to carry ink."[7] Beyond this literal application, harrowing also alludes to Christian resurrection – to Christ's Harrowing of Hell. In this light, the harrow as a figure for writing implies that Blake is working in an apocalyptic register. This register is, as Steven Goldsmith has compellingly argued, deeply troubling both aesthetically and ethically.[8] While it claims a kind of revelatory knowledge, such ostensible insight comes at the cost not only of simultaneous destruction of the putatively "inessential" but, equally disturbingly, a concomitant institutionalization of hierarchical power. Apocalypse tends toward a complete form that ends – by claiming to achieve an absolute, perfectly self-relating state – any further artistic, historical, or intellectual development. In *Milton,* Blake does indeed harrow up the past (textual predecessors from his Lambeth period, from English history, and from John Milton's poetry) in what can look like a consolidating, totalizing effort. But in conceiving of Christian redemption as citation, he also hints at the way figures for recuperation can themselves be altered and used differently – for citation and redemptive harrowing follow very different kinds of logics. In fact, Blake reimagines harrowing so completely that it becomes the operation that introduces *disorder* in and through its efforts at spiritual management.

The classes into which, for instance, harrowing is supposed to cast groups of people – elect, redeemed, and reprobate – themselves turn out to be completely reshuffled by text's end. As with Shelley's inversion of his own figures of historical synthesis in *Hellas*, Blake continually reorganizes his systems of organization, a key factor in producing the often dizzying experience of reading his work. When Blake tries, for example, to write his poem as history, then as biography, then as autobiography, then as spiritual quest, and then as prophecy, this overlapping of genres does not produce a final form but rather works against any sort of fixed genre definition. In Blake's own terms, if "states" describe the particular way in which individuals are determined, *Milton* is very concerned to point out that states change. In terms of historiography it is then no surprise that, even as the text does recycle characters and passages from Blake's earlier work in what looks like an attempt to put them, finally, into their fit places, this apparently redemptive, apocalyptic act tends, in fact, to illustrate the always provisional status of its products. Ultimately, as Morton Paley observes, "Whether apocalypse and millennium are envisaged on the historical plane, in nature, or within the self, cracks and fissures develop in the seeming continuous strata."[9]

Perhaps the clearest instance of how determination loses its purely formative function is presented in spiritual "self annihilation" (*M.*, 14:22, E., 108). Self annihilation is Blake's expression for the imagination as such. This imagination does not merely generate representations, historical or aesthetic: it also, so to speak, de-generates them. Rather than reconciling the gap in and of desire, this formulation of the imagination *exposes* that gap as a way to redefine prophetic imagination as constant re-vision rather than pre-vision. "To step out of heaven," as Milton does, "is to make oneself vulnerable to revision."[10] Rewriting John Milton's politics as a literary and historical aesthetic, the "State about to be Created" called "Milton" is the state of re-stating, the state in or of revolution inhabited by the artist (*M.*, 32:26, E. 132). Echoing but also inverting Wordsworth's spots of time, Blake's "Moment in each Day that Satan cannot find" does not restore but rather reinvents the subject and the work of art (*M.*, 35:42, 45; E. 136). Despite similarities of language, there is a major difference between how Wordsworth and Blake approach the concept of "renovation" – a difference reflective of their conflicting attitudes toward prophecy. For Wordsworth, renovation overlaps with restoration. For Blake, however, this renovating moment is itself mutable, is an urgency that demands the invention of a new historical style. Rather than a quality belonging to a subject, renovation changes "every Moment of the Day if rightly placed," becoming an autonomous force for change, a moment of momentum that interrupts the circularity of restoration (*M.*, 35:45, E.136).

But before looking at how imagination in *Milton* displaces the very states it creates, we should consider more closely Blake's concept of history as a tissue of impossibilities. The deeply uncanny nature of history, as Blake understands it, is partly what motivates the spasmodic style in *Milton* (and other of his works), where actions are sudden and extreme even as their motivations remain obscure. In fact, the text seems desperate to catch up with itself, often offering causes for effects retroactively. Leutha, for example, takes responsibility for the disaster with the harrow well after the fact; and Satan tries to justify his anger by revealing, in a scene that feels tacked on, that his Mills have been damaged by Palamabron – that he is, in other words, also a victim. But these belated rationalizations never quite even things out. Indeed, the text never adequately accounts for the major rupture: "What cause at length mov'd Milton to this unexampled deed[?]" – that is, his descent from Eternity, the action around which the whole poem turns (*M.*, 2:21, E., 96). The text suggests the motive was the Bard's Song. And yet, we hear the Song *after* learning of Milton's act. In addition, the Song's content does not effectively clarify Milton's motivation anyway. Thus, one senses in the poem the same kind of sudden jump from the impossible to the actual that, for Blake, characterizes history itself. Blake's formulation of imagination as both creation and negation is an attempt, then, to emulate – rather than represent – history as a narrative always suspended in the act of representation. The notion that "Milton" names the state of the annihilation of states – and that this is the essence of the prophetic imagination, just as forgetting is the essence of Shelley's memory – presents the imagination in a paradoxical form *analogous to* actuality in history. This can be so since, for Blake, the actual does not exclude the impossible.

Permutations of the Impossible

Terms such as "possible," "actual," and "impossible" appear to hold fairly clear relationships with each other. Normally, we would think that for something to be actual, it must have been, prior to its realization, possible. Similarly, if something is impossible it would seem absurd to say that it should ever be actual. Possible and impossible look like absolute terms and thus ought to be resistant to gradations as introduced by, for instance, talk of probability. It would be odd to say that the impossible is more or less probable; likewise, if something is possible it remains so regardless of its likelihood. And yet, in the course of his *Poetics* Aristotle observes that a "likely impossibility is always preferable to an unconvincing possibility" and that stories "should never be made up of improbable incidents."[11] So, *improbable* incidents are bad but *impossible* incidents are fine. Put otherwise, Aristotle asserts that a probable impossibility is more aesthetically satisfying than an improbable possibility. An utterly fantastic scenario of the sort encountered in, say, utopian fiction, that nevertheless remains true to a principle of probability within that fictional world is preferable to an artwork set within our own apparently possible (because actual) world but composed of actions or details that strain credulity. The salient point here respecting Blake is that Aristotle sees the relationship between the possible and the impossible as more than a mere binary opposition or a one-sided relation of "Negation" (*M.*, 41:32, E., 142). Drawing out the implications of Aristotle's analysis we could, in fact, identify four categories: probable possibility, improbable possibility, probable impossibility, and improbable impossibility. Blake appeals to the third category listed – probable impossibility, the same one Aristotle approves of from an aesthetic perspective – in his commentary on Watson and Paine's argument concerning the historical accuracy of Moses' putative authorship of the Torah.

	Possible	Impossible
Probable	Enlightenment history	Well-crafted fiction, poetry. (Also, the Torah)
Improbable	Bad realism	Blake's history

In his annotations to Watson's *Apology for the Bible,* Blake insists that "He who writes things for true which none could write. but the actor. such are most of the acts of Moses. must either be the actor or a fable writer or a liar. If Moses did not write the history of his acts, it takes away the authority altogether it ceases to be history & becomes a Poem of probable impossibilities fabricated for pleasure as moderns say but I say by Inspiration" (E., 616). At first glance, it is difficult to determine where exactly Blake stands. Initially it sounds as if he would reject the authority of the Mosaic books were it determined that they were composed, as Paine suggests and as early exponents of the higher criticism argued, by someone other than Moses. However, Blake says that such a revelation would merely change the work's genre. Rather than history, the books would be poetry. If this sounds like a demotion, Blake is quick to add that, to his mind, poetry is no mere entertainment but the product, rather, of "Inspiration." So, in a curious way, Blake takes Paine's secularizing argument – that the books of Moses are *not* historically accurate – as a path to the re-enchantment of the Bible understood as inspired poetry. As texts written in harmony with Aristotle's advice – the Mosaic books constitute a "Poem of probable impossibilities" – they retain aesthetic and, as such, spiritual value.

What then marks off history proper as a genre? According to an entry for his 1809 *Descriptive Catalogue,* history is defined by acts; and yet, questions of cause and effect that would seem to fall under the purview of the historian remain off limits:

> Acts themselves alone are history, and these are neither the exclusive property of Hume, Gibbon nor Voltaire, Echard, Rapin, Plutarch, nor Herodotus. Tell me the Acts, O historian, and leave me to reason upon them as I please; away with your reasoning and your rubbish. All that is not action is not worth reading. Tell me the What; I do not want you to tell me the Why, and the How; I can find that out myself, as well as you can, and I will not be fooled by you into opinions, that you please to impose, to disbelieve what you think improbable or impossible. His opinions, who does not see spiritual agency, is not worth any man's reading; he who rejects a fact because it is improbable, must reject all History and retain doubts only. (E., 544)

Blake thinks that historians are not well suited to the task of translating acts into causal narrative – ironically, the very practice that ostensibly sets Enlightened forms of narrative history apart from simple chronicles. Left to the official canons of history, Blake complains, one might think that the world in which we live is the product of a historical process that develops only along the lines of the probable and possible. This, however, would be the illusion of hindsight, indeed, what Deleuze, reading Bergson, will call the "*retrograde movement* of the true."[12] But, Blake suggests, a given historical moment is no more probable or, in a sense, even possible for being actual. By the same token, actuality cannot discipline the past by supposing that the status quo is evidence that one lives in the only possible present of that past, or that the future must follow in order from possibilities calculated in the present. In a well-known passage, Blake asserts instead that "The historical fact in its poetical vigour [or] as it always happens" is not as "some Historians pretend, who being weakly organized themselves, cannot see either miracle or prodigy; all is to them a dull round of probabilities and possibilities; but the history of all times and places, is nothing else but improbabilities and impossibilities; what we should say, was impossible if we did not see it always before our eyes" (E., 543). Blake says that only the artist, with her more supple sense of the relations of possibility and impossibility, probability and improbability, is able to read history since historical facts always remain poetically vital or radically open to reversibility.

It is for this same reason that prophecy in Blake cannot be reduced to historical prediction. Rather, as he remarks in his annotations to Watson,

> Prophets in the modern sense of the word have never existed Jonah was no prophet in the modern sense for his prophecy of Nineveh failed Every honest man is a Prophet he utters his opinion both of private & pubic matters Thus If you go on So the result is So He never says such a thing Shall happen let you do what you will. a Prophet is a Seer not an Arbitrary Dictator. It is mans fault if God is not able to do him good. for he gives to the just & to the unjust but the unjust reject his gift[.] (E., 617)

Rejecting the fatalism of prediction, Blake suggests that prophecy is always open to revision through action, in other words, through history itself. All prophecy can predict is what is likely to happen if nothing substantial changes, putting it on par with stating the obvious. The historians Blake abuses all aim to be "prophets" in this attenuated sense wherein the future is merely a copy of the past. The other side of this statement, though, is that history is, in reality, radically unpredictable since one cannot anticipate what happens on the hither side of an effective action. As Jonah finds out, not even God can foresee what free humans will do and what kind of future they will produce. This, as noted in chapter 3, is what makes his prophecy truly generous.

So, when Blake says that Jonah "was no prophet in the modern sense for his prophecy of Ninevah failed," we ought not to take this for a rejection of Jonah's prophetic power. Rather, Blake is rejecting the *modern sense* of prophecy, the narrowed and anemic idea, as Voltaire puts it, that "All predictions are [i.e., can be] reduced to calculations of probabilities."[13] For Blake, prophecy could go beyond parroting a history of probabilities and possibilities and articulate, instead, history's impossibility only as long as it *preserves* its paradoxical and self-undercutting structure. When Blake's prophecy makes the acute *failure* of prediction into its primary mode of speech, he projects impossibility onto the present as a way of shaking confidence in prevailing notions of art's and life's limitations.

Blake here, in his own way, articulates the sort of historical sensibility that emerges on account of the widening fissure between the "space of experience" and the "horizon of expectation" discussed in the preceding chapter. Unlike Gadamer and Wordsworth's dialectical concepts of experience, where novelty's clash with expectation merely expands the subject's store of knowledge,[14] Koselleck suggested that temporalization – the sudden confluence of non-synchronous speeds, a "sense of time as fractured and unevenly heterogeneous"[15] – in Romanticism might result in the creation of a new historical subject, one sensitive to the hither side of the experienceable, to the impalpable conditions of possible experience. This subject would be somehow sensitive, like Kant's enthusiast, to what is *outside* sensation; he would be able to feel, like Wordsworth's hyper-affective self, his own impalpable impressionability; and his history may be rooted in a certain past, as in Shelley's *Hellas*, though that past would appear like a ghost: impressive, yet also strangely fleeting. Put otherwise, this subject is not only constituted by his possibilities but also by his impossibilities – that is, by *potentialities that do not, strictly, belong to him*. Such a subject, defined by his vulnerability to a future that is outside all expectation – a subject for whom there is a radical rift in experience so profound that it may annihilate that very self-appropriating subject of experience altogether – registers his very dispossession of experience as his historical essence. This ongoing derealization of life demonstrates what it means to live in a time where the future has become both utterly strange and yet, for that very reason, all the more pressing, such that thinking historically does not provide us with knowledge for the future but rather a deeper sense of the instability of the contemporary moment.

Common sense will object to this line of discussion. If something happens actually that was deemed to be impossible, then it must have simply been misidentified, it must have only *seemed* impossible. Is this objection, however, not really an evasion of impossibility as such? By adopting a retrospective point of view, the "reasonable" historian simply denies the reality of impossibility – no matter how effective, how real it may be at a given moment – by treating impossibility as something subjects in the past have been unable accurately to identify. But what, for the historical subject, would distinguish a real impossibility from a merely disguised possibility? One can mark such a difference only from a distance, leaving the historically situated subject always late to her own "correct" understanding of what is and what is not possible for her. In a sense, then, the sober historian who presents history as a series of the most likely events, as a narrative composed within the bounds of the possible, casts doubt on any assertion of historical impossibility made today or any day even in light of palpably intractable conflicts or immovable obstacles. From this putatively conservative stance it is, curiously, no longer safe to say that something in the present moment is impossible. This is not much different from the other extreme: that anything, then, *is* possible – even what is impossible now. This "impossibility," so the logic goes, could just be very effective at obscuring the full range of possibilities – it might actually be a camouflaged possibility. So, if the objection is that it is absurd to call the actual impossible, this complaint can only be made by taking a speculative, future position that elides the experience of impossibility in historical life at a given moment in light of a future where all change from the past can be dressed up as the progeny of the possible.

This refusal to see anything as really impossible from the perspective of a future that contradicts such an assessment seems to be wonderfully optimistic. What requires special attention, however, is how the relentless positivity of such thought can have the effect of denying the real suffering that accompanies the effort to live through a deeply discordant reality. Such discord is not simply a mistake of perception. Simply calling something "possible all along" following the sudden actuality of what was experienced as impossible does not inspire consciousness – and should not inspire historians of probabilities and possibilities – with a great deal of self-confidence. At the same time, insisting on the reality of the impossible is not to suggest that, say, major and ongoing political or social conflicts in the present cannot ever be ameliorated. The point is, rather, that if in a speculative future wherein such conflicts have been resolved, historians imagine resolution always to have been latent, they would in fact misrepresent how history moves. The assumption of a basically smooth transition assumes there is some kind of history-in-itself, something deeper or inside appearances, that is merely (mis) represented by events, rather than seeing history as immanently productive: an act in self-creation, a form of simulation, a reality that is also a virtual reality. By insisting on the reality of impossibility, Blake aims to revive the intensity of this creativity as it is lived, of the reality of historical situatedness over which one has rather limited control. This in no way precludes change; it does, however, mean seeing history as the result of strange and mighty forces capable of short-circuiting the difference between the possible and impossible, seeing history as pregnant with what Goldsmith, in a recent paper, calls "the inconsistent movement of violence in history."[16] The historical subject continues to live amidst actual impossibilities; but, in this view, impossibility is no barrier to the invention and reinvention of life. The difficult idea here is that we have to think of the impossible as real and actual – until it is not. Blake removes the mediating function whereby consciousness covers over a disjunctive, unprethinkable alteration in life by inserting a nice, rational transition where, in fact, one does not exist. Blake is thus sensitive to forces at work in producing genuinely, qualitatively novel forms of life, powers beyond calculation and closed systems.

Blake's paradox might be clarified (though, crucially, rendered no less paradoxical) by comparison with Deleuze's concept of virtual reality. As Žižek remarks, "It was Gilles Deleuze – another great Schellingian – who, long before the fashion of Virtual Reality, elaborated the status of virtuality apropos of the mystery of *event*."[17] Deleuze follows Bergson, who sees the virtual not as a pseudo-reality but as actuality plus its potentiality. As with Kant's sign of history, our virtual reality is always more than an empirical tabulation could account for; in Žižek's examples, this is why historicism can never entirely account for why specific cultural or artistic events (film noir, or courtly romance) should emerge precisely when and as they do. The same can be said, as noted previously, for the rise of historicism as such, suggesting that this field of thinking might be unable to write its own history as a shape of consciousness without some acknowledgment of its obscene, interiorized other: prophetic negativity. As Brian Massumi describes, "The body," in a parallel fashion, "is as immediately virtual as it is actual. The virtual, the pressing crowd of incipiencies and tendencies, is a realm of *potential*."[18] *Potentiality* names the incalculable power of becoming (just pure difference) whereas *possibility* is the name attached, *ex post facto*, to potential: a gesture that regressively fixes becoming as being. Possibility is potential depotentiated, sapped of its potency. So, "the distinction between potential and possibility is a distinction between conditions of emergence and re-conditionings of the emerged."[19] In fact, there is a rhythm to this reciprocal play that could be thought of as the action typical of historiography (or, of typical historiography) according to Blake. In Massumi's words:

> Possibility is back-formed from potential's unfolding. But once it is formed, it also effectively feeds in. Fedback, it prescripts: implicit in the determination of a thing's or body's positionality is a certain set of transformations that can be expected of it by definition and that it can therefore undergo without qualitatively changing enough to warrant a new name. These possibilities delineate a region of nominally defining – that is, normative – variation. [By contrast,] [p]otential is unprescripted. It only feeds forward, unfolding toward the registering of an event[.][20]

From this angle, the concept of the possible (as distinct from the potential) is limiting because it tries to codify and make narrative sense out of the chaos of becoming. Like a snapshot of a dance, this condensation of "potential" into "possible" will always miss what is essential.

The virtual, however, offers a way to try to think about becoming that does not subordinate process to product. We might be tempted to think of "virtual reality" as a kind of hollowed-out reality – "virtual" in the sense that it lacks something or is not fully real. But the virtual is just as real as the actual, though it also opens beyond the actual along lines of becoming according to potentialities that cannot be sketched out in advance. Indeed, like Blake, Deleuze rejects the supposition that something actual must have been, at some point in its history, possible, since this submits becoming to nothing but "a succession of states in a closed system."[21] We might, then, say of Blake something similar to what Deleuze says of Bergson: "the same author who rejects the concept of *possibility* – reserving a use for it only in relation to matter and to closed systems, but always seeing it as the source of all kinds of false problems – is also he who develops the notion of the *virtual* to its highest degree and bases a whole philosophy of memory and life on it."[22]

Blake sees history as no less impossible for being actual, which is just another way of saying that the past, present, and future never lose their miraculous quality. Since this is habitually overlooked, it is the task of the poet-prophet not just to record acts but to cleanse the doors of perception. Hence, while *Milton* could be read as a monument to Blake's literary past, it could also be read as an expression of history's virtual reality. By rewriting John Milton's foray into "Things unattempted yet in Prose or Rhyme"[23] as the "unexampled deed" of Milton's descent from Eternity, Blake makes the difficult question of "what cause at length mov'd Milton" into a frame for thinking about how history – while certainly shot through by various cause–effect relationships – remains irreducible to a logic of possibility. As much as the poem is clearly embedded in literary tradition, this history in no way renders the acts of the poem predictable; nor does it make the actual events expressed in the poem look more possible after the fact. The only thing predictable about Blake's revision of *Paradise Lost* is that he inverts the moral valence attached to the "cause" that "Move'd our Grand Parents in that happy State, / Favour'd of Heav'n so highly, to fall off / From thir Creator": Blake's Milton is not disobedient but heroically self-sacrificing.[24] What is "predictable," then, is only that the literary precedent Blake alludes to for explaining unexampled deeds cannot be a simple model. This is analogous to how Shelley's allusiveness, discussed last chapter, turns into elusiveness when his literary–historical references reproduce not a stable canon but a series of missed encounters. With Blake, in a precise way, we can only expect the unexpected. Considering, in fact, how the poem dramatizes Blake's own writing practice, the text suggests that the apparent effort to determine the past through "redemptive" citations of his earlier work does not produce a complete book. Rather than casting his earlier productions as the natural precursors to this "major prophecy" and so composing a narrative of his *oeuvre* according to probabilities and possibilities, the key trope for composition, the Harrow of the Almighty, turns into an instrument of disorganization, something productive of only provisional states.

"Things unattempted"

One popular critical narrative of Blake's *oeuvre* suggests that his early texts, including the Lambeth books, represent defective or at least incomplete efforts at a systematic mythology, one adequately realized only in the later illuminated books, *Milton* and *Jerusalem*, where "Every word and every letter" experimented with in the putatively primitive works finally "is studied and put into its fit place" (*J.*, 3, E., 146). This idea of retroactive arrangement operates on a model of apocalyptic redemption – the promise of the millennium – as if the major books rescue their own prefatory materials from perdition. Northrop Frye, for instance, argues that "all of Blake's poetry, from the shortest lyric to the longest prophecy, must be taken as a unit and, *mutatis mutandis*, judged by the same standard. This means that the longer and more difficult prophecies will have to bear the weight of the commentary."[25] David Erdman echoes this position, arguing that what makes Blake's *Gwin* and *America* prophetic is that "in both prophecies Blake warns kings, nobles, and bishops: If you go on binding the nations, oppressing the poor, and ravaging the countryside with war, the result must be revolt."[26] Harold Bloom understands Blakean prophecy, similarly, as an updated version of Ezekiel's warning and threatening.[27] When this sense of prophecy is applied reflexively to Blake's corpus it means that the virtual reality, the chaotic potentiality of the Lambeth books, must finally be arrested or, in Deleuze's terms, territorialized by later works that aspire to the "perfect coincidence between form and content."[28] Typifying this narrative, Joseph Anthony Wittreich argues that "Blake's rather nebulous conception of epic evolves to the point where he can attempt a meaningful coalescence of epic and prophetic elements, a coalescence that is grandly realized in *Milton* and *Jerusalem*."[29]

Admittedly, *Milton* does attempt in several ways to absorb and re-organize the often chaotic productions typical of Blake's art up to the major prophecies, suggesting – at least at first glance – that the later work aspires to spur apocalypse in order to hasten the millennium. Such (re)creation *ex Deo*, as it were, happens in *Milton* most clearly by way of citation and the reincorporation of earlier characters, passages of text, and concepts. As early as *Milton*'s third plate, for instance, Blake's Bard offers a condensed version of *The [First] Book of Urizen*. In fact, upon observing Urizen's (de)formation, Los seems to re-embody the speaker from the "Memorable Fancy" in *The Marriage of Heaven and Hell* who identifies the Angel's "dark visions of torment" – a conglomeration of nightmare images including "black & white spiders" and "the head of Leviathan" – as something "owing to [the Angel's] metaphysics," confirming that the "Eye altering alters all" (*U.*, 2:7, E., 70; *MHH.*, 18, E., 41; 19, E., 42; E., 485). For when Los looks upon Urizen's formation "his immortal limbs / Grew deadly pale; he became what he beheld," effectively intellectualizing and in some sense ameliorating the confusion of agent and patient in *Urizen* described more traumatically and mythopoetically in terms of bodily violence: "Urizen was rent from his [Los'] side" and the wound "heal'd not" (*M.*, 3:28–9, E., 97; *U.*, 6:4, E.,74; Ibid., 7.4, E., 74). The description of human formation similarly seems to combine the language of involution and vegetable growth familiar from *Urizen* with the notion that "mans desires are limited by his perceptions" asserted not only in short prose tracts like "There is no Natural Religion" and "All Religions are One" but also explored dramatically in *The Book of Thel* and in the reciprocal relationship between innocence and experience in the *Songs* (E., 2). For if "the five Senses" are "the chief inlets of Soul in this age," the language in *Milton* presents these inlets also as barriers that "shut" perception "in narrow doleful form[s]": the "Eye of Man a little narrow orb closd up & dark" and "the Ear, a little shell in small volutions shutting out / All melodies" (*MHH.*, 4, E., 34; *M.*, 5:19, E., 99; 5:21, E., 99; 5:23–4, E., 99). In fact, the entire tenor of the Bard's Song detailing the destruction of Palamabron's harrow and Satan's mills elaborates on the destructiveness of "Satans mildness" and "pity false" warned of more briefly in "A Poison Tree" (*M.* 7:21, E., 100; 7:42, E., 101). And yet, as David Riede says, ultimately, *Milton* "does not end with a seamless vision, but with a woven garment of language that prevents, or defers, revelation."[30]

With Los' declaration of sorrow – "this mournful day / Must be a blank in Nature" – he attempts to mourn the trauma of the Lambeth books, suggesting that *Milton*'s return to the literary past is also a kind of textual or artistic self-therapy (*M.*, 8:20–1, E., 102). The damage occasioning this day of mourning follows from the failure properly to divide and organize labour – a problem that echoes Blake's own artistic and professional challenges. The difficulty begins when Satan

> soft intreated Los to give him Palamabrons station;
> For Palamabron returnd with labour wearied every evening
> Palamabron oft refus'd; and as often Satan offer'd
> His service till by repeated offers and repeated intreaties
> Los gave to him the Harrow of the Almighty[.] (*M.*, 7:16–20, E., 100)

This role reversal proves disastrous: Satan leaves Palamabron's "horses [...] mad! his Harrow confounded! his companions enrag'd!" (*M.*, 8:18, E., 102). Blake rewrites the Satanic hubris of *Paradise Lost* as failed apprenticeship. But the tool at the centre of the conflict, Palamabron's harrow, is semantically over-freighted. As noted earlier, harrowing resembles Blake's artistic practice while also recalling Christ's Harrowing of Hell. If this represents the ultimate act of redemptive inscription, its rhetorical overdetermination introduces a serious instability. This operation of organization itself undergoes revision, suggesting ultimately that redemption is less about restitution and more about substantial transformation.

Christ's Harrowing is supposed, for instance, to separate the eternally damned from the elect. As the text says, there are

> Three Classes of Men regulated by Los's Hammer.
> The first, the Elect from before the foundation of the World:
> The second, The Redeem'd. The Third, The Reprobate & form'd
> To destruction from the mothers womb: follow with me my plow!
> (*M.*, 7:9–12, E., 100)

Later, however, the text scrambles these same categories or, as Paley says, subjects these classes to "ironical inversions of meaning."[31] When "Los stood & cried to the Labourers of the Vintage" that they "must bind the Sheaves not by Nations or Families" but by "Three Classes," he re-classes the groups (*M.*, 25:16, E., 121; 25:26, 27, E., 122):

> The Elect is one Class: You
> Shall bind them separate: they cannot Believe in Eternal Life
> Except by Miracle & a New Birth. The other two Classes;
> The Reprobate who never cease to Believe, and the Redeemd,
> Who live in doubts & fears perpetually tormented by the Elect
> These you shall bind in a twin-bundle for the Consummation[.]
>
> (*M.*, 25: 32–7, E., 122)

Here the Elected individual proves to be the self-satisfied hypocrite Milton, in *Aeropagitica*, described as a "heretick in the truth," one who "beeleve[s] things only because his Pastor sayes so."[32] Blake revises the meaning of the second class as well: the Redeemed, contrary to the sense of successful rescue denoted by the name, are here described as perpetually striving toward the status denied them by the Elect; the Redeemed masochistically and repeatedly victimize themselves, becoming like spectres. Finally, it is the Reprobate, whom one would expect, given the sense of criminality the word connotes, to be damned, that proves most faithful. In reorganizing these classes Blake revises the concept of organization itself, suggesting that "faithfulness" means not passivity (something possibly implied in both *Paradise Lost* and *Paradise Regained*) but rather ongoing self re-creation. That Los, the figure of prophecy and poetry, can reorganize these classes by fiat illustrates how, for Blake, with the full force of paradox, the impossible – such as the election of the reprobate – is an actual, historical reality and yet can suddenly give way, though in a manner that preserves rather than sublates the negativity of impossibility.

Milton develops this negativity in the discussion not only of classes but also of states. While classes (dis)organize different groups of people, states (dis)organize individuals. Blake insists that we "Distinguish [...] States from Individuals in those States. / States Change: but Individual Identities never change nor cease" (*M.*, 32:22–3, E., 132). The "state" here is a way of being that includes not only psychological conditions but also material, physical, affective, political, and geographical conditions. Milton's difficult task, one that rewrites his investment in Cromwell's political revolution as subjective transformation, is to change his "state" in this broader meaning. More precisely, Milton's redemption is "complete" only when he has become the very state of re-stating. The redeemed Milton will be the state in or of revolution:

> And thou O Milton art a State about to be Created
> Called Eternal Annihilation that none but the Living shall
> Dare to enter[.] (*M.*, 32:26–8, E., 132)

"Milton" names the state wherein the individual touches his or her radical individuality, a state that pushes beyond its own initial limitation *qua* state to become identical with individuality. But with this, Milton does not fall into Satanic self-possession. This is because the individual itself is understood not to be a mode of permanence but, rather, merely the punctual location of the power of self-annihilation. What Blake calls the *individual* could just as well be called the *imagination*: "The Imagination is not a State: it is the Human Existence itself/ Affection or Love becomes a State, when divided from Imagination" (*M.*, 32.33–4, E., 132). The individual *as* imagination is, then, the power of restating as such. So, this is a power that will "never change nor cease" and yet will never ossify either, since it is a negativity that remediates itself endlessly. As Goldsmith remarks of *Milton*, here "Blake presents 'Man' as an always extendable work in progress," not "an a priori form [...] but a critical agency, a permanent ability to modify and extend the lineaments of received human being by 'exploring' their limits."[33] In this respect Blake's (and Moses') wish "that all the Lords people were prophets" (1.17) is granted, but only in the sense that the self-less individual, like the prophet, lives on into the future as the displacement of his own apparent states and ends. The result is a rhythm that succumbs neither to the empty repetition Blake sees as typical of nature, nor a simple Judeo-Christian teleology.

This state of restating describes a process that Deleuze would call "becoming-imperceptible." In *A Thousand Plateaus*, becoming-imperceptible describes the "immanent end of becoming," a "cosmic formula" that prescribes casting off "molar" and fixed determinations of the self in favour of a "molecular" flexibility.[34] It is not, in other words, that someone named "Milton" becomes someone else, so much as "Milton" names a process – it is a vital, immanent force that is both transcendental (in the sense of exceeding an existing state) and yet also immanent (since this transcendence is not tethered to any particular pre-formed ideal). Milton is a virtual state, a way of *being potential* – a state, as we will see later, Schelling also attempts to imagine when he describes God in *Ages of the World*. Such power of re-creation, as something that includes but goes beyond the subject, is exactly what Satan does not grasp. "All the Living Creatures of the Four Elements" that "in the aggregate are named Satan / And Rahab" are one-dimensional since they "know not of Regeneration, but only of

Generation" (*M.*, 31:17, 18–19, 19; E., 130). Pure generation lacks the substantial, qualitative difference – guaranteed, in Blakean language, by impossibility – that makes revision truly new, whereas generation alone tends to form into oppressive habits. As Milton himself says in the poem, his return from eternity foreshadows the moment when "Generation is swallowd up in Regeneration," when various stale forms of "the not Human" will be "cast off" to reveal not finished selfhood but "the Human Existence": that is, active standing out from being (*M.*, 41:38, E., 143; 32:32, E., 132).

As should be clear, it would be a major mistake at this point to gloss over the resistances to revolution and transformation that give history its sometimes depressing inertia. Difficulties do not disappear simply with the recognition that states can change; nor does Deleuzian thought, with its profoundly affirmative thinking of creativity and the virtual, suddenly change the lived conditions of history. Indeed, "Milton," this state of restating, remains at a distance: it is a state *about to be* created rather than one actually instantiated or something one could take up at will. And it must always hover in this anticipation. The creativity of restating is impossible to represent since such concretization denudes that same power. Only as a fracture in the edifice of the actual, as something impossible until – suddenly – it is not, does Milton (the "state") exist. Revolution in the state cannot follow logically, according to probabilities and possibilities, from things as they are. And yet if we accept Blake's idea that history is composed of lurching movements from impossibilities to actualities, the state of Milton is no less actual for being impossible – for being *the* impossible that marks actual history as not-all, as always incomplete. In other words, for Blake, part of ensuring that substantial change can happen, that genuine and qualitative revolution can gain traction, requires, paradoxically, that the actual not lend itself so easily to the possible. If we are seduced, especially today thanks to the fantasies maintained through liberal capitalism, into the belief that "anything is possible," then the concept of possibility itself will suffer a near total evacuation of meaning. Blake's great contemporary value stems, thus, from how he enables a return to impossibility as the foundation for the virtual.

"a fructifying virtue"

Milton pursues a rhythm of (dis)organization, subtly undermining the purely recuperative sense of prophecy typically associated with the major prophecies, that is, the apocalyptic idea that "the prophetic poet sees all aspects of time – past, present, and future – collapsing into a single moment."[35] Aside from its revision of the act of harrowing (and Harrowing), the poem also overburdens systems of spatial organization in its redundant and layered forms of mapping.

Throughout the text Blake writes psychodrama as geography, then again as history, as personal vision, as biography, and finally as autobiography. The "body" of *Milton* is written over with so many glosses that this produces not a transparent view of historical or poetic truth but rather a collage of incompatible systems; if *Milton* edges toward apocalypse, toward the immediacy of Revelation, it also hypermediates that Revelation, expanding and elaborating and enriching the sensuous world apocalypse would cancel out. Consider, for instance, geography. Blake takes his cue from Jacob's renomination and metamorphosis in the Hebrew Bible.[36] There, Jacob is parcelled out geographically and socially according to the biological dictates of Israel's progeny. Likewise, Blake maps the universe through spiritual entities, the Four Zoas:

> Four Universes round the Mundane Egg remain Chaotic
> One to the North, named Urthona: one to the South, named Urizen:
> One to the East, named Luvah: One to the West named Tharmas[.]
> (*M.*19:15–17, E., 112)

This mapping becomes more complex when Blake turns various human institutions into cities: Allamanda is commerce (*M.*, 27:42, E., 125), Bowlahoola is law (*M.*, 24:48, E., 120), and Golgonooza is "namd Art & Manufacture by mortal men" (*M.*, 24:50, E., 120). But then this schema is again transposed onto the body when "the City of Golgonooza/ Which is the spiritual fourfold London" is located "in the loins of Albion" (*M.*, 20:39–40, E., 114). Indeed, Milton's spatial trajectory or "track" that describes his descent through the universe passes through these variously determined "states" – understood as politically defined nations, physical organs of the body, and psychological categories – providing him with, literally, a new perspective on life:

> And the Four States of Humanity in its Repose,
> Were shewd them. First of Beulah a most pleasant Sleep
> On Couches soft, with mild music, tended by Flowers of Beulah
> Sweet female forms, winged or floating in the air spontaneous
> The Second State is Alla & the third State Al-Ulro;
> But the Fourth State is dreadful; it is named Or-Ulro:
> The First State is the Head, the Second is in the Heart:
> The Third in the Loins & Seminal Vessels & the Fourth
> In the Stomach & Intestines terrible, deadly, unutterable (*M.*, 34:8–16, E., 143)

This redundancy of organization, one that goes so far as to take organ-ization literally, does less to establish a single, simplified picture – an apocalyptic

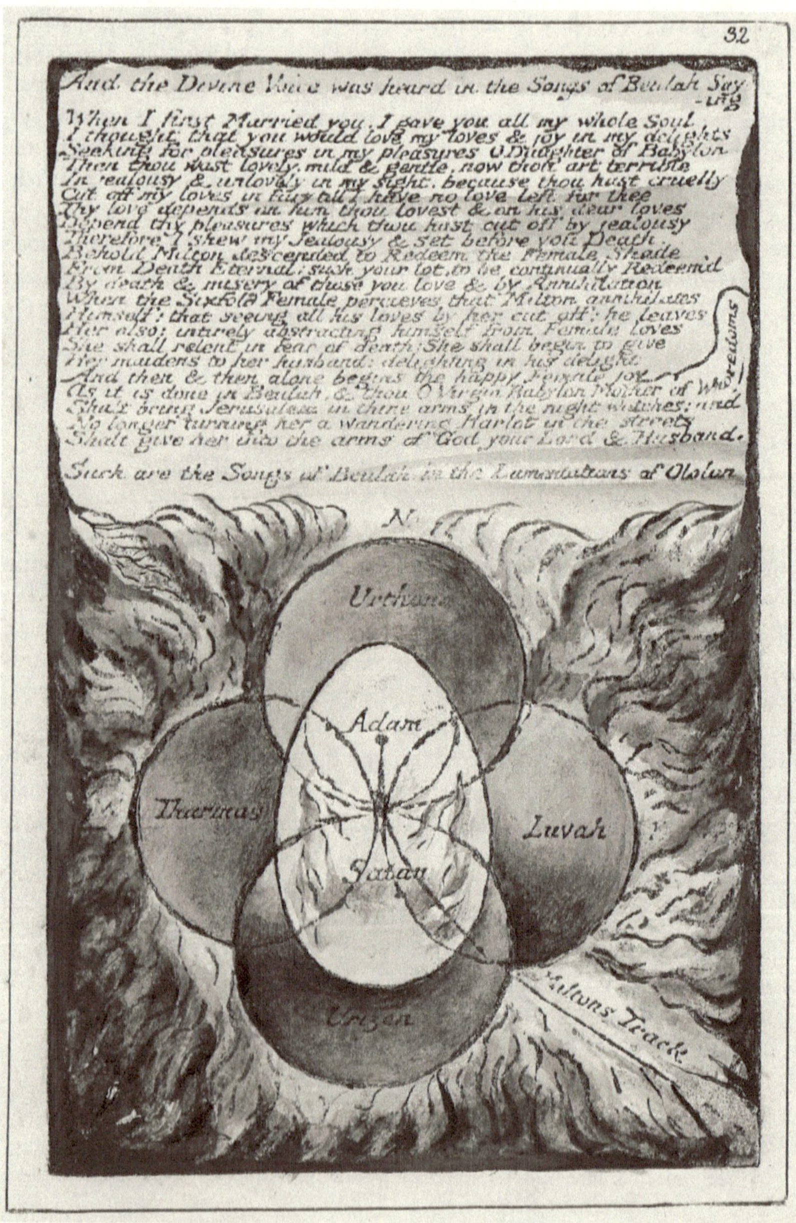

Figure 2. Milton's track, William Blake. *Milton, a poem in 12* [i.e., 2] *books*. Plate 33. *The author and printer W. Blake*. Copy D. [London:] 1804 [i.e., 1815?]. Rosenwald Collection, Library of Congress. Catalogue Number 48031331.

totality – than to suggest a perpetual sliding between systems of organization themselves, the next coming to supplement the previous like Shelley's messengers in *Hellas*. Writing psychodrama as geography, history, personal vision, biography, psychology, and so forth in an effort to appropriate the internal order of each system, undermines *Milton*'s drive for narrative simultaneity and displaces total conceptual and visionary unity. Allowed to approach what seems to be a state of absolute and universal correspondence, Blake's vision reveals its prophetic negativity: the effort to *represent* such totalization appears unable to find a way to combine, into one simple shape, multifarious forms of systematization.

Such difficulty also plays out at the level of the image. This is particularly important since visual arts implicitly promise the kind of simultaneity *Milton* apparently strives toward. Indeed, if a system is presented as an image, one might reasonably expect to benefit from the form, just as a map can prove more intuitively orienting than a list of directions. Yet, even at their most diagrammatic, Blake's images interrupt their own comprehensiveness in various ways. For instance, the "Four intersecting Globes. & the Egg form'd World of Los" (*M.*, 34:33, E., 134) illustrated on the bottom half of Plate 33 presents an attractive symmetry that promises, at first glance, clarification of *Milton*'s metaphysics. But it quickly becomes apparent that the image poses more questions than it answers. The central problem is that, despite appearing in the same visual space, we have no universal, mediating term for all the different kinds of coordinates. This leaves one to wonder, for instance, how the map directions (North, East, South, West, inscribed at the outer edge of the design) relate to apparently corresponding, spherical realms (Urthona, Luvah, Urizen, and Tharamas, respectively). What, moreover, is the significance of shape in this diagram? The spherical realms overlap each other and are, again, overlain by an egg-shaped field defining the opposed states of Adam and Satan. Why this geometry that, first, creates so many zones of intersection that remain undefined and, second, contrasts perfect spheres with the egg's asymmetry? None of this, finally, is effectively tied together by the one element that cuts across the image, the "track" of Milton's descent. Curving asymptotically toward an invisible limit, we are left to ponder how this line illustrates "descent," "fall," or the move from Eternity to self-annihilation. A map without a legend, this image produces the impression of a system even as it ultimately inhibits elucidation – not for an absence of codes but for being overloaded.

Consider also the mutability and re-coding of one of the key images in *Milton* – the star of inspiration – through comparison with *Jerusalem*. This star that famously falls on Blake's left foot, entering at the tarsus, is fused with the plow in the later work. While Blake never depicts the harrow of the almighty

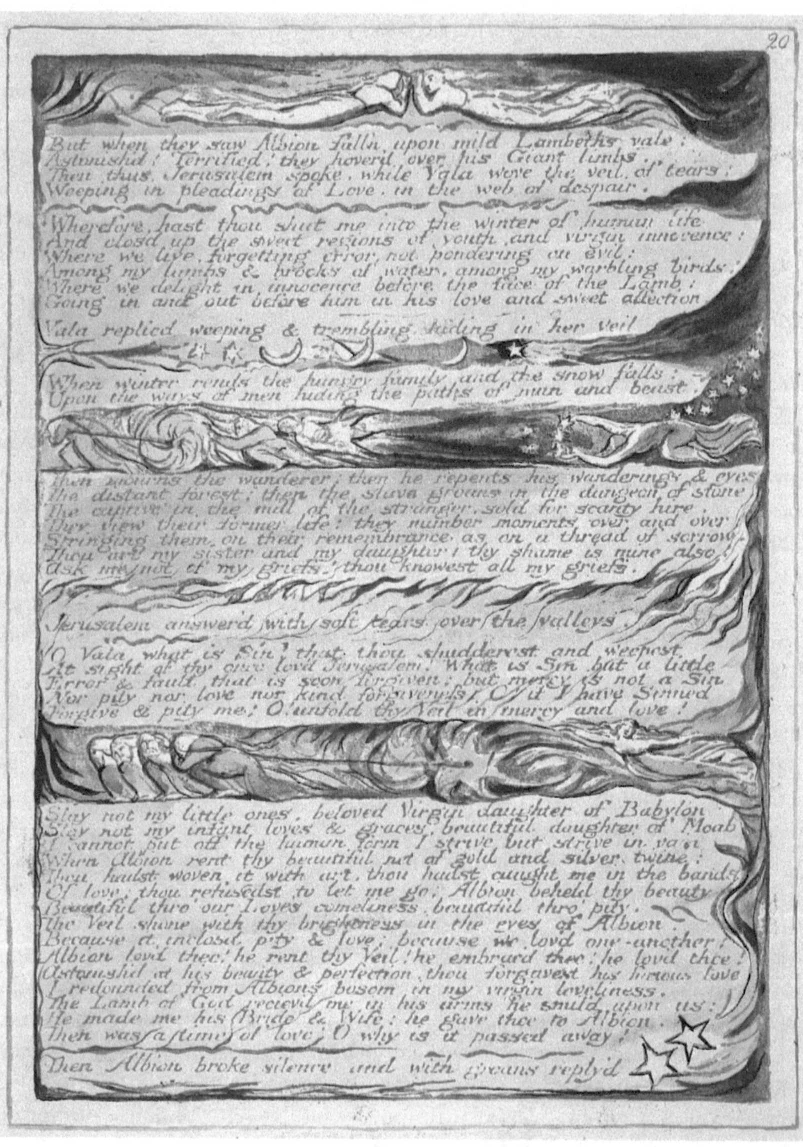

20

But when they saw Albion fall'n upon mild Lambeths vale:
Astonish'd! Terrified, they hover'd over his Giant limbs.
Then thus Jerusalem spoke, while Vala wove the veil of tears:
Weeping in pleadings of Love, in the web of despair.

Wherefore hast thou shut me into the winter of human life
And clos'd up the sweet regions of youth and virgin innocence:
Where we live, forgetting error, not pondering on evil:
Among my lambs & brooks of water, among my warbling birds:
Where we delight in innocence before the face of the Lamb:
Going in and out before him in his love and sweet affection.

Vala replied weeping & trembling, hiding in her veil.

When winter rends the hungry family and the snow falls:
Upon the ways of men hiding the paths of man and beast,

Then mourns the wanderer: then he repents his wanderings & eyes
The distant forest; then the slave groans in the dungeon of stone.
The captive in the mill of the stranger, sold for scanty hire.
They view their former life: they number moments over and over;
Stringing them on their remembrance as on a thread of sorrow.
Thou art my sister and my daughter! thy shame is mine also!
Ask me not of my griefs! thou knowest all my griefs.

Jerusalem answer'd with soft tears over the valleys.

O Vala what is Sin? that thou shudderest and weepest
At sight of thy once lov'd Jerusalem! What is Sin but a little
Error & fault that is soon forgiven; but mercy is not a Sin
Nor pity nor love nor kind forgiveness! O! if I have Sinned
Forgive & pity me! O! unfold thy Veil in mercy and love!

Slay not my little ones, beloved Virgin daughter of Babylon
Slay not my infant loves & graces, beautiful daughter of Moab
I cannot put off the human form I strive but strive in vain
When Albion rent thy beautiful net of gold and silver twine;
Thou hadst woven it with art, thou hadst caught me in the bands
Of love; thou refusedst to let me go: Albion beheld thy beauty
Beautiful thro' our Loves comeliness, beautiful thro' pity.
The Veil shone with thy brightness in the eyes of Albion,
Because it inclosd pity & love; because we lov'd one-another!
Albion lov'd thee! he rent thy Veil! he embrac'd thee! he lov'd thee!
Astonish'd at his beauty & perfection, thou forgavest his furious love:
I redounded from Albions bosom in my virgin loveliness.
The Lamb of God reciev'd me in his arms he smil'd upon us:
He made me his Bride & Wife: he gave thee to Albion.
Then was a time of love: O why is it passed away!

Then Albion broke silence and with groans reply'd

Figure 3. Harrowing the page with starplows, William Blake. *Jerusalem: The Emanation of The Giant Albion.* Plate 20. Bentley, Copy E. Yale Center for British Art, Paul Mellon Collection. Accession Number B1992.8.1(20).

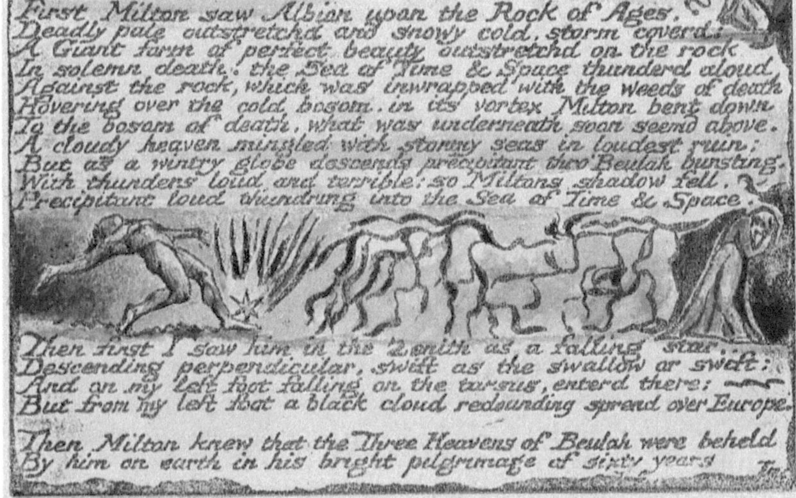

Figure 4. Inspiration and Alteration, William Blake. *Milton, a poem in 12* [i.e., 2] *books. The author and printer W. Blake*. Plate 17 (detail). Copy D. [London:] 1804 [i.e., 1815?]. Rosenwald Collection, Library of Congress. Catalogue Number 48031331.

in *Milton*, he seems to return to and finally visually express this image on Plate 20 of *Jerusalem*. The interlinear images combine the action of harrowing and of stellar inspiration in what looks like a kind of visual citation of *Milton*, though one that creates the original image for the first time. In both instances, figures rake across the page a star-like plow whose design recalls those scenes of inspiration depicted in *Milton*, not only on the full-page designs of William and Robert, but also the star illuminating the first page and the smaller insert depicting Blake in his garden in Lambeth on Plate 15. Indeed, the spatial composition of the latter image closely resembles Plate 20 of *Jerusalem*, inviting one to read the scenes as mirrors of each other. Each forms a kind of triptych. Read left to right, like the text in which it is nested, the scene on Plate 15 of *Milton*, between lines 47 and 48, depicts Blake's inspiration by the star-formed Milton, an altar of rocks in the middle – punning perhaps on the "alteration" at hand – and finally a female being, possibly Catherine Blake, on the right-hand margin, turning away and shielding her eyes from the event. Plate 20 of *Jerusalem* copies this layout. In the second of the two scenes, four figures – perhaps an attempt to render the fourfold spiritual man – plow the page using the very star that in *Milton* represents Milton as a communicable power, this having supplanted and altered the alter in *Milton*. Again, in what might be a literalization of the action of *Milton*, the star becomes the plow or harrow that is, now, drawn through the page of *Jerusalem*. Completing the visual echo is the female figure on the right-hand margin. Yet the differences are as interesting as the similarities. This woman is no longer cowering; transformed from a terrestrial to an ethereal being, she regards the scene in spite of its more manifestly dangerous appearance. Moreover, the star is no longer entering Blake's foot but, converted into a machine of broader spiritual scope, now harrows Albion as a whole. Picking up on the scene of mortality Milton immediately encounters in his descent from Eternity –

> First Milton saw Albion upon the Rock of Ages,
> Deadly pale outstretched and snowy cold, storm coverd:
> A Giant form of perfect beauty outstretchd on the rock
> In solemn death (*M*. 17:36–9, E., 109–10)

– the text on and around Plate 20 of *Jerusalem* concerns an Albion part Job, part Lear, fearful of death, and struggling to classify and order his sons and daughters. Suffering "the seven diseases of the Soul" that make "Albions Cliffs" into "a rocky form against the Divine Humanity," Albion cuts himself off from others and descends into a brooding, Urizenic paranoia (*J*. 19:27, 34, 36, E., 164).

Having defensively "fled inward among the currents of his rivers" (*J*. 19:40, E., 164), Albion's redemption, if indeed signalled by the star-shaped harrow, falls not to Milton but, appropriately enough, to Jerusalem. Channelling the strength of Oothoon in *Visions of the Daughters of Albion*, Jerusalem entreats Vala to break the cycle of sexual-political violence, to "slay not [Jerusalem's] little ones" in a sad repetition of biblical history but rather to trade sin for forgiveness, just as Vala "foregavest [Albion's] furious love" in spite of a violence so great that it "rent [her] Veil" (*J*., 20:28, 38, 37, E. 165). Allowed to revive within Albion, Jerusalem might manage to dissuade Albion from persisting in his "dark despair & everlasting brooding melancholy!," his insistence on a pompous martyrdom – "But come O Vala with knife & cup! drain my blood/ To the last drop! then hide me in thy Scarlet Tabernacle" (*J*. 22:26, 31–2, E. 167) – that perpetuates his addiction to selfhood. Yet, the process of redemption here is in some respects reversed: where Milton consciously and intentionally resumes the human form, Jerusalem admits that she, inversely, "cannot put off the human form" (*J*. 20:30, E., 165). A reluctant hero, Jerusalem's redemption of Albion does not happen through a straightforward self-sacrifice, then, but rather works *against* the *false* "sacrifices of cruelty" (*J*. 23:18, E., 168), going in this sense against the grain of the action of *Milton* just as the plow in *Jerusalem* moves right to left across the page, counter to the direction of reading.

Blake's complication of systems of organization both textually and visually goes to the heart of the paradox identified by Jerome McGann: "why Blake should have created his own elaborate system and how he expected it to serve the arts of creation rather than destruction" is difficult to say given his explicit effort "to deliver Individuals from those Systems" (*J.* 11:5, E. 154).[37] McGann's response to the apparent impasse is to argue that Blake's poems are systems in creation, that they are the antitheses of changeless eternity and so solicit their own cancellation by subsequent imaginations. Hence, if Blakean prophecy is "a call to judgment," a genre wherein the prophet "declares that the time of choice has come," this judgment is not a simple, determinative operation but a form of reflection that – as in Kant's third *Critique* – invents new ideas to account for unprecedented minute particulars.[38] W.J.T. Mitchell's reading of *Milton* takes a similar position, arguing that the poem is "designed to destroy the system it contains in the interest of imaginative freedom, and this results in a sense of the poem as experience not concept."[39] Blake thus seems to agree in spirit with Friedrich Schlegel who solves the conflict between the necessity of systematization and the necessity of freedom through a schizophrenic sort of duality: "It's equally fatal for the mind to have a system and to have none. It will simply have to decide to combine the two."[40] *Milton* is an effort to present just such a marriage of heaven and hell.

Recognizing these internal tensions helps to account for the architecture of time in Blake's poem and sets the stage for a contrast to Wordsworth's apparently analogous interest in prophetic, restorative moments. "Architecture" should be understood here somewhat literally. Like structures in a city, "the Sons of Los build Moments & Minutes & Hours/ And Days & Months & Years & Ages & Periods; wondrous buildings" (*M.*, 28:44–5, E., 126). Times are nested within each other, the "Moment" being "a Couch of gold for soft repose" that sits in the centre of "times" that radiate outward in grander and grander estates:

> And every Minute has an azure Tent with silken Veils.
> And every Hour has a bright golden Gate carved with skill.
> And every Day & Night, has Walls of brass & Gates of adamant,
> Shining like precious stones & ornamented with appropriate signs:
> And every Month, a silver paved Terrace builded high:
> And every Year, invulnerable Barriers with high Towers.
> And every Age is Moated deep with Bridges of silver & gold.
> And every Seven Ages is Incircled with a Flaming Fire. (*M.*, 28:50–7, E., 126–7)

Each unit of time defends itself against the infiltration of the other. Where we might expect time's dynamic, fluid nature to find expression as smooth ingress and egress, we are faced, instead, with gates, walls, moats, towers – all forms of barriers. The passage stresses that time's internal, structural elaboration consists of firm boundaries that mobilize against homogenization. We have here not one time divided into different sized units so much as qualitatively different times, each with its own shape, colour, texture, and density. Like the discordant rhythms of history resonating ever more loudly in the 1790s, these times could only be forced into agreement by a comparatively violent act – a "loud prophetic blast of harmony," perhaps, the sort of messianic energy of

> An ode in passion uttered, which foretold
> Destruction to the children of the earth
> By deluge now at hand.[41]

In *Milton*, that violent, totalizing instant is the "Moment," the apocalyptic "Pulsation of the Artery" that encompasses "all the Great/ Events of Time" (*M.*, 29:3, E., 127; *M.*, 29:1–2, E., 127).

Importantly, though, it is impossible exactly to determine in Blake what the duration of this moment is. We know that "Every Time *less* than a pulsation of the artery/ Is equal in its period & value to Six Thousand Years" (*M.*, 28:62–3, E. 127; my emphasis) but this leaves no indication of what the period and value *of* the grand moment, the total pulsation, would be. This means one cannot measure the gap between one's own time and the date of the apocalypse, or – even more important – the gap between apocalypse and recuperative millennium. If this is the catastrophic point in time that the text is building toward, it is also the point from which the apocalypse unravels. Drawing on a long tradition, Blake names Jerusalem the New City. Given Blake's tendency to see time as architecture, what then might Jerusalem's architecture tell us about historical and prophetic time, especially about the final encompassing moment equal to the pulsation of the artery? Specifically, how might the difficulty with *founding* Jerusalem complicate the apocalyptic moment?

> The Surrey hills glow like the clinkers of the furnace: Lambeths Vale
> Where Jerusalems foundations began; where they were laid in ruins
> Where they were laid in ruins from every Nation & Oak Groves Rooted
> Dark gleams before the Furnace-mouth a heap of burning ashes
> When shall Jerusalem return & overspread all the Nations
> Return: return to Lambeths Vale O building of human souls
> Thence stony Druid Temples overspread the Island white
> And thence from Jerusalems ruins[.] (*M.*, 6:14–21, E., 99)

On the one hand, the passage suggests that Jerusalem is the original foundation of England, that Druid temples are the material traces of this original culture, and that it is a matter not of Jerusalem's arrival but rather its return to Albion. The foundations, in this reading, remain preserved beneath the fray of historical change, like Greece's footings, "Built below the tide of war," in *Hellas.*[42] On the other hand, the passage repeats, almost obsessively, that these foundations "were laid in ruins." This could mean that the foundations were *set* amidst the ruins of a previous civilization or amidst Blake's own artistic productions associated with his time living in "Lambeths Vale" – that is, the fragmentary but also mighty forms of the Lambeth Books. But, it can also mean that the foundations in question were *destroyed.* Given Blake's language, it is impossible to quarantine one sense of the phrase from the other, to separate grounding from demolition. The two tendencies, the two fatalities of having and not having a system, occupy the same space; like the stone and the shell in Wordsworth's dream of the Arab, Jerusalem is both itself and not itself at the same time. The text does not waver between these two positions but, more troublingly, turns the basic notion of architectural organization *into* disorganization.

Read back into the architecture of time, the "rotary motion" – to borrow a Schellingian phrase, to which we will turn in the next chapter – of the apocalyptic moment changes the "period & value" of the "Moment," beyond Satan's ken, so celebrated in the text:

> There is a Moment in each Day that Satan cannot find
> Nor can his Watch-Fiends find it, but the Industrious find
> This Moment & it multiply. & when it once is found
> It renovates every Moment of the Day if rightly placed[.] (*M.*, 35:42–5, E. 136)

Taken out of context, this could sound like one of Wordsworth's spots of time. As we saw in chapter 3, a spot of time has a "renovating virtue" and so, in its own way, "renovates every Moment of the day" by converting loss into profit. Wordsworth's moment is alchemical, transformative, dialectical: negativity does not simply damage the subject but becomes "food for future years." But as we also saw, the spots are also self-cancelling: as numbing medicine the speaker can imbibe to dull acute suffering, the "abundant recompense" renders the subject less sensitive, less alive to his world, and thus less able to experience the extraordinary in the ordinary. Blake moment, however, says nothing about deadening sensitivity or of closing oneself off from the threat of new experience. *Milton* makes self-annihilation, not self-development, the aim of the heroic subject. The cut that alienates the subject from himself in Wordsworth is always registered as a wound to be stitched back together. For Blake, however, suturing is a Satanic response. Satan is that state of preserving in selfhood. Riffing on *Paradise Lost* where Satan admits, "Which way I flie is Hell; my self am Hell," Blake's Milton both realizes and repudiates the notion that he is "of the Devils party" when he says, "I in my Selfhood am that Satan: I am that Evil One!" before exiling himself – in a curious repetition of Adam and Eve's fate – from eternity (*M.*, 14:30, E. 108).[43] Hell in *Paradise Lost* is a state of the self; in *Milton*, Blake rewrites this to mean that the state of selfhood itself is Satanic. Satan and his minions cannot find the renovating moment because it is, by definition, where they are not, and not where they are: the instant of experience that breaches expectation. Milton's decision to "go to Eternal Death" does not, then, promise to reconstitute the self but, precisely, to escape from its narcotic, intoxicating haze. Rather than shore up the teetering subject, Blake's renovating moment destroys the same foundations it makes.

As noted earlier, Blake's moment is also auto-renovating, suggesting that time might open up into affects and experiences that do not, strictly, belong to a subject. This expressivity of time is badly hampered when it is funnelled into nostalgia, the closed circuit that curtails renovation to restoration, revision to regression. In fact, Wordsworth is at his most Blakean in the 1799 *Prelude* when the key adjective is not "renovating" but the more interesting "fructifying." Wordsworth comes back to this key word, modifying "virtue," several times in his revisions of *The Prelude*, trying "vivifying" before settling on "renovating." The vegetable vitality of fructification suggests a time that is literally disseminative, that spreads seeds, that spends without securing a return. Less a product than the action of generation and regeneration, time's fructifying virtue might escape the control of its origin, might become Blake's "Wild Thyme" that serves as "Los's Messenger to Eden" (*M.*, 35:54; E., 136). Unlike the clock-time implicit in Satan's "watch-fiends" that regulates the industrial workday, Blake here gestures toward a time that is "wild," that is, both unregulated and rural. And while this time is identified with a function, it has a life beyond its mere utility. This life is expressive and even artistic when spreading "over the Rock of Odours his bright purple mantle" (*M.*, 35:57; E., 136).

In a letter to Thomas Butts on 23 September 1800, immediately following his move to the more rustic environs of Felpham, Blake expresses confidence that his "Work will go on here with God speed." As if to explain this optimism he relates how "A roller & two harrows lie before my window. I met a plow on my first going out to my gate the morning after my arrival, & the Plowboy said, to the Plowman, 'Father, The Gate is Open.'"[44] This is not only the gate of paradise but also the gate of hell. And what passes through this portal is not the kind of historical knowledge that would sedate the anxious, modern subject – it is not merely redemption. This harrowing, rather, will be harrowing, will involve opening to a future that cannot be predicted and from which one might not recover. Blake's prophetic art performs a kind of historiography but aims not to produce clarifying narratives of historical development, elucidations of cause-and-effect relationships, or any kind of easily readable record of his time. Instead, he stresses history's recalcitrant impossibility and amplifies the negativity within history that resists the dialectical conversion of the unknown into knowledge or positive experience. Blake's impossibility is never secretly possible or redeemable, even if it sets the stage for and offers limited encouragement to such processes. In the case of historiographical reflection, this resistance to knowledge might be productive but only insofar as it demands a change in the concepts of historical knowledge and historiography themselves. To give the concept of future possibility renewed force, Blake insists not just on resuscitating unrealized possibilities of the past – though he does do this, as when Milton's wives and daughters are revived as "the Six-fold Miltonic Female."[45] But more than this, and counterintuitively, Blake dilates the sense of actual life's impossibility: the realities of limitation, depression, and failure. While apparently pessimistic, these efforts in fact reveal a potentiality in history, what we could call the virtual, that foregrounds forces in history capable of totally renovating every moment of the day, of reformulating our most basic expectations about time, probability, and impossibility. Blake's prophetic writing resists turning history into depotentiated fact by preserving, rather than eliminating, impossibility.

Chapter Seven

The Preface and Other False Starts: Prophesying the Book to Come

"Germany is to the French Revolution, then, as Achilles to the tortoise – forever postponing its encounter with an object that it had already overtaken, and constantly running ahead of a thing with which it could never quite catch up"

Rebecca Comay, *Mourning Sickness: Hegel and the French Revolution*

"Against the 'official' notion of Kierkegaard as *the* 'anti-Hegel,' one should assert that Kierkegaard is arguably the one who, through his very 'betrayal' of Hegel, effectively remained faithful to him. He effectively *repeated* Hegel, in contrast to Hegel's own pupils, who 'developed' his system further"

Slavoj Žižek, *Organs without Bodies*

Among other things, a prophet is a herald of the future to come. It should be unsurprising, then, if they gravitate toward this genre of writing or even embody the role in their manner of speaking. Blake's Bard in *Milton* plays this role, singing an allegorical preface – strange as it is – to the larger event of Milton's descent from eternity. Wordsworth's *Prelude* is also conceived as a preface to an epic, though one that eclipses the work it would announce. As we will see in the next chapter, the Sibyl of Cumae and Beatrice, from *Valperga*, both preface, literally and figuratively, Mary Shelley's *The Last Man*. Refocusing on Blake for the moment, recall that his Lambeth Books are sometimes thought of as prefaces to the major prophecies – an idea, I suggested in chapter 6, in need of reconsideration given that its teleological implications are ill-suited to Blake's most fundamental thinking about history. Blake's art resists the concept of progressive development, following instead a deeply disjunctive itinerary drawn from his thinking about history as reflected in his *Descriptive Catalogue,* the marginalia to Watson, and elsewhere. Working through this argument involved illustrating how a major prophecy, *Milton,* displaced the apocalypse it also announced. In so doing, the text reformulated key concepts such as imagination, the state, history, prophecy, renovation, and time itself. Another way to explore Blake's impossible history would, however, follow the inverse track. Rather than focus on how *Milton*'s techniques of auto re-vision undermine apocalyptic pre-vision, we could interrogate *by pushing further* the idea that the Lambeth books *are* prefaces – those works "laid in ruins" that are also the foundations of Jerusalem (and of *Jerusalem*) – but not of the sort that easily give themselves over to the work they introduce. This means reconceptualizing the literary preface along the lines of how prophecy has been reconsidered thus far. That is: What if the preface does not invite but rather obstructs the book to come?

Blake's Lambeth "prefaces" keep the future, insofar as it apocalyptically accomplishes the work of mourning the past, always at a distance. Mourning is the process by which the past is constituted as a whole object that can finally be put, decisively, past. But, as noted in chapter 3 in the case of Wordsworth and in the last chapter of Blake's *Milton*, both artists cannot – nor would Blake, specifically, want to – completely reabsorb the traumatic origin. Both, rather, can begin their respective works only thanks to an inaugural alienation on which their art then feeds. In Blake, for instance, history's impossibility and the re-creative moment of renovation are never "worked out"; in fact, he sees the efforts to stabilize and smooth over the jagged corners of history as a sort of anaesthetic that addles and befogs an awareness of life's richness. Instead of folding negativity into production, work, or the proper subject of Enlightenment representation, history's impossibility in Blake's art is accorded new weight as the historiographical counterpart to an imagination that revises itself so turbulently that it draws the subject into this chaos rather than permitting him a safe distance, like that enjoyed by Kant's observer of the sign of history. Blake's history writes the actual as impossible, such that what appears to be normal, natural, and inevitable is revealed as not only miraculous but also multiple and heterogenous – a world overfilled and onto which no single metric, no ratio, no "one law" or legend or system of coordinates can be successfully imposed.

In his *The Life of William Blake,* Alexander Gilchrist is irritated by Blake's strange temporality, complaining that *America, A Prophecy* "has no distinctly seizable pretensions to a prophetic character, being, like the rest of Blake's 'Books of Prophecy,' rather a retrospect, in its mystic way, of events already transpired."[1] Like the prophet who revokes certainty in the present rather than proffering knowledge of the future, Blake's prefaces do not pave the way to the future but rather dig ever deeper into the impossibility of their own function as foundations. Blake is not alone in this regard. Both Søren Kierkegaard and Friedrich Schelling think of the preface as a starting point that, nevertheless, cannot properly begin. The division between the preface and the work proper, like that between the beginning and the start elaborated on below, represents an effort at dividing labour. As noted in the previous chapter, what Blake's *Milton* suggests is that while such a division is ideal – this is one take on the Bard's cautionary parable – nevertheless the lines of demarcation and hierarchies of order through which roles are determined prove to be mobile and perhaps positively disorienting. Similar problems develop in Schelling and Kierkegaard: the division of labour between preface and body in the work of art and philosophy ends up halting production. Formulated as the literary preface, prophecy's ambivalence becomes a preface that invokes *and* revokes what it promises. In other words, the kind of preface that emerges in all three writers "does not run errands on behalf of the system."[2] Rather, the preface becomes absolute. We face an absolute preface when the preface becomes the shape taken by the total work, when the work proper is a form of its own anticipation. Like Milton in Blake's eponymous poem, the work gestured toward by such prophetic inauguration is always "a State about to be Created."[3] It is around this darkest elaboration of Romantic prophecy that Kierkegaard and Schelling join company with Blake in thinking the impossibility not merely of predicting the future but of beginning history at all.

Whereas, in Geoffrey Hartman's words, "the Bible's 'in the beginning' [is] a limiting concept, which tells us not to think about what went before," Blake's Book of Genesis, by contrast, relentlessly calls attention to its founding contradiction.[4] In its role as an inaugurating book, *The [First] Book of Urizen* complicates the division of labour between preface and work, especially when it is shrunk down into a homunculus of sorts and transplanted into the opening pages of *Milton*.[5] This book, as preface, seems in some sense to un-work the whole it is supposed to introduce, or to represent what Blanchot calls "the work of the absence of (the) work": not merely non-work, but the *work of* non-work, or what he terms *disoeuvrement.* In Mary Jacobus' words, we can think of *disoeuvrement* as "a restless unworking that refuses totalization and proceeds, not by way of critique, but rather by juxtaposition, divergence, and difference. This is dialectic without negation, yet capable of responding to disaster and of broaching the unknown of one's own thought through repetition, return and response."[6] Indeed, Blanchot goes so far as to see the workless preface as something like the exemplary mark of Romanticism:

> *Romanticism, it is true, ends badly, but this is because it is essentially what begins* and what cannot but finish badly: an end that is called suicide, madness, loss,

> forgetting. And certainly it is often without works, but this is because *it is the work of the absence of (the) work*; a poetry affirmed in the purity of the poetic act, an affirmation without duration, a freedom without realization, a force that exalts in disappearing and that is in no way discredited if it leaves no trace, for this was its goal: to make poetry shine, neither as nature nor even as work, but as pure consciousness of the moment.[7]

Worklessness is neither work nor non-work, but rather the action of idleness, a project that coincides with its own entropy, just as Georges Bataille says of his *Inner Experience*: "The opposition to the idea of project – which takes up an essential part of this book – is so necessary within me that having written the detailed plan for this introduction, I can no longer hold myself to it."[8] The negativity of self-annihilation imported though the inaugurating citation of *Urizen* and formalized as the absolute preface in *Milton,* begins to look like Bataille's *Inner Experience* – an abject project – or like Schelling's strange picture of history in *Ages of the World*: a history trapped in the preface to history. Whereas Los is Blake's "Eternal Prophet,"[9] *Milton* remains divided between its organizing work and *Urizen*'s disorganizing introduction, the project of prophetic apocalypse delayed by *Urizen*'s confusion of self-generation with self-destruction. This confusion manifests as a doubled time, one that runs ahead of another to which it cannot ever catch up. Even as *Milton* approaches temporal simultaneity – all the action in *Milton* seems to happen in the same moment[10] – the text distends itself, gesturing in the final lines to a moment that is always outstanding rather than identical to the action described. Similarly, Schelling's appeal to temporal simultaneity in an effort to ameliorate the ontological and epistemological contradictions that attend the Godhead's revelation in actual history prove more problematic than he had anticipated. Blake's absolute preface is, thus, manifested in both literary and metaphysical terms through a reading of Kierkegaard and Schelling; both philosophers explore forms of negativity that fall outside the efficiency of Hegel's historical dialectic and this enables a new perspective on Blake's complex treatment of prophetic labour.

Prelude to Beginning

The discussion of Blake's prefaces benefits from a distinction between beginnings and starts. A start is one kind of temporal formulation and distinct from that of the beginning. A start would be comparatively unproblematic: one could locate a start wherever one pleased and could precipitate a start without major inconvenience. A start, to use the terms of the preceding chapter, is always possible. A beginning, on the other hand, would involve a point of absolute precedence and anteriority, and in this sense would involve a different temporal matrix from the start – that is, would not be on the same horizon as a start. One can always make a start; people, every day, can and do make starts. And one can always abandon something and start again. This was evident earlier as Wordsworth, for instance, seems always to be starting *The Excursion* over again by rewriting its prelude. A start, however, cannot make the same existential claims as a beginning: it does not relate to the things that emerge from the start in the same way as the beginning does, since the start is annihilated by the work to come. A beginning, then, is in some sense eternal or beyond time, as Schelling writes of an eternal beginning in the *Ages of the World*, one that "never ceases to be a beginning."[11] This is not a start that one can move away from or beyond, but a radical positing that has to contend endlessly with the abyss that is its logical condition of possibility. The beginning is what holds open the perpetual possibility of a start without, itself, starting, without itself falling into a history of the possible and probable, of cause and effect; this is why it demands its own temporal architecture, why it is gated or perhaps moated around like one of Blake's times, separating itself from the structure of starting. So, when Wordsworth and Blake both try in their respective works to recuperate the *beginning*, the difficulty with such projects presents itself symptomatically, namely, in terms of the more discrete, literary conundrum of how to *start* a text about *beginning*. Hence, the false starts witnessed in several of Blake's Lambeth books, Wordsworth's series of *Preludes*, and Shelley's repeated invocation of the Wandering Jew, who seems always to stand on the threshold of a history that will properly begin the work of healing and mourning.[12] Because these works seek the more radical beginning – either cosmic in Blake, subjective in Wordsworth, or historical in Shelley – they offer a way for what cannot be figured in chronological sequence (i.e., *beginning*) to appear, but only as a kind of unfeasibility, unreadability, or impossibility. Perpetual *starting* figures the failure to recuperate *beginning*. This is registered in the effort exerted by both Wordsworth and Blake to start the text from a place of sufficient but ultimately impossible anteriority. Wordsworth gestures at this anteriority most explicitly in the "Intimations Ode," although it is also behind the linguistic sleight of hand that is the "prophetic" call to prophecy, the invocation to inspiration. This is the effort to solicit and to claim artistic authority in the same breath, which leads to the temporal problem whereby the future seems to open only though a gesture of retrospection. This is an attempt to contain time through experience even as the experience *of* time's impalpable impression betrays the futility of such delicate webs of tenses.

The preludia in question – i.e., Blake's Lambeth books – are, then, the disfigured figurations of a radical beginning, where beginning is a force that exceeds any kind of finite localization. The beginning is what creates the possibility of starting but also what makes every particular start into a kind of betrayal of the beginning. The beginning as such does not start because it is the very *ability* to start, to negate, to inaugurate. As this power, the beginning must always remain in the beginning: it can never be reduced to or appropriated by the particular projects that might make a start. If the beginning started, if it took on flesh, as it were, and became past, it would foreclose the possibility of any new starts, would revoke the horizon it opens for new starts, and existence would be rendered completely, sequentially determined. Hence, from a practical perspective, if there is to be existential freedom, the beginning must not start. This is not because the beginning is some kind of transcendental signified or idea – if it does not start, that does not mean that it rests in self-sufficiency. Rather, it is because the beginning does *not* have being itself that it can function as the ground of starts. The temporality of beginning recalls the abyss of anteriority that would solicit the infinite regression of prefaces to prefaces that, noted earlier, Blanchot sees as the paradox whereby one can start writing only if one has already written. The start, by contrast, is the cut that ruptures this same dull round, like the emergence of the Godhead out of Schelling's rotary motion of the potencies, calming primordial turbulence into a dialectical process – at least temporarily. Such a fiat inaugurates a development only *temporarily* because ultimately it cannot quite silence the beginning, or cannot quite overcome and absorb the impossibility of beginning. The start cannot put the beginning in its proper place. Hence, when starts themselves become the centre of attention, they reveal their susceptibility to regression.

With Blake, we see how prefatory negativity resists complete chronological discipline through his struggles with starting his so-called minor prophecies – that is, with initiating those texts that are supposed, in turn, to constitute the prefatory material for *Milton* and other "major" works. When we consider Blake's attempts to initiate various texts, we see how the abyss of the beginning irritates and even revokes the starts it makes possible. The very struggle to start would then be a sign of the beginning, not the beginning itself. Blake's preludia represent locations of mediation where eternity (as eternal beginning) intersects time (punctual, discrete starts), just as the prophet is the immediate mediator of the divine Word, just as the sign of history traces and yet leaves indeterminate the freedom it signifies. The anteriority that the prelude or preface claims, therefore, echoes the prophet's complex position not merely in terms of her ostensible anteriority respecting historical events.[13] The analogy between preface and prophet, in addition, discloses a common traumatic economy: just as the prophet is traumatized not so much by simply missing an experience but by the attempt to *encounter*, by narrating, the missed experience with the unconditional, so too do Blake's prefaces writhe under the impossible demand to reconcile eternal beginning with chronological starts – a problem Michel Foucault will see, more broadly, as "the foundation for our experience of time, and, since the nineteenth century, as the starting-point of all our attempts to re-apprehend what beginning and re-beginning, the recession and the presence of the beginning, the return and the end, could be in the human sphere."[14] When this *aporia* reaches its most reflexive, insane point in the abyssal regression of prefaces to prefaces, Blake's prophetic time overlaps with Kierkegaardian irony as perpetual inauguration, revealing itself as neither predictive nor apocalyptic.

Blake is full of false starts because he cannot start properly. But what would it even mean to start "properly"? Blake's relentless rewriting, recycling, and internal citation, witnessed especially, as discussed above, in *Milton*, leads to the question: what if there is no such thing as a *proper* start? Can there really be a start that is perfectly self-appropriating, self-contained, complete? Would this containment not preclude the action of self-transgression or self-transcendence that defines starting, the moment of breaking away from one state toward something new? The fact is that there are only ever false starts. One cannot start except falsely, or through a loss of total coherence and the dispersal of property. This is because a start places the very notions of the "total" and "coherent" into crisis: a start interrupts that from which it breaks. Every start is also an end to whatever it departs from. Hence, Ian Balfour, following Blanchot, will make much of the sense that prophecy is, in the first instance, already "pervasively citational":[15] the prophet *repeats*, or cites, the words of the God in her "original," inspired, and ostensibly *immediate* utterance. The "presence" of prophetic speech is fractured by this referentiality that gestures toward an always anterior power or proper being and beginning. For instance, Blake's prefaces in *Europe, A Prophecy* and *America, A Prophecy* reflect this fracturing such that not only do the individual texts struggle with the placement of the preface but the question of priority also arises *between* the texts, as they enter into a dizzying series of reciprocally prefatory relationships. While we might expect texts nominated as prophecies at least to attempt to stride into the future, these texts are conspicuously belated. Blake, then, suggests that there are only ever false starts; as such, the sense of error the word "false" carries has to be ejected. Starting and starting imperfectly, inappropriately, or through temporal discontinuity – so, in other words, starting traumatically, split from identity like the prophet's "original citation" – are one and the same.

This kind of inaugural negation is particularly overdetermined in the Preludium of *Europe*. The "nameless shadowy female" who gives birth to the revolutionary forces of Orc seems, herself, barely to exist.[16] If she is the figure who would "labour into life" other figures, it is also clear that this prodigality does not preserve her own life: each birth will, she laments, "cause [her] name to vanish, that [her] place may not be found."[17] The shadowy female is "consumed" and "devoured" in her productivity, leaving her only a brief glimpse of her "fruits": "I see it smile & I roll inward & my voice is past."[18] What Saree Makdisi notes in his reading of *America* also applies to this moment in *Europe*, namely that "it is not production or even work as such that is being stigmatized [...] but rather a particular process of production that requires a minute and highly orchestrated social division of labour and the reification of particular labouring roles within that division."[19] The difference between healthful prodigality and "enslavement has to do with confinement and restriction to a particular identity and a particular role within a productive process [...] so that the labourer's very identity is commensurate with his or her labour, and has no ontological independence from labour, potential or actual."[20] As the nameless female perfectly illustrates, "Outside of such work time, labour not only has no value: it has no existence."[21] But if it is the explicitly exploitative nature of labour's organization that damages the subject of production and (re) producibility, there may be a way from within that negativity – as brutal as it certainly is – also to recognize something powerfully resistant to work. Perhaps what Blake's female represents is not only the injustice of labour division; perhaps she, too, presents something more radically other, a kind of production that cannot be either saved or violated by consumption but rather operates beyond such determinants:

> I bring forth from my teeming bosom myriads of flames.
> And thou [Enitharmon] dost stamp them with a signet, then they roam abroad
> And leave me void as death:
> Ah! I am drown'd in shady woe, and visionary joy.[22]

This female becomes the void or the negativity of a preface; she is nothing but a point of departure. In other words, she is, herself, a prelude – a (dis)embodied figure of *Europe*'s Preludium, where that introductory text is itself already divided from its beginning by another preface: its own fairy tale (i.e., a tale told by a fairy) beginning. In addition, she resembles Shelley's Ahasuerus, disfigured in her attempt to mediate between eternal beginning and finite starting. In fact, like "an incarnation of the to-come," she reappears in chapter 8 as Mary Shelley's vanished Sibyl in the preface to *The Last Man*: the formless figure of the future.

This passage from *Europe* is temporally overdetermined not only because the female's existential evacuation and the Preludium's preface protract the text's proper beginning but also because *Europe* (1794) is anticipated at the end of *America* (1793): "Till Angels & weak men twelve years should govern o'er the strong,/ And then their end should come, when France receiv'd the Demon's light."[23] *America*, then, is a prophecy of a prophecy. But if such redundancy seems to promise historical synthesis – to stabilize chronology or to establish one thing as definitively precedent and another as definitively subsequent – the effect is, as witnessed in *Milton*'s redundant organization, quite the reverse. Once the abyss of the origin is discovered, attempts to close over such negativity look desperate. The historical, material conditions of production suggest a significant *inversion* of *America*'s apparent priority: it is Blake's experience of the French, not the American, Revolution that inspires his imagery and serves as the affective foundation for *America*. If *America* acts as a preface for *Europe* in terms of the order of composition and historical chronology, it is a preface that is itself the product of what it ostensibly anticipates, projecting its own beginning out ahead of itself and into the future. Rather than a smooth temporal progression, Blake's texts short-circuit the creative fiat in what could be described as – anticipating the discussion of Schelling's historiography below – a vertiginous "rotatory movement," leaving us with a series of preludia that do not steadily evolve into a grand system but rather perpetually displace each other, flickering in and out of existence like the shadowy female.[24] They also produce a text structurally analogous to one of Kierkegaard's lesser-known parodies of Hegel.

The Work to Come

As Todd Nichol argues, Kierkegaard's little-studied *Prefaces* (1844) "continues in comic mode the attack on Danish Hegelianism initiated in earlier works and soon to be more fully developed in *Stages* and *Postscript*."[25] Similarly, Neils Thulstrup notes that *Prefaces* "showed the comical aspect of [Hegel's] energetic system building."[26] The comedy stems from the fact that this book is composed only of a series of prefaces, authored by one "Nicholas Notabene," in a paradigmatic instance of remediation producing hypermediation: with each preface, the distance between the beginning and the work proper dilates. Dwelling on what Hegel considered to be a philosophically dubious genre – a position he articulates in his own preface to the *Phenomenology* – Kierkegaard performs a clever, parodic repetition of Hegel's complaint. According to Hegel, the preface to a completed philosophical system is not merely unnecessary but worse: it is deceptive since it circumvents the necessarily protracted operation of dialectical unfolding by presenting the conclusions before the book even starts.[27] In such texts time and history are disjointed, with narrative running ahead of itself and yet failing to catch up to the substantial body. Hegel famously begins his own preface to the *Phenomenology* thus:

> It is customary to preface a work with an explanation of the author's aim, why he wrote the book, and the relationship in which he believes it to stand to other earlier or contemporary treatises on the same subject. In the case of a philosophical work, however, such an explanation seems not only superfluous but, in view of the nature of the subject-matter, even inappropriate and misleading. For whatever might appropriately be said about philosophy in a preface – say a historical *statement* of the main drift and the point of view, the general content and results, a string of random assertions and assurances about truth – none of this can be accepted as the way in which to expound philosophical truth.[28]

Since, for Hegel, knowledge is not merely a product of thinking "but rather the result together with the process through which it came about," the preface, as an immediate statement of the essence of the work, "by itself is a lifeless universal, just as the guiding tendency is a mere drive that as yet lacks an actual existence."[29] For Hegel, an abstraction is just that – abstract. In common parlance, "abstract" connotes complexity but philosophically it signifies the reverse: the abstract is a simplification of complex reality that collapses time and development into a superficial product. Hence the mere existence of a preface to a philosophical work suggests a certain failure to think the concrete rigourously.

As if intentionally to aggravate the patient dialectician, Notabene's whole work will focus on "the preface as such, the liberated preface."[30] In a strange sort of agreement with Hegel's labour of the negative, this is a type of writing, he says, that "must then have no subject to treat but must deal with nothing, and insofar as it seems to discuss something and deal with something, this must nevertheless be an illusion and fictitious motion."[31] Notabene's liberated prefaces, a collection of prefaces to books that do not exist, do not function as typical prefaces: they do not repress themselves in the interest of another project. Rather, *Prefaces* foregrounds the recalcitrant worklessness of the preface in order subtly to question Hegel's confidence in spiritual and historical progress. The text performs this questioning parasitically by insisting on and agreeing with Hegel's own insight. In fact, Notabene's first words in the preface to *Prefaces* flag for the reader that this is indeed a text concerned centrally with Hegel even if his name never appears: "It is a frequently corroborated experience that a triviality, a little thing, a careless utterance, an unguarded exclamation, a casual glance, an involuntary gesture have provided the opportunity to slip into a person and discover something that had escaped more careful observation. Lest, however, this insignificant remark be distorted and become pompous, I shall for the moment forego further pursuit of it and get on with my project."[32] This observation on observation recalls a pertinent remark in Kierkegaard's letters (III C 31) that connects this matter of insight via accident specifically to Hegel: "One often grasps Hegel best," Kierkegaard writes, "in his casual remarks."[33] Notabene's opening "casual remark," his carefully scripted unguarded utterance, does indeed offer a greater insight to *his* book of prefaces than might be expected by setting up *Prefaces* as a conversation with Hegel.

Behind this playing with prefaces lies a substantial friction. As Thulstrup notes in his important study, *Kierkegaard's Relation to Hegel*,

> In Kierkegaard there is no metaphysically necessary stride toward the higher stage [of consciousness or life] such as we find in Hegel. [...] According to the present text [i.e., *Papirer*, I A 75] of Kierkegaard, there is a possibility that man *can* pass from the stage in question [i.e., the moral stage] to another and higher one, from morality with its place for the irony of life in self-knowledge. For Hegel there is a necessity that man *must* progress along the dialectical way of development.[34]

Hence, the preface is only *inappropriate* if there is a process of work assumed to be *proper.* The preface can only be misleading or superfluous if a certain development is considered to be necessary. Kierkegaard's existentialism, however, loosens these assumptions. The "theory of stages" is, for instance, "in total discord with Hegel's philosophy [since] the norm [in Hegel] for personality was speculative insight, not as for Kierkegaard an ethical position toward one's self and to the self's given reality as a task."[35] As a specific phenomenon through which to express a different sense of subjective development and, with that, a different kind of negativity or non-work, Kierkegaard's *Prefaces* inverts its relationship to the kind of future presumed by Hegel in the same manner as Shelley's Ahasuerus and Blake's prophecies displace apocalypse in and through the very act of its apparent solicitation.

It is not surprising, then, that *Prefaces* seems obsessed with different forms of emptiness, with the gaps that, like the shadowy female in Blake, persist within the texture of positive generation. The original inspiration for this book of prefaces stems, for one, from an amusing line of reasoning conducted by Notabene's wife. She forbids him to be a proper writer since, in her estimation, writing is equivalent to philandering. "Her view is *in contento* [in substance] as follows: a married man who is an author is not much better than a married man who goes to his club every evening, yes, even worse, because the one who goes to his club must himself still admit that it is an infraction, but to be an author is a distinguished unfaithfulness that cannot evoke regret even though the consequences are worse."[36] While this is in part comedic, there may well be a more substantial truth to the notion that writing and infidelity share a common ground. As a comment on the nature of writing itself, Kierkegaard perhaps anticipates modern notions of dissemination, displacement, and tracing – the sense that what is most essential to language is its ability to break from its own origin. So if it is by way of apparent compromise that Notabene is permitted to write prefaces – and prefaces only – to works that do not exist, in another sense this restriction is really an unsurpassable limit: *all* writing is rewriting, which is also to say that *all* writing is a kind of preface to future rewritings. Kierkegaard's analogy for this condition is appropriately inane: "I thus reserved for myself," says Notabene, "permission to venture to write 'Prefaces.' In this connection I appealed to analogies, that husbands who had promised their wives never to use snuff any more had as recompense obtained permission to have as many snuffboxes as they wished."[37] To write (prefaces) is then to indulge in a measured impropriety. And where better to reflect on this inappropriate practice than in the preface to *Prefaces*? "I will without delay tell the reader how all this hangs together, since it is in exactly the right place here, and just as defamation belongs at a coffee party, this [i.e., the explanation for his writing prefaces without complete works] is something that very properly belongs in a preface."[38] Just as irony's reflexivity never manages to result in concrete totalization, the preface to *Prefaces* turns its ostensible appropriation and mastery of the beginning into yet another false start.

In a sense, then, Notabene parodies Hegel not simply by agreeing that prefaces are superfluous – it is of course only because they *are* trivial that he is permitted to write them – but also by framing the preface as the appropriate place *for* the inappropriate. This is to suggest, in a move anticipating Bataille's concept of unemployable negativity – the inevitable remainder of dialectical operations – that what Hegel's system cannot account for is precisely what it *dis*counts: that which is resistant to utility, that which is manifestly useless. Notabene embodies this recalcitrance in the form of idiocy. In the eighth chapter (i.e., the eighth preface) of *Prefaces*, Notabene contemplates starting a "philosophical journal in Denmark."[39] He imagines aiding the spread of philosophy through his very stupidity, his dim wits actively spurring the dialectic of enlightenment. He says, "My purpose, then, is to serve philosophy; my qualification for this is that I am obtuse enough not to understand it [...]. And yet my enterprise can only benefit philosophy, since no harm can come to it from the fact that even the most obtuse person can make it out; it thereby wins its most complete victory and demonstrates the rightness of making all into philosophers."[40] Through his self-annihilating resignation to the superiority of Hegelian thought, Notabene becomes – like Blake's shadowy female – a kind of casualty of work's perfection, of its total efficiency.

However, this very concession to production leaves an indivisible remainder. For Notabene can finally assert,

> There is one thing I do know quite definitively: it is that I do not understand [Hegelian thought]. There is one thing that I do desire of my contemporaries: it is an explanation. Consequently I do not deny that Hegel has explained everything; I leave that to the powerful minds who will also explain what is missing. I keep my feet on the ground and say: I have not understood Hegel's explanation. [...]. I plead, I plead for an explanation, an explanation, note well, that I can understand, because it would scarcely help me if there were to be an explanation that explains everything in Hegel, but in such a way that I cannot understand it.[41]

This complaint, like Byron's in the Dedication to *Don Juan* that Coleridge should "explain his Explanation," is somewhat juvenile. In fact, Notabene is willing to concede, later on, that "perhaps it is for another reason that philosophy cannot have anything to do with me; perhaps the explanation of my obtuseness is the same as the explanation regarding philosophy, that is, that one who cannot understand philosophy also cannot understand the explanation of why he cannot understand it."[42] Here, Notabene would take responsibility for his own ignorance rather than expect another somehow to educate him. But even if the inadequacy of Notabene's thought is neither the fault of the system nor something that must necessarily be explicable to Notabene, it indicates a kind of deficit of or depression in thought that cannot be properly systematized or organically sublated by Hegel's dialectic. It can only be left out. It is a negativity that becomes problematic not because it represents wrong ideas but because it is *not even wrong*. As Plato's dialogues demonstrate, for stupidity to be useful it still has to be wrong in the right way. What Kierkegaard describes, however, is a negativity that remains awkwardly askew and so forms an absolute preface to spirit's development, a development into which it can never properly enter.

Hegel serves here as the common link for paring Kierkegaard with Schelling, as each thinker explores modes of negativity – irony, stupidity, prehistory, the unconscious – that are not neatly dialectical. Rather than simply introducing the work, the preface for both these thinkers enters onto a regressive course, such that prefaces preface only other prefaces, the work's foundations repeatedly, as Blake put it, "laid in ruins" in the simultaneously affirmative and negative sense of that phrase. Combining Blake's treatment of labour and Bataille's distinction between restricted and general economy, this absolute preface could be read as an example of what Blanchot calls the work of the absence of (the) work. In "Literature and the Original Experience," a long essay in the middle of *The Space of Literature,* Blanchot describes literature's beginning as just this kind of absolute preface, a prophecy that suspends the work to come in perpetual anticipation: "The work says this word, beginning, and what it claims to give to history is initiative, the possibility of a point of departure. *But for its own part it does not begin.* It is always anterior to any beginning, it is always already finished. As soon as the truth one thinks one draws from it comes to light, becomes the life and the action of daytime's clarity, the work closes off on itself as if it were a foreigner to this truth and without significance."[43] There is an insuperable gap between the work's infinite power to initiate and its limited incarnation in a particular work – a difference recalling Claire Colebrook's observation that since "*apocalyptic representation* could only occur within history while apocalypse itself would break with all its worldly anticipation," any such representation must necessarily misrepresent the actual, extra-historical event.[44] The reticence of the beginning resists the work's reduction of negation to "*determinate* negation," a form of finitude that facilitates "the transition [...] through which the progress through the complete series of forms comes about of itself."[45] Blanchot reformulates the work's negativity not by denying the dialectical unfolding of spirit or the existence of particular works or projects, but by investigating the potential of turning the work into the very absence of the work, by putting the work to work *at* worklessness. Blake and Kierkegaard prove exemplary in this respect, as each dwells on a mode of inauguration that is not simply the start of a project but rather precisely the reversal of work and preface. The work-as-preface in Blake and Kierkegarrd *is* the work of the absence of (the) work that Blanchot describes. For, as Blanchot insists, the work's becoming-absent relies on a return to its own origin understood not as what is most proper to it but as a radical exclusion: "The work says the word *beginning*," and yet "in itself it remains mysterious, excluded from the initiation and exiled from the clear truth."[46] If the division of labour according to a preface/work opposition is supposed to enhance productivity and efficiency, what happens, in these cases, is that prefatory negativity infects labour itself. The preface prevents the work from getting to work. The absolute preface – or the preface under its abyssal rather than positive, productive aspect – performs the work of work's absence, where this means neither work nor non-work, but the work *of* idleness, of putting work to work against itself.

This "absence of the work" emerges in another way in *Milton*'s fraught relationship to its own originating materials. On the one hand, the poem actively and explicitly pursues an apocalyptic vision, ending with a terrifying crescendo that seems to teeter on the brink of the End:

> Rintrah & Palamabron view the Human Harvest beneath
> Their Wine-presses & Barnes stand open; the Ovens are prepar'd
> The Waggons ready: terrific Lions & Tygers sport & play

> All Animals upon the Earth, are prepard in all their strength
> To go forth to the Great Harvest & Vintage of the Nations[.][47]

On the other hand, the poem blurs the division of labour it thematizes. Blake's treatment of time, as we saw in chapter 6, offered a way to read this self-conflicting gesture as a case study in Romantic prophecy where the work of history is, likewise, trapped in its traumatic past. The preceding chapter concluded with a discussion of how time in *Milton* becomes autonomous, how it fractures into qualitatively different temporal structures, eludes regulation, and becomes "Wild." Rather than a tool to measure things other than itself, this wild time is concerned first with its own life and growth. In stark contrast to Newtonian abstract or universal time, "Wild Thyme" in Blake produces qualitatively different sorts of itself. Again, we are dealing not with a single substance called "time" that could be cut up into different units or used as a mechanism for measuring something outside itself; rather, time is a temporal multiplicity, different forms of which correlate to qualitatively different states and structures. This would make it a mistake to treat time as some kind of common denominator that might mitigate traumatic negativity by absorbing all events into the same system. When Blake calls time "the mercy of Eternity" this comfort is really a delusion of Beulah.[48] Schelling's treatment of time's internal differences in *Ages of the World* is similar and has an analogous effect on how the work of historiography gets snagged in rather than clarified by temporality. That is, for Schelling, "*Eternity itself begets time in order to resolve the deadlock it became entangled in.*"[49] *Ages*, like Blake's major prophecies, seems at first to aspire to a total picture of history. Indeed, it invokes the standard prophetic historiography where the future will be unfolded on the basis of a comprehensive explication of the past and the present. However, the text succumbs to a persistent counterplot where time's ability to ameliorate onto-theological contradictions proves instead to intensify those contradictions. Like the turbulent state Blake calls "Milton," Schelling's history becomes the displacement of the states it describes; like Shelley's *Hellas*, *Ages* performs rather than simply describes this prophetic revision; and like Kierkegaard's *Prefaces*, the work proper is endlessly folded back into the preface to itself, into an action of starting that can never really begin.

"the question of all the ages"

The three ages of Schelling's *Ages of the World* never resolve themselves into an unproblematic narrative of progression despite the implicit promise of coherence contained in the past, present, future structure into which his project, in its introduction, is broken. Schelling parallels forms of knowledge and means of expression with these ages: "The past is known, the present is discerned, the future is intimated. The known is narrated, the discerned is presented, the intimated is prophesied."[50] This tidy logic that treats prophecy as a form of prediction and reinforces a broader sense of order among temporalities becomes, however, fatally complicated when Schelling enters into a closer analysis of the past. Ultimately, to what extent can "narration" express the past when the beginning is a form of intense negativity? For "the beginning," says Schelling, "really only lies in the negation. [...] It is a negation of the starting point and the actually emerging moment is an overcoming of this negation [...]. Negation is [...] the necessary precedent (*prius*) of every movement. [...] What wants to grow must foreshorten itself and hence, negation is the first transition whatsoever from nothing to something."[51] Later on, this past is characterized in fact not as the "known" but, rather, as precisely what is *un*known: "There is no dawning of consciousness (and precisely for this reason no consciousness) without positing something past. There is no consciousness without something that is at the same time excluded and contracted."[52] Indeed, "left to itself, nature would still lead everything back into that state of utter negation."[53] Hence, the past, as the ground of consciousness – as something that is absolutely past in the sense that it was never once present, ever – is unconscious, even as it enables knowledge and, in fact, forestalls God's psychosis by incarcerating the ground that He contains but is non-identical with. In other words, in the preface to Schelling's *Ages*, the text projects a linear historical and narrative ordering in terms that imply a regular progression from past to present to future; but, when it comes to unfolding the work proper, consciousness seems unable to move forward, as it does so confidently in Hegel, or elude the spectre of regression.

Especially in the third version of *Ages*, Schelling remains committed to the promise of total vision, imagining a future when something like Blake's illuminated book will successfully unfold the unity of the real and ideal in a positive philosophy of revelation. For Slavoj Žižek, the third iteration of Schelling's text is less interesting than the second because it aims for a "compromise formation" that would tame the more radical sense, foregrounded in the second version, of freedom's (and God's) internal contradictions by introducing a split between positive and negative philosophy.[54] Yet, while Žižek is disappointed by this retreat from paradox, it is the key operation for an analysis of prophecy's ostensibly regulative function. The third version of *Ages* is thus the most important version for the present study. In his preface to the first book of *Ages*, "The Past," Schelling says quite confidently that his text "contains some preparation for that future objective presentation of science."[55] At the same time, with a curious sort of hesitation, he describes that presentation as something messianically to-come when he muses, "Perhaps the one is still coming who will sing the greatest heroic poem, grasping in spirit something for which the seers of old were famous: what was, what is, what will be. But this time has not yet come."[56] Like the conventional reading of *Milton*'s timeframe, Schelling places his own work in the instant immediately preceding Revelation. Yet, upon closer inspection this instant is not as pregnant as initially supposed. Just as *Milton*'s additive and organizing exigency displaces total vision and perfect redemption – for if Milton redeems himself it is not by achieving a unified or greater selfhood but precisely by entering into the state of radical re-stating, otherwise called self-annihilation – so too does Schelling's effort to unify "the world of thought and the world of actuality" suggest that that unification is always only a provisional arrangement: pro-visional taken in the double sense of prophetically intimated (rather than knowingly narrated) as well as temporary (rather than permanent).[57] Schelling finds it impossible to follow his initial plan and winds up trapped in the beginning. Failing to work out from its own age, the book of "The Past" – or what could be called Schelling's absolute preface to absolute history – radiates worklessness, undermining anything like the actual "recollection of the primordial beginning of things" through a reading of "history according to its external forms."[58]

The text not only makes this point in the content of its argument but also in its form. Jason Wirth points out that "Schelling composed multitudinous versions of *Die Weltalter*, including numerous versions of the first book (*The Past*)" – there were, in fact, "more than twelve quite different handwritten versions of the first book."[59] At the level of textual production, this difficulty with beginning the system recalls Blake's Lambeth period. While the same or similar names of characters reappear in a series of works – *America, Europe, The Song of Los, The Book of Los, The Song of Ahania*, etc. – there is no sense of global development, no sense that characters remember their history from one text to the next. Nor is there a clear sense of a shared or stable universe. While it may be safe to associate, say, Orc with revolutionary violence, Urizen with oppression, Los with art, these types remain abstract precisely in the Hegelian sense. In effect, then, Blake and Schelling's continual rewriting performs materially the kind of "rotatory movement" the latter describes as the (an)archaic foundation of being.[60] For Schelling, "the first nature is, with regard to itself, in contradiction."[61] This is because there are three mutually excluding original forces or "potencies" that constitute the primordial scene of metaphysical reality. For there to be any kind of development, Schelling reasons, there must be an original opposition, an originary difference that would create the conditions *for* differentiation and therefore, eventually, knowledge of this. Based on the threefold nature of God as [1]"the outpouring, outstretching, self-giving being, [...] [2] an equivalently eternal force of selfhood, of retreat into itself, of Being in itself," and [3] the unity of these two principles, Schelling offers a triadic model of "the eternal Yes," the "eternal No," and a "third term or the unity of the Yes and the No."[62]

While each of these potencies "has the same claim to be that which has being," each claim is urged against the claim of the other two.[63] The result is a temporal pattern of promotion and relegation. While the potencies are "equipotent," still "a Before and an After," a "prior and posterior [...] between the forces" must emerge, otherwise there would be nothing but eternal stasis – something denied by human experience.[64] Like the strangely "unprolific" offering that inaugurates *Milton*, Schelling argues that "the beginning only really lies in the negation," where negativity is understood as "not a mere feebleness or lack in the being, but active negation": "that God negates itself, restricts its being, and withdraws into itself, is the eternal force and might of God."[65] Indeed, we ought not to forget that *The [First] Book of Urizen* plays, as noted above, a special role within *Milton*. *Urizen* is Blake's Genesis, the book describing the origination of the universe. Interpolated within *Milton*, *Urizen* finally becomes the "first book" it was originally billed as. Through seven "Ages" that parallel the seven days of creation, the text describes the formation of Urizen as a "State of dismal woe."[66] This is the created state Orc attacks crudely and physically when he "stamp[s] to dust" the "Stony law" but that Milton overcomes spiritually through self-annihilation.[67] Like Schelling's primordial history, Blake's Urizen is a state of internal violence; from "hot burning" globules to the "deep darkness & petrified" organs of a growing form, we come eventually not to a healthy organism but rather a life in "ghastly torment sick" growing ever more both "Enraged & stifled."[68] Origination is here described as torturous, even strangely mortifying, elaborating the same affect that radical creation has for Schelling.

Because negation is the primordial act of existence, positive evolution will never escape its depressing influence. Schelling's foundations are, like Jerusalem's, perpetually "laid in ruins." While the order of the potencies can be established as the No, the Yes, and the unity of No and Yes, Schelling thus sees this continuum of progressive amelioration as not a Hegelian spiral but a circle: "That originary, necessary, and abiding life hence ascends from the lowest to the highest. Yet when it has arrived at the highest, it retreats immediately back to the beginning in order again to ascend from it."[69] What follows is a perfectly Urizenic picture of chaos. The "unremitting movement that goes back into itself and recommences" constitutes an "annular drive," an ongoing contest between each potency's *mere being* and each potency's desire to *have being*, wherein

> There is only an unremitting wheel, a rotatory movement that never comes to a standstill and in which there is no differentiation. Even the concept of the

> beginning, as well as the concept of the end, again sublimates itself in this circulation. There is certainly a beginning of the potency in accordance with its inherent possibility, but this is not an actual beginning. An actual beginning is only one that posits itself as not having being in relationship to that which should actually be. But that which could be the beginning in this movement does not discern itself as the beginning and makes an equal claim with the other principles to be that which has being.[70]

Recalling the tide-like rhythms of Shelley's *Hellas* and *Triumph of Life*, as well as Kierkegaard and Blake's serial prefacing, nature for Schelling acts as "an allegory of this perpetually advancing and retreating movement": "One generation comes, the other goes. Nature goes through the trouble to develop qualities, aspects, works, and talents to their pinnacle, only again to bury them for centuries in oblivion, and then start anew."[71]

Nevertheless, as the progressivism of his introduction suggests, Schelling attempts to illustrate how historical, actual progression finally does break from the orbit of this annular drive. He does so by developing a concept of existential temporalities that emerge under the auspices of the eternal Godhead – temporalities that, as in Koselleck's analysis, will fracture the purely cyclical concept of revolution and introduce qualitative change. Specifically, "the blind obsession and craving of the first [nature] only grows silent before something higher."[72] This "Other that is outside" the "insensate movement" of rotation is able to convince the potencies to form a truce since it offers a state of being that is more attractive to all but identical to none.[73] The Godhead's strange ontological status as "that which in itself neither has being nor does not have being" is, specifically, an example of blissful "pure equivalence (indifference)" – that is, not passivity or ignorance but a kind of distilled calmness, a Zen-like "will that wills nothing" and therefore does not suffer.[74] Indeed, the Godhead acts as a salve: "That which is higher, magically, so to speak, rouses in that life [i.e., the "eternally commencing" life of the potencies] the yearning for freedom. The obsession [*Sucht*] abates into yearning [*Sehnsucht*], wild desire turns into a yearning to ally itself, as if it were its own true or highest self, with the will that wills nothing, with eternal freedom."[75] Put differently, the Godhead performs a cut and projects – or perhaps abjects – the potencies, creating in this instant the distinction between God's ground as nature (necessity) and God's essence as spirit (freedom). Or, in Žižek's psychoanalytic formulation, this is the move from drive to desire. This distinction is also essentially temporal. The Godhead puts the cyclical itinerary of the annular drive into the Past, into the unconscious, absolute prehistory of history: a past that was never present even once, a past that comes into being *as* past. At the same time this scission opens up an absolute future, one that comes into being *as* future. Like Ahasuerus' evocation of a ghostly, paradoxical "incarnation" of the future in *Hellas*, this is a future always to-come, truly open because it can never – not even in the future – be narrated. In contrast to the compulsive existence of the annular drive, "yearning nature has in itself the possibility to come to Being, to subject [...], to the stuff of actualization"[76]; and yet the future in which this possibility glimpses its own actuality remains, at this point, purely formal.

"How the pure Godhead, in itself neither having being nor not having being, can have being is the question of all the ages."[77] The question, in other words, of how the Godhead can be both indifferent (pure potential) and actual (determinate) at the same time – how God can be actual–potential – is a question that the division into eternal and yet temporally differentiated Ages is supposed to explain. Schelling argues that it is not at all paradoxical to suggest that different times exist, in their difference from one another, at the same time. Time for Schelling is problematically related to representation, as he hints at in his turn, near the end of *Ages*, toward the positive philosophy. Typically, it would be correct to think of eternity not as a very long time but as *outside* time altogether. This is why St Augustine says it is absurd to ask what God was doing *before* the creation of the universe, since Creation includes the creation of time – and so of any "before" or "after" – itself. But Schelling thinks of time as enfolding eternity. He argues, for instance, that "the true eternity does not exclude all time but rather contains time (eternal time) subjugated within itself. Actual eternity is the overcoming of time";[78] "It is not empty (abstract) eternity, but that which contains time subjugated within itself."[79] Eternity is not merely separated from but includes, exceeds, and overflows time; eternity is time plus time's outside. As Žižek puts it, "Eternity is not a modality of time; it is rather time itself that is a specific mode (or rather modification) of eternity."[80] Hence, it is not absurd to refer to the negating potency as "eternal beginning" for Schelling, as the eternal is now a modification of what is an essentially temporal predicament.[81] The eternal – God Himself – can have a beginning in the sense of a qualitative distinction from His eternal present or eternal future. And yet that beginning is never or was never completely *within* time. So, there is a *beginning* that is *eternal* in the sense that it would, from time's point of view, span and include all punctual instants while remaining non-present. This is close to how Blake imagines the infinite within the finite, the eternal in the temporal: as Isaiah says in *The Marriage of Heaven and Hell*, from the right perspective he "discover'd the infinite in every thing."[82]

Time is especially important to Schelling for how it helps to navigate the ontological conflicts in God's historical revelation. For instance, we reach "the highest conceivable contradiction," says Schelling, when God, if He is to reveal

Himself, must accord being both to the Yes and the No – God's power of positive revelation and His power to abstain from the limitations that attend any determination – at the same time: a blatant contradiction that can be ameliorated "only though a closer determination of it."[83] God must be both actual (and thus submit to the necessities of nature) and yet remain somehow also, and at the same time, free. Time proves to be the key that allows Schelling's God to have it both ways. The Absolute, he reasons, can indeed *have being* simultaneously as "the No and the Yes" if "one of them is prior, as ground, and the other is posterior, as grounded."[84] In this reasoning, the No is the ground of the Yes or is the abyssal (un)grounding that is the condition for any grounding whatever. Hence, if "God as the Yes and God as the No cannot have being *at the same time*," God can have His being as both at different times.[85] The trick is that *these different times* can exist *simultaneously*: "If A is posited, then B must simply still persist *as the prior*, and hence, in such a way, that they are nonetheless at the same time, *in different times*."[86] We might imagine Schelling speaking with Blake's voice: "Time is the mercy of Eternity; without Times swiftness/ Which is the swiftness of all things: all were eternal torment."[87]

Treating time this way means that the Yes – God's positive revelation – gains a degree of consistency or stability, although it is never completely free from the dissolving ground of the No. Indeed, Schelling refers to the same physiological process as Blake in order to describe this organization of the negative and positive into past and future: namely, pulsation. Both Schelling and Blake rewrite God's complicated ontology as human physiology, in effect incarnating eternity while also spiritualizing incarnation. Schelling's use of the analogy is similar to Blake's and both stand opposed to apocalyptic atemporality. As noted in the last chapter, Blake imagines history's apocalypse as a single spasm, though we cannot measure the length of time equal to this pulsation. Apocalypse remains therefore always in the future:

> For in this Period the Poets Work is Done: and all the Great
> Events of Time start forth & are conceived in such a Period
> Within a Moment: a Pulsation of the Artery.[88]

According to Paul Tillich, "While chronos designates the continuous flux of time, kairos points out a significant moment of time [...], unique moments in the temporal process, moments in which something unique can happen or be accomplished."[89] Blake does seem drawn to this concept of a time that is specially enriched or that stands out from secular history's narrative levelling. Others have described this moment – like that in which Milton enters "Blake's" left foot in *Milton* – as epiphany.[90] Yet, this would restrict the moment to an intellectual or cognitive event. Kairos, by contrast, marks a change in the forms of time itself. Blake stresses this latter notion by describing the moment of potential renovation as a "Moment in each Day that Satan cannot find," as something existing in time's own nature and structure that remains, in the terms of chapter 6, virtual: that is, actual and yet more than the actual, irreducible to a tabulation of what is.[91] Indeed, that this moment is "in *each day*" goes some way to dispelling the apocalyptic tone of the great "Pulsation of the Artery." This potentiality, existing in the being of time, is thus both revolutionary and yet non-final: the moment does not signal the last day so much as a kind of lasting, a revolutionary potency that both changes history in unforeseeable ways and yet remains resolutely historical in this changing.

Schelling's consideration of pulsation illustrates something similar; for him, it is impossible to invoke this process as an image of perfect totality since the heart's rhythm involves two equipotent, opposed, and sequentially ordered forces. According to Schelling, the temporal organization of the potencies into a prior and a posterior

> can be represented as a systole and a diastole. This is a completely involuntary movement that, once begun, makes itself from itself. The recommencing, the re-ascending is systole, tension that reaches its acme in the third potency. The retreat to the first potency is diastole, slackening, upon which a new contraction immediately follows. Hence, this is the first pulse, the beginning of that alternating movement that goes through the entirety of visible nature, of the eternal contraction and the eternal re-expansion, of the universal ebb and flow.[92]

According to this logic, Blake's appeal to a pulmonary temporality to "organize" the history of his artistic work, similar to his effort in *Urizen*, cannot be successfully totalizing, at least not in the mode of apocalypse. Like other attempts in *Milton* to order its prefatory materials – "for each matter only flourishes when it is in its place,"[93] says Schelling, sounding rather like Blake – the operation of pulsation, suggesting a literally vital historical process and works actively against apocalyptic arrest.

Does this mean that Schelling's organization of time manages successfully to ameliorate the kinds of contradictions he and Blake identify between nature and spirit, between finite sense and infinite perception? Or, does "advancing" the contradiction in this way indicate, rather, that there is no final resolution? The fact is that Schelling's description of different times remains unresolved and irresolvable. For, in what sense can something be said to *have being* when the condition in which it can have that being is, say, the past or the future – that is, a condition that itself *does not have being*? As Jason Wirth observes, we "can speak of the Being of what has being (presence) and the being of what does not, *strictu sensu*, 'have' being," namely, "the past, the future."[94] In fact, the having-being of the No *is* being's negation: the No has its being as that which annihilates being. So, if time allows God to move out of pure indifference (i.e., the state of neither having nor not having being), the actuality of the Yes is countered by the activated negation of the No. The goal will not be, then, to find a way for the No and the Yes to *have* being at the same time, since the No never really has being: its having-being is identical to its negation of determinate existence. Rather, the aim is to think of a way to place the No and Yes into a relation that does not instantly deteriorate into static contradiction, something Schelling hints at when he overlaps temporal succession with the logic of the "ground" and "grounded." Time is a way to insulate the Yes from the corrosive power of the No without necessarily separating the two. Hence, the past becomes the (un) ground of the future. Time offers Schelling not so much a conduit from age to age as a way to quarantine the No from the Yes, to elude the perpetual suspension of the actual that happens in Kierkegaard's irony when the No "has its being" as active negation, such that the positive unfolding of the Godhead (the Yes) is not immediately annulled. The No, then, is not simply past (for it never was in the present, never made past by time's passage) but an absolute past, is always already past, or forms the absolute preface to history as God's "proper work." And yet, this past coincides with the Yes of the present: the No is distinct from but never more or less distant, as it were, from the Yes; really, they are coeval. Again, as the ground–grounded logic suggests, the two terms maintain a symbiotic relationship. Hence, with the concept of "different times" Schelling can imagine the Absolute as assuming being in all its forms – even if those forms are mutually cancelling – at the same time, because the different times, in which the Absolute has different forms of being, are, themselves, "different, at the same time, nay, to speak more accurately, they [i.e., the different times and, *ergo*, the forms of being in those times] are necessarily at the same time."[95]

This problem of temporality's coordination with actuality and possibility finds another mode of expression in Schelling's attempt to unify and yet compartmentalize God through the process of historicization. As Tilottama Rajan notes, "Schelling's sense of history in the 1813 *Ages*, as a process of 'constantly re-embody[ing]' 'archetypes' that are visions of 'the innermost thoughts of God' and 'visions of future things'" continues in the 1815 version as well.[96] For instance, toward the beginning of Part B – a section that reverts to the beginning of Part A in an effort to detail more clearly the "life of the individual potency" – Schelling describes a deep connectivity between the opposed forces, suggesting that even within the primordial night of contraction there is something that reaches out and "seeks in a natural way to attract its higher self."[97]

However, just as Blake's *Milton* is hyper-organized such that each particular "organ" tries to determine the text absolutely, ensuring, ironically, that the work never quite merges into a full body, so does Schelling overdetermine his dialectic of forces. For instance, the negating potency develops psychoanalytically into the unconscious, the grounding alterity that is abjected in the moment that consciousness emerges: "There is no dawning of consciousness (and precisely for this reason no consciousness) without positing something past. There is no consciousness without something that is at the same time excluded and contracted."[98] Hence, we move with this psychology also into history, for "the unconscious is posited as the *past* of consciousness."[99] Then, on top of this determination, Schelling will also formulate his distinction in terms of a difference between spirit and nature: "In nature, the spirit knows itself as the one who *was* because it posits nature as its *eternal* past."[100] So, the unity of the whole system will demand quilting points that function in these different though overlapping registers of psychology (unconscious/conscious), history (past/future), and metaphysics (nature/spirit). Enter the language of "types." Thinking "typically" provides a medium in which to formulate temporal sedimentation, a *lingua franca* that makes sense within and across the different systems involved. This terminology, moreover, marks Schelling's attempt to deliver on the predictive prophecy of his introduction.

In an effort to propel history out of its past, Schelling argues that something like the future inheres within primordial negation in the form of a prototype: "The soul, awakening from the depths of the unconscious, does not accomplish its graduated course without higher guidance. For already in its first awakening it is deeply stirred by the dark intimation that its actual model is in the world of spirits."[101] Schelling casts the differentiated ages of the world into a scene of desire where "everything prototyptical" is "pulled toward its ectype" as if "through a natural and irresistible inclination."[102] In a strange way, this regressive trajectory becomes, ultimately, progressive. As "the higher order (A^2) is pulled toward nature [i.e., A^1], it is pulled away in the same proportion from its superior order (from the A^3)."[103] The prototype's attraction to its "earlier" self generates, out of this very regression, a coincident progression by activating the attraction of its own higher potency to itself. When a potency retreats, it creates a vacuum into which its prototype is consequently drawn. In essence, Schelling repeats the logic of the 1813 version of *Ages* where "history develops unproblematically through nature as a 'ladder of formations' that is still conceived as a prophetic poem, in which the 'creative spirit' sees the 'spirits of things' and 'make[s] them corporeal' so as to 'unfold a complete image of the future world.'"[104] With this rhythm, where history ascends through spiritual peristalsis, the Godhead, Schelling notes, "beh[olds], as if in a glimpse or vision, the entire ladder of future formations."[105] However, a closer look at this "ladder" suggests that there is some doubt about the completeness of this transition from possibility to actuality. This, in turn, casts doubt on the appeal to predictive prophecy as an attempt to determine the future.

The predictive sedimentation of types begins to unravel "in the being of the second potency or of that which is the substratum of the spirit world."[106] Reviewing how the ages are ordered by types, Schelling notes,

> As the spirit world is the prototype of nature and all things of this external world are depictions of what nature beheld in the inner world, so, in turn, that universal soul is the immediate prototype of that which is creating the spirit world. What is thereby produced in the spirit world is just the ectype, or what is actual, of that which lay in the universal soul as prototypical or possible.[107]

Nature is the ectype of the spirit world. From the perspective of nature, the spirit world is prototypically embedded in nature and allows nature to reach forward, through obscure prophetic signs, to its higher potentiality. At the same time, the spirit world is the ectype – a less-perfect copy – of the universal soul. From the perspective of the spirit world, the universal soul is prototypically embedded in the spirit world. Arrayed in this manner, the spirit world is the actuality of the universal soul, just as the universal soul is the possibility of the spirit world. Similarly, nature is the actuality of the spirit world just as the spirit world is the possibility of nature. The middle term, or the spirit world, is under one aspect the *prototype* of nature, a mere *potentiality* toward which nature tends. Under another aspect, however, the same spirit world is the *ectype* of the universal soul, is the *actuality* that grounds the potential. Put more starkly, this means that the middle, mediating term or A^2 located between nature (A^1: necessity, unconscious, past) and the Godhead (A^3: possibility, consciousness, future) turns out to be *actual and potential at the same time*. Recalling the language of the last chapter, A^2 is a virtual state. It is also a similar, if more convoluted, formulation of Blake's impossible history. To say that the historical present is *both* actual *and* possible inverts but maintains a Blakean sense that the actual is a deeply fractured field of forces irreducible to a narrative of the probable and possible; in *both* having being *and* not having being, actual history overflows the limitations that would attend it as *either* merely actual (unchangeable) *or* merely possible (limited by probability). Schelling here overlaps the potential and the actual such that the contradiction between the two locates the abyss of freedom within history. In his refusal, however, to annul the uncanny contradiction of this situation – the actual is in no simple way provisional here but just as robust as the potential – Schelling, like Blake, stresses the reality of history's impossibility, a negativity that never disappears in light of positive unfolding.

This uncanny, double identification of the intermediate concept circles back to the problem, noted above, of different times, where the past and future – as dimensions that do not have being – are, strangely, supposed to enable God to have being in different, contradictory ways in different times, while those different times themselves exist at the same time. Schelling, in fact, in what seems like a desperate effort to ensure the possibility of a transition from negative to positive philosophy, suddenly reverses the alignment of ectype-actuality and prototype-potentiality. As if passing through the vortex of the second potency's ambivalent mediation as *both* actual *and* potential, Schelling recasts the moment as *neither* actual *nor* potential. In this way, he projects *actuality* into the future while at the same time retaining the notion that the future is embedded in the present and past *as* actuality. Returning to his distinction between having and not having being, Schelling argues that the "initial life of blind necessity," or the torturous rotation of the potencies, "could not be said to have being because it never actually attained continuance, Being, but rather just remained in striving and desire for Being."[108] This is a surprising statement since, as noted, it seems to turn the actuality of the spirit world's ectype – that is, nature – into a prototype. The Godhead's indifference, which had initially been considered the purest potentiality, begins to look like the only kind of actuality because it is the only real consistency. Ultimately, the *condition of actuality* in which the prototype is supposed to reside, as a potentiality, becomes itself *prototypical* in the face of a *prototype* that has been re-determined as what is most *actual*. Prophecy once again manifests in an irreducibly ambivalent manner that revokes the present as much as it predicts the future.

The notion of different times is supposed to mean God can have being and yet maintain the freedom of neither having nor not having being, insofar as time distances *and* gathers these contradictory positions together. This concept interrupts even as it tries to repair what had been, in Schelling's introduction to *Ages*, the very uniform trajectory from past, to present, to future. If what might have being – God's historical revelation – is posited prophetically in the future, then it is posited as being and not being at the same time. This is because the future itself is determined as not-having-being and yet also as the only dimension wherein being achieves the continuity necessary to achieve actuality. What started as a prophetic itinerary following a restricted economy of prediction begins to look increasingly unstable. The simultaneity within difference or the difference within simultaneity that the concept of different times is supposed to offer – as a way through the *aporia* of God's dual nature, as both necessary and yet also "the most voluntaristic being" – reveals an ontological schizophrenia.[109]

God can have being in mutually exclusive ways only within a system of order (time) that cannot, itself, claim anything but mere being. This makes Schelling's predictive prophecy look remarkably similar to Blanchot's prophecy: the retraction of actuality, the evacuation of presence. The mechanics of how these ages are supposed to be embedded in each other reveals also that, within the tissue of prophetic connectivity – that is, within the logic of ectype and prototype – the potentiality usually associated with the future reverses position with the past's usual association with actuality. Schelling's prophetic prototype becomes indistinguishable from ectypal regression, such that the actuality of God's revelation in the future can be confirmed only insofar as this assurance revokes nature's actuality, or subtracts the past that is supposed to be the unconscious ground of consciousness, the absolute Past that is supposed to open the eternal Future.

Chapter Eight

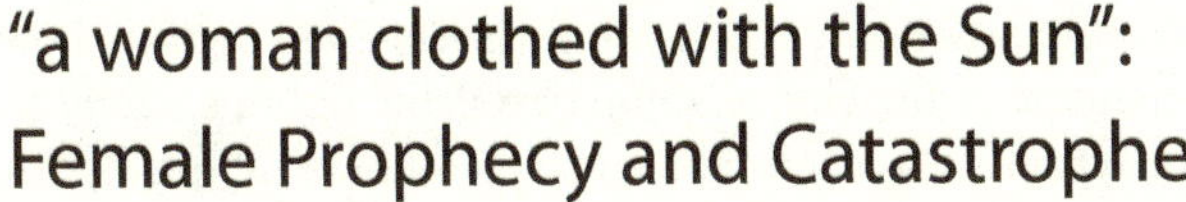

"a woman clothed with the Sun": Female Prophecy and Catastrophe

"The apocalypse is disappointing"

Maurice Blanchot

When Blake's Milton descends from Eternity, he strips from himself layer after layer of confining dress. "I come," he announces,

in Self-annihilation & the grandeur of Inspiration
To cast off Rational Demonstration by Faith in the Saviour
To cast off the rotten rags of Memory by Inspiration
To cast off Bacon, Locke & Newton from Albions covering
To take off his filthy garments, & clothe him with Imagination
To cast aside from Poetry, all that is not Inspiration[.][1]

This divestment cleanses the doors of perception by eliminating ideas and ideals that, held in high esteem by the named "Enlightened" figures, are in fact but "The Poison of the Honey Bee."[2] This sceptical attitude toward ostensible goods – rational demonstration, memory, Enlightened philosophy – suggests that Blake has a complicated relationship to Romantic utopianism. Specifically, there is a line of thinking that says the best kind of utopia is a dystopia, since it works to illustrate the limitations of an imagination conceived on a strictly empirical, indeed Lockean, model of combination. Dystopia shows us the weakness of our own ability to imagine difference as really different. In Fredric Jameson's words, if normally our "imaginations are hostages to our own mode of production" then "the best Utopia can serve the negative purpose of making us more aware of our mental and ideological imprisonment," or "the best Utopias are those that fail the most comprehensively" because in them the prevailing modes of production get exposed and terminated.[3] Failure here would mark a kind of advance over fantasy. Positive utopia merely reproduces the future through what is established as possible and probable; in the absence of a radical event, even the utopian will remain limited to being the inverse of the status quo, and so basically continuous with the past. For Blake, this would reduce utopia to the same dull round as the history produced by historians. Failed utopia, however, illustrates this very limiting of the imagination and exposes how disabling "freedom," reduced to the choice among available options, really is. To be more precise: the type of art most interesting would not be simply dystopia, that is, the depiction of a horrible future. The more significant formulation is *dystopic utopia* – a utopia that, in its very perfection, proves to be dystopic. In such texts, the ideal of the political imagination is fully realized; like the Classical phase of art in Hegel's *Aesthetics*, there is no problem with the adequacy of the idea's embodiment.[4] Yet, this very adequacy of realization makes it possible to see how far short the idea or ideal itself falls.

Understood in this way, a failed utopia forms a background against which radical newness comes into sharper focus. In this context, certain representations of the end of history are, then, politically effective – in spite of apparently transcending politics – if they work out to completion dominant ideas of the political and social sphere in ways that make possible new conditions for imagination. Achieving the full embodiment of a prevailing ideal, even fictionally, is a way of exhausting that same ideal. We saw this, for example, in Blake's *Milton*. Because *Paradise Lost* is so successful in presenting its theodicy, because it is the most complete and nuanced expression of Divine justice according to Christian orthodoxy, it becomes possible, subsequently, to establish its systemic limitations and, so, to open a totally new space for thinking about subjectivity, ethics, inspiration, faith, and history. Blake can shatter *Paradise Lost* because Milton crystallizes his vision so completely. Writing the failure of utopia can, then, reorient the discussion of social conflicts by recalibrating fundamental ideas about the good. As social and political reality changes, the basic idea of what is or is not the ideal good – what is or is not the ideal state: what is heaven, what hell – will need revision. Indeed, this revision may become so thoroughgoing that previously progressive positions are seen as comparatively regressive. Such a pattern emerges, for instance, in Blake's shifting reactions to the French Revolution. In 1789, like so many observing enthusiasts, for Blake "the French Revolution was the herald of the Millennium"; after 1792, however, he "tore off his white cockade, and assuredly never wore the red cap again."[5] The necessity for deep, personal revision can be clarified by repeatedly asking rather simple but important questions such as: Who decides what is good? For whom is this good really good? What is good about the good? It is into this field of concerns that Mary Shelley's *The Last Man* makes its intervention. This is a text that presents, sequentially, utopia, then dystopia, then ultimately utopia's dystopian reality. Reread through the lens of the dystopic latter half of the book, the preceding, utopian story is unmasked as, in fact, a sinister ideal, one that has to be exposed before a new future – beyond either dystopia or conventional utopia – is possible. Like Blake's Milton, Shelley's utopian patriarchs descend from eternity, become emphatically mortal, and enact a painfully literal sort of self-annihilation. This opens the future to a minimal sort of optimism by promising a history that is beyond prediction and knowledge – a history that is outside of the history of "man," what Maurice Blanchot in *Le Dernier Homme* also quietly approaches.

But before getting to the last man we have to begin with Shelley's first women. In contrast to Blake's optimistic rewriting of the English Revolution as self-annihilation in *Milton*, Shelley's prophetess, Beatrice, in *Valperga, or, the Life and Adventures of Castruccio, Prince of Lucca,* aligns prophetic prospecting with violent bondage. Shelley's treatment of prophecy in *Valperga* and *The Last Man* appears, indeed, deeply pessimistic. It is bad enough that prophecy is figured as predictive and binding; but, in addition, the particular future to which history is bound – in *Valperga*, personal history, in *The Last Man*, world history – is decidedly unhappy. Expanding on the question of prophecy and gender also touched on by Kant in his allusion to Tiresias,[6] Shelley stresses how prophecy is the form that restriction, punishment, and regulation often take when women, especially, attempt to assert historical agency. Yet, Shelley does not, ultimately, understand prophecy only as a repressive discourse. Read as failed utopia – as immanently dystopic utopia – her works remain intellectually closer to those Romantics for whom prophecy is a drive for renovation, a vitality expressed in the face of a new future where the stress lay not on determining that future but on revealing the tenuousness of prevailing norms. Specifically, *The Last Man,* rather than just materializing the violence of the prophetic imagination – introduced in *Valperga* – in the form of the plague, embodies a Blakean, revisionary power, the sort that hesitates to produce total or final visions. So, while Morton Paley is surely correct that the imagination in *The Last Man* "presents itself as a saviour only to be revealed as a creator of phantasms," we should add that if the plague presents itself as the end of a Romantic ideology, the fictional editor's preface reveals this end as yet another kind of phantom.[7] In its effort to think its own termination, the imagination does not – cannot – die but is, rather, spurred to reinvent itself. Yet, the mood in which Shelley approaches this reinvention is remarkably subdued. The journey to the end of man is coloured neither by Beatrice's anger nor Blake's human vitality but rather a silent, almost passive contemplation: neither pessimistic nor optimistic.

Blake's state of re-stating is, as discussed earlier, ultimately liberating since it names that minimal gap in the putatively totalized state that keeps it open to more than superficial change. The essence of the prophetic imagination in *Milton* is not the establishment of some final form but perpetual revolution, to which the "redeemed" subject is joyfully vulnerable. However, Shelley's prophetess in *Valperga*, Beatrice, is denied any such (re)creative possibilities. In spite of genuine clairvoyance, Beatrice is made to disbelieve her powers and exiles herself in despair, only to be kidnapped, tortured, and enslaved. In other words, "holy women with pretensions to charismatic power have always provoked fear along with awe," and the narrative in *Valperga* aims to limit Beatrice's power by using prophecy as a form of punishment that leads, literally, to confinement.[8] In this respect, Beatrice's fate recalls that of the Cumaean Sibyl who frames *The Last Man*, reducing prophecy to what Ernst Bloch identifies as a "passive type of augury."[9] The Sibyl resembles Cassandra who "could only foresee the curse of the Atrides, without being able, by any appeal for conversion, to forestall it."[10] Classical scholars believe that the figure of Cassandra shades into the figure of the Sibyl, suggesting that we might more precisely identify Shelley's prophetesses as versions of Cassandra.[11] This opens a line of thought that provides a crucial, specific context for Anne Mellor's argument that *Valperga* demonstrates "the inability of women, whether adoring worshippers (like Beatrice) or active leaders (like Euthanasia) to influence political events or to translate an ethic of care – whether embodied in the domestic affections or in a political program of universal justice and peace – into historical reality."[12]

In *Sibyls and Sibylline Prophecy in Classical Antiquity*, H.W. Parke offers a useful summary of the mythical origin of this archetypal prophet in relation to Apollo and notes the important role sexual difference plays in the development of Cassandrian or sibylline prophecy:

> The theme of the gift of prophecy combined with the curse of failure to convince the hearers may well have been invented for this context [i.e., Aeschylus' *Agamemnon*] in the Epic cycle, but it would be equally useful if attached to Sibylla, who similarly foretold disasters which were never averted. [...]. [Beyond this common curse,] [t]he legend of Apollo, the frustrated lover, is joined [in the case of the Sibyl] with the second motif which we have mentioned – the mistaken prayer for long life, not immortal youth. It appears first in a late narrative in Ovid, who tells in his own vividly sophisticated manner what must have been a long-established legend. The Cumaean Sibyl explains to Aeneas that she is not a goddess, though she has been offered immortality if only she would yield her virginity to Apollo. The god, wooing her, promised her the fulfilment of her wish, and she grasped a handful of sand and asked for as many years as it contained grains. This was

> granted, but she had forgotten to ask for eternal youth. Although she would have obtained that also, if she had yielded herself to him, she refused, and therefore was fated to grow older and older until she had reached the number of the grains of sand. When she was speaking to Aeneas, she had lived seven hundred years and had still three hundred remaining. By then she would have shrunk to the tiniest scale until there was nothing left but her voice.[13]

Like Blake's shadowy female, the sibyl becomes a voice and nothing more.[14] This background frames female prophecy in particular as a curse – and as a specific kind of curse. Apollo imposes this punishment when Cassandra breaks her sexual contract with him. What is remarkable is not that Apollo should retaliate but that his retaliation should consist of eliminating Cassandra's historical agency. Reneging on her promise of sexual favours means that Cassandra is permitted to "conceive" history intellectually but denied the power to bring that conception, as it were, to term. Apollo's curse aborts the productivity of the imagination and denies the materiality of the female body by submitting all historical insight to rigorous limitations that ensure the gestating idea never enters the world of historical actuality. The unnaturally long life the sibyl enjoys only testifies all the more vividly to her infertility. A figure so utterly deprived of a fruitful engagement with the world, Cassandra's protracted existence, like that of the Wandering Jew discussed previously, amounts to a mockery of life, a living death.

The sexual politics of female prophecy is not something confined to Classical myth. Shelley would have been more directly familiar with Joanna Southcott who in 1792, at the age of forty-two, had a religious awakening and a streak of compelling predictions preceding the publication, in 1801, of her first of several books. Southcott was well enough recognized in the early 1800s for "Keats, Southey, Blake and Byron each [to write] disparagingly" of her.[15] Given William Godwin's "intimate friend[ship]" with William Tooke Harwood, one of the "leading figures in the Southcottian movement," it is all the more likely that Shelley was cognizant of the rise of this unusual woman from Devonshire.[16] Indeed, given Shelley's own traumatic experiences with difficult births, Southcott's claim, in 1814 – her sixty-four years of age and virginity notwithstanding – to be pregnant with the Messiah would have been particularly arresting. Could the unnatural labours of Victor Frankenstein, written about two years later, owe anything to Southcott's sensational claim? Might Southcott have informed Shelley's depiction of Wilhelmina of Bohemia, the leader of a feminist sect and virgin mother of Beatrice in *Valperga*? Or could the public display of Southcott's body – that is, the widely published details of her examination by doctors and, eventually, records of her autopsy – could this policing of the prophetess' body by "enlightened" sceptics, be reflected in Beatrice's incarceration and subjective dissection?[17] As Juster remarks, "The ritual defilement of the prophetesses's dead body, like the examination of [the] body for signs of criminality and sexual deviance, stand as a fitting symbol of the fate of the mystical female body in the Age of Enlightenment."[18] That this fourteenth-century character, Beatrice, might, as Emily W. Sunstein asserts, be "drawn from Joanna Southcott" makes additional sense in that Southcott stands out from the veritable pantheon of eighteenth-century prophets by hearkening back to a concept of the mystical body popular in the early modern era in which *Valperga* is set.[19] From roughly the twelfth to the fifteenth century, "the intense physicality of female piety" was commonly expressed by "ecstatic nosebleeds and weepings, periodic stigmatic bleedings, mystical lactations" and other such phenomena indicative of the "extreme porousness" of women's bodies. But by the late eighteenth century this "grotesque" female body faced a "campaign to tame and domesticate the inspired behavior of women by 'sealing up the female body through the maintenance of virginity, a more strictly cloistered life, and rigid control over the visible self.'"[20] Southcott, like Blake, is thus a prophet both ahead of and behind her times.

Control over the visible self is precisely what satirists like Charles Williams, Thomas Rowlandson, and George Cruikshank sought to exercise through their caricatures of Southcott. For instance, in Rowlandson's "A Medical Inspection. Or Miracles Will Never Cease," a grossly caricatured Southcott hikes up her petticoats before three ogling doctors. "Aged 64/ Bladders of Corruption/ and Blasphemy Sealed up and/ Ready to Burst" is stamped on her backside. The aim here is not only to submit Southcott to disciplinary inspection – an inspection by the reading public even more than the doctors, who are themselves extremely caricatured. It is also to make her literally legible and thus subject to the letter of the law. As one overheated critic argued, Southcott enjoys the "inactivity of the law," a freedom afforded by a kind of loophole that fails to hold her accountable for her supposedly damaging though difficult-to-trace influence:

> While the petty thief, and the timid or occasional swindler, are condemned to the house of correction and the pillory, this profane and systematic depredator on the public credulity, this blasphemer of her God, this propagator of every description of indecency and impiety, is permitted to circulate her pamphlets and her tickets, to cajole the dupes of her cunning into the gift of valuable presents, to delude the poor, and cheat the rich, and to become the indirect instrument of fraud and murder.[21]

In the absence, however, of official charges, William N. Jones' satirical periodical, *The Scourge* (1811–16), sought – along with pieces like Rowlandson's – a kind of vigilante justice. Southcott is a central figure of ridicule, especially in the eighth

Figure 5. Doctors inspecting Joanna Southcott, Thomas Rowlandson. "A Medical Inspection. Or Miracles Will Never Cease." Number 111, Cheapside, London: Thomas Tegg, 8 September 1814. British Museum, Satires, 12333. Registration number 1868,0612.1267. © Trustees of the British Museum.

edition (1814), where she features in three elaborate, coloured satirical drawings by Charles Williams and is the much-abused subject of several poems and articles over the course of six published issues.[22]

While she was known popularly for well over a decade, the rise in high-profile attacks on Southcott around 1814 seem correlated to her mystical pregnancy;[23] indeed, many of the satirical images of Southcott from that time are sure to represent her as pregnant.[24] But what is the special danger of this particular stunt? One possibility is that it represents the Frankensteinian prospect of unregulated reproduction. "If Shiloh be in reality enabled to propagate the means of procreation, without the usual intercourse between the sexes" then not only might "barren wives and unfortunate husbands [...] be rejoiced" but so too might this lead down a slippery slope to sexual perversion, as when "The antiquated batchelor [*sic*] of seventy-two, who is tempted by the inclinations of the flesh, to engage in holy matrimony with some seductive female of twenty-one, will no longer be afraid that his labors may prove unproductive."[25] Recalling Kant's fears of monstrous reproduction,[26] Southcott promotes a delusive and dangerous form of self-insemination that ignores the limits of possible knowledge. Moreover, Southcott's claims could be viewed as attacks on the family structure and, with that, on one of the principal institutions through which patriarchal authority is reproduced. She is also routinely accused of charging money for her "seals," guaranteeing heavenly election. As one poetical satire puts it,

Great JOANNA, brother TOZER,
  Chosen from this sinful nation,
Bids you to mankind propose her
  Genuine tickets for salvation.
Call the giddy world, and tell 'em

  They are all of Satan's leaven;
But that, cheap as dirt, you'll sell 'em
  Seals to frank 'em all to Heaven.[27]

While many assaults note Southcott's putative financial gain, the focus is more often on a broader sense of her danger to the community. Indeed, critics were not above accusing Southcott of facilitating the crimes of others who called themselves her followers: "If any evidence were required of the total perversion of understanding and of principle that distinguishes her followers," writes one critic, "it would be found in the history of Mary Bateman, who was executed on Saturday the 18th of March, 1809, for the murder of Mrs. Perigo of Bramley."[28] As when Beatrice gets effectively lumped in with the wicked Fior di Mandragola in *Valperga* – discussed in more detail below – the disciplinary strategy here is to discredit Southcott by associating her with witchcraft.[29]

Southcott's pregnancy could also be seen as especially disconcerting to her critics for how she was able to exercise a kind of veto to male authority as represented by medical doctors such as Richard Reece. "The fact to which we allude is," notes the preface to a brief "Life of Joanna Southcott," "the publication of a letter from Dr Richard Reece, containing a copy of her register, by which it appears she is sixty-five years of age, and a statement that he has himself examined her, and *that she is pregnant!*"[30] In an effort to defend his "professional character" from the "infatuated imposter," Reece, in 1815, published a detailed explanation of how he arrived at and why he publicly defended his diagnosis that Southcott did appear to be pregnant – an explanation that literally dissects her to produce the closest, coldest possible observation in the service of rehabilitating his name.[31] By attacking reputation, Southcott's stunt threatens medicine as an institution. If a poor, basically uneducated woman can place the reputations of highly respected men in danger – not just Reece but several other doctors as well – the question is: who is the real fraud? Indeed, who is more dangerous to society, Southcott – who remains always on the fringe – or those men who are licensed and accredited by the state, allowed to undertake the serious task of diagnosing illness and prescribing remedies? What this episode makes clear is that, at this point in medical history, the empirical analysis of the body faces a crisis of legitimacy – analogous to the sort Southcott herself faced. Medicine has to distance itself from such crises as problems of a pre-Enlightened, unscientific world. Hence, Southcott becomes an especially charged case in the history of medicine's cultural fashioning: for medical doctors to come under the same kind of doubt and scrutiny as a prophet represents a moment of intolerable recognition, of potentially fatal contagion, where the kinds of uncertainty ostensibly eliminated by the new truth of Enlightenment "method" return like the repressed.

Valperga and the Curse of Female Prophecy

The politics of sex and gender that, in different ways, translate potential agency back into regulation for both Southcott and the Cassandra re-emerge brutally in *Valperga*. Beatrice offers a vivid example of how institutions formed by men – whether it is the Inquisition, political state, or hospital – attempt to control charismatic, influential women by laying claim specifically to their bodies. This struggle looms large in Beatrice's own back-story. Beatrice, reared for years in secret, is the child of Wilhelmina (Guglielma) of Bohemia. The historical Wilhelmina founded a religious sect in 1262, though kept this secret so closely guarded that nothing was suspected until eighteen years after her death.

In 1300, the Inquisition denounced her as a heretic following an investigation and executed the living heads of the movement, a woman named Manfreda and a man named Andreas Saramita. The central tenet of the sect was that "as the Word had been incarnate in a Man, so the Holy Spirit had become incarnate in a woman, Guglielma."[32] The implication here is that "all authority has [...] departed from the existing ecclesiastical hierarchy and Boniface VIII is no true pope."[33] The movement also takes a powerfully feminist shape since, as Marjorie Reeves notes, the Guglielmite's "daring logic" insisted that "if the revolution was to be absolute, there must be a new incarnation of the Godhead, and this must be in the opposite sex."[34] In *Valperga*, Castruccio, while preparing to invade Ferrera in the first of several military campaigns to reclaim not only his hometown of Lucca – whence he was as a youth exiled by the Guelphs – but eventually also the castle Valperga on his way to a greater conflict with republican Florence, learns something of this history from the Bishop of Ferrera, an inside agent who supports Castruccio. As they plan the assault, an immediate and intense sympathy forms between the bishop and Castruccio. So, when Castruccio, awed by the beauty and mystery of Beatrice, asks the bishop about her prophetic aspirations, the bishop reveals the secret of her birth. This private history is but one of several that come to supplement and displace the official, male-dominant history with which *Valperga* – insofar as it places Castruccio's life and exploits at its narrative centre – is ostensibly concerned. The first volume of the text centres on Castruccio's boyhood: the death of his father, his education by Frances Guinigi, and his time in Venice which leads to a trip to England. It also details how, after fleeing England for murdering a noble in a fit of pride, Castruccio meets and serves under Alberto Scoto, the exiled former ruler of Piacenza, from whom he imbibes a doctrine of militaristic terrorism and political cunning that – following a kind of latency period wherein Castruccio seems to develop into a noble, moderate, and benevolent young man – later resurfaces. Attesting to this early sensitivity, he is for instance shocked by the excesses of Henry VII's imperial army and resigns from that service. He then spends three years of campaigning "under one or another of the Ghibeline lords" in Lombardy (130), and eventually is able – thanks to various political turns of fortune – to return to a Lucca ripe for the reassertion of Ghibelline authority. Castruccio, putting to use Scoto's training, eventually grows more callous and aggressive, turning "towards the final establishment of the Ghibeline ascendancy" and casting himself as "prince or imperial vicar of Tuscany" (132, 250).

It is, however, at this point in the narrative that Euthanasia de Adimari re-enters, introducing a feminist "plot" into this history of male ambition. Indeed, the vile Battista Tripalda will later complain of Euthanasia's role in the conspiracy to depose Castruccio in language significant for a reading of the novel as a whole: "Women, women! [...] By the body of Bacchus! I wonder what Bondelmonti meant by introducing a woman into the plot!" (414). A foil for Beatrice, Euthanasia is "passionless, yet full of enthusiasm" (134), the "fair" woman who plays off Beatrice's "dark" beauty in a typically gothic mirroring. Through the deaths of her father and brothers she becomes sole heiress to the castle Valperga; as queen, the people under her government prosper and she establishes the fortress as a kind of neutral ground between Castruccio, in whom she sees – better than most – the potential for gracious nobility, and the Florentine republic: her cherished home but the state with which Castruccio is in direct political opposition. As a minor character, Ludovico de'Fondi, notes, "Although she has been sought by the first nobles of Italy," Euthanasia nevertheless "glories in her independence and solitude" (137). Given her "enthusiasm for the liberties of [her] country" (146), a conflict with Casstruccio is inevitable in spite of their mutual, romantic affection. It is through Euthanasia's agent, Bindo – a servant who "has by heart [...] every prophecy that has been made since the time of Adam" (171) and whose name again pairs prophecy with bondage – that her narrative intersects with a third and final articulation of female authority, the witch Fior di Mandragola. While she claims a certain kind of power over inanimate objects and knows "the fortunes of men," Mandragola concedes that "man himself is not to be ruled, unless he consent to obey" (324). These limitations notwithstanding, Mandragola manipulates both Beatrice and Bindo in an effort to maintain whatever slight power she can over the gullible and vulnerable. Ultimately, however, Mandragola is a parody of female prophecy and her proximity to Beatrice marks the text's effort to discredit the latter's agency by her association with this villain.

The notion that prophecy should amount to bondage is one of the first and most consistent ideas established in *Valperga*. Early in the text, Castruccio, at just fourteen years of age, journeys from Ancona – his family's refuge following exile from Lucca – to Florence, lured by an advertisement for a dramatic presentation of Dante's *Inferno*. Beginning a cautionary motif that will traverse the novel and code imagination as excessive, dangerous, and prone to self-destruction – indeed, will align such imagination with prophecy – this performance not only "fired the imagination of Castruccio" (65) but gained its intense effect through its externalization of the collective interior: "The infernal drama was acted to the life; and the terrible effect of such a scene was enhanced, by the circumstance of its being no more than an actual representation of what then existed in the imagination of the spectators, endued with the vivid colours of a faith inconceivable in these lethargic days" (66). But, in what Castruccio cannot help but feel as Divine reprimand, the scene suddenly transforms from an imaginary into a real Hell – a substitution that will be repeated later in the text when Beatrice's recurring nightmare is suddenly realized. While Castruccio looks on helplessly, "the bridge of Carraia, on which a countless multitude stood, one above the other, looking on the river, fell" (66). Fleeing the "fearful screams" of the victims and onlookers, Castruccio, in what looks like unconscious penance for surrendering too entirely to his imagination, enters a local church to compose himself and to thank God that he had "escaped from Hell!" (66, 67).

As frightened as he is, Castruccio fares much better than his fellow Ghibelline, Farinata degli Uberti, whom Dante torments in Canto Ten of his *Inferno*. The history of Farinata – one that intersects with Castruccio's – is particularly relevant since it is through Dante's treatment of him that *Valperga* finds a contemporary (i.e., contemporary to the setting of the action) and authoritative precedent for figuring prophecy as torture. As Allen Mandelbaum notes,

> Farinata was the name used for Manente, son of Jacopo degli Uberti, a famous leader of the Ghibellines of Florence. At the meeting of the victorious Ghibellines at Empoli after the battle of Montaperti in September 1260, he vehemently opposed the proposal to destroy Florence. He returned to Florence after Montaperti and died in 1264, one year before Dante's birth. In 1283, [two years after the birth of Castruccio, according to Tegrimi[35]] Farinata and his wife were posthumously excommunicated by the Franciscan inquisitor; their bones were exhumed and dispersed, and the earthly goods of their heirs confiscated.[36]

Farinata's heresy – echoing the Paterin heresy adopted by Beatrice later in *Valperga* – consists of a rejection of Christian metaphysics. Hence, Dante locates him with "Epicurus and all his followers,/ Who hold the soul dies with the body."[37] What is most important in the context of *Valperga*, however, is not so much the behaviour of Farinata, although he prefigures and markedly contrasts with Castruccio's own – for Castruccio, grown into a man and, eventually, a tyrant, *will* demolish the castle of Valperga, Florence's proxy in the plain of Lucca. Rather, it is the specific nature of his torment. Since "the punishments in the Inferno follow the law of *contrapasso* – that is, the punishment is commensurate with the fault"[38] – there is a darkly comic irony that Farinata should be transformed into a Cassandrian prophet.

After some confusing, initial exchanges with Farinata's shade in hell, Dante asks, "Pray untie for me this knot [...]/ Which has entangled and confused my judgment," and remarks:

> From what I hear, it seems
> You see beforehand that which time will bring,
> But cannot know what happens in the present.[39]

To which Farinata responds,

> We see, like those with faulty vision,
> Things at a distance [...]. That much,
> For us, the mighty Ruler's light still shines.
> When they draw near or happen now,
> Our minds are useless. Without the words of others
> We can know nothing of your human state.
> Thus it follows that all our knowledge
> Will perish at the very moment
> The portals of the future close.[40]

If Farinata denies the immortality of the soul, it is fitting, according to Dante's form of poetic retribution, that a particularly disabling version of prophecy should become Farinata's form of bondage: he will, for eternity, see only an eternity that divorces him from finite embodiment. In *Valperga*, prophecy follows this Dantean formulation: foresight comes at the expense of freedom and historical agency in the present.

This is nowhere clearer or more tragic than in the history of Beatrice. Adopted by Marsilio, the Bishop of Ferrara, upon the death of her guardian, Magfreda, Beatrice as a child displays an active imagination full of "enthusiasm" and "wild dreams." When she begins to prophesy and wins followers, Marsilio indulges what he sees as delusion for fear that the truth might entirely crush her spirit. As Beatrice's reputation as a seer grows, however, she attracts the attention of the Inquisition. This leads to her trial. In fact, still confident in her powers and unaware of the bishop's manipulation, Beatrice proposes a test, one where she must navigate, blindfolded, a maze of white-hot ploughshares. Unbeknownst to Beatrice, Marsilio, however, arranges to rig the event by appealing to the abbot whose men are charged with its staging. The abbot agrees and when Beatrice does indeed manage to emerge unscathed, forcing the Inquisitors to retreat, Marsilio suffers from a guilty conscience, given the perpetuation of what, in his mind, is a fraud. Afterward, Marsilio narrates this history to Castruccio: "Beatrice herself is wrapt up in the belief of her own exalted nature, and really thinks herself the *Ancilla Dei*, the chosen vessel into which God has poured a portion of his spirit: she preaches, she prophesies, she sings extempore hymns, and entirely fulfilling the part of *Donna Estatica*, she passes many hours of each day in solitary meditation, or rather in dreams, to which her active imagination gives a reality and life which confirm her in her mistakes" (212). Eventually, Marsilio reveals all this to Beatrice. The result is, as expected, catastrophic. Beatrice is convinced that her life has been a lie and exiles herself from Ferrera, an exile that leads her briefly to the castle Valperga but, ultimately, on to an earthly inferno.

Her subsequent experiences suggest that we should pause over her day of judgment and Bishop Marsilio's claim to have fixed the test. Given the data available in the text, can we be *sure* that she is not, in fact, clairvoyant? While critics seem quick to accept the Marsilio's word[41] – his assertion that Beatrice is deluded – the question is more difficult to answer than might be expected. Despite the bishop's claims, and despite the modern reader's own willingness quickly to ingest his demystification of the scene, it is impossible to determine how exactly this test was faked. There is no explicit or even implicit explanation of how precisely the Brothers of the Church are able to ensure Beatrice's safety or success, especially since she is not aware of any mundane interventions and does not herself knowingly participate in any trickery. Indeed, when the bishop undertakes the scheme, he is entreated by the abbot "not to ask an explanation": the abbot assures Marsilio "that he and his monks [have] the charge of the preparation for the Judgment and that [...] she [i.e., Beatrice] should receive no injury" (216). Later on, after her escape from Tripalda and rescue by Euthanasia from the Inquisition in Lucca, Beatrice's own narrative of events does little to elucidate the matter. She recalls addressing the bishop: "Tell me then, by your hopes of heaven, [...] whether fraud was used in the *Judgment of God* that I underwent, or how I escaped the fearful burning of the hot shares" (353). When he delays his explanation, she insists again that he "tell [her] truly how it happened" (353). "That I cannot, my child" replies the bishop, "for I was myself kept in the dark" (353). Oddly, this crucial episode of putative enlightenment seems, under closer examination, to become more and more mysterious and inexplicable.

One explanation for its resistance to elucidation is that Beatrice *does* have powers that cannot be explained in simple, rational terms. Indeed, given the belatedness of various revelations, the narrative seems reluctant to admit that Beatrice falls into the hands of Batista Tripalda in a scene that she has prophetically dreamt – a scene she dreams "always on the eve of some great misfortune" (358). This merger of dream and reality validates her visionary power and suggests that its earlier denial is part of a larger scheme to curb and revoke her agency. Defining the repressive economy of the text even more sharply, the validation of her prophetic power coincides with the instant of her abduction, as if the text, finally unable to keep her under control through rhetorical and narrative means, resorts to physical violence. In the midst of a powerful depression, Beatrice is "haunted by a prophecy," by "the memory of a dream":

> there was a plain flooded by the waters of an overflowing river, the road was dry, being on the side of a hill above a level of the plain, and I kept along a path which

> declined, wondering if I should come to an insurmountable obstacle; at a distance before me they were driving a flock of sheep; on my left, on the side of the hill, there was a ruined circuit of wall, which inclosed the dilapidated houses of a deserted town; at some distance a dreary, large, ruinous house, half like a castle, yet without a tower, dilapidated and overgrown with moss, was dimly seen, islanded by the flood on which it cast a night-black shade; the sirocco blew, and covered the sky with fleecy clouds; and the mists in the distance hovered low over the plain; a bat above me wheeled around. Then something happened, what I cannot now tell, terrific it most certainly was; Euthanasia, there is something in this strange world, that we none of us understand. (358)

While this recurrent vision is unsettling in itself, its significance exponentially increases when one day during her exile, Beatrice, descending into the plain surrounding Rome, slowly recognizes that she is walking, awake, into this very scene. As it slowly dawned on her, she "grew dizzy and sick" and when she finally noticed "a large, old, dilapidated house islanded in the flood," the whole vision comes suddenly rushing back: "The dream flashed across my memory; I uttered a wild shriek, and fell lifeless on the road" (358–9). The "something" that remains obscure in Beatrice's recollection of the prophetic dream is made savagely clear when she regains consciousness in the clutches of "a wicked and powerful enemy" who keeps her as a slave for three years to service a "carnival of devils" (359, 360). His name is Battista Tripalda and was introduced earlier in the narrative as an "uncouth and arrogant" canon who insinuates himself into Castruccio's government in spite of suspicions that he is a spy (299). The truth, however, is more monstrous. This cunning, hypocritical man about whom "worse stories had been whispered" (299) operates some kind of den of depravity and it is this into which Beatrice falls. Here Tripalda's exceptional contempt for women, so apparent in his embassy to Euthanasia in advance of Castruccio's assault on Valperga, becomes the rule. Tripalda is allowed literally to dominate "women's eloquence [and] obstinacy" (302). In Beatrice's mind he becomes "the god of evil" incarnate (360).

Beatrice confirms her genuinely prophetic powers at the moment of her infernal imprisonment. Prophecy, rather than opening prospects, leads to captivity. Echoing its Dantean and Cassandrian forms, prophecy, as a revelation of what is inevitable, seems more like a form of cruelty than a source of power. Indeed, this sense of powerlessness in the face of a shadowy agent who issues out of one's own mind invites a psychoanalytic treatment.[42] But it also invites a reconsideration of the apparent polarization of male and female characters in *Valperga* through a subterranean allusion to Percy Shelley's own prophetic imagination. It appears that Mary Shelley bases Beatrice's terrifying revelation on an episode Percy describes in the final pages of *Speculations on Metaphysics*. Returning in a different way to the sort of questions with which Kant was occupied in his reading of Swedenborg, the final chapter of Percy's *Speculations* presents a "Catalogue of the Phenomena of Dreams, as Connecting Sleeping and Waking."[43] Here he recalls a particularly thrilling experience identical in structure to Beatrice's. "I have beheld scenes," says Percy, "with the intimate and unaccountable connexion of which with the obscure parts of my own nature, I have been irresistibly impressed."[44] In what sounds much like a Wordsworthian spot of time – a moment that might seem unremarkable but, thanks to radical agitation, leaves an indelible impression – Shelley notes that the scene in question initially "produced no unusual effect on [his] thought."[45] Things get very strange, however, when this scene begins to stalk his dreams: "After a lapse of many years I have dreamed of this scene. It has hung in my memory, it has haunted my thoughts, at intervals, with the pertinacity of an object connected with human affections."[46] This creates the conditions for a paradoxically obscure revelation:

> the most remarkable event of this nature, which ever occurred to me, happened five years ago at Oxford. I was walking with a friend, in the neighborhood of that city, engaged in earnest and interesting conversation. We suddenly turned the corner of the lane, and the view, which its high banks and hedges had concealed, presented itself. The view consisted of a windmill, standing in one among many plashy meadows, inclosed with stone walls; the irregular and broken ground, between the wall and the road on which we stood; a long low hill behind the windmill, and a grey covering of uniform cloud spread over the evening sky. It was that season when the last leaf had just fallen from the scant and stunted ash. The scene surely was a common scene; the season and the hour little calculated to kindle lawless thought; it was a tame uninteresting assemblage of objects, such as would drive the imagination for refuge in serious and sober talk, to the evening fireside, and the dessert of winter fruits and wine. The effect which it produced on me was not such as could have been expected. I suddenly remembered to have seen that exact scene in some dream of long – – – –[47]

Like Beatrice's prophecy, this narration of the scene is traumatically belated. The dreams in each case become prophetic in a moment of powerful *déja vu,* in the instant that acting in anticipation of the scene becomes impossible. Like Beatrice, Percy swoons, the text breaking off in what marks the jagged "conclusion" of the entire work on metaphysics. Indeed, Mary's editorial note on this passage indicates that the effect was not merely rhetorical but that, in his revisiting of the moment wherein his dream was revealed as somehow prophetic, the uncanny power of the experience really returned to Percy. Whereas "forgetful memory," as we saw in *Hellas*, brings back forgetting in the instant of putative recollection, here the memory cannot insulate the subject from the trauma of prophecy's realization. Memory's narrative exigency, its power retroactively to organize discontinuity, cannot help but find itself overcome in the instant its content expresses itself. Like a wound inflicted to the very action of mourning, it appears that not even framing prophecy's revelation as an event in the past can defuse the surprise of realizing, too late, one's own prophetic unconscious. As in the Wordsworthian "experience" of missing experience, or with the "sense" of having touched on one's own senseless sensitivity, the belatedness of the subject's recognition of her or his prophetic power must always be missed – there is no catching up to it. "I remember well," writes Mary in her editorial gloss, Percy "coming to me from writing [the final passage of *Speculations* in 1815], pale and agitated, to seek refuge in conversation from the fearful emotions it excited," emotions "wound up by the delicacy of his health to an intense degree of sensibility [...], even to physical pain."[48] Percy thus appears in some respects to provide Mary with an inspiration for Beatrice's imagination, though in the latter's case there is no easy release from "physical pain" through either conversation or poetic invention. Beatrice is shattered by the same prophetic sensitivity that Wordsworth and Shelley translate into poetic–prophetic election.[49]

In chapter 3 we saw how the episode of the gibbet-mast wrought consciousness into such a state of sensitivity that even a banal scene could leave its mark. In both Percy's personal and Mary Shelley's fictional rendition of this psychological complex, consciousness is braced-up, is rendered especially impressionable, through the repetition of a dream. What sets this mode of sensitization apart from Wordsworth, though, is that the winding up of consciousness happens *unconsciously*. And yet, this ought not to be entirely surprising since, as we saw in Wordsworth, becoming impressionable does not, itself, leave an impression; to be rendered more and more sensitive happens through the *absence* of experience. Indeed, as dramatized both in *Valperga* and *Speculations on Metaphysics*, the shock of a mundane moment is all the more penetrating since the recurring dream is not recognized to be prophetic until after the fact. The priming process, the affective charging of the self, happens silently, secretly. When Beatrice concludes her conversation with Euthanasia she remarks that "there is something in this strange world, that we none of us understand" (358). In *Frankenstein*, Walton expresses his unaccountable compulsion for exploration in nearly the same words, though he moves the mystery from the world at large to his inner life: "There is something at work in my soul that I do not understand."[50] Beatrice, later, makes this same, interiorizing move. When she retells her dream to Fior di

Mandragola, Beatrice recalls more about it than she was able to with Euthanasia. This time, the scene is rife with tropes of reflection and depth:

> There was a vast, black house standing in the midst of the water; a concourse of dark shapes hovered about me; and suddenly I was transported into a boat which was to convey me to that mansion. Strange! another boat like to mine moved beside us; its prow was carved in the same manner; its rowers, the same in number, the same in habiliment, struck the water with their oars at the same time with ours; a woman sate near the stern, aghast and wild as I; – but their boat cut the waves without a sound, their oars splashed not the waters as they struck them, and, thought the boats were alike black, yet not like mine did this other cast a black shadow on the water. We landed together; I could not walk for fear; I was carried into a large room, and left alone; I leaned against the hangings, and there advanced to meet me another form. It was myself; I knew it; it stood before me, melancholy and silent; the very air about it was still. I can tell no more; – a few minutes ago I remembered none of this; a few moments, and I distinctly remembered the words it spoke; they have now faded. Yes; there is something mysterious in my nature, which I cannot fathom. (379–80)

In this rendition, Beatrice comes face to face with her own mysterious interiority. In a disturbing twist, it is not Tripalda who confronts her in this chamber, as in the actual scene from her life, but her own future self, the "melancholy and silent" person she becomes following an imprisonment that "much changed" her (359). Could this mean that Beatrice's own unconscious is tyrannical, evil, murderous? The ostensibly imposed experience of imprisonment and torture could be the external manifestation of her prophetic power, casting Tripalda as merely the public name for that spirit – identified, as we will see in a moment, as the imagination – lurking within her own deepest self.

Amazingly, Beatrice survives her torment. But unlike Wordsworth who attempts masochistically to transform trauma into food for future years and thus swell his ego on the verge of its annihilation, Beatrice's experience leads her to a kind of anti-Romanticism. Given that, in her experience, the prophetic imagination is tantamount to imprisonment, it is not surprising that she sees nothing redemptive in imagination; rather than call on imagination to ameliorate a blunder, Beatrice experiences this appeal as itself a stumbling block. Hence, in a scathing indictment of false hope, she casts "the imagination" as nothing but a "masterpiece of malice" that

> spreads honey on the cup that you may drink poison; that strews roses over thorns [...]; [it is] that semblance of beauty which beckons you to the desert; that apple of

> gold with the heart of ashes; that foul image, with the veil of excellence; [...] that diadem of nettles; that spear, broken in the heart! He, the damned and triumphant one, sat meditating many thousand years for the conclusion, the consummation, the final crown, the seal of all misery, which he might set on man's brain and heart to doom him to endless torment; and he created the Imagination. And then we are told the fault is ours; good and evil are sown in our hearts, and ours is the tillage, ours the harvest. (343)

Adopting a Paterin outlook following her imprisonment, Beatrice "believes in the ascendancy of the evil spirit in the world" (340). Considering "the strife, the hatred and uncharitableness" of "domestic life," the "midnight murders, envy [...], ingratitude, cruelty" of human society, to say nothing of "disease, plague, famine, leprosy, fever," Beatrice interprets the kind of optimism urged by the imagination as, at best, false consciousness. "Bitter experience," she says, has "let [her] into the truth of things," rather like the forbidden fruit in Eden (344). Indeed, she sounds in this moment something like Milton's Satan, promulgating an anti-theodicy, determined to reveal all positive forms of the prophetic imagination as versions of the same ideology that pretends the Fall to have been fortunate. And she has good reason for thinking this: not only does she know firsthand how Prometheus unbound just leads to another state of bondage but so too does Castruccio's increasingly tyrannical and bloody rule stem from a concept of "the state" that is "a fiction, which sacrifices that which constitutes it, to the support of a mere name" (261).

Beatrice's anti-prophecy – her determined rejection of all better prospects – would be deeply sceptical of those readings of Romantic imagination that see it as simply healing the rift between ideal and real conditions. "The imagination is [often] assigned the responsibility," Forest Pyle argues, "of making a linkage, an articulation" between discordant realms.[51] And it is this power to reconcile difference into a smooth surface that, for Beatrice, is a lie. Imagination's ability to transform chaos into order, Beatrice fears, means it might also be deployed to create alibis for wrongs that are indefensible. Yet, it is not clear that the imagination does produce seamless wholes from fragmented experience. As Pyle continues, while it is "Deployed as a principle of coherence [...] or a medium of translation for the discourse of Romanticism, the imagination is simultaneously a principal site of its division and disjunction."[52] Much the same can be said of prophecy: just as the Romantic imagination undermines its identification with the blind optimism that turns all trauma into subjective election, so does prophecy disperse – more or less consciously and dramatically – the future it dictates. When Shelley returns to the prophetic imagination in *The Last Man*, she does so with every intention of heeding Beatrice's warning.

"introducing a woman into the plot": *The Last Man*

Presenting the bulk of the work as the redaction of a nineteenth-century editor who, as the text's fictional "Introduction" explains, discovers and translates prophetic leaves found in a hidden chamber of the cave of the Sybil of Cumae,[53] Shelley's *The Last Man* presents an apocalyptic prophecy of the history of the future as told by Lionel Verney, the sole survivor of a global plague that leaves him, at the end of the twenty-first century, the last man on earth.[54] The Sybil framing prophecy finds her textual correlate in the Greek woman Evadne Zaimi. Despite the brevity of her appearance, Evadne is crucial to understanding how Shelley negotiates the fraught relationship between sexual and historical agency and for uncovering a reading of *The Last Man* that does not fall victim to what appears to be a completely depressing, closed, and destructive picture of the future. Evadne is something like a reincarnation of Beatrice: not only does she suffer a similar fate (rejection, abjection) but her curse on Raymond inaugurates "man's" decline. This curse activates Beatrice's pessimism and offers Cassandra a measure of revenge, if belatedly. As a young man, Adrian falls in love with Evadne. She, however, rejects Adrian, for it is Adrian's friend "Raymond, the deliverer of Greece, the graceful soldier, who bore in his mien a tinge of all that, peculiar to her native clime Evadne cherished as most dear."[55] Yet, in this case, too, love remains unreciprocated. Evadne thus stands in the midst of a series of unrequited loves and unsatisfied desires, effectively repeating Adrian's psychological experience though in a manner that does not generate any sympathetic intimacy between them. Given this instability – Evadne's precarious position between Adrian and Raymond – there is a certain irony that she should be rediscovered in the text as the mysterious prize-winning architect.

Upon ascending to the office of Lord Protector of England, Raymond "projected the erection of a national gallery for statues and pictures" (76). An emblem of British history and culture, "the edifice was to be the great ornament of his Protectorship" (76). After reviewing hundreds of unsatisfactory proposals, "at length a drawing came [...]. The design was new and elegant, but faulty; so faulty, that although drawn with the hand and eye of taste, it was evidently the work of one who was not an architect" (77). For some reason Raymond is fascinated with this design and his inquiries into its provenance lead him eventually to "the dwellings of want" (78) and Evadne's wasted form. Moved by her series of misfortunes since her departure from England years earlier, Raymond begins secretly visiting Evadne – a decision that, like St Leon's decision in William Godwin's eponymous text to keep secrets from his wife, Marguerite, leads eventually to domestic catastrophe.[56] But when Raymond eventually rejects Evadne in an effort to return to his original political and domestic responsibilities, it becomes impossible to do so. Recalling the capaciousness of Blake's language in *Milton*, Raymond finds it impossible to secure his "state," in political, emotional, and even physiological terms. This is because Evadne, like Dido in Virgil's *Aeneid*, curses the would-be politician and contaminates the state's claim – announced by political philosophers from Plato to Hegel to Adrian – to serve as the material expression of rationality itself. In the *Philosophy of Right*, for instance, Hegel asserts that "The state is the actuality of the ethical Idea. It is ethical spirit as the substantial will manifest and clear to itself, knowing and thinking itself, accomplishing what it knows and insofar as it knows it."[57] Evadne's curse on Raymond, however, illustrates how something deeply unreasonable remains hidden behind this eminently reasonable facade. The state is pregnant with negativity that gets forcefully expressed in Evadne's curse: "Many living deaths have I borne for thee, O Raymond, and now I expire, thy victim! – By my death I purchase thee – lo! the instruments of war, fire, the plague are my servitors. I dared, I conquered them all, till now! I have sold myself to death, with the sole condition that thou shouldst follow me – Fire, and war, and plague, unite for thy destruction – O my Raymond, there is no safety for thee!" (131). This revenge follows a kind of *contrapasso* logic by turning all "mankind" into the host for an invasive, alien life, by making "man" pregnant – Southcott-like – with death.

It is tempting to think of *The Last Man* as Beatrice's next prophecy, that the scattered, Sibylline leaves the fictional editor discovers are Beatrice's own "hideous progeny."[58] For Evadne's curse on Raymond seems overcharged, spilling out across the whole world with the fury of Beatrice's infinite absolute negativity. Reborn as plague, Beatrice becomes a force of nature that bends universal human history to her will, gaining the agency she was so brutally denied in *Valperga*. Yet, *The Last Man* marks a significant refinement of Beatrice's suspicion toward the prophetic imagination – a refinement that succumbs *neither* to imagination's identification with false consciousness *nor* to the apocalyptic empiricism that finds (or thinks it finds) the real in the elimination of the ideal. While the text retains a large measure of Beatrice's justified rage, gone is the naive assumption that truth lies in some self-evident "bitter experience." In its place is, first, a Blakean, dynamic sense of the imagination as the power of revision. Second, rather than actually achieving cosmic redress for Beatrice through universal destruction – the eye-for-an-eye logic operative in the historical world of *Valperga* – the plague is most remarkable for how it does not, how it cannot, achieve the complete end it seems so relentlessly to pursue. Neither as optimistic nor as pessimistic as it has been interpreted previously,[59] Shelley's text evolves a strangely powerful neutrality. Ultimately, Shelley's text marks what Blanchot calls a "limit-experience," a state of being where the Hegelian end of history encounters a kind of disappointment with its own success, the sort of workless negativity discussed in chapter 7.[60] This dissatisfaction discloses a negativity that does not get drawn up into dialectical activity and that calls for, in Michel Foucault's phrase, a "non-positive affirmation."[61] It is in this twilight that Shelley's text finally leaves what is remaining of the historical subject.

How, then, does Shelley mitigate pure nihilism in the direction of this affirmation without affirmation? For one, she uses prophetic catastrophe to terminate not history or the future as such but only a particular, idealized state – one that, in its very perfection, proves indeed less egalitarian that it seems. Twenty-first-century London as depicted in the text could be called utopian only if that concept includes the pervasive marginalization of female desire. That such marginalization is widespread in spite of having achieved the "perfect system of government" (68) becomes clear when we hear story after story of women suddenly freed from patriarchal domination by, of all things, the plague. There is, for instance, the history of Juliet, whom the plague frees from domestic authority such that she can pursue a relationship with her lover. There is, also, the story of Lucy: a young woman separated from her preferred lover and forced into marriage with a brutal man who attempts to alienate her from her family. The plague liberates her, too, and she enters the troop of English emigrants along with her aged mother. Finally, there is the "simple history" (307) of the nameless Swiss organist. Like the other young women mentioned, the plague removes class barriers and allows her, "the fair daughter of a poor musician" (307), temporarily to unite with a young nobleman. This is not to say that the plague is less damaging than it seems – ultimately it also kills all of these women. The point, rather, is that in the course of its destruction it makes visible major shortcomings of an ostensibly egalitarian utopia. It also suggests – given the imposter-prophet's scheme to manipulate and control the vulnerable – that in order to work effectively as a purgative, the plague must be totally negating.

Echoing Mark Canuel's reading, we can understand the plague as something horrible and heartbreaking and, yet, also, as a force not entirely unproductive. "The plague is not merely to be understood in terms of its destructive effects," he argues, "but also in terms of the way those effects continually produce a new evaluation of the formation of community."[62] By erasing social and class difference, for example, "the plague redefines the social meaning of personhood."[63] As noted above, the plague enables social and romantic re-formations (short-lived though they may be). Similarly, in purging idealism, the text does not bring us to the Hegelian end of history so much as to the end of only one possible history of "man," to only one possible notion of "the end of man." As Barbara Johnson notes, the text seems to ask, "How indeed can one survive humanism? How can one create a language that is postplague, that is, postuniversal?"[64] The answer to these questions remains suspended. But the text's prophetic gift is to create the conditions for their asking. Merely outlining these inquiries takes us beyond the discourse of existential authenticity and into a renegotiation of the "human." For "man" in Shelley's text seems to signify a fairly narrow category and, once recognized as such, we might be rather less concerned about its loss. As Johnson observes, the "image of England [in Lionel's opening description] as mental mastery, inviolable insularity, self-sufficient centrality, is in fact the image of a certain conception of *man* which will be progressively demystified throughout the novel that follows."[65] The plague infects hope to the core to induce a crisis in the very ideals that we hope for. Rather than palliate an ailing humanism that seems inevitably to produce patriarchs, nationalists, and martyrs, the strategy here is, in Benjamin's words, to induce "a real state of emergency."[66]

Shelley revives the so-called plague of liberty (198), that is, the republican state Galeazzo Visconti and Castruccio both seek to *repress* in *Valperga*, as an *actual* plague. And we might think of this plague as the deadly, vengeful, but inevitable offspring of the contradictions that remain embedded in the idealized state. Rather than the "plague of *liberty*" we have a "*plague* of liberty," a story where the imaginary realization of the liberal state brings that limited notion of liberty – of liberalism – to its end. For within this state there also remain significant socioeconomic divisions, most obvious in Evadne's desperate living conditions following her father's loss of wealth. Given the megalomaniacal designs of "the methodist," it appears that ethical improvement also remains, at best, uneven across the population. In fact, this English society is still insular, nationalistic, and educationally stratified (recall Lionel's early poverty and ignorance): the culture is both somehow perfected and yet underdeveloped. Indeed, the same war between the Greeks and Turks contemporary to Shelley (and inspiration for Percy Shelley's *Hellas*) continues even in this distant future. Shelley's presentation of the realized republican state thus reveals *that ideal itself* as a lure.

Consider, for instance, what passes for a perfected electoral policy: "Every thing in the English constitution had been regulated for the better preservation of peace. On the last day, two candidates only were allowed to remain; and to obviate, if possible, the last struggle between these, a bribe was offered to him who should voluntarily resign his pretensions; a place of great emolument and honor was given him, and his success facilitated at a future election" (73). Indeed, Raymond is not so much elected Lord Protector as appointed when "the member who had nominated Ryland, rose and informed us that this candidate had resigned his pretensions" (73). This peace-preserving code eliminates the very act of decision; in the name of perpetual peace, this constitution confuses what Blake calls "Mental Fight" with "Corporeal Strife." While it may appear more "civilized" than argument, what this gentleman's agreement really does is eliminate any avenue for robust critique on grounds that critique disturbs the peace. This "emphasis on civility and cultivation is strong enough to erase virtually every trace of political tension" and thus tends dangerously toward social and political homogeny.[67] In fact, the entire process is rigged more fundamentally and is even more deeply violent than genuine debate could ever be. It is not merely that we trade democratic decision for appointment but that once a candidate gets to this stage his political victory is ensured, if slightly deferred. Differences between candidates prove to be totally superficial – which effectively eliminates election as a viable route for unconventional parties – as evidenced by the fact that "resignation" secures future "election." Government in this ostensible utopia proves to be entirely insular. Thus, by calling progressive ideals themselves into question, the text, in essence, "attacks all conventional stratifications, civic as well as individual."[68]

Taking aim at such faulty ideals, *The Last Man* functions as a negating sort of prophecy rather than an apocalypse. Unlike, say, a poison that simply destroys its host, the text is a purgative that works its way through the system. It upsets the system by forcing it to its limit, to the point where it resorts to total evacuation. In political terms, we might recall Tocqueville: "As the object of the French Revolution was not only to change an ancient form of government, but also to abolish an ancient state of society, it had to attack at once every established authority, to destroy every recognized influence, to efface all traditions, to create new manners and customs, and, as it were, to *purge the human mind of all the ideas upon which respect and obedience had hitherto been based*. Thence arose its singularly anarchical character" (7, emphasis added). To adopt Tocqueville's terms, this purgation would not destroy the human but neither would it simply return, nostalgically, to a previous state of humanity. Instead, it would help the imagination encounter what is typically unthought within ideas normally taken to be utopian – that is, the ideology of utopia. Like Blake, Shelley is sensitive to the flaws within Republican ideals, both the flaws of commission and of omission. The most egregious of these problems is that historical agency remains the exclusive property of men or, more insidiously, of a masculinized subjectivity. And yet, Shelley's response is not merely to afford greater so-called agency to women. Rather, the text draws humanity as a whole toward what it cannot master. The text does not expand human agency, does not grant a wider range of subjects access to "the human," but rather illustrates the weakness of this agency, a weakness dramatized by its concentration in a single person, the last man, who is master of everything – and nothing.

As with Blake's impossible history, it would be mistaken to attempt to transform the trauma of Shelley's text into a mere lesson, into some kind of data one might instrumentally refine in an effort – genuine, though naive – incrementally to improve things as they are. This is because Shelley's text questions more radically what "improvement" really means. This is not to say that the amelioration of suffering is pointless and that one, beautiful soul-like, ought to retreat from making what worldly interventions one can. That said, Shelley's target in this work has the philosophical courage to question the sinister dimensions of what look like universal goods. Like Percy Shelley's Wandering Jew, there is a sense that progress might overlap with regression or, to paraphrase Walter Benjamin, that civilization may progress only through barbarism. In cutting this knot, however, Shelley does not submit to sheer pessimism. While she does not provide a representation of new goods or what a society committed to different goods might look like, she nevertheless retains the possibility of a future wherein this might take shape. Like Schelling's notion of an intermediate phase between being and nothingness – an existence that is less than actual but more than nothing – the utopian strain in Shelley's thought is of this minimal, barely utopian sort. Rather than depict an ideal future in terms that must inevitably repeat the thought (and limitations) of the present and past, Shelley's utopian thought is extremely delicate, presenting an almost impalpable affirmation of the mere future.

In other words, *The Last Man* puts any defense of humanity, humanism, and history into question. By taking us to the limit of these concepts and resisting the impulse to offer consolation (God, truth, enlightenment), we enter a space for thinking the slippery negativity of Blanchot's "contestation." Both Shelley and Blanchot,[69] performing a thought experiment, agree with Hegel to begin at the end: history is over, man is everything, thought is absolute. In such a state, says Blanchot, "We all live more or less from the perspective of a terminated history."[70] "Man accomplishes himself because he carries through completely all his negations."[71] Yet, Blanchot will not accept this translation of all negativity into productivity, insisting rather on a sort of residue or waste that Hegel does not account for in this overripe state of man:

> No, man does not exhaust his negativity in action; no, he does not transform into power all the nothingness that he is. Perhaps he can reach the absolute by making himself equal to the whole and by becoming conscious of the whole. But then more extreme than this absolute is the passion of negative thought; for faced with this response, negative thought is still capable of introducing the question that suspends it, and, faced with the accomplishment of the whole, still capable of maintaining the other exigency that again raises the issue of the infinite in the form of contestation. [...] The limit-experience is the experience of what is outside the whole when the whole excludes every outside; the experience of what is still to be attained when all is attained and of what is still to be known when all is known: the inaccessible, the unknown itself.[72]

There is an "essential lack" in humanity that perhaps shows itself most clearly when humanity seems to be totally complete. The dissatisfaction of the last man, the ultimate man, derives not from having something yet unaccomplished but rather from the malaise of having nothing now to do. "A strange surplus," indeed. For, "What is this excess that makes the conclusion ever and always unfinished?"[73] Shelley answers this question with the plague and its own "product," the last living person and his story. For the last man makes concluding impossible – he draws us toward the end but does not permit ending.

As Morton Paley observes, "The imagination resists the idea of Lastness, an idea that presupposes a recipient or reader whose very existence negates the Lastness of the narrating subject."[74] It is on this very point that we might return, one last time, to Blanchot. In his novella *Le Dernier Homme*, Blanchot explores the impossibility of conceptualizing and representing the last man and the state or condition of calm attentiveness that this impossibility generates. In the midst of a vague, meandering narrative, Blanchot's speaker asks the titular, silent last man, "Who are you?" only to answer his own query immediately: "You can't be what you are."[75] Just as the gift, which we saw in chapter 3, in order to be a gift and not a debt, must not be what it is, so the last man, once recognized as such, is no longer alone. The last man in Blanchot or Shelley, by virtue of being recognized as such, cannot be last. Indeed, even were he to recognize himself, he would have to divide into Wordsworth's "two consciousnesses," conscious of himself "And some other being." Blanchot's text thus inverts expectations by affording this figure a strange sort of resiliency: what is horrible is not that the last man might die and with him humanity end, but precisely that he *cannot*, properly, die. "The most anguishing idea," the speaker confesses, is that the last man "can't die, because he has no future."[76] As Jan Plug notes, Adrian's humanism subordinates individuals' deaths to an idea of the human that is transcendent: "Humanity is always 'full,' never leaving even a trace of a remainder, because it registers no loss, precisely because it is not conceived as adhering in its composite parts (individuals, human beings), but is rather a 'full number,' transcendent, even transcendence. [...] Death has no other function here than to reconfirm the dialectical power of humanism to subsume all loss or negativity to its own fullness."[77] The death of the last man would mean the end of this humanistic economy. As such, death, as something history feeds on, becomes impossible: because there is no more history. For death to continue to fill the humanist's coffers, there has to be a future wherein the human can look back on death as a negation well within the power of humanism. No future, no death; no death, because no future.

To hover on the edge of humanity gestures toward an existence – though not a humanism – that picks up beyond the end of "man." Shelley's history of the future is therefore, in Blake's sense, impossible just as "a book entitled *The Last Man* is manifestly an impossible book."[78] In limiting destruction to humanity, Shelley subtly affirms another, even broader vitality – both of nature and of the plague itself. As Blanchot writes in *Friendship*, "The apocalypse is disappointing. The power to destroy, with which science has invested us, is still very weak. We could perhaps annihilate life on earth, but we can do nothing to the universe. This inability should make us patient."[79] This weakness and disappointment does not diminish the traumatic reality of human death; yet, Shelley's text makes us patient, makes us negatively capable (as it were) of turning to a future that outlives us and about which we can determine nothing. The lastness at issue in *The Last Man* is thus not total and complete annihilation. Shelley reveals another, hitherto unobserved horizon of existence precisely by taking political possibility to its limits and imagining what Kant in *The Conflict of the Faculties* calls a "natural revolution."[80] In fact, in order to *represent* the lastness of humanity, Shelley's text has to be on both sides of "the end." We are left not simply with bare life after the end of "man" but with a cognition that, in order to think the end, has somehow to outlive itself. This is a conceptual problem that Shelley deals with rhetorically and structurally via Sibylline prophecy, a mind that can be both before and after the end of consciousness. "The end" as a *concept* necessitates consciousness, even if the concept is the *end of* consciousness.

Yet, we should not forget that *The Last Man* is not only conceived by a mind that is partly inhuman (the Sibyl), but that the narrative we have is the product of a complex mediation of that inhuman thought by an anonymous editor. This editor does not merely collect and passively translate but, rather, gives "form and substance to the frail and attenuated Leaves of the Sibyl," entirely and by necessity "transforming them" since "they were unintelligible in their pristine condition" (4). The narrative that makes up the body of the novel is not so much discovered as produced in and through the free act of "translation." Hence, this "edition" of prophecy cannot be analysed by comparison with its "pristine" manuscript since, in its untouched form, the pages are utterly meaningless. This prophetic history exists only in the space between manuscript and imagination. The editor's own analogy stresses the speculative quality of the work. Imagine Raphael's *Transfiguration of St. Peter.* Disaggregate "the painted fragments which form the mosaic" and give them to another artist (4). "He would," says the editor, "put them together in a form, whose mode would be fashioned by his own peculiar mind and talent" (4). The prophetic imagination might, then, play out one "ideal" history but it is never permitted to make more than *provisional images*. If *The Last Man* defensively rebinds Prometheus by explicitly predicting the future, it also treats this picture as infinitely decomposable.

As Charlotte Sussman points out, "Because of its resemblance to Mary Shelley's world and because it was written after the deaths of Percy Shelley, Byron, and others in her circle, *The Last Man* has often has been read as a personal memoir written in the key of apocalypse."[81] What the foregoing has argued contests this assessment. The history with which the text leaves us is radically anonymous in origin and end. The space of history it clears through its (near) self-annihilation is devoid of any ideas, precedents, or plans – there is no apocalyptic revelation. If humanism manages to hang on by a thread, what *The Last Man* really brings to an end is any recourse to apocalypse. For Wordsworth and Kant, apocalypse was still a possibility – and an attractive one – because, for each, there is a world "beyond" appearances, beyond history as mere distortion. While Percy Shelley holds similar ideas in much of his writing, in *Hellas,* by contrast, history is decidedly *not* a cover or mask for some deeper but occluded truth. It is for this reason that prophetic prediction is a moot point. Similarly, Blake's thinking about historical redemption through harrowing is never purely recollective or restitutive. Rather, in *Milton* he calls on an imagination that is inspired to reinvent itself and history in ways that explode precedent and prevailing identities. Rather than map out the future, we observed how prophecy often turned us back to the paradoxes of the past: instead of the future, we face the impossibility – with Kierkegaard and Schelling as well – of even beginning history, the challenge of writing history in the breach of time when all ends, all "works," seem to have dispersed.

Likewise, Mary Shelley's *The Last Man* is a prophecy of an apocalypse that never happens. Its origin in the cave of the Sybil is as hypermediated as its end is impossible. That is, the text illustrates an impossible history, a story about how history really is impossible. In affirming this impossibility, Shelley does the only thing one can do at the end of history and the end of man, or in the wake of what Bataille called "interior experience," the moment when "radical negation that no longer has anything to negate *is affirmed.*"[82] Shelley's prophecy thus takes us toward what is unthought and unthinkable, not by positing ideas that outstrip comprehension but, rather, by gaining proximity to something beyond the idea of history. What we read is a history, our history, made vulnerable to an inhuman end. By embracing what Blanchot in *Le Dernier Homme* calls "unlimited weakness," Shelley's history trades ideas of the future for much leaner fare. Indeed, Shelley's affirmation is the affirmation of Blanchot's last man: an "assent to mere presence without anything that could appear, on the margin of the world constituted by man."[83] A prophecy to end apocalypse.

Afterword

It is clear that contemporary Western culture remains fascinated by prophecy and prophecies of massive destruction especially. Post-apocalyptic films, television shows, and novels abound, furnishing us with a seemingly endless series of global plagues and environmental disasters, of zombies and Terminators, of Thunderdomes and Hunger Games. The irony of this proliferation of endings – an endless series of endings – is something we are, in light of the foregoing study, better positioned to understand as part of a broader literary and cultural trend that includes the Romantic period in an important way. But beyond these most obvious forms of cultural production, we might also think about the realities of economic apocalypse and the varieties of prophecy to which it gives rise. While the economic collapse in 2008 was brought about by a series of factors beyond the scope of this project to address, suffice it to say that many problems stemmed from a remarkable short-sightedness in spite of an obsession among investors with predicting future trends. In a particularly ironic turn, futures contracts, designed to bring stability to markets by fixing future prices, only exacerbated problems when they themselves became objects of rampant speculation. Banking on the future has never been so literal or so costly. In such climates, Mary Shelley's imposter prophet returns as Bernie Madoff and any number of other "advisors" who are only too happy to prophesy for profit. There are also, to be sure, more recognizably religious prophets as well. Harold Camping – repeatedly predicting the Rapture for the better part of three decades, up until his death in December of 2013 – maintained and even gained followers over the course of his career.[1] The rise of so-called megachurches in the United States, helmed by charismatic leaders, also suggests that the biblical mode of prophetic performance remains important today for many. Something, however, of that fascination with destruction also inheres in these institutions, whose popularity seems undiminished in spite of not infrequent scandal and occasional collapse.[2]

To what extent is thinking about Romantic prophecy helpful for framing the variety of apocalypses that occupy contemporary culture? Indeed, that we have to talk about apocalypses in the plural suggests the need for some clarification. The finality and totality that traditionally defined apocalypse is displaced and fragmented, as if there are multiple endings in a variety of different registers that still could be understood as, somehow, apocalyptic. That this is so may be one of the most tangible and lasting effects of prophecy's repeated failures, something that this study has argued comes to consciousness with special force in the Romantic period. It also seems to inform the confusion we witness with post-apocalyptic art as a genre. That is, the term most often connotes ruined worlds, situations where the earth, the human race, or the values we hold most dear are at risk of extinction. That the genre does *not* signify a blissful, utopian world and a redeemed, enlightened humanity testifies to the degree to which the term "apocalypse" has been hollowed out. It is as if Romantic prophecy's resistance to historicism's crypto-apocalypticism has, through this very pressure, contributed to the evolution of apocalypse into something less spectacular but equally insidious. Displacing the stultifying and tyrannical logics and politics of apocalypse, prophecy's fragmentation of the End into various and incomplete ends has not liberated human potential. Instead, the proliferation of false endings has engendered a new sort of inertia, a changelessness that trades imminent terror for pervasive boredom.

While the timelines proposed in seminal texts such as *The Limits of Growth* (1972) have been revised in subsequent editions,[3] experts in geology, population biology, paleontology, ecology, and system modelling argue that the earth is on the brink of an ecological "tipping point."[4] Yet, like so many modern-day Cassandras, these experts appear unable to spur significant change in policy and practice. It is as if prophecy's historical tendency to fail has sapped any urgency surrounding prospective catastrophes in contemporary culture. We suffer an exhaustion born from historical unpredictability; we have, like Percy Shelley's Mahmud, dismissed Ahasuerus, sure he has nothing to tell us about the outcome of impending conflicts. Refusing to be duped by the writing on the wall, Western liberal democracy has become particularly vulnerable to the lure of what Fredric Jameson, Slavoj Žižek, and Alenka Zupančič have all identified as a particularly idiosyncratic understanding of the possible: while "anything is possible" in the medical–technological enhancement of consumption, it has become impossible to imagine a genuine change in political, economic, social, or environmental reality. As Jameson has it, today "it is easier to imagine the end of the world than the end of capitalism."[5] Put slightly otherwise, it is entirely possible to imagine that capitalism will usher in the end of the world and yet impossible to imagine mitigating that eventuality; in attempting to intervene to save the dying patient we are warned off on grounds that we might accidentally kill him. Yet, if you go on so the result will be so. As Blake notes, this is not really a prophetic statement, just common sense. And yet, contemporary culture has grown so numb to alarming pronouncements that the obvious threats to continued existence seem utterly impossible to hear or heed.

If prophecy's failure was a resource for Romantics, it was so because it helped to dismantle the prevailing ideology of apocalypse. But the future's foreclosure with which we are threatened today is not apocalyptic in that older sense. What we need is a sharper distinction between apocalypse and disaster. Morton Paley's discussion, touched on above, of apocalypse without millennium suggests, indeed, that destruction severed from its recuperative moment (millennium) is something qualitatively different from apocalypse. This different sort of threat – we could call it disaster – is precisely what contemporary culture faces and yet seems unable to respond to. Disasters are not the result of divine intervention. As such, they do not include any of the promised gifts of apocalypse: knowledge, revelation, redemption, atonement, recuperation. If contemporary culture is unresponsive to imminent disaster, it is at least in part because we have confused the portents delivered by scientists with those delivered by prophets. *Apocalypse* has cried wolf so many times, there is no longer any collective response when *disaster* – humanitarian, ecological, ethical – begins to sound in reminiscent tones. The resources gleaned from a reconsideration of Romantic prophecy will be useful in this new context to the extent that they may help us to distinguish productive uncertainty from crippling precariousness, economic revolution from technical innovation, and critical scepticism from gutless deferral. A new prophecy will have to contend with and help to dismantle the neoliberal future: a future that seems endlessly open and infinitely plastic – provided no real change in social, economic, political, or environmental reality derails existing networks of privilege and power. This future seems bright but its brightness is, like the shape all light, blinding. Romantic prophecy today would have to darken this empty radiance as the first step to thinking the future beyond the pantomime of false choices. Exposing rapid alteration as the counterfeit of evolution, the new prophecy will have to make plain what is in many ways an obvious and yet currently unthinkable fact: states, as Blake insists, can actually change.

Notes

Introduction

1 Wesley, *The Journal of the Rev. John Wesley*, 432. Wesley makes this comment in 1789.
2 "A Convert" [Anon.], *The Age of Prophecy!*, 2. Hereafter "Convert."
3 See Hill, *The World Turned Upside Down*, 91.
4 Weber, *The Sociology of Religion*.
5 Ibid., 49.
6 Blake, *The Poetry and Prose of William Blake*, *J.* 10:20, E. 153. Along with the standard abbreviations of Blake's works, including, where applicable, plate and line number, these notes follow the practice of indicating the page number in Erdman's edition as well, abbreviated "E."
7 Ibid., 58–9.
8 Blake, "THERE is NO Natural Religion" [b], *The Poetry and Prose of William Blake*, E. 2. On probable and possible history pp. 144–51.
9 See Paley's *Apocalypse*, 21–2, for additional sources for this kind of mapping of the millennium onto the political moment of the 1790s.
10 Brothers, *God's Awful Warnings*.
11 Ibid., my emphasis.
12 [Anon.] "Analogy of sacred history and prophecy.
13 Ibid., 28, 29.
14 Dobbs, *A concise view from history and prophecy*, 201, 206.
15 Dukes, *Religious politics*, 18–19.
16 Franks, *Memoirs of Pretended Prophets*, iii.
17 Paine, *The Age of Reason, Part the Third*, 44.

18 Oliver, *Prophets and Millennialists*, 43.

19 See chapter 1 for a more sustained discussion of Enlightenment historiography and the rise of the philosophy of history. See Bradley's *The Presuppositions of Critical History* (1874) for an example of how the Higher Criticism, following Spinoza but gaining wider traction in the eighteenth century, informs positivistic historical methods in the later nineteenth century.

20 See for instance Blair's *Lectures on Rhetoric and Belles Lettres*, 259–60. For an analysis of Blair in the context of the Scottish Enlightenment's historiographies, see Phillips, *Society and Sentiment.*

21 See Collingwood, *The Idea of History*, 132–3.

22 See, for instance, von Ranke's *History of the Latin and Teutonic Nations*; Ranke places special emphasis on what we would call primary sources.

23 Collingwood, *The Idea of History*,144.

24 Edinburgh: William Creech, 1795.

25 Ibid., 41, 42.

26 Ibid., 37.

27 Speaking of the sense of history in a parallel context around 1800, Rebecca Comay writes: "German history scans as a dissonant counterpoint of divergent rhythms running along separate tracks, each set to a different tempo and a different beat. Racing forever ahead of an event to which it can never catch up, forever Achilles to the tortoise, Germany, around 1800, presents the perfect model of historical nonsynchronicity." Comay, *Mourning Sickness*, 2.

28 Blake, *The Complete Poetry*, E. 481.

29 Comay, *Mourning Sickness*, 5.

30 Wordsworth, *The Prelude*, 5.96. Unless otherwise noted, all citations from *The Prelude* are from the 1805 version.

31 Tocqueville, *The State of Society*, 192. Hereafter *State.*

32 Ibid.

33 Tocqueville, *Democracy in America*, 883. Hereafter *Democracy.*

34 Ibid., 1106.

35 Lefort, *Democracy and Political Theory*, 258.

36 *Democracy*, 884.

37 *State*, 22. My emphasis.

38 Herder, "This Too a Philosophy of History for the Formation of Humanity" (1774), *Philosophical Writings*, 341.

39 Paine, 67.

40 Ibid., 66, 65.

41 Ibid., 20.

42 Ibid., 65.

43 Koselleck, *Zeitschichten.*

44 Koselleck, *Futures Past*, 56. Hereafter *Futures.*

45 Thompson, *The Making of the English Working Class*, 191.

46 *Futures*, 240.

47 Ibid., 203.

48 Bakhtin, "Forms of Time and of the Chronotope in the Novel," in *The Dialogic Imagination*.

49 *Futures*, 243.

50 Whipple, *North American Review*, 359.

51 Ibid., 359–60. The point here is not that one must agree with Whipple that there really are no parallels to the events circa 1790–1820. That is a fairly extravagant claim. The present study is, rather, concerned with the prevalence of the *belief* that this is so, with the growing sense – whether this is "true" or not, however one might determine this – that life is losing its historical coordinates.

52 James Chandler, *England in 1819*, 78. See also his "Introduction" (with Maureen McLane) to *The Cambridge Companion to British Romantic Poetry*, 2. Other historians, like John Zammito, also endorse this periodization of historiography's self-reflection. See "Historians and Philosophy of Historiography," in *A Companion to the Philosophy of History and Historiography*, 63–84, especially pages 65–6; and Stephen Bann's *The Clothing of Clio*. On the philosophy of history as a context for Romantic prophecy, see chapter 1, pp. 38–45.

53 Williams, *Culture and Society*, 36.

54 Ibid., 277–8.

55 Copjec, "The Tomb of Perseverance: On Antigone," in *The Ethics of History*, 118–54, 125.

56 Ibid., 125–6.

57 Blake, *MHH*, 14, E., 39.

58 Goldsmith, *Unbuilding Jerusalem*, 5. Hereafter *Unbuilding*.

59 Balfour, *The Rhetoric of Romantic Prophecy*.

60 Ibid., 46, 18.

61 Goldsmith, *Blake's Agitation*, 5. Hereafter *Agitation*.

62 Quoted in *Agitation*, 3.

63 Bruns, *Maurice Blanchot*, 127.

64 Ibid., 136.

65 See Fry, *Wordsworth and the Poetry of What We Are* as another example of a contemporary study of Romanticism from a phenomenological-existential point of view.

66 Erdman, *Blake*, 203.

67 *Agitation*, 7.

68 Ibid.

69 Blumenberg, *The Legitimacy of the Modern Age*, 224.

70 Ibid., 28, my emphasis. For instance, the Millerites remain active today in the form of the Seventh-day Adventist Church not merely in spite of the so-called Great Disappointment of 22 October 1844 but, this argument goes, thanks to it.
71 See chapter 8, pp. 199–203, for more on Southcott.
72 Reece, *A Correct Statement*, 105–6.
73 Bolter and Grusin, *Remediation*, 5. By "double logic" they mean the conflicting impulse where "our culture wants both to multiply media and to erase all traces of mediation: ideally, it wants to erase its media in the very act of multiplying them" (5).
74 Markley, "New Media and the Natural World: The Dialectics of Desire," 33–57, 34.
75 "Medium," Oxford English Dictionary Online. The first use of this term to designate a spiritualist given in the OED dates from 1851. However, this example does not read as a coinage, suggesting the term had been in circulation prior to that time.
76 Langan and McLane, "The Medium of Romantic Poetry," 239–62, 241. Hereafter "Medium."
77 Langan, "Understanding Media in 1805," 49–70, 69, 70.
78 Goldsmith, *Agitation*, 60.
79 "Medium," 240, 241.
80 Scott, "My Aunt Margaret's Mirror," 1–44.
81 Ibid., 12.
82 Ibid., 23.
83 Ibid.
84 Ibid.
85 Langan, "*Telepathos*: Medium Cool Romanticism," 35 par., par. 16.
86 Pyle, *The Ideology of the Imagination*, 2.
87 Sha, "Imagination," *A Handbook of Romanticism Studies*, 19–36, 19.
88 White, *Romantic Returns*, 5.
89 Pyle, *The Ideology of the Imagination*, 10.
90 Von Rad, *Old Testament Theology*, 1.66.
91 All references are to *The Bible: Authorized King James Version with Apocrypha* unless otherwise noted.
92 Gleig, "Prophecy," *Encyclopædia Britannica*, 15. 595, 596; Smith, "Prophetical Books of the Old Testament," *Encyclopædia Britannica*.
93 E., 898.
94 See Abrams, *Natural Supernaturalism*, 12.
95 Ibid., 31.
96 Ibid., 255.
97 Shelley, *Defence of Poetry*, in *Shelley's Poetry and Prose*, 535. All references to Percy Shelley's poetry and prose are to this edition, abbreviated *SPP*, unless otherwise indicated.

98 See Wittreich's *Angel of Apocalypse*, *Visionary Poetics*, and his edited collections, *Blake's Sublime Allegory* and *Milton and the Line of Vision*. Harold Bloom's *The Visionary Company* also organizes its approach to Romanticism's prophetic mode in terms similar to Wittreich's.

99 Wittreich, "'A Poet Amongst Poets': Milton and the Tradition of Prophecy," in *Milton and the Line of Vision*, 97–142, 99. Hereafter "A Poet."

100 Ibid., 101.

101 Ibid., 102, 104.

102 Koselleck, *The Practice of Conceptual History*, 127.

103 McGann, "The Aim of Blake's Prophecies and the Uses of Blake Criticism," in *Blake's Sublime Allegory*, 3–21, 6.

104 Wittreich, "A Poet," 105.

105 Mary Shelley, *Valperga*, 344.

1 Secularization and the New Ends of History

1 Carra, *System de la raison*, iv.

2 In Koselleck, *Futures*, 18.

3 Ibid.

4 John Milbank, *Theology & Social Theory*, 9.

5 Monod in Pecora, *Secularization and Cultural Criticism*, 5.

6 Ibid.

7 Carl Schmitt, *Political Theology*, 36. Compare Abrams, *Natural Supernaturalism*, 13.

8 Hans Blumenberg, *The Legitimacy of the Modern Age*, 20.

9 Charles Taylor, *A Secular Age*, 86.

10 Blumenberg, *The Legitimacy of the Modern Age*, 48.

11 Ibid., 48–9.

12 Abrams, *Natural Supernaturalism*, 12.

13 Blumenberg, *The Legitimacy of the Modern Age*, 466. My emphasis.

14 Hayden White, *Tropics of Discourse*, 102.

15 Ibid., 110–11.

16 Ibid., 106. Compare Bann, *The Clothing of Clio*, 9.

17 Phillips, *Society and Sentiment*, 45.

18 Blanchot, *The Book to Come*, 79. Hereafter *Book.*

19 Ibid.

20 In terms of critical interlocutors, Blanchot has not, historically, been central to Romantic studies, appearing most often in discussions of Romantic fragmentation and aphorism. See Lacoue-Labarthe and Nancy's *The Literary Absolute* and Strathman's *Romantic Poetry and the Fragmentary Imperative*. Yet, in spite of his relative marginality, there is an ongoing – if niche – interest in Blanchot as a

reader of Romanticism. See Khalip's *Anonymous Life* and McKeane and Opeiz's recent essay collection, *Blanchot Romantique*. Closer to home, Balfour in *The Rhetoric of Romantic Prophecy* also briefly discusses Blanchot's "On Prophetic Speech."

21 See "*The Last Man*: Apocalypse Without Millennium," in *The Other Mary Shelley*, ed. Fisch, Mellor, and Schor, 107–23.
22 *Book*, 82–3.
23 Jacobus, *Romantic Things*, 96.
24 *Book*, 82.
25 Ibid., 81–2.
26 Ibid., 79.
27 See Joshua 13:33; Genesis 49:5–7.
28 Kierkegaard, *The Concept of Irony*, 259.
29 Collings, *Monstrous Society*, 41.
30 Hegel, *Aesthetics*, 1.68–9.
31 Ibid., 2.1209.
32 Ibid., 1.159, 1.160.
33 Ibid., 1.160.
34 In fact, in the *Philosophy of Right*, Hegel will define Romantic irony explicitly as a product of Fichte's attempt to unify intuition and intellect in pure subjectivity. See *Hegel's Philosophy of Right*, 258.
35 Kojève, *Introduction to the Reading of Hegel: Lectures on the Phenomenology of Spirit*, 109.
36 Kierkegaard, *The Concept of Irony*, 254.
37 Ibid., 259.
38 Ibid., 259.
39 Ibid., 261.
40 Ibid., 248.
41 de Man, *Aesthetic Ideology*, 179.
42 Voltaire, *The Philosophy of History*, 123. In the interests of gauging how Voltaire was presented to an English readership, the present study engages with this early translation. For the standard modern edition see *The Complete Works of Voltaire*.
43 Ibid., 221.
44 See Markus, *Saeculum*.
45 Phillips, *Society and Sentiment*, 177.
46 Voltaire, *The Philosophy of History*, 1.
47 Markus, *Saeculum*, 192.
48 Adler and Menze, "Introduction," in *On World History, An Anthology*, 3–22, 9.
49 Voltaire, *The Philosophy of History*, 211.
50 In Löwith, *The Meaning in History*, 17.
51 Ibid., 18.

52 See also Rudwick: "What in the eighteenth century is called 'history' embraced all those sciences that aimed to *describe* the diversity of the world; 'philosophy' incorporated those that sought to *explain* how the world works." *Bursting the Limits of Time*, 49.
53 Phillips, *Society and Sentiment*, 171.
54 Bann, *Romanticism and the Rise of History*, 3–4.
55 Herder, "Older Critical Forestlet," *Philosophical Writings*, 257–67, 259.
56 Ibid., 260.
57 Koselleck, *Futures*, 17.
58 Schlegel, *Philosophy of History*, 1.lxxix.
59 Hegel, *The Philosophy of History*, 79.
60 Ibid., 34.
61 Ibid., 29.
62 Ibid., 47.
63 Ibid., 39.
64 Ibid., 47–8.
65 Dupré, *Passage to Modernity*, 10.
66 Dupré, *The Enlightenment*, 4.
67 Ibid., 12.
68 Herder, "This Too a Philosophy of History for the Formation of Humanity," in *Herder: Philosophical Writings*, 272–360, 285–6. All emphasis is Herder's unless otherwise indicated. Hereafter "This Too."
69 Ibid., 286.
70 Ibid.
71 Ibid. 286, 289.
72 Ibid., 298.
73 Ibid.
74 Ibid., 320.
75 Ibid., 299.
76 Ibid., 298–9.
77 Ibid., 299.
78 Herder, "Letters for the Advancement of Humanity," *Herder: Philosophical Writings*, 380–424, 396.
79 Ibid., 414.
80 Ibid., 395.
81 As Friedrich Schlegel puts it in his Vienna lectures, "the Philosophy of history, as it is the spirit or idea of history, must be deduced from real historical events" (65). The idea of history, he continues, "must be the pure emanation of the great whole" (65), must in other words be shaped by – rather than determine preemptively and impose upon – the historical scene. *The Philosophy of History*.
82 Eichner, "The Rise of Modern Science and the Genesis of Romanticism," 8–30, 16.

83 William Wordsworth, *The Prelude*, 6.542. All citations from *The Prelude* are, unless otherwise noted, from the 1805 version.

84 Ibid.

85 See ch. 8, pp. 214–22.

86 Baker, "Natural Science and the Romanticisms," 387–412, 390.

87 Forster, "Introduction," *Herder*, xxvii.

88 Herder, "This Too," 335.

89 Vašíček, "Philosophy of History," in *A Companion*, 26–43, 27–8.

90 Herder, "This Too," 296.

91 Ibid., 258, 259.

92 Ibid., 259.

93 Ibid., 260.

94 Ibid. In the passage here quoted, Herder is phrasing these points as leading questions. For the sake of clarity, I have phrased what I take to be Herder's aim more directly. This is not to suggest, however, that the form of the text is unimportant. My sense is that the rhetorical choice in this case is determined by Herder's attempt not to alienate the historical society in Göttingen. By posing his criticisms as questions for investigation and phrasing the task as one concerned with "*our* thinking," collectively, Herder is being prudent rather than harbouring genuine doubts about his own conclusions.

95 Ibid., 260.

96 See Schelling, *Ages of The World [1815]*, xl.

97 Von Rad, *Old Testament Theology*, 2.13.

98 Shaffer, *Kubla Khan and the Fall of Jerusalem*, 22. It is important to note that while this sensibility gains traction in the late eighteenth century and develops greatly through the nineteenth century, this was by no means the first time scholars interrogated the Bible in this fashion. Spinoza's 1670 *Tractatus Theologico-Politicus*, for instance, is an important early work that attempts to read the Bible according to a secular hermeneutic standard.

99 Eichhorn, *Introduction to the Study of the Old Testament*, xi.

100 Ibid., 114.

101 Ibid.

102 See Stuart Weeks, "Predictive and Prophetic Literature: Can *Neferti* Help Us Read the Bible?" in *Prophecy and Prophets in Ancient Israel*, 25–46, 29.

103 Nissinen, "Comparing Prophetic Sources: Principles and a Test Case," in *Prophecy and Prophets*, 3–24, 9.

104 Ibid., 12. See also *Writings and Speech in Israelite and Ancient Near East Prophecy*, Zvi and Floyd, eds.

105 Von Rad, *Old Testament Theology*, 332.

106 Ibid., 45.

107 Ibid., 45–6.
108 Ibid., 46.
109 Ibid.
110 Carroll, *When Prophecy Failed*, 40.
111 Ibid., 58.
112 Ibid.
113 See Derrida, *Of Grammatology*, 61.
114 Nissinen, "Comparing Prophetic Sources," 12.
115 Löwith, *The Meaning in History*.
116 Schlegel, *Philosophical Fragments*, 27. See Benjamin's well-known adaptation of this image in "Theses on the Philosophy of History," *Illuminations*, 253–64.
117 Carroll, *When Prophecy Failed*, 41–2.
118 Plug, *Borders of a Lip*, 50.

2 Prophecy within the Limits of Reason Alone

1 Larsen, *Emanuel Swedenborg*, 45.
2 See ch. 6, pp. 144–51.
3 See Kant, "On a Recently Prominent Tone of Superiority in Philosophy [1796]," in *Theoretical Philosophy after 1781*, 425–46.
4 Kant, *Prolegomena to any future metaphysics that will be able to come forward as a science (1783)*, in *Theoretical Philosophy after 1781*, 29–170, 57.
5 Immanuel Kant, "Dreams of a Spirit-Seer Elucidated by Dreams of Metaphysics" [1766], in *Theoretical Philosophy, 1755–1770*, 301–60, 322. Subsequent citations noted in-text.
6 See *Critique of Pure Reason*, A780/B808, 664.
7 Sewall refers to "the half serious, half ironical style which characterizes this remarkable work" that is "Dreams of a Spirit-Seer" (11).
8 Cassirer, *Kant's Life and Thought*, 77–8.
9 Shell, *The Embodiment of Reason*, 116.
10 Cassirer, *Kant's Life and Thought*, 90.
11 See "Preface" to first edition of *The Critique of Pure Reason*, A: ix.
12 *Callimachus*, ed./trans. Bulloch, 99.
13 Ibid., 101.
14 Ibid.
15 Ovid, *Metamorphoses*, 149.
16 See ch. 8, pp. 206–7.
17 Bulloch, "Introduction," *Callimachus*, 23.
18 Blanchot, *Book*, 81–2.
19 Blanchot, *The Work of Fire*, 120. Hereafter *Fire*.

20 Gadamer, *Truth and Method*, 25, 36–7.
21 Gadamer, *Truth and Method*, 260, 270.
22 Ibid., 274.
23 Ibid.
24 Kant, *Critique of the Power of Judgement*, 20:197, 4.
25 Ibid.
26 Ibid.
27 Shell, *The Embodiment of Reason*, 117.
28 Lucretius, *On the Nature of Things*, 41.
29 Gadamer, *Truth and Method*, 273.
30 Ibid., 179.
31 Ibid.
32 Dupré, *The Enlightenment*, 16.
33 Ibid., 31.
34 Shelley, *Zastrozzi & St. Irvyne*, 252.
35 Tarbet, "The Fabric of Metaphor in Kant's *Critique of Pure Reason*," 257–70, 259.
36 See ch. 4, p. 103.
37 Kant, *Critique of Pure Reason*, [A6/B10] 129.
38 Ibid., [A7/B11] 130.
39 Ibid.
40 Palmquist, *Kant's System of Perspectives*, 115.
41 Shell, *The Embodiment of Reason*, 118.
42 [Bxxx] 117.
43 [B12] 142.
44 Palmquist, "A Priori Knowledge in Perspective," 255–82, 271.

3 Ghostlier Demarcations: Mysticism, Trauma, Anachronism

1 Wordsworth, "Essays upon Epitaphs," *21st-Century Oxford Authors*, 535–54, 537. Hereafter "Epitaphs."
2 Ibid., 539.
3 Wordsworth, *The Prelude*, 6.542. All citations from *The Prelude* are, unless otherwise noted, from the 1805 version.
4 "Epitaphs," 540, 541.
5 *The Prelude* 6.151–2, "Tintern Abbey," 100, 102–3. Wordsworth, *The Collected Poetry*. All in-text citations of Wordsworth's poetry refer to line numbers.
6 On Wordsworth's avoidance of apocalyptic consciousness, see Hartman, *Wordsworth's Poetry*. On reinvesting apocalyptic revelation into nature itself, see also Hartman's "A Poet's Progress" in *Modern Philology*, 214–24.

7 See Steven Goldsmith's reading of Joseph Mede's 1642 *The Key of Revelation*. Mede stresses the "interior, nonlinear, spatial logic" of apocalyptic representation, an event best captured as a "harmonious, mathematical order." Goldsmith, *Unbuilding*, 98–9.

8 Strictly speaking, Aristotle's law, noted in *Metaphysics*, Book XI(K), states that "There is a principle in things, about which we cannot be deceived, but must always, on the contrary, recognize the truth, - vis. that the same thing cannot at one and the same time be and not be, or admit any other similar pair of opposites" ([1026a19–1677] 2.155). *The Complete Works of Aristotle*, ed. Barnes.

9 Ibid.

10 Like the "indisputable shapes" (11.381) that recall King Hamlet's "questionable shape," we should not be surprised to see Wordsworth treat poetic precursors as haunting spirits. See Jonathan Wordsworth's *William Wordsworth*, page 63, and Bate's *Shakespeare and the English Romantic Imagination*, page 116.

11 Liu, *Wordsworth*, 13, 223.

12 Bann, *Romanticism*, 3.

13 Žižek, "The Abyss of Freedom," 62.

14 Numbers 11:29.

15 The editors' note to this passage suggests an allusion to Acts 2:3–4. While that is perfectly reasonable, it seems that it might also gesture toward Numbers, especially given the context, in the Old Testament, of state-founding and formation.

16 See Madden, "The Religious Politics of Prophecy," 270–84, 272.

17 Derrida, *Given Time 1*, 27.

18 Ibid.

19 Benjamin, *Illuminations*, 222.

20 Jonah 3:4–10. For a discussion of Jonah's prophecy alongside Blake, see Balfour's *The Rhetoric of Romantic Prophecy*, 129–30.

21 Deuteronomy 18:21–2. See also Swedenborg, *Arc. Col.* 5.2493, #3698.

22 See Frye, *Fearful Symmetry*, 403.

23 To be discredited and dismissed is also the fate of Cassandra. See ch. 8, pp. 198–9.

24 Blanchot, *Fire*, 303.

25 "Prelude: 3. *Music*. Originally: a short, often extemporized, piece of music played before another in order to tune an instrument or allow an instrumentalist to warm up (*obs.*). Now: (*a*) a piece designed as the formal introduction to a musical work, *esp.* a movement preceding a fugue or forming the first piece of a suite" (Oxford English Dictionary Online).

26 Blanchot, *Fire*, 305.

27 Larkin, "Wordsworth's Maculate Exception," 30–5, 30.

28 Blanchot, *Book*, 85.

29 These lines (and all subsequent citations of "Home at Grasmere," unless otherwise indicated) are taken from Manuscript D as reproduced in Beth Darlington's parallel

text edition of "Home at Grasmere." The only significant variation from his later version of the poem – i.e., that reproduced in the posthumous 1888 *Complete Poetical Works of William Wordsworth* – with respect to the passage quoted, is that here Wordsworth's invocation opens with "*come* thou prophetic Spirit" whereas later versions begin "*descend* thou prophetic Spirit." The earlier Manuscript D version – dating likely somewhere between 1812 and 1814 (Darlington 25) – has the virtue of echoing the apocalyptic language characteristic of the Book of Revelation, again suggesting that Wordsworth sees himself in some respects akin to the biblical prophets.

30 Compare Weiskel, *The Romantic Sublime*, 154.

31 Blanchot, *The Infinite Conversation*, 355. Hereafter *Infinite*.

32 See ch. 7, pp. 171–6.

33 Given their importance in *The Prelude,* most studies of Wordsworth advance readings of the spots of time. Of texts directly and consistently focused on the spots, the present study has found the following most helpful: Ellis' *Wordsworth, Freud, and the Spots of Time*; Simpson's *Wordsworth and the Figurings of the Real*; Hartman's *Wordsworth's Poetry* and *The Unremarkable Wordsworth*. Thinking of these and other studies, Peter Larkin notes that "a critical consensus has tended to maintain that Wordsworth's childhood memories are marked more by trauma than mystic import" (30). The present reading does not deny this consensus but asks only why mystic import and trauma should be thought as opposed experiences. In stressing the curious immutability of these mutable, refigurable moments, the following understands the spots in terms closest perhaps to Paul H. Fry's. In his discussion of the ostensive mode in literature as what precedes rhetorical or historical signification, he describes the spots of time as "semantically underdetermined moments of uncanny intensity from which historical meaning and social context are [...] excluded." Fry, *A Defense of Poetry*, 35. This very exclusion, however, creates the conditions – a demand – for subsequent analysis, both rhetorical and historical. At the same time, such responses will always miss the essence of that radically underdetermined subjective priming or sensitization.

34 Richardson, "Wordsworth at the Crossroads," 15–20, 15.

35 Blake, *The Marriage of Heaven and Hell*, Plt. 15, E. 40. Along with the standard abbreviations of Blake's works, including, where applicable, plate and line number, these notes follow the practice of indicating the page number in Erdman's edition as well, abbreviated "E."

36 As Collings notes, the speaker's feverish, obsessive gesturing to the home – "here ... here" – in lines 136–40 of "Home at Grasmere" sound panicked, alarmed, and, indeed, alarming, recalling what he calls Wordsworth's "Masochistic Repetition" (69). Collings, *Wordsworthian Errancies*.

37 Collings, *Wordsworthian Errancies*, 123.
38 Ibid., 151.
39 Ibid., 118.
40 De Quincey, "On Wordsworth's 'There was a boy,'" 641.
41 This follows Collings' reading of what Douglas Kneale describes as the "'monumental' letters" (137) inscribed by "Some unknown hand" (11.294) at the base of the moldering gibbet-mast. Kneale, *Monumental Writing*. See Collings, *Wordsworthian Errancies*, 145–6.
42 "Epitaphs," 547. For another discussion centred more on Burke and the question of public execution that takes up the *Essays upon Epitaphs* in connection to the gibbet-mast episode, see Bringham's "Frail Memorials," 15–31.
43 Ibid.
44 Larkin, "Wordsworth's Maculate Exception," 33.
45 Locke, *An Essay Concerning Human Understanding*, 2.1.2.
46 Davies, "Wordsworth and the Empirical Philosophers," 153–74, 162.
47 Ibid.
48 Ibid., 157.
49 Locke, 1.1.15, 2.11.17.
50 Ibid., 2.10.5.
51 Burke, *Attitudes Toward History*, 59.
52 Milton, *Paradise Lost*, *The Complete Poems*, 2.1026–8. Hereafter *Paradise Lost*.
53 Hartman, *The Unremarkable Wordsworth*, 24.
54 Ibid., 24.
55 *MHH*, 24, E., 44.
56 Weber, *The Sociology of Religion*, 47.
57 Kant, "Dreams of a Spirit-Seer," 301–60, 306.

4 Beyond the Sign of History: Prophetic Semiotics and the Future's Reflection

1 De Quincey, "The Last Days of Immanuel Kant," 3.99–166, 3.111. On the political see also Kant, *Anthropology from a Pragmatic Point of View*, 186. Hereafter *Anthropology*.
2 See Alison's "Introduction," in *Theoretical Philosophy after 1781*, 1–28.
3 Kant, *Theoretical Philosophy after 1781*, 417.
4 Ibid.
5 Ibid.
6 Ibid.
7 Kant, *The Conflict of the Faculties*. Hereafter *Conflict*.
8 Balfour, *The Rhetoric of Romantic Prophecy*, 19. Kant, "On a Recently Prominent Tone of Superiority in Philosophy [1796]," 425–46, 439, 443.

9 See Clark, "We 'Other Prussians,'" 261–87. Hereafter "Prussians."
10 Kant, *Critique of the Power of Judgement*, [5:276] 157. Hereafter *Judgement.*
11 *Anthropology*, 59.
12 Kant, *The Critique of Pure Reason*, [A vii] 99.
13 Kant, *The Metaphysics of Morals*, [6.485] 227.
14 "Prussians," 266.
15 Comay, *Mourning Sickness*, 26; Khalip, *Anonymous Life*, 27.
16 See Clark, "Kant's Aliens," 201–89: 206, 207. Hereafter "Aliens."
17 *Conflict*, 143.
18 Fenves, *A Peculiar Fate*, 185.
19 *Conflict*, 169.
20 Ibid., 141, 149.
21 Comay, *Mourning Sickness*, 35.
22 *Anthropology*, 79.
23 *Conflict*, 151. Emphasis added.
24 Deleuze, *Kant's Critical Philosophy*, 12.
25 *Conflict*, 151.
26 Ibid.
27 *Anthropology*, 86–7.
28 Ibid., 87.
29 *Conflict*, 159.
30 Ibid.
31 *Judgement*, 62–3
32 Paul Guyer, "Introduction," *Kant's Critique of the Power of Judgement*, x. See also *Judgement*, 81–2.
33 Kant, *Grounding for the Metaphysics of Morals*, 43.
34 Plug, *Borders of a Lip*, 24.
35 Ibid., 25.
36 Ragussis, "Language and Metamorphosis in Wordsworth's Arab Dream," 148–65, 148, 149.
37 *Judgement*, 71.
38 Guyer, *Kant's Critique of the Power of Judgement*, xvi.
39 Ibid., xv.
40 *Judgement*, 128.
41 Snow, *Schelling and the End of Idealism*, 170.
42 Clark, "Aliens," 208.
43 *Conflict*, 153.
44 Aylesworth, "Lyotard, Gadamer, and the Relation between Ethics and Aesthetics," 84–99, 92.
45 *Conflict*, 151.

46 Ibid., 141.
47 Baucom, *Spectres of the Atlantic*, 115.
48 Abbeele, "Introduction," iv–xiv, xi, my emphasis.
49 Ibid., xii.
50 Lyotard, *Enthusiasm*, 12. Hereafter "Enthusiasm."
51 See Mee, *Romanticism, Enthusiasm, and Regulation.*
52 Cooper, *Shaftesbury*, 10.
53 *Conflict*, 155.
54 *Judgement*, 154.
55 Ibid.
56 Ibid.
57 Guyer, x.
58 Lyotard, *The Differend*, 163.
59 *Conflict*, 159.
60 Lyotard, "The Sign of History," 162–82, 168. Herafter "Sign."
61 *Conflict*, 159.
62 "Sign," 171, 172.
63 Ibid., 172.
64 *Judgement*, 156.
65 Benjamin, "Theses on the Philosophy of History," 253–64, 256.
66 "Sign," 173.
67 "Enthusiasm," 25.
68 Benjamin, 264.
69 Goldsmith, *Agitation*, 2, 67.
70 Ibid., 72.
71 Ibid., 77.
72 Ibid., 74.

5 The Future of an Allusion: Temporalization and Figure in Lyrical Drama

1 Koselleck, *Futures.*
2 Blake, *The Poetry and Prose of William Blake*, *M.*, 2.21, E., 96; *M.*, 32.26., E., 132. Along with the standard abbreviations of Blake's works including, where applicable, plate and line number, these notes follow the practice of indicating the page number in Erdman's edition as well, abbreviated "E."
3 Percy Shelley, *Shelley's Poetry and Prose*, 430, 431. All references to Shelley's poetry and prose are to this edition unless otherwise noted. Poems and dramas are cited by line number, prose by page number.
4 Koselleck, *Geschichtliche Grundbegriffe.*
5 *Futures*, 243.

6 Ibid., 270.
7 Koselleck, *The Practice of Conceptual History*, 4. Hereafter *Practice.*
8 Gadamer, *Truth and Method*, 342.
9 Ibid., 347.
10 Ibid., 350.
11 Ibid.
12 Koselleck, *Futures*, 275.
13 Ibid., 276.
14 Blanchot, *Infinite*.
15 Koselleck, *Practice*, 120.
16 See Ulmer, "*Hellas* and the Historical Uncanny," 611–32.
17 Shelley, *The Triumph of Life*, 334.
18 Wordsworth, *The Prelude*, 2.35–6. All citations from *The Prelude* are, unless otherwise noted, from the 1805 version.
19 de Man, *The Rhetoric of Romanticism*, 98.
20 *Infinite*, 353.
21 On fragmentary accomplishment see Lacoue-Labarthe and Nancy, *The Literary Absolute*.
22 Blanchot, *Infinite*, 315.
23 Ibid.
24 Jacobs, *Uncontainable Romanticism*, 25.
25 Blanchot, *The Step Not Beyond*, 112.
26 See Ulmer, "*Hellas* and the Historical Uncanny, 618–19, for his reading of this complex, layered analogy.
27 Hogle, *Shelley's Process*, 290.
28 "The oracle at Dodona is regarded by ancient writers as the first prophetic centre." Morrison, "The Germanic World," 96.
29 Keats, *Selected Letters*, 41–2.
30 Koselleck, *Futures*, 5.
31 Ibid., 14.
32 Aeschylus, *The Persians*, 164.
33 Ibid., 181–97.
34 Shelley, *Triumph of Life*, 42, 47.
35 Ibid., 409–11.
36 Goldsmith, *Unbuilding*, 235.
37 Comay, *Mourning Sickness*, 58.
38 Gibbon, *The History of the Decline and Fall of the Roman Empire*, 7.197.
39 White, *Tropics of Discourse*, 106.
40 Ibid., 7.212.
41 Goldsmith, *Unbuilding*, 241–2.

6 Auguries of Experience: Impossible History and Infernal Redemption

1 Makdisi, *William Blake and the Impossible History of the 1790s*, 1.

2 Herder, "Older Critical Forestlet," 257–67, 259.

3 Gilchrist, *The Life of William Blake*, 27.

4 Ibid., 113.

5 Blake, *The Poetry and Prose of William Blake*, *M.*, 14.29, E., 108. Along with the standard abbreviations of Blake's works, including, where applicable, plate and line number, these notes follow the practice of indicating the page number in Erdman's edition as well, abbreviated "E."

6 Collings, *Monstrous Society*, 41.

7 Richman, "Milton Re-membered, Graved and Press'd," 385–401, 388. See also Hilton's *Literal Imagination*.

8 See Goldsmith, *Unbuilding*.

9 Paley, *Apocalypse and Millennium*, 2.

10 Goldsmith, *Agitation*, 18.

11 Aristotle, *Poetics*, 1460a27–1460b5.

12 Deleuze, *Bergsonism*, 34.

13 Voltaire, *The Philosophy of History*, 172.

14 See ch. 5, pp. 125–6.

15 Makdisi, *William Blake and the Impossible History of the 1790s*, 1.

16 Goldsmith, "'Cracked Across,'" 305–42, 308.

17 Žižek, "The Abyss of Freedom," 61–2.

18 Massumi, *Parables for the Virtual*, 30.

19 Ibid., 9.

20 Ibid.

21 Deleuze, *Bergsonism*, 18.

22 Ibid., 43.

23 Milton, *Paradise Lost*, 1:16.

24 Ibid., 1:28, 29–31.

25 Frye, *Fearful Symmetry*, 5.

26 Erdman, *Prophet Against Empire*, 29.

27 See Bloom, *The Ringers in the Tower*, 65–79.

28 Wittreich, "Opening the Seals: Blake's Epics and the Milton Tradition," 27.

29 Ibid.

30 Riede, "Blake's *Milton*," 257–77, 275.

31 Paley, *Apocalypse and Millennium in English Romantic Poetry*, 237.

32 Milton, *The Complete Prose Works of John Milton*, 2.543.

33 *Agitation*, 34.

34 Deleuze and Guattari, *A Thousand Plateaus*, 279.

35 Wittreich, "Opening the Seals," 23–58, 47.
36 Renamed "Israel," Jacob becomes identical to the nation itself. See Genesis 32:24–32.
37 McGann, "The Aim of Blake's Prophecies and the Uses of Blake Criticism," 3–21, 9.
38 Ibid., 11.
39 Malekin, rev. *Blake's Sublime Allegory*, 339–43, 340.
40 Schlegel, *Philosophical Fragments*, 24.
41 Wordsworth, *The Prelude*, 5.96–9.
42 Shelley, *Shelley's Poetry and Prose*, 697.
43 *Paradise Lost*, 4.75.
44 Blake, *Complete Writings*, 803.
45 *M.*, 41:30, E., 143.

7 The Preface and Other False Starts: Prophesying the Book to Come

1 Gilchrist, *The Life of William Blake*, 110.
2 Kierkegaard, *Prefaces; Writing Sampler*, 6. Hereafter *Prefaces.*
3 William Blake, *The Complete Poetry and Prose*, *M.*, 32:26, E., 132. Along with the standard abbreviations of Blake's works, including, where applicable, plate and line number, these notes follow the practice of indicating the page number in Erdman's edition as well, abbreviated "E."
4 Hartman, *Criticism in the Wilderness*, 119.
5 On *Urizen* as an inaugural book, see Mann, "The Book of Urizen and the Horizon of the Book," 49–86.
6 Jacobus, *Romantic Things*, 96.
7 Blanchot, *Infinite*, 352–3, my emphasis.
8 Bataille, *Inner Experience*, 6.
9 *U.*, 10:17; *J.*, 75.7. In *Milton*, Los is called "the Prophet of Eternity" (7.38).
10 Fox, *Poetic Form in Blake's* Milton, xii.
11 Schelling, *Ages of The World [1815]*, 17.
12 On Blake and false starts, see Rajan, "(Dis)Figuring the System," 383–411.
13 The etymology of the word "inaugurate" – "To make auspicious or of good augury" (OED 3) – suggests that the notion of starting is linguistically and historically related, in English, to the action of prophecy.
14 Foucault, *The Order of Things*, 362–3.
15 Balfour, "The Future of Citation," 115–28, 117.
16 *Eur.*, 1:1, E., 60.
17 Ibid., 1:9, 5, E., 60.
18 Ibid., 1:10, 2:5, 2:16, E., 61.
19 Makdisi, *William Blake*, 99.
20 Ibid.

21 Ibid.
22 *Eur.*, 2:9–12, E., 61.
23 *Am.*, 16:14–15, E., 57.
24 Schelling, 20.
25 Nichol, "Introduction," vii–xviii, xi.
26 Thulstrup, *Kierkegaard's Relation to Hegel*, 366.
27 Hegel, *Phenomenology of Spirit*, 29.
28 Ibid., 1.
29 Ibid., 2.
30 *Prefaces*, 5.
31 Ibid.
32 Ibid., 3.
33 Thulstrup, *Kierkegaard's Relation to Hegel*, 264.
34 Ibid., 69.
35 Ibid., 260.
36 Kierkegaard, *Prefaces*, 8.
37 Ibid., 12.
38 Ibid., 6.
39 Ibid., 47.
40 Ibid., 51.
41 Ibid., 56.
42 Kierkegaard, *Prefaces*, 59.
43 Blanchot, *The Space of Literature*, 228–9, my emphasis. Hereafter *Space*.
44 Colebrook, "The End of Redemption and the Redemption of Ends," 79–92, 80.
45 Hegel, *Phenomenology of Spirit*, 51.
46 *Space*, 229.
47 *M.*, 42:36-43:1, E., 142–3.
48 Ibid., 24:72, E., 121.
49 Žižek, "The Abyss of Freedom," 30. Original emphasis.
50 Schelling, *Ages of the World*, xxxv.
51 Ibid., 16.
52 Ibid., 44.
53 Ibid., 31.
54 Žižek, "The Abyss of Freedom," 36.
55 Schelling, *Ages of the World*, xl.
56 Ibid.
57 Ibid.
58 Ibid., xxxix.
59 Wirth, "Introduction," in *Ages of The World [1815]*, vii–xxxii, vii.
60 Schelling, *Ages of the World*, 20.

61 Ibid., 12.
62 Ibid., 6, 11.
63 Ibid., 10.
64 Ibid., 33.
65 *U.*, 3:2, E., 70; Schelling, *Ages of the World*, 16, 32, 15.
66 *M.*, 3:10, E., 97.
67 *Am.*, 8:5, E., 54.
68 Ibid.
69 Schelling, *Ages of the World*, 19.
70 Ibid., 21, 20. Schelling frequently distinguishes between "mere Being," or being in itself, and "having being" in the sense of an existent being (22–3). Mere being, or pure being, is an "intermediate" (64) concept, in that it generates a third option between the extremes of having being and nothingness.
71 Ibid., 21.
72 Ibid., 22.
73 Ibid., 23.
74 Ibid., 24.
75 Ibid., 28.
76 Ibid.
77 Ibid., 40.
78 Ibid., 43.
79 Ibid., 44.
80 Žižek, "The Abyss of Freedom," 29.
81 Schelling, *Ages of the World*, 17.
82 *MHH.*, 12, E., 38.
83 Schelling, *Ages of the World*, 75.
84 Ibid., 76.
85 Ibid., 76.
86 Ibid.
87 *M.*, 24:72–3, E., 121.
88 *M.*, 29:1–3, E., 127.
89 Tillich, "Kairos," 194. See Edward J. Rose's "Los, Pilgrim of Eternity" in *Blake's Sublime Allegory: Essays on The Four Zoas, Milton, Jerusalem*, 83–99. Rose makes the connection between Blake's work and Tillich's discussion of Christian temporality.
90 See Barfoot's "'Milton Silent Came Down My Path,'" 61–84.
91 *M.*, 35:43, E., 136.
92 Schelling, *Ages of the World*, 21.
93 Ibid., 29.
94 Wirth, "Introduction," in *Ages of the World [1815]*, xxxi.
95 Schelling, *Ages of the World*, 76.

96 Rajan, "'The Abyss of the Past,'" 35 paragraphs, par. 7. Rajan also gestures to the philosophical background of the key terms addressed below: "the idea of the prototype or ectype derives from Jean-Baptiste Robinet's post-Spinozist *De la Nature,* which sees nature as a historical process of working out an original 'prototype' through time, although Robinet is arguably less anthropological than his successors" (§7).
97 Schelling, *Ages of the World*, 55, 56.
98 Ibid., 44.
99 Ibid., my emphasis.
100 Ibid., 45.
101 Ibid., 59.
102 Ibid.
103 Ibid.
104 Rajan, "Abyss of the Past," par. 8
105 Schelling, *Ages of the World*, 59.
106 Ibid., 64.
107 Ibid., 65.
108 Ibid. 48.
109 Ibid., 5.

8 "a woman clothed with the Sun": Female Prophecy and Catastrophe

1 Blake, *The Poetry and Prose of William Blake, M.*, 41.2–7, E., 142. Along with the standard abbreviations of Blake's works, including, where applicable, plate and line number, these notes follow the practice of indicating the page number in Erdman's edition as well, abbreviated "E."
2 Blake, "Auguries of Innocence," 49, E. 491.
3 Jameson, *Archaeologies of the Future*, xiii.
4 See Hegel, *Aesthetics*.
5 Gilchrist, *The Life of William Blake*, 95, 96.
6 See ch. 2, pp. 57–8.
7 Paley, "Mary Shelley's *The Last Man*," 1–25, 12.
8 Juster, "Mystical Pregnancy and Holy Bleeding," 249–88.
9 Bloch, *Atheism in Christianity*, 89.
10 Ibid.
11 See Waszink's "Vergil and the Sibyl of Cumae," 43–58, 52–3. See Barbara Jane O'Sullivan's "Beatrice in *Valperga*: A New Cassandra," in *The Other Mary Shelley*, 140–58.
12 Mellor, *Mary Shelley*, 210.
13 Parke, *Sibyls and Sibylline Prophecy*, 57.

14 "A man plucked a nightingale and, finding but little to eat, said: 'You are just a voice and nothing more." Plutarch, *Moralia: Sayings of Spartans.* Cited as epigram in Mladen Dolar's *A Voice and Nothing More*, 3.

15 Sigler, "Dead Faith and Contraband Goods," 405–25, 406. Between 1801 and 1814, Southcott published approximately sixty-five pamphlets. According to some estimates, there were over 100,000 copies of her various works circulating from 1801 to 1816, making her one of the most prolific and popular writers in the period. See Hopkins, *A Woman to Deliver Her People*, 84.

16 Hopkins, *A Woman to Deliver Her People*, 151.

17 See Reece, *A Correct Statement of the Circumstances that attended the Last Illness and Death of Mrs. Southcott*, note 31, concerning Southcott's autopsy.

18 Juster, "Mystical Pregnancy and Holy Bleeding," 287.

19 Sunstein, *Mary Shelley*, 189.

20 Juster, "Mystical Pregnancy and Holy Bleeding," 254, 255, 257.

21 Anon., "Joanna Southcott's Pregnancy," 163–8, 164.

22 Issues 1, 3, and 5 include Williams' fold-out "embellishments" of Southcott. They are, respectively, "Spirits at Work – Joanna Conceiving – i.e., *Blowing up Shiloh*"; "A Paradice [*sic*] for Fools, *A Nocturnal Trip – or – The Disciple of Johanna* [*sic*] *Benighted,*" a triptych divided into "The Summons to Paradise," "The Set Down," and "The Return to Reason"; and "Delivering a Prophetess."

23 Ibid., 168.

24 Aside from William Sharp's engraved portrait of Southcott, all extant representations of Southcott available in the British Museum, which includes those published in *The Scourge*, depict her as pregnant, with her pregnancy being the central theme in most of them.

25 P.P., "Joanna Southcott," 197–200, 198.

26 See ch. 2, pp. 57–8.

27 Anon., "Celestial Visitation. A Poetical Epistle," 3–6, 3.

28 Ibid., 166.

29 On Mary Bateman, see Mackay, *Extraordinary Popular Delusions and the Madness of Crowds* and "Batemen, Mary," the *Oxford Dictionary of National Biography*.

30 A.R., "Life of Joanna Southcott," 233–7, 233.

31 Reece, *A Correct Statement of the Circumstances that attended the Last Illness and Death of Mrs. Southcott*, 3, vi. Reece also reproduces his letter, noted in the *Scourge* piece, to the *Sunday Monitor* for August 25, 1814, along with several other letters published in various newspapers. He names several other professionals who "all declared her in a state of pregnancy, after making a full and satisfactory examination" (18).

32 Reeves, *The Influence of Prophecy in the Later Middle Ages*, 249.

33 Ibid.

34 Ibid., 250. Also quoted in Rajan's notes in *Valperga*, 457n10.

35 See Rajan's chronology in *Valperga*, page 47. Mary Shelley makes Castruccio younger than he might actually have been, imagining his birth to be in 1289.

36 Mandelbaum, *The Divine Comedy of Dante Alighieri: Inferno*, 360.

37 Dante, *Inferno*, 10.13–14.

38 Mandelbaum, *The Divine Comedy of Dante Alighieri: Inferno*, 350.

39 Dante, 10.95–6; 10.97–9.

40 Ibid., 10.100–8.

41 To name but two of many, Sharon M. Twigg, for instance, refers to "Beatrice's false prophetic status" (495) as if this is obvious and Daniel E. White, similarly, sees her as suffering from "an illusion." Twigg, "'Do You Then Repair My Work,'" 481–505, 495. White, "'The god undeified,'" 34 paragraphs, par. 23. This is not to say that the aforementioned studies do not make cogent, interesting, and helpful arguments – they certainly do. The point here, however, is that by focusing on the phenomenon of prophecy more closely – on its social and epistemological paradoxes – Beatrice can be read in a substantially new light. Rather than a naive failure who is quick to deify Castruccio and believe all manner of supernatural nonsense she is, rather, a genuinely powerful woman with ambitions to historical agency against whom the text mobilizes, as an extension of Castruccio's paranoid, imperial egoism, in an effort to deflate and control her through a kind of character assassination.

42 William D. Brewer suggests something along these lines when he points out that "as a study of human psychology, *Valperga* can be compared to *Caleb Williams* (1794), William Godwin's 'analysis of the private and internal operations of the mind' (339)." "Mary Shelley's *Valperga*," 133–48, 133. Also see Sunstein, above, who argues that Euthanasia's concept of the mind anticipates Freud's in *A General Introduction to Psycho-Analysis*.

43 Shelley, *The Prose Works of Percy Bysshe Shelley*, 6.295.

44 Ibid., 6.296.

45 Ibid.

46 Ibid.

47 Ibid., 6.297.

48 Mary Shelley, Annotations to *Speculations on Metaphysics*, *The Prose Works of Percy Bysshe Shelley*, 6.297 n1.

49 See Joseph W. Lew, "God's Sister: History and Ideology in *Valperga*," in *The Other Mary Shelley*, 159–84, 163.

50 Shelley, *Frankenstein*, 22. This particular line does not appear in the original 1818 version of *Frankenstein*, suggesting that Walton may have, as it were, quoted Beatrice rather than Beatrice Walton.

51 Pyle, *The Ideology of the Imagination*, 2.

52 Ibid., 10.

53 For a reading of this scene as an inversion of Plato's allegory of the cave, see Gilbert and Gubar, *The Madwoman in the Attic*, 95–9.
54 Four people, in fact, survive the plague: Lionel, Adrian, Clara, and Evelyn. However, Evelyn dies from typhus fever and Clara and Adrian die in a shipwreck from which only Lionel escapes.
55 Shelley, *The Last Man*, 31. Hereafter cited in-text.
56 For a reading of how *The Last Man* hearkens back to *St Leon*, see the chapter "Crossing Culture: *The Last Man*" in Plug's *Borders of a Lip*.
57 Hegel, *Outlines of the Philosophy of Right*, 228 [§275].
58 This is to repurpose Mary Shelley's well-known description of *Frankenstein* in the 1831 "Author's Introduction" to the Standard Novels Edition.
59 Those readings sensitive to the biographical dimension of the novel frequently, and naturally enough, read the text in pessimistic terms. See, for a classic example, Peck, "The Biographical Element in the Novels of Mary Wollstonecraft Shelley," 196–219. More recently, several critics have taken much more optimistic stances. To take but one example: Bennett argues that what *The Last Man* illustrates is how "through imagination one can re-see the world" because the text "enfranchises a new world order and a new world understanding." Bennett, *Mary Wollstonecraft Shelley*, 54, 82. The present study suggests that both extremes are somewhat off the mark. *The Last Man* approaches, rather, a kind of indifference, disinterest, or neutrality, where each of these terms is understood, via Blanchot, as a form of engagement with something other or what he calls "outside."
60 Blanchot, *Infinite*, 203.
61 Foucault, "A Preface to Transgression," 24–40, 26.
62 Canuel, "Acts, Rules, and *The Last Man*," 147–70, 161.
63 Ibid., 165.
64 Barbara Johnson, "The Last Man," in *The Other Mary Shelley*, 258–66, 263.
65 Ibid., 265.
66 Benjamin, "Theses on the Philosophy of History," in *Illuminations*, 253–64, 257.
67 Canuel, "Acts, Rules, and *The Last Man*," 156.
68 Bennett, "Radical Imaginings, 147–52, 149.
69 See Blanchot, "Affirmation and the Passion of Negative Thought," in *The Infinite Conversation*, 202–11.
70 *Infinite*, 204.
71 Ibid., 205.
72 Ibid.
73 Ibid., 207.
74 Paley, "Mary Shelley's *The Last Man*," 2.
75 Blanchot, *The Last Man*, 63. Hereafter *Last*.
76 Ibid., 26.

77 Plug, *Borders of a Lip*, 156.
78 Johnson, "The Last Man," 265.
79 *Friendship*, 106.
80 Kant's assurance that the human race is progressing remains haunted by a parenthetical gesture toward this absolute rupture in nature. That is, Kant qualifies his optimism when he notes that "all the peoples on earth [. . .] will gradually come to participate in progress [. . .] provided at least that there does not, by some chance, occur a second epoch of natural revolution which will push aside the human race to clear the stage for other creatures." Kant, *The Conflict of the Faculties*, 161.
81 Sussman, "'Islanded in the World,'" 268–301, 268.
82 *Infinite*, 208.
83 Frey, "The Last Man and the Reader," 252–79, 270.

Afterword

1 McFadden, "Harold Camping, Dogged Forecaster of the End of the World, Dies at 92."
2 See Welch, "The rise and fall of Mars Hill Church"; Weber, "C.J. Mahaney Breaks Silence on Sovereign Grace Ministries Abuse Allegations; Turner, "Megachurch."
3 Meadows et al., *The Limits to Growth: A Report for the Club of Rome's Project on the Predicament of Mankind*; Meadows et al., *Limits to Growth: The 30-Year Update.*
4 Morello, "Is Earth Nearing an Environmental 'Tipping Point'?"; Boerlijst et al., "Catastrophic Collapse Can Occur without Early Warning," n.p.
5 Jameson, *Archaeologies of the Future*, 199.

Bibliography

Abbeele, Georges van den. "Introduction." *Enthusiasm: The Kantian Critique of History*. Stanford: Stanford UP, 2009. ix–xiv.

Abrams, M.H. *Natural Supernaturalism: Tradition and Revolution in Romantic Literature*. New York: Norton, 1971.

Adler, Hans, and Ernest A. Menze. "Introduction." *On World History, An Anthology: Johan Gottfried Herder*. New York: M.E. Sharp, 1997. 3–22.

Aeschylus. *The Persians*. Trans. Edith Hall. Warminster: Aris & Phillips, 1996.

[Anon.] *The Age of Prophecy! Or, Further Testimony of the Mission of Richard Brothers, by A Convert*. London: Printed for the Author, 1795.

[Anon.] "Analogy of sacred history and prophecy, with the events and principles of modern times: exemplified in a remarkable passage of the prophet Isaiah: a discourse, written in Ireland during the late rebellion there, 1798." London: W. Bulmer and Co., 1800.

[Anon.] "Celestial Visitation. A Poetical Epistle: *From Miss Townley to the Rev. Mr. Tozer, Minister of the Southcott Chapel, Duke-street, St. George's-fields*." *The Scourge* 8[1] London: William N. Jones (1814): 3–6.

[Anon.] "Joanna Southcott." *The Scourge* 8[3] London: William N. Jones (1814): 197–200.

[Anon.] "Joanna Southcott's Pregnancy." *The Scourge* 8[3] London: William N. Jones (1814): 163–8.

[Anon.] "Life of Joanna Southcott." *The Scourge* 8[3]. London: William N. Jones (1814): 233–7.

Alison, Henry. "Introduction." *Theoretical Philosophy after 1781*. Trans. Gary Hatfield et al., Ed. Henry Allison and Peter Heath. Cambridge: Cambridge UP, 2002. 1–28.

Aristotle. *The Complete Works of Aristotle*. Ed. Jonathan Barnes. 2 Vols. Princeton: Princeton UP, 1991.

Aylesworth, Gary. "Lyotard, Gadamer, and the Relation between Ethics and Aesthetics." *Lyotard: Politics, Philosophy, and the Sublime.* Ed. Hugh Silverman. New York: Routledge, 2002.

Baker, Jennifer J. "Natural Science and the Romanticisms." *ESQ* 53.4 (2007): 387–412.

Bakhtin, Mikhail. *The Dialogic Imagination: Four Essays.* Ed. Michael Holquist, Trans. Caryl Emerson. Austin: University of Texas Press, 1981.

Balfour, Ian. *The Rhetoric of Romantic Prophecy.* Stanford: Stanford UP, 2002.

– "The Future of Citation: Blake, Wordsworth, and the Rhetoric of Romantic Prophecy." *Writing the Future.* Ed. David Wood. London: Routledge, 1990.

Bann, Stephen. *Romanticism and the Rise of History.* New York: Twayne, 1995.

– *The Clothing of Clio: A Study of Representation of History in Nineteenth-Century Britain and France.* Cambridge: Cambridge UP, 1984.

Barfoot, C.C. "'Milton Silent Came Down My Path': The Epiphany of Blake's Left Foot." *Moments of Moment: Aspects of Literary Epiphany.* Ed. Wim Tigges. Amsterdam: Rodopi, 1999.

Bataille, *Inner Experience.* Trans. Leslie Anne Boldt. Albany: SUNY Press, 1988.

Bate, Jonathan. *Shakespeare and the English Romantic Imagination.* Oxford UP: Clarendon 1986.

Baucom, Ian. *Spectres of the Atlantic.* Durham: Duke UP, 2005.

Benjamin, Walter. *Illuminations: Essays and Reflections.* Trans. Harry Zohn. Schocken: New York, 1968.

Bennett, Betty T. *Mary Wollstonecraft Shelley: An Introduction.* Baltimore: Johns Hopkins UP, 1998.

– "Radical Imaginings: Mary Shelley's *The Last Man.*" *The Wordsworth Circle* 26.3 (Summer 1995): 147–52.

The Bible: Authorized King James Version with Apocrypha. Oxford: Oxford UP, 1997.

Blair, Hugh. *Lectures on Rhetoric and Belles Lettres* [1783]. Ed. F.H. Harding, 2 vols. Carbondale: U of Southern Illinois P, 1965.

Blake, William. *The Poetry and Prose of William Blake.* Ed. David V. Erdman, rev. ed. New York: Anchor, 1988.

– *Complete Writings: With Variant Readings.* Ed. Geoffrey Keynes. Oxford: Oxford UP, 1966.

Blanchot, Maurice. *The Book to Come.* Trans. Charlotte Mandell. Stanford: Stanford UP, 2003.

– *The Work of Fire.* Trans. Charlotte Mandell. Stanford: Stanford UP, 1995.

– *The Infinite Conversation.* Trans. Susan Hanson. Minneapolis: University of Minnesota Press, 1993.

– *The Step Not Beyond.* Trans. Lycette Nelson. Albany: SUNY Press, 1992.

– *The Last Man.* Trans. Lydia Davis. New York: Columbia UP, 1987.

– *The Space of Literature.* Trans. Ann Smock. Lincoln: University of Nebraska Press, 1982.

Bloch, Ernst. *Atheism in Christianity: The Religion of the Exodus and the Kingdom.* Trans. J.T. Swann. 2nd ed. London: Verso, 2009.

Bloom, Harold. *The Ringers in the Tower: Studies in Romantic Tradition.* Chicago: Chicago UP, 1971.

– *The Visionary Company: A Reading of Romantic Poetry.* New York: Anchor, 1961/1963.

Blumenberg, Hans. *The Legitimacy of the Modern Age.* Trans. Robert M. Wallace. Cambridge, Mass: MIT Press: 1983.

Boerlijst, Maarten C., Thomas Oudman, and Andre M. de Roos. "Catastrophic Collapse Can Occur without Early Warning: Examples of Silent Catastrophes in Structured Ecological Models." *PLoS ONE* 8.4 (2013): n.p.

Bolter, Jay David and Richard Grusin. *Remediation: Understanding New Media.* Cambridge: MIT Press, 1999.

Brewer, William D. "Mary Shelley's *Valperga*: The Triumph of Euthanasia's Mind." *ERR* 5.2 (1995): 133–48.

Bringham, Linda C. "Frail Memorials: 'Essays upon Epitaphs' and Wordsworth's Economy of Reference." *Philosophy and Literature* 16.1 (1992): 15–31.

Brothers, Richard. *God's Awful Warnings to a Giddy, Careless, Sinful World, Being a Revealed Knowledge of the Prophecies and Times, Particularly of the Present Time, the Present War, and the Prophecy Now Fulfilling (Year of the World 5913.) Written under the Direction of the LORD GOD. And Published by his Sacred Command.* London: S. Green, 1794.

Bruns, Gerald L. *Maurice Blanchot: The Refusal of Philosophy.* Baltimore: Johns Hopkins UP, 1997.

Bulloch, A.W. Ed. and trans. *Callimachus: The Fifth Hymn.* Cambridge: Cambridge UP, 1985.

Burke, Kenneth. *Attitudes Toward History.* 3rd ed. Berkeley: University of California Press, 1984.

Canuel, Mark. "Acts, Rules, and *The Last Man.*" *Nineteenth-Century Literature* 53.2 (September, 1998): 147–70.

Carra, Jean-Louis. *System de la raison; ou, le prophète philosophe.* 3rd ed. Paris: Buisson, 1791.

Carroll, Robert P. *When Prophecy Failed: Reactions and Responses to Failure in the Old Testament Prophetic Traditions.* London: SCM Press, 1979.

Cassirer, Ernst. *Kant's Life and Thought.* Trans. James Haden. New Haven: Yale UP, 1981.

Chandler, James. *England in 1819: The Politics of Literary Culture and the Case of Romantic Historicism.* Chicago: Chicago UP, 1998.

Chandler, James and Maureen McLane, "Introduction," *The Cambridge Companion to British Romantic Poetry.* Cambridge: Cambridge UP, 2008. 1–9.

Clark, David L. "We 'Other Prussians': Bodies and Pleasures in De Quincey and Late Kant." *ERR.* 14.2 (2003): 261–87.

– "Kant's Aliens: The *Anthropology* and its Others." *CR: The New Centennial Review* 1.2 (2001): 201–89.

Colebrook, Claire. "The End of Redemption and the Redemption of Ends: Apocalypse and Enlightenment in Blake's Prophecies." *Southern Review: Literary and Interdisciplinary Essays* 27.1 (1994): 79–92.

Collings, David. *Monstrous Society: Reciprocity, Discipline, and the Political Uncanny, c. 1780–1848.* Lewisburg: Bucknell UP, 2009.

– *Wordsworthian Errancies: The Poetics of Cultural Dismemberment.* Baltimore: Johns Hopkins UP, 1994.

Collingwood, R.G. *The Idea of History.* Ed. Jan van den Dussen, rev. ed. Oxford: Clarendon, 1993.

Comay, Rebecca. *Mourning Sickness: Hegel and the French Revolution.* Stanford: Stanford UP, 2011.

Cooper, Anthony Ashley. *Shaftesbury: Characteristics of Men, Manners, Opinions, Times.* Ed. Lawrence E. Klein. Cambridge: Cambridge UP, 1999.

Copjec, Joan. "The Tomb of Perseverance: On Antigone." *The Ethics of History.* Ed. David Carr, Thomas R. Flynn, and Rudolf Makkreel. Evanston: Northwestern UP, 2004.

Dante, Alighieri. *The Divine Comedy of Dante Alighieri: Inferno.* Trans. Allen Mandelbaum. New York: Bantam, 1980.

Davies, Hugh Sykes. "Wordsworth and the Empirical Philosophers." *The English Mind: Studies in the English Moralists Presented to Basil Willey.* Ed. Hugh Sykes Davies and George Watson. Cambridge: Cambridge UP, 1964.

Day, John, Ed. *Prophecy and Prophets in Ancient Israel: Proceedings of the Oxford Old Testament Seminar.* London: T&T Clark International, 2010.

Deleuze, Gilles. *Bergsonism.* Trans. Hugh Tomlinson and Barbara Habberjam. New York: Zone Books, 1991.

– *A Thousand Plateaus: Capitalism and Schizophrenia.* Trans. Brian Massumi. Minneapolis: University of Minnesota Press, 1987.

– *Kant's Critical Philosophy: The Doctrine of the Faculties.* Trans. Hugh Tomlinson and Barbara Habberjam. London: Athlone, 1984.

De Man, Paul. *Aesthetic Ideology.* Minneapolis: University of Minnesota Press, 1996.

– *The Rhetoric of Romanticism.* New York: Columbia UP, 1984.

De Quincey, Thomas. "On Wordsworth's 'There was a boy.'" *Romanticism: An Anthology.* Ed. Duncan Wu. 2nd ed. Oxford: Blackwell, 1998.

– "The Last Days of Immanuel Kant." *The Works of Thomas De Quincey.* 4th ed. 16 Vols. Edinburgh: Adam and Charles Black, 1878.

Derrida, Jacques. *Of Grammatology.* Trans. Gayatri Chakravorty Spivak. Baltimore: Johns Hopkins UP, 1997.

– *Given Time 1: Counterfeit Money.* Trans. Peggy Kamuf. Chicago: University of Chicago Press, 1992.

Dobbs, Francis. *A concise view from history and prophecy, of the great predictions in the sacred writings, that have been fulfilled; also of those that are now fulfilling, and that remain to be accomplished.* Dublin: John Jones, 1800.

Dolar, Mladen. *A Voice and Nothing More.* Cambridge, Mass.: MIT Press, 2006.

Dukes, W. *Religious politics; or The present times foretold, by the Prophet Micah; being a plain solution of that prophecy, by W.D.* London: D.I. Eaton, 1795.

Dupré, Louis. *The Enlightenment and the Intellectual Foundations of Modern Culture.* New Haven: Yale, 2004.

– *Passage to Modernity: An Essay in the Hermeneutics of Nature and Culture.* New Haven: Yale, 1993.

Eden, William. "Some remarks on the apparent circumstances of the war in the fourth week of October 1795." Edinburgh: William Creech, 1795.

Eichhorn, J.G. *Introduction to the Study of the Old Testament: A Fragment Translated by George Tilly Gollop.* London: Spottiswoode and Co, 1888.

Eichner, Hans. "The Rise of Modern Science and the Genesis of Romanticism." *PMLA* 97.1 (1982): 8–30.

Ellis, David. *Wordsworth, Freud, and the Spots of Time: Interpretation in* The Prelude. Cambridge: Cambridge UP, 1985.

Erdman, David V. *Blake: Prophet Against Empire.* New York: Anchor, 1969.

Fenves, Peter D. *A Peculiar Fate: Metaphysics and World-History in Kant.* Ithaca: Cornell, 1991.

Fisch, Audrey A., Anne K. Mellor, and Esther H. Schor, Ed. *The Other Mary Shelley.* Oxford: Oxford UP, 1993.

Forster, Michael N. "Introduction." *Herder: Philosophical Writings.* Cambridge: Cambridge UP, 2002. vii–xxxv.

Foucault, Michel. "A Preface to Transgression." *Bataille: A Critical Reader.* Ed. Fred Botting and Scott Wilson. Oxford: Blackwell, 1998.

– *The Order of Things: An Archaeology of the Human Sciences.* New York: Vintage, 1973.

Fox, Susan. *Poetic Form in Blake's* Milton. Princeton: Princeton UP, 1976.

Franks, James. *Memoirs of Pretended Prophets, who have Appeared in Different Ages of the World, and Especially in Modern Times.* London: J. Johnson, 1795.

Frey, Hans-Jost. "The Last Man and the Reader." Trans. Georgia Albert. *Yale French Studies* 93 (1998): 252–79.

Fry, Paul H. *Wordsworth And the Poetry of What We Are.* New Haven: Yale, 2008.

– *A Defense of Poetry: Reflections on the Occasion of Writing.* Stanford: Stanford UP, 1995.

Frye, Northrop. *Fearful Symmetry: A Study of William Blake.* Princeton: Princeton UP, 1947/69.

Gadamer, Hans-Georg. *Truth and Method.* Trans. Joel Weinsheimer and Donald G. Marshall. 2nd rev. ed. New York: Continuum, 2004.

Gibbon, Edward. *The History of the Decline and Fall of the Roman Empire*. 10 Vols. London: W. Allason, 1823.

Gilbert, Sandra M., and Susan Gubar. *The Madwoman in the Attic: The Woman Writer and the Nineteenth-Century Literary Imagination*. 2nd ed. New Haven: Yale, 2000.

Gilchrist, Alexander. *The Life of William Blake*. Ed. W. Graham Robertson. London: John Lane, 1863/1907.

Gleig, George. "Prophecy." *Encyclopædia Britannica*. 3rd ed, 1797.

Goldsmith, Steven. *Blake's Agitation*. Baltimore: Johns Hopkins UP, 2013.

– "'Cracked Across': Blake, Milton, and the Noise of History." *Studies in Romanticism* 51.3 (2012): 305–42.

– *Unbuilding Jerusalem: Apocalypse and Romantic Representation*. Ithaca: Cornell UP, 2003.

Guyer, Paul. "Introduction." *Kant's Critique of the Power of Judgement: Critical Essays*. Ed. Paul Guyer. Lanham: Rowman & Littlefield, 2003. vii–xxii.

Hartman, Geoffrey. *The Unremarkable Wordsworth*. Minneapolis: University of Minnesota Press, 1987.

– *Criticism in the Wilderness: The Study of Literature Today*. New Haven: Yale UP, 1980.

– *Wordsworth's Poetry: 1787–1814*. New Haven: Yale UP, 1964.

– "A Poet's Progress: Wordsworth and the *via naturaliter negative*." *Modern Philology* 59.3 (1962): 214–24.

Hegel, G.W.F. *Outlines of the Philosophy of Right*. Trans. T.M. Knox. Ed. Stephen Houlgate. Oxford: Oxford UP, 2008.

– *The Philosophy of History*. Trans. J. Sibree. Kitchener: Batoche Books, 2001.

– *Phenomenology of Spirit*. Trans. A.V. Miller. Oxford: Oxford UP, 1977.

– *Aesthetics: Lectures on Fine Art*. Trans. T.M. Knox. 2 Vols. Oxford: Clarendon, 1975.

Herder, J.G. *Philosophical Writings*. Trans. Michael N. Forster. Cambridge: Cambridge UP, 2002.

Hill, Christopher. *The World Turned Upside Down: Radical Ideas During the English Revolution*. London: Penguin, 1975.

Hilton, Nelson. *Literal Imagination: Blake's Vision of Words*. Berkeley: University of California Press, 1983.

Hogle, Jerrold E. *Shelley's Process: Radical Transference and the Development of His Major Works*. New York: Oxford UP, 1988.

Hopkins, James L. *A Woman to Deliver Her People: Joanna Southcott and English Millenarianism in an Era of Revolution*. Austin: University of Texas Press, 1982.

Jacobs, Carol. *Uncontainable Romanticism: Shelley, Brontë, Kleist*. Baltimore: Johns Hopkins UP, 1989.

Jacobus, Mary. *Romantic Things: A Tree, A Rock, A Cloud*. Chicago: University of Chicago Press, 2012.

Jameson, Fredric. *Archaeologies of the Future: The Desire Called Utopia and Other Science Fictions.* London: Verso, 2005.

Johnson, Barbara. "The Last Man." *The Other Mary Shelley: Beyond* Frankenstein. Ed. Audrey Fisch, Anne K. Mellor, and Esther H. Schor. Oxford: Oxford UP, 1993. 258–66.

Juster, Susan. "Mystical Pregnancy and Holy Bleeding: Visionary Experience in Early Modern Britain and America." *William and Mary Quarterly* 57.2 (2000): 249–88.

Kant, Immanuel. *Theoretical Philosophy after 1781.* Trans. Gary Hatfield et al. Ed. Henry Allison and Peter Heath. Cambridge: Cambridge UP, 2002.

– *Critique of the Power of Judgement.* Ed. and trans. Paul Guyer. Cambridge: Cambridge UP, 2000.

– *Critique of Pure Reason.* Trans./Ed. Paul Guyer and Allen W. Wood. Cambridge: Cambridge UP, 1998.

– *The Metaphysics of Morals.* Ed. and trans. Mary Gregor. Cambridge: Cambridge UP, 1996.

– *Grounding for the Metaphysics of Morals: On the Supposed Right to Lie because of Philanthropic Concerns.* Trans. James W. Ellington. Indianapolis: Hackett, 1993.

– *Theoretical Philosophy, 1755–1770.* Ed. and trans. David Walford. Cambridge: Cambridge UP, 1992.

– *The Conflict of the Faculties.* Trans. Mary J. Gregor. New York: Abaris, 1979.

– *Anthropology from a Pragmatic Point of View.* Trans. Victor Lyle Dowdell. Ed. Hans H. Rudnick. Carbondale: Southern Illinois University Press, 1978.

Keats, John. *Selected Letters.* Ed. John Mee. Oxford: Oxford UP, 2002.

Khalip, Jacques. *Anonymous Life: Romanticism and Dispossession.* Stanford: Stanford UP, 2009.

Kierkegaard, Søren. *Prefaces; Writing Sampler.* Trans. Todd Nichol. Princeton: Princeton UP, 1997.

– *The Concept of Irony: With Constant Reference to Socrates.* Trans. Lee M. Capel. London: Collins, 1966.

Kneale, J. Douglas. *Monumental Writing: Aspects of Rhetoric in Wordsworth's Poetry.* Lincoln: University of Nebraska Press, 1988.

Kojève, Alexander. *Introduction to the Reading of Hegel: Lectures on the Phenomenology of Spirit.* Trans. James H. Nichols, Jr. Ed. Allan Bloom. Ithaca: Cornell UP, 1980.

Koselleck, Reinhart. *The Practice of Conceptual History: Timing History, Spacing Concepts.* Trans. Todd Samuel Presner et al. Stanford: Stanford UP, 2002.

– *Zeitschichten: Studien zur Historik.* Frankfurt: Schrkamp, 2000.

– *Futures Past: On the Semantics of Historical Time.* Trans. Keith Tribe. Cambridge: MIT Press, 1985.

– *Geschichtliche Grundbegriffe: historisches Lexikon zur politisch-sozialen Sprache in Deutschland.* Ed. Otto Brunner, Werner Conze, and Reinhart Koselleck. 9 vols. Stuttgart: E. Klett, 1972–97.

Lacoue-Labarthe, Philippe, and Jean-Luc Nancy. *The Literary Absolute: The Theory of Literature in German Romanticism.* Trans. Philip Barnard and Cheryl Lester. Albany: SUNY, 1988.

Langan, Celeste. "*Telepathos*: Medium Cool Romanticism." *Romanticism on the Net.* 41–2 (February–May 2006): 35 par.

– "Understanding Media in 1805: Audiovisual Hallucination in *The Lay of the Last Minstrel.*" *Studies in Romanticism* 40.1 (2001 Spring): 49–70.

Langan, Celeste, and Maureen N. McLane. "The Medium of Romantic Poetry." *The Cambridge Companion to British Romantic Poetry.* Ed. James Chandler and Maureen N. McLane. Cambridge: Cambridge UP, 2008.

Larkin, Peter. "Wordsworth's Maculate Exception: Achieving the 'Spots of Time.'" *Wordsworth Circle* 41.1 (2010): 30–5.

Larsen, Robin. *Emanuel Swedenborg: A Continuing Vision.* New York: Swedenborg Foundation, 1988.

Lefort, Claude. *Democracy and Political Theory.* Trans. David Macey. Cambridge: Polity, 1988.

Liu, Alan. *Wordsworth: The Sense of History.* Stanford: Stanford UP, 1989.

Locke, John. *An Essay Concerning Human Understanding.* Ed. Peter H. Nidditch. Oxford: Clarendon Press, 1975.

Löwith, Karl. *The Meaning in History: The Theological Implications of the Philosophy of History.* Chicago: University of Chicago Press, 1949.

Lucretius. *On the Nature of Things.* Trans. Martin Ferguson Smith. Indianapolis: Hackett, 1969/2001.

Lyotard, Jean-François. *Enthusiasm: The Kantian Critique of History.* Trans. Georges van den Abbeele. Stanford: Stanford UP, 2009.

– *The Differend: Phrases in Dispute.* Trans. Georges van den Abbeele. Minneapolis: Minnesota UP, 1988.

– "The Sign of History." *Post-Structuralism and the Question of History.* Ed. Derek Attridge, Geoff Bennington, and Robert Young. Cambridge: Cambridge UP, 1987.

Mackay, Charles. *Extraordinary Popular Delusions and the Madness of Crowds* [1841/52]. Philadelphia: Templeton Foundation Press, 1999.

Madden, Deborah. "The Religious Politics of Prophecy: Or, Richard Brothers' *Revealed Knowledge* Confuted." *History of European Ideas* 34 (2008): 270–84.

Mandelbaum, Allen. "Notes." *The Divine Comedy of Dante Alighieri: Inferno.* Trans. Allen Mandelbaum. New York: Bantam, 1980.

Makdisi, Saree. *William Blake and the Impossible History of the 1790s.* Chicago: University of Chicago Press, 2003.

Malekin, Peter. rev. *Blake's Sublime Allegory. Review of English Studies* 26.103 (1975): 339–43.

Mann, Paul. "The Book of Urizen and the Horizon of the Book." *Unnam'd Forms: Blake and Textuality.* Ed. Nelson Hilton and Thomas Vogler. Berkeley: University of California Press, 1986. 49–86.

Markley, Robert. "New Media and the Natural World: The Dialectics of Desire." *Bucknell Review* 46.2 (2003): 33–57.

Markus, R.A. *Saeculum: History and Society in the Theology of St Augustine.* Cambridge: Cambridge UP, 1970.

Massumi, Brian. *Parables for the Virtual: Movement, Affect, Sensation.* Durham: Duke UP, 2002.

McFadden, Robert D. "Harold Camping, Dogged Forecaster of the End of the World, Dies at 92." *The New York Times* (17 December 2013).

McKeane, John, and Hannes Opeiz, eds. *Blanchot Romantique.* Oxford: Peter Lang, 2011.

Meadows, Donella H., et al. *Limits to Growth: The 30-Year Update.* New York: Earthscan, 2004.

– *The Limits to Growth: A Report for the Club of Rome's Project on the Predicament of Mankind.* New York: Universe Books, 1972.

Mee, Jon. *Romanticism, Enthusiasm, and Regulation: Poetics and the Policing of Culture in the Romantic Period.* Oxford: Oxford UP, 2003.

Mellor, Anne K. *Mary Shelley: Her Life, Her Fiction, Her Monsters.* New York: Routledge, 1988.

Milbank, John. *Theology & Social Theory: Beyond Secular Reason.* 2nd ed. Oxford: Blackwell, 2006.

Milton, John. *Paradise Lost, The Complete Poems.* Ed. John Leonard. London: Penguin, 1998.

– *The Complete Prose Works of John Milton.* Ed. Don M. Wolfe et al. 8 vols. New Haven: Yale UP, 1953–82.

– *Complete Poems and Major Prose.* Ed. Merritt Y. Hughes. New York: Odyssey Press, 1957.

Morello, Lauren. "Is Earth Nearing an Environmental 'Tipping Point'?" *Scientific American* (7 June 2012).

Morrison, J.S. "The Germanic World." *Oracles and Divination.* Ed. Michael Loewe and Carmen Blacker. New York: Random House, 1981.

Nichol, Todd. "Introduction." *Prefaces; Writing Sampler.* Trans. Todd Nichol. Princeton: Princeton UP, 1997.

Nissinen, Martti. "Comparing Prophetic Sources: Principles and a Test Case." *Prophecy and Prophets in Ancient Israel: Proceedings from the Oxford Old Testament Seminar.* Ed. John Day. New York: T&T Clark, 2010.

Oliver, W.H. *Prophets and Millennialists: The Uses of Biblical Prophecy in England from the 1790s to the 1840s.* Auckland: Auckland UP, 1978.

Ovid. *Metamorphoses.* Trans. Frank Justus Miller. Ed. E.H. Warmington. 2 vols. Cambridge, Mass.: Harvard UP, 1971.

Paine, Thomas. *The Age of Reason, Part the Third: Being an Examination of the Passages in the New Testament Quoted from the Old, and Called Prophecies Concerning Jesus Christ: To Which is Prefixed an Essay on Dream, with an Appendix, Containing my Private Thoughts on a Future State.* London: R. Carlile, 1818.

Paley, Morton D. *Apocalypse and Millennium in English Romantic Poetry.* Oxford: Clarendon, 1999.

– "Mary Shelley's *The Last Man*: Apocalypse without Millennium." *Keats-Shelley Review* 4.1 (1989): 1–25.

Palmquist, Stephen R. *Kant's System of Perspectives: An Architectonic Interpretation of the Critical Philosophy.* Lanham: University Press of America, 1993.

– "A Priori Knowledge in Perspective: (II) Naming, Necessity and the Analytic A Posteriori." *The Review of Metaphysics* 41:2 (1987): 255–82.

Parke, H.W. *Sibyls and Sibylline Prophecy in Classical Antiquity.* Ed. B.C. McGing. London: Routledge, 1988.

Peck, Walter E. "The Biographical Element in the Novels of Mary Wollstonecraft Shelley." *PMLA* 38 (1923): 196–219.

Pecora, Vincent P. *Secularization and Cultural Criticism: Religion, Nation, and Modernity.* Chicago: University of Chicago Press, 2006.

Phillips, Mark Salber. *Society and Sentiment: Genres of Historical Writing in Britain, 1740–1820.* New Jersey: Princeton UP, 2000.

Plug, Jan. *Borders of a Lip: Romanticism, Language, History, Politics.* New York: SUNY Press, 2003.

Pyle, Forest. *The Ideology of the Imagination: Subject and Society in the Discourse of Romanticism.* Stanford: Stanford UP, 1995.

Ragussis, Michael. "Language and Metamorphosis in Wordsworth's Arab Dream." *Modern Language Quarterly* 36.2 (1975): 148–65.

Rajan, Tilottama. "'The Abyss of the Past': Psychoanalysis in Schelling's *Ages of the World* (1815)." *Romantic Circles Praxis* (2008): 35 paragraphs.

– "(Dis)Figuring the System: Vision, History, and Trauma in Blake's Lambeth Books." *Huntington Library Quarterly* 58.3–4 (1996): 383–411.

Reece, Richard. *A Correct Statement of the Circumstances that attended the Last Illness and Death of Mrs. Southcott, With an Account of the Appearances Exhibited on Dissection: And the Artifices that were Employed to Deceive her Medical Attendants.* London: Sherwood, Neely, and Jones, 1815.

Reeves, Marjorie. *The Influence of Prophecy in the Later Middle Ages: A Study in Joachimism.* Oxford: Clarendon, 1969.

Richardson, Alan. "Wordsworth at the Crossroads: 'Spots of Time' in the 'Two-Part Prelude.'" *The Wordsworth Circle* 19.1 (1988): 15–20.

Richman, Jared. "Milton Re-membered, Graved and Press'd: William Blake and the Fate of Textual Bodies." *ERR* 19.4 (October 2008): 385–401.

Riede, David. "Blake's *Milton*: On Membership in the Church Paul." *Re-Membering Milton: Essays on the Texts and Traditions.* Ed. Mary Nyquist and Margaret W. Ferguson. New York: Methuen, 1987.

Rudwick, Martin. *Bursting the Limits of Time: The Reconstruction of Geohistory in the Age of Revolution.* Chicago: Chicago UP, 2005.

Schelling, Friedrich. *Ages of The World [1815].* Trans. Jason M. Wirth. Albany: SUNY Press, 2000.

Schlegel, Friedrich. *Philosophical Fragments.* Trans. Peter Firchow. Minneapolis: University of Minnesota Press, 1991.

– *Philosophy of History, in a Course of Lectures, Delivered at Vienna.* Trans. James Burton Robertson. 2 vols. London: Saunders and Otley, 1835.

Schmitt, Carl. *Political Theology: Four Chapters on the Concept of Sovereignty.* Trans. George Schwab. Chicago: University of Chicago Press, 2005.

Scott, Walter. "My Aunt Margaret's Mirror." *The Keepsake for 1929.* Ed. Frederic Mansel Reynolds. Peterborough: Broadview, 2006. 1–44.

Sewall, Frank. "Introduction." *Dreams of a Spirit-Seer Illustrated by Dreams of Metaphysics.* London: Swan Sonnenschein & Co., LIM, 1900. 3–33.

Sha, Richard. "Imagination." *A Handbook of Romanticism Studies.* Ed. Joel Faflak and Julia M. Wright. Malden: Wiley, 2012.

Shaffer, E.S. *Kubla Khan and the Fall of Jerusalem: The Mythological School in Biblical Criticism and Secular Literature, 1770–1880.* Cambridge: Cambridge UP, 1980.

Shell, Susan Meld. *The Embodiment of Reason: Kant on Spirit, Generation, and Community.* Chicago: Chicago UP, 1996.

Shelley, Mary. *The Last Man.* Ed. Hugh J. Luke, Jr. and Judith Tarr. Lincoln: University of Nebraska Press, 2006.

– *Frankenstein, Or, The Modern Prometheus.* Ed. Maurice Hindle. rev. ed. Oxford: Penguin, 1992.

– *Valperga: or, The Life and Adventures of Castruccio, Prince of Lucca.* Ed. Tilottama Rajan. Peterborough: Broadview, 1985.

– Annotations. *Speculations on Metaphysics* [Vol 6]. *The Prose Works of Percy Bysshe Shelley.* 8 vols. Ed. Harry Buxton Forman. London: Reeves and Turner, 1880.

Shelley, Percy. *Shelley's Poetry and Prose.* Ed. Donald Reiman and Neil Fraistat. 2nd ed. New York: Norton, 2002.

– *Zastrozzi & St. Irvyne; or, The Rosicrucian.* Ed. Stephen C. Behrendt. Peterborough: Broadview, 2002.

– *The Prose Works of Percy Bysshe Shelley.* Ed. Harry Buxton Forman. 8 vols. London: Reeves and Turner, 1880.

Sigler, David. "Dead Faith and Contraband Goods: Joanna Southcott and the Logic of Sexuation." *Studies in Romanticism* 49.3 (2010): 405–25.

Simpson, David. *Wordsworth and the Figurings of the Real.* New Jersey: Humanities Press, 1982.

Smith, William Robertson. "Prophetical Books of the Old Testament." *Encyclopædia Britannica.* 9th ed. 1878–89.

Snow, Dale. *Schelling and the End of Idealism.* Albany: SUNY Press, 1996.

Spinoza, Benedictus de. *Tractatus Theologico-Politicus.* Trans. Samuel Shirley. Leiden: E.J. Brill, 1989.

Strathman, Christopher A. *Romantic Poetry and the Fragmentary Imperative: Schlegel, Byron, Joyce, Blanchot.* Albany: SUNY, 2006.

Sunstein, Emily W. *Mary Shelley: Romance and Reality.* Boston: Little, Brown, 1989.

Sussman, Charlotte. "'Islanded in the World': Cultural Memory and Human Mobility in *The Last Man.*" *PMLA* 118.2 (2003): 268–301.

Swedenborg, Emanuel. *Arcana Coelestia: The heavenly arcane contained in the Holy Scripture or Word of the Lord unfolded, beginning with the book of Genesis.* Trans. John Clowes. Ed. John Faulkner Potts. Standard Edition, 12 vols. Pennsylvania: Swedenborg Foundation, 2009.

Tarbet, David W. "The Fabric of Metaphor in Kant's *Critique of Pure Reason.*" *Journal of the History of Philosophy* 6.3 (1968): 257–70.

Taylor, Charles. *A Secular Age.* Cambridge, Mass: Belknap Press, 2007.

Thompson, E.P. *The Making of the English Working Class.* New York: Vintage, 1966.

Thulstrup, Niels. *Kierkegaard's Relation to Hegel.* Trans. George L. Stengren. Princeton: Princeton UP, 1980.

Tillich, Paul. "Kairos." *A Handbook of Christian Theology.* Ed. Marvin Halverson and Arthur Cohen. New York: Meridian, 1985.

Tocqueville, Alexis de. *Democracy in America* [1835]. Ed. Eduardo Nolla. Trans. James T. Schleifer. Indianapolis: Liberty, 2010.

– *The State of Society in France Before the Revolution of 1789 and the Causes which Led to That Event.* 3rd ed. Trans. Henry Reeve. London: John Murray, 1888.

Turner, Matthew Paul. "Megachurch: Stay With Your Kiddie Porn-Watching Husband – or face 'Discipline.'" *The Daily Beast* (31 May 2015).

Twigg, Sharon M. "'Do You Then Repair My Work': The Redemptive Contract in Mary Shelley's *Valperga.*" *Studies in Romanticism* 46.4 (2007): 481–505.

Ulmer, William. "*Hellas* and the Historical Uncanny." *ELH* 58.3 (1991): 611–32.

Vašíček, Zdeněk. "Philosophy of History." *A Companion to the Philosophy of History and Historiography.* Sussex: Blackwell, 2009.

Voltaire. *The Complete Works of Voltaire.* Ed. Theodore Besterman et al. 8 vols. Geneva: Institut et musée Voltaire, 1968.

– *The Philosophy of History.* London: I. Allcock, 1766.

von Rad, Gerhard. *Old Testament Theology.* Trans. D.M.G. Stalker, 2 vols. Louisville: John Knox Press, 1965.

van Ranke, Leopold. *History of the Latin and Teutonic nations from 1494 to 1514.* London: Bell, 1887.

Waszink, J.H. "Vergil and the Sibyl of Cumae." *Mnemosyne.* 4th Series, 1 (1948): 43–58.

Weber, Jeremy. "C.J. Mahaney Breaks Silence on Sovereign Grace Ministries Abuse Allegations." *Christianity Today* (22 May 2014).

Weber, Max. *The Sociology of Religion.* Boston: Beacon Press, 1922/1993.

Weiskel, Thomas. *The Romantic Sublime: Studies in the Structure and Psychology of Transcendence.* Baltimore: Johns Hopkins UP, 1976.

Welch, Craig. "The rise and fall of Mars Hill Church." *Seattle Times* (15 September 2014).

Wesley, John. *The Journal of the Rev. John Wesley, A.M., Sometime Fellow of Lincoln College, Oxford.* 4th vol. London: J. Kershaw, 1827.

Whipple, E.P. *North American Review.* Ed. Jared Sparks et al. vol 59. Boston: Otis, Broaders, and Co, 1844.

White, Daniel E. "'The god undeified': Mary Shelley's *Valperga,* Italy, and the Aesthetic of Desire." *Romanticism on the Net* 6 (1997): 34 paragraphs.

White, Deborah. *Romantic Returns: Superstition, Imagination, History.* Stanford: Stanford UP, 2000.

White, Hayden. *Tropics of Discourse: Essays in Cultural Criticism.* Baltimore: Johns Hopkins UP, 1978.

Williams, Raymond. *Culture and Society: 1780–1950.* New York: Columbia UP, 1983.

Wirth, Jason. "Introduction." *Ages of The World [1815].* Trans. Jason M. Wirth. Albany: SUNY Press, 2000. vii–xxxii.

Wittreich, Joseph Anthony. *Visionary Poetics: Milton's Tradition and His Legacy.* San Marino: Huntington Library, 1979.

– Ed. *Milton and the Line of Vision.* Madison: University of Wisconsin Press, 1975.

– *Angel of Apocalypse: Blake's Idea of Milton.* Madison: University of Wisconsin Press, 1975.

– Ed. *Blake's Sublime Allegory: Essays on the Four Zoas, Milton, Jerusalem.* Madison: University of Wisconsin Press, 1973.

Wordsworth, Jonathan. *William Wordsworth: The Borders of Vision.* Oxford: Clarendon, 1982.

Wordsworth, William. *21st-Century Oxford Authors: William Wordsworth.* Ed. Stephen Gill. Oxford: Oxford UP, 2010.

– *The Collected Poetry of William Wordsworth.* London: Wordsworth Editions, 1994.

– *The Prelude: 1799, 1805, 1850.* Ed. Jonathan Wordsworth, M.H. Abrams, and Stephen Gill. New York: Norton, 1979.

– "Home at Grasmere [ms D]." Ed. Beth Darlington. Ithaca: Cornell UP, 1977.

Zammito, John. "Historians and Philosophy of Historiography." *A Companion to the Philosophy of History and Historiography.* Sussex: Blackwell, 2009. 63–84.

Žižek, Slavoj. "The Abyss of Freedom." *The Abyss of Freedom/Ages of the World.* Ann Arbor: University of Michigan Press, 1997.

Zvi, Ehud Ben and Michael Floyd, Ed. *Writings and Speech in Israelite and Ancient Near East Prophecy.* Atlanta: Society of Biblical Literature, 2000.

Index

Abrams, M.H., 13, 19, 20, 29, 31
absence, 44, 67, 82, 87–8, 91, 98, 110, 118, 129, 132, 139, 159, 170–1, 180–1, 196, 200, 211
abstraction, 13, 36, 43, 177
abyss, 12, 33, 37, 81, 87, 126, 172–3, 174, 176, 181, 188, 192
acceleration, 21, 28, 124, 134
Adler, Hans, 39
Aeneas, 198–9
Aeschylus, 57, 134–6, 198, 242
aesthetic, aesthetics, 4, 7, 20, 41, 44, 63, 101, 109, 111–12, 113, 116, 118, 141–6
affect, 116, 119–20, 124, 185
age, 5, 8–9, 11, 16, 42, 99, 105, 153, 155, 162–3, 171–2, 182–5, 187, 190–4, 199–200, 203, 205
agency, 120, 146, 155, 203, 205, 218; historical, 24, 197, 199, 207, 214, 218
Ahasuerus, 22, 30, 32, 124, 128–9, 133, 136, 138–9, 175, 178, 187, 224. *See also* Wandering Jew
allusion, 22, 57, 123, 125, 127, 129, 131, 133–5, 137, 139, 197, 209
analogy, 18, 53, 61, 64, 110–11, 128–30, 132–4, 173, 179, 188, 221
anxiety, 11, 91, 93, 95, 96, 115; historical, 12, 14, 18; of hope, 89, 100, 119
apocalypse, 6, 13, 20, 29, 31, 34, 80, 87, 131, 142–3, 152, 156, 157, 164, 169, 181, 188–9, 195, 218, 221–2, 224–5
Aristotle, 28, 80, 139, 144–6, 237n8
art, artist, 10, 15, 17, 20, 38, 40, 44, 45, 65, 97, 133, 140, 141, 143, 146, 147, 149, 153, 163, 165, 169–70, 184, 196, 221; post-apocalyptic, 224
Augustine, 38–9, 41, 187
Aylesworth, Gary, 113

Badiou, Alain, 114
Baker, Jennifer J., 44
Bakhtin, Mikhail, 10
Balfour, Ian, 13, 105, 174
Bann, Stephen, 39, 83
Bataille, Georges, 171, 179, 180, 222
Bateman, Mary, 202, 248
Baucom, Ian, 114
Baumgarten, Alexander, 53
being, 4, 8, 11, 13–15, 18, 21, 34, 36–7, 41, 48, 54–5, 58–61, 63–5, 76, 88, 91, 93, 110–11, 120, 123, 126, 130–1, 134, 146, 150–1, 154–6, 159, 169, 173, 175, 184–90, 192–4, 196, 198, 205, 208, 215, 219–20

Ben Zvi, Ehud, 47
Benjamin, Walter, 49, 86, 118, 217, 219, 235n116
Bennett, Betty T., 250n59
Bergson, Henri, 146, 149–50
Blake, Catherine, 161
Blake, William, 4, 6–7, 12, 14–15, 17, 19, 23, 32, 34, 45, 51, 62, 76, 85, 87, 92, 101, 116, 120, 123, 139–47, 149–59, 160–1, 163–75, 178, 180–4, 185, 187–9, 192, 195–7, 199–200, 217–18, 225, 227–9, 237–8, 241, 243–4, 246–7; Blakean prophecy, 14, 152, 163; *Jerusalem*, 23, 151–2, 159–62, 164–5, 169; Lambeth books, Lambeth period, 23, 142, 151, 152, 153, 161, 164, 165, 168, 169, 172, 184; *Milton*, 14, 22–3, 32, 35, 81, 92, 110, 123, 141–4, 151–67; *Urizen*, 23, 85, 152, 157, 159, 162, 170, 171, 184, 185, 189
Blanchot, Maurice, 13–14, 23, 27, 33, 34–5, 48, 62, 87–8, 90, 98, 103, 111, 123, 130–3, 137, 141, 170, 173, 174, 180–1, 195, 197, 215, 219–22, 231–2n20; and prophecy/prophetic speech, 37, 130, 194
Bloch, Ernst, 198
Bloom, Harold, 152, 231n98
Blumenberg, Hans, 29–31, 48
body, 20, 55–7, 60, 62, 106, 129, 150, 157, 168, 170, 177, 191, 199–200, 203, 205–6, 221; female, 199–200
Boerhaave, Herman, 59
Bolter, Jay David, 16, 230n73
Brewer, William D., 249n42
Brothers, Richard, 4, 5
Burke, Kenneth, 99, 239n42
Butts, Thomas, 166
Byron, Lord (George Gordon), 180, 199, 222
Camping, Harold, 223
Canuel, Mark, 216
Carra, Jean-Louis, 27
Carroll, Robert, 48–9
Cassandra, 24, 198–9, 203, 206, 209, 214, 224
Chandler, James, 11
childhood, 9, 42, 89, 91, 94
chimeras, 52, 59, 61
Christian, Christianity, 29, 40, 138; Christian metaphysics, 206
clairvoyant, 4, 17, 107, 208
Clark, David, 105
Cohen, Herman, 39
Colebrook, Claire, 181
Collings, David, 35, 93–4
Comay, Rebecca, 7, 105, 107, 168, 228n27
consciousness, 6–7, 36, 40, 46, 53, 56, 59, 64–5, 73, 77, 82–3, 95, 105, 108, 124, 129–34, 149–50, 171, 178, 183, 191–2, 194, 211, 221, 224
Copjec, Joan, 12
Critical philosophy, 22, 50, 54, 60, 69–70, 72, 75, 104, 105, 110

Dante Alighieri, 57, 59, 81, 132, 205–7
death, 16, 64, 66, 99–100, 106, 108, 139, 162, 175, 203–5, 207, 215, 220, 221, 222–3; living, 199, 215
Deleuze, Gilles, 13, 107, 146, 149–50, 155
de Man, Paul, 13, 38, 130, 131, 134
De Quincey, Thomas, 70, 95, 100, 103, 105
Derrida, Jacques, 85–6
Descartes, René, 65
de Tocqueville, Alexis, 7–8, 9, 12, 14, 218
dreams, 21, 51–5, 58–9, 61–3, 66, 68–72, 74, 78–80, 82, 92, 110, 119, 129–30, 133, 136, 207–11
Dupré, Louis, 41, 68, 69

ectype, 191, 192, 193, 194, 247n96
Eden, William, 6
Eichhorn, J.G., 46
Eichner, Hans, 43–4
Ellis, David, 238n33
empiricism, 53–4, 98–9, 125; apocalyptic, 24, 215
Enlightenment, 5, 27, 29, 41–3, 50, 54, 64–8, 142, 179, 200, 203, 208, 219; historiography, 49; philosophy of history, 44; progressivism, 40
enthusiasm, 15, 22, 54, 75, 77, 105, 109, 113, 115–19, 124, 142, 196, 205, 207
Erdman, David, 14–15, 152
eternity, 6, 12, 138, 144, 151, 156, 159, 162, 163, 166, 168, 173, 182, 187–8, 195, 197, 207

Festinger, John, 15–16
Flaxman, John, 135–6
Floyd, Michael, 47
Forster, Michael N., 44
Foucault, Michel, 174, 216
freedom, 28, 33, 40–1, 55–6, 66, 72, 73, 83, 107, 109–11, 114, 117, 120, 124, 163, 171, 173, 183, 186, 192–3, 196, 200, 207
French Revolution, 5, 7–8, 11–12, 82–3, 85, 102, 106–8, 113–14, 117, 120, 137, 168, 196, 218
Fry, Paul H., 238n33
Frye, Northrop, 12–13, 152, 229n65

Gadamer, Hans-Georg, 13, 54, 64–5, 67, 125–7, 147
Gibbon, Edward, 5, 139, 146
Gilchrist, Alexander, 141, 169
God, 4, 19, 30, 34–5, 40–1, 53, 72, 80, 86, 94, 106, 133, 138, 147, 155, 166, 174, 183–8, 190, 193–4, 200, 206–8, 219, 227
Godwin, William, 103, 199, 214, 249n42
Goldsmith, Steven, 13, 15, 17, 119–20, 136, 142, 149, 155
Greece, Greeks, 11–12, 38, 43, 127, 135–9, 214, 217
Greek Revolution, 22, 124, 140
Grusin, Richard, 15, 230n73

Hartman, Geoffrey, 100, 170
Harwood, William Tooke, 199
heaven, 6, 44, 76, 81–2, 84, 92, 108, 127, 152, 163, 187, 196, 202, 208
Hebrew prophets, prophecy, 47, 49–50, 106
Hegel, G.W.F., 5, 7, 18, 23, 28, 31, 32, 33, 36–7, 40–1, 46, 124, 168–94, 196, 215, 216, 219, 232n34; critique of prophecy, 37
Heidegger, Martin, 13, 54, 62, 126; *Dasein*, 64–5
hell, 12, 57, 59, 76, 127, 139, 142, 152–3, 163, 166, 187, 196, 206
Herder, J.G., 4, 5, 9, 31, 38, 39, 40–6, 50, 141, 234n94
Hilton, Nelson, 142
historiography, 5, 9, 11, 14–15, 18, 21–2, 28, 30–1, 33, 38, 45–6, 50, 83, 85, 127, 142–3, 150, 167, 182
Hogle, Jerrold E., 132
Hume, David, 5, 33, 37, 45, 52, 146

imagination, 18–19, 20, 24, 43, 52, 59–61, 63, 82, 94, 112, 118, 132, 134, 140, 143–4, 155, 163, 169, 195–7, 199, 205–7, 210, 212–13, 215, 220–2
impossibility, 21, 23, 35, 70–1, 126, 133, 137, 140, 144–6, 148–9, 154, 156, 167, 169–70, 172–3, 220, 222; history's, 22–3, 141, 147, 169, 192, 193, 218
inspiration, 89–90, 94, 142, 145, 159, 161, 172, 195–6, 211, 217

intuition, 55, 57, 60, 71, 83, 109–10, 113, 124, 131; intellectual, 36–7, 53, 75; spiritual, 56
irony, 23, 32–3, 35–8, 48–9, 64, 71, 102, 106–7, 129, 140, 178, 179, 180, 206, 214, 223

Jacobs, Carol, 131
Jacobus, Mary, 34, 170
Jameson, Fredric, 13, 195, 224
Jerusalem, 21, 23, 151–2, 159–62, 164, 165, 169, 185
Johnson, Barbara, 216–17
Jonah, 86–7, 147, 237
Jones, William N., 200
Juster, Susan, 200

Kant, Immanuel, 5, 12–14, 21–2, 34, 36–7, 41, 50, 52–72, 74–5, 77, 83, 101–9, 111–20, 123–4, 131, 133, 141, 163, 197, 210, 221–2, 251n80; *Begebenheit*, 108, 113, 116; *Conflict of the Faculties, The*, 22, 74, 102, 104, 106, 107–8, 116, 221; *Critique of Pure Reason* (First *Critique*), 51, 70, 71–3, 105, 107, 109, 110; *Critique of the Power of Judgment* (Third *Critique*), 65, 104, 105, 106, 108, 109, 110, 111, 114, 116, 118, 163; Kantian sublime, 13, 126; Kant's System, 105, 111, 115
Khalip, Jacques, 105
Kierkegaard, Søren, 7, 13, 28, 33, 35–7, 62, 87, 111, 168–94, 222; irony, 33, 37, 174, 178, 190; *Prefaces*, 14, 23, 176–80, 182
Kneale, Douglas, 239n41
Koselleck, Reinhart, 10–11, 13, 22, 28–9, 40, 88, 125–6, 132, 134, 147, 186

Langan, Celeste, 17–18, 40
Larkin, Peter, 96, 238n33
lastness, 24, 220–1
Lefort, Claude, 8, 12
Liu, Alan, 82–3
Locke, John, 97–8, 195
Löwith, Karl, 49
Lowth, Robert, 4
Lyotard, Jean-François, 114–19

Macpherson, James, 141
Makdisi, Saree, 15, 141, 175
Mandelbaum, Allen, 206
Martin, Dorothy (aka Marian Keech), 16
Massumi, Brian, 150
McGann, Jerome, 23, 163, 231n103, 244n37
McLane, Maureen N., 17
McLuhan, Marshall, 16, 47
Mede, Joseph, 237n7
Mee, John, 15
Mellor, Anne, 198
memory, 14, 75–8, 95, 98, 115, 129–34, 137, 150, 195, 209–11
Menze, Ernest A., 39
metaphysics, 21, 50, 52–3, 60, 68–71, 103–4, 115, 152, 191, 210–11
Milbank, John, 29
Milton, John, 14, 20, 22–3, 32, 35, 81, 92, 123, 142–4, 151–9, 161–6, 168–71, 173–4, 176, 182, 184–5, 188–9, 197–8, 215, 222; *Paradise Lost*, 99, 140, 151, 153, 154, 166, 196. *See also under* Blake, William
Mitchell, W.J.T., 163
Monod, Jean-Claude, 29

nature, 8, 20, 32, 49, 54–7, 64, 66, 68–9, 71, 73, 77–8, 82, 85, 91, 104–5, 109–12, 116–17, 138, 143–4, 153, 155, 171, 177, 179, 183–4, 186, 188–9, 191–3, 206, 210, 212, 215, 221

negation, 14, 32, 36, 87, 144–5, 170, 181, 183, 185, 190, 219–20
negativity, 7, 23, 28, 33–7, 48–9, 87–8, 93–4, 115, 126, 141, 154–5, 165, 167, 171, 175–6, 178, 180, 185, 193, 215–16, 219–20; prophetic, 37, 150, 159
Nichol, Todd, 176
Nissinen, Martti, 47

Old Testament, 4, 19, 35, 46
Oliver, W.H., 5
Orient, Oriental, 9, 12, 42, 43
Ovid, 57–8, 61, 198

Paine, Thomas, 5, 9–10, 145
Paley, Morton D., 34, 143, 154, 197, 220, 225, 227n9
Palmquist, Stephen, 71, 73
paradox, 11, 14, 21, 62, 70, 85–6, 87, 90, 93, 98, 102, 118, 140, 144, 147, 149, 154, 156, 163, 173, 183, 187, 210, 222, 249n41
Parke, H.W., 198
phenomenology, 13–14, 36, 100, 176–7
philosophy, 15, 31–2, 38–41, 50, 52, 60–1, 65, 69–70, 72, 75, 103, 104–5, 110, 150, 170, 177, 179–80, 215; of history, 5, 9, 15, 27–8, 31–2, 38–40, 42, 106
Plug, Jan, 50, 110, 220
preludes, preludia, 171–6. *See also under* Wordsworth, William
Priestly, Joseph, 4
progress, 5, 7, 27, 40, 42–3, 104, 107–8, 113–15, 117–19, 124, 141, 155, 178, 181, 219; historical, 74, 113, 118, 177; human, 102, 113, 116
prophecy: apocalyptic, 134, 214; biblical, 5, 46–50; failed, 16, 47, 49, 140; female, 24, 195, 199, 203, 205
prophetic imagination, 23–4, 143, 144, 197–8, 209, 212–13, 215
prophetic speech, 34–5, 48–9, 130, 174
pulsation, 164, 188–9
Pyle, Forest, 18, 213

Ragussis, Michael, 110
Rajan, Tilottama, 190, 247n96, 249n35
reason, 5, 7–11, 21–2, 50–1, 53–7, 59–61, 63–9, 71–6, 92, 103–5, 107, 109–12, 114, 116, 118, 120, 132, 134, 146–8, 180, 183, 191, 222, 227, 235–6, 248
redemption, 40, 89, 92, 153, 155, 162, 166, 225, 245; apocalyptic, 151; historical, 222
Reece, Richard, 16, 203, 248n31
Reeves, Marjorie, 204
remediation, 17, 28, 49, 62, 77, 110, 140, 176
representation, 9, 13, 17–18, 31, 115, 132–3, 143–4, 169, 181, 187, 196, 219
revelation, 13, 19–20, 32, 40, 73, 93, 145, 153, 157, 183–4, 194, 208–9, 222, 225
revolution, 4, 7–8, 62, 75, 82, 85, 106, 113, 120, 123–4, 133, 136–7, 140, 143, 155–6, 176, 186, 204. *See also* French Revolution
Richardson, Alan, 90
Richman, Jared, 142
Riede, David, 153
Rink, Friedrich Theodor, 103
Robinet, Jean-Baptiste 247n96
Romanticism, 5, 7, 9, 13–19, 21, 28–30, 34, 37, 39–41, 43, 45–6, 49–50, 72, 125, 130, 147, 170, 213
Romantics, 4, 11–12, 15, 18, 21, 43–4, 50, 123, 130, 134, 197, 225
Rose, Edward J., 246n89
Rousseau, Jean-Jacques, 56, 131

Rowlandson, Thomas, 200, 201
Rudwick, Martin, 233n52

Satan, 99, 143–4, 153, 155, 159, 165–6, 189
Schelling, F.W.J., 7, 8, 13, 34, 45, 46, 62, 87, 116, 129, 168–94, 182–3, 185, 189, 246n7; *Ages of the World*, 14, 22, 23, 110, 155, 171, 172, 182
Schlegel, K.W.F., 46, 49, 233, 235, 244
Schmitt, Carl, 29
Schwärmerei, 116, 118, 119. *See also* enthusiasm
Scott, Walter, 17–18
Scottish Enlightenment, 39, 46, 228n20
selfhood, 156, 162, 166, 184–5
Shaffer, E.S., 46
Shell, Susan Meld, 54
Shelley, Mary, 6–7, 14, 18, 24, 44, 169, 196–222, 223; *Frankenstein*, Frankenstein's Creature, 5, 106, 199, 202, 211, 249n50, 250n58; *Last Man, The*, 14, 24, 44, 168, 175, 196–7, 198, 213, 214–22; *Valperga*, 18, 24, 168, 197–213, 215, 217, 249n35
Shelley, Percy Bysshe, 7, 9, 14, 18, 22, 32, 34, 35, 45, 69, 84, 110, 120, 124–40, 142, 143, 144, 148, 151, 159, 172, 175, 178, 182, 186, 224; *Hellas*, 14, 22, 110, 124, 127–34, 136–40; and prophecy, 221; *Triumph of Life*, 9, 128, 130, 131, 134, 186
Sibyl (of Cumae), 24, 168, 175, 198–9, 221
Smith, William Robertson, 19
Snow, Dale, 112
Southcott, Joanna, 5, 16, 24, 199–203, 215, 248nn15, 24
space of experience, 22, 28, 88, 123, 125–6, 132, 147
spirit, 6, 8, 11, 16, 18, 20, 22, 49, 52–3, 55–6, 58–60, 62, 66–9, 76, 81–2, 84, 96, 127, 129, 136–7, 163, 181, 184, 186, 189, 191, 207, 212
subjectivity, 12, 18, 20, 62, 85, 91–2, 196; masculinized, 218
sublime, 34, 63, 78, 92, 112, 107, 115–18, 140
Sunstein, Emily W., 200
Sussman, Charlotte, 222
Swedenborg, Emanuel, 5, 21–2, 50, 51–2, 53, 60, 61, 68, 69, 75, 76, 101, 103, 105, 210
Sykes Davies, Hugh, 97
sympathy, 37, 51, 75, 102, 104, 108–9, 113, 115
system, systematization, 5, 9, 13, 20, 27, 41, 50, 80, 101, 104, 105, 149, 151, 156, 157, 159, 165, 169, 170, 176, 180, 182, 184, 191, 194, 196, 200, 218, 224; Blake, 4, 23, 143, 163; Hegel, 168, 176, 179; Heidegger, 126; Kant, 54, 70, 74, 102, 105, 111, 115, 118; of government, 4, 6, 216. *See also* Carra, Jean-Louis

Tarbet, David, 70
temporality, temporalization, 9, 10, 22, 23, 35, 77, 91, 100, 101, 108, 114, 115, 123, 125, 131, 133, 134, 139, 140, 147, 169, 173, 182, 186, 189, 190
Thompson, E.P., 10, 75
Thulstrup, Neils, 176, 178
Tillich, Paul, 188, 246n89
time, spots of, 75, 83, 85, 88, 90–2, 94, 97, 98, 102, 111, 115, 126, 130, 143, 165, 238n33
Tiresias, 21, 52, 54, 57–8, 61, 62, 63, 65, 66, 70, 114, 197
transcendence, 20, 29, 38, 39, 49, 52, 94, 154, 155, 174, 220
"transcendence was put aside," 45
transcendental illusion, 53, 116–17, 119

translation, 14, 17, 19, 79, 80, 103, 108, 119, 136, 213, 219, 221
trauma, traumatic, 6, 7, 21, 75–102, 104, 123, 124, 152, 153, 169, 173, 174, 182, 199, 210, 211, 212, 213, 218, 221, 238n33
Twigg, Sharon M., 249n41

Ulmer, William, 128, 129
utopia, 18, 24, 62, 83, 136, 145, 195–7, 216, 218, 219, 224

Valéry, Paul, 51–2
van den Abbeele, George van den, 115
vision, 140; allegorical, 136; apocalyptic, 140, 181
voice, 13, 34, 43, 48, 79, 89–90, 140, 175, 199, 248
Voltaire, 5, 32, 38–9, 40, 42, 45, 146, 147, 232n42
von Rad, Gerhard, 19, 27, 46, 47, 48
von Ranke, Leopold, 228n22

Wandering Jew, 30, 35, 128, 172, 199, 219. *See also* Ahasuerus
Wasianski, E.A.C., 103
Watson, Richard, 19, 145, 147, 168
Weber, Max, 3, 101
Weever, John, 76
Wesley, John, 3, 228n1
Whipple, E.P., 11
White, Daniel E., 249n41
White, Deborah, 18
White, Hayden, 33, 139
Williams, Charles, 200, 202, 248n22
Williams, Raymond, 11
Wirth, Jason, 184, 189
Wittreich, Joseph Anthony, 20–1, 23, 152, 231n98
Wolff, Christian, 53, 103
Wordsworth, Dorothy, 77
Wordsworth, William, 6, 7, 11, 12, 14, 20, 21, 22, 32, 34, 45, 50, 59, 74, 75–102, 103, 104, 105, 110, 111, 114, 115, 118, 119, 120, 123–6, 129, 130, 131, 133, 140, 143, 147, 148, 163, 165–6, 168, 169, 172, 210, 211, 212, 220, 222, 236n6, 237n10, 238n33; "Home at Grasmere," 21, 89–90, 92–3, 94, 237–8n29; *Prelude*, 21, 32, 78, 82, 84, 87–91, 93–6, 101, 110, 166, 168, 172; "Tintern Abbey," 21, 74, 77–9
workless, worklessness, 14, 35, 37, 170, 171, 177, 181, 184, 215

Žižek, 13, 149, 183, 187, 237, 243, 245–6
Zupančič, Alenka, 224

www.ingramcontent.com/pod-product-compliance
Lightning Source LLC
LaVergne TN
LVHW090154080826
844660LV00013B/799/J

* 9 7 8 1 4 4 2 6 3 0 7 0 3 *